SPLENDID! SPLENDID!

SPLENDID! SPLENDID!

The Authorized Biography of
Willie Whitelaw

MARK GARNETT AND IAN AITKEN

JONATHAN CAPE
LONDON

Published by Jonathan Cape 2002

2 4 6 8 10 9 7 5 3 1

First published in Great Britain in 2002 by
Jonathan Cape
Random House, 20 Vauxhall Bridge Road,
London SW1V 2SA

Random House Australia (Pty) Limited
20 Alfred Street, Milsons Point, Sydney,
New South Wales 2061, Australia

Random House New Zealand Limited
18 Poland Road, Glenfield,
Auckland 10, New Zealand

Random House South Africa (Pty) Limited
Endulini, 5A Jubilee Road, Parktown 2193, South Africa

The Random House Group Limited Reg. No. 954009
www.randomhouse.co.uk

A CIP catalogue record for this book
is available from the British Library

ISBN 0–224–06311–1

Papers used by The Random House Group Limited are natural,
recyclable products made from wood grown in sustainable forests;
the manufacturing processes conform to the environmental
regulations of the country of origin

Typeset by Palimpsest Book Production Limited,
Polmont, Stirlingshire
Printed and bound in Great Britain by
Mackays of Chatham PLC

CONTENTS

To the memory of Toby Low, Lord Aldington, MC

LIST OF ILLUSTRATIONS

A rare glimpse in the Cabinet room, 1985 (*Lady Whitelaw*).

Willie with the Queen and the Chairman of Lloyd's, Peter Miller (*Peter Kain/Camera Press*).

Willie and Celia at Ennim after Willie's resignation, January 1988 (*Lady Whitelaw*).

Lord Tebbit poses with two Willie look-alikes on holiday in Portugal (*Lord Tebbit*).

Three Whitelaw generations at Ennim (*Lady Whitelaw*).

ACKNOWLEDGEMENTS

The greatest problem bequeathed by Willie Whitelaw to his biographers is the seemingly endless roll-call of his friends and colleagues. We have tried to contact as many as possible of these. Some felt that they could not help, others thought it best to remain anonymous; and we are acutely conscious of the hoardes who were left unconsulted through lack of time or our inability to trace them. But we are enormously grateful for the cooperation of those listed below, and Willie would have been glad to know that many of the conversations proved to be as enjoyable as they were enlightening.

We would like to record our thanks to Andrew Alexander; Lord Biffen; Lord Brittan; David Butler; Lord Campbell of Croy; Lord and Lady Carr; Lord Carrington; Kenneth Clarke; Peter Clarke; John Cole; Viscount Cranborne; Lord Deedes; Lord Denham; Nirj Deva; Michael Dobbs; James and Mary Douglas; Major Charles Farrell; Garret Fitzgerald; Michael Foot; Lord Garel-Jones; Dr John Gayner; Sir Martin Gilbert; Lady Caroline Gilmour; Geoffrey Goodman; the late Lord Hailsham; Simon Heffer; Peter Hennessy; Simon Hoggart; Lord Howe; Lord Howell; Liz Huckle; Lord Hurd; Sir Bernard Ingham; Robert Jackson; Lord Jenkin; Lord Jopling; Trevor Kavanagh; Sir Ludovic Kennedy; Jack Liddiard, OBE; Keith McDowall; Michael Mates; Sir Carol Mather; Sara Morrison; Andrew Neil; Sir Fraser and Lady Noble; Sir Jack Page; Lesley Pallett; Lord Parkinson; Jeremy Paxman; Joy Pemberton-Pigott; Lord Peyton; Lord Prior; Sir Timothy Raison; David Rogers; Andrew Roth; the late Lord Runcie; James Russell; Dili Satha; Lady Soames; Peter Stothard; Sir Teddy Taylor; Lord Tebbit; Lady Thatcher; Stella Thomas; Geoffrey Tucker; Sir Brian Unwin; Lord Waldegrave; Sir Dennis Walters; Lord Wetherill; Francis Wheen; David Wilson; Lord Windlesham; Lord Young of Graffam.

Individual chapters were read by Sir Robin Chichester-Clark, Sir John

Chilcot; the late Sir Frank Cooper, Michael Crick, Andrew Denham, Lord Gilmour, Lord Merlyn-Rees, and Lord Pym. Although they have saved us from numerous howlers and suggested many improvements, any remaining errors of fact or interpretation are entirely our responsibility. Sadly the late Lord Aldington was already in very poor health when the chapters began to take shape. But despite his discomfort in the weeks before his death, he was always ready to discuss the friend he had known since his schooldays, and to argue over details of his own remarkable career. We only hope that he would have found a recognisable portrait of Willie in the finished book.

We were extremely fortunate in being allowed to consult government papers which have yet to be made available to other researchers. For this we have to thank the lasting goodwill generated by Willie over nearly two decades as a senior minister. But we are aware of our debts to several senior officials, who ensured a favourable hearing for our unusual request. At the Cabinet Office Records section Tessa Sterling and Richard Ponman were extraordinarily helpful and patient during an exercise which took far longer than we originally expected. We are particularly grateful to the staff at the Northern Ireland Office for working so hard to deliver papers to us when they faced other important distractions. For Sir John Chilcot, who found time amidst numerous commitments to oversee the research, no thanks can really be sufficient. Those days in the Cabinet Office will always be a treasured memory; our conversations were always great fun, as well as instructive.

More predictable was the assistance accorded to us by the usual archival suspects. The efficiency of the Public Record Office never ceases to amaze. At the Bodleian, Jill Davidson turned into Jill Spellman but remained as friendly and helpful as ever. We are also very grateful to the staff at Churchill College (especially Andrew 'Cummerbund' Riley), and the British Library of Political and Economic Science. We have been given access to unpublished material by David Butler, Lord Carr, John Cole, Michael Crick, Lord Gilmour, Miles Hudson, Geoffrey Tucker and Lord Young; we thank them all for their help. Mark Garnett would also like to record his grateful thanks to Carole and Ian Taylor, who offered him shelter during research trips to London.

At Random House, we have been very fortunate to work with Will Sulkin, Jörg Hensgen and Poppy Hampson who have gone well beyond the call of duty to assist with this project. Even the unannounced arrival of a harassed author was invariably greeted with a welcome as warm as the coffee.

Obviously our greatest debt is to Lady Whitelaw. She never lost confidence in the book, and it was always a delight to travel up to Cumbria to discuss the latest chapter with her. Finishing a book always brings a tinge of regret, and no one could dream of associating with a political family which exudes a greater sense of warmth and loyalty. Although Willie always made a point of paying tribute to Celia, her importance in his life could only be appreciated by those who saw them together during the last illness. However confused Willie might be, Celia was still 'the ever-fixed mark' who brought love and stability to his life. While sifting through boxes of old papers at their beloved home near Penrith, we discovered a dusty old file of letters to Celia from the wives of Willie's fellow Guardsmen. No doubt the wives of many senior officers kept up some form of correspondence with the loved ones of those who shared dangers and hardships after D-Day; but no one could have matched Celia's energy and efficiency in discharging the task. Almost every interviewee who knew the couple expressed the view that she was the ideal political wife; one old friend even suggested that she would have made a better Prime Minister than Willie. Throughout the composition of the book she retained a keen interest, often saving us from factual errors but never making the slightest effort to dictate our conclusions. This was exactly the approach that Willie had taken before his incapacitating illness, and we are most grateful for it.

Mark Garnett
Ian Aitken
June 2002

Whitelaw Family Tree

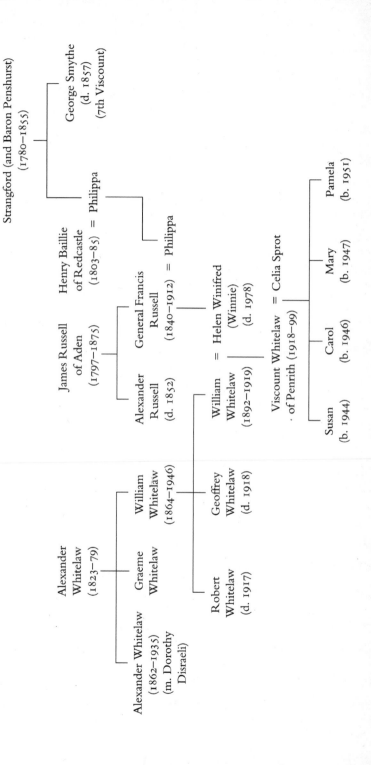

Percy Smythe, 6th Viscount
Strangford (and Baron Penshurst)
(1780–1855)

George Smythe
(d. 1857)
(7th Viscount)

James Russell
of Aden
(1797–1875)

Henry Baillie
of Redcastle
(1803–85) = Philippa

Alexander
Russell
(d. 1852)

General Francis
Russell
(1840–1912) = Philippa

Alexander
Whitelaw
(1823–79)

Alexander Whitelaw
(1862–1935)
(m. Dorothy
Disraeli)

Graeme
Whitelaw

William
Whitelaw
(1864–1946)

Robert
Whitelaw
(d. 1917)

Geoffrey
Whitelaw
(d. 1918)

William
Whitelaw
(1892–1919)

= Helen Winifred
(Winnie)
(d. 1978)

Viscount Whitelaw = Celia Sprot
of Penrith (1918–99)

Susan
(b. 1944)

Carol
(b. 1946)

Mary
(b. 1947)

Pamela
(b. 1951)

INTRODUCTION

Willie Whitelaw began to write his memoirs almost as soon as he retired from the Cabinet in January 1988. Before the book appeared it was rumoured that the lynchpin of Mrs Thatcher's government had turned his pen against his former colleague, to devastating effect. According to 'friends', the ex-Deputy Prime Minister was furious because Mrs Thatcher had hardly spoken to him since he left office. He was said to want a change of leadership, favouring the Chancellor, Nigel Lawson.[1]

When the *Sunday Times* bought the serialisation rights to the book, they discovered that it was something less than a premeditated act of revenge. From the finished text, it seemed that the author had liked almost everyone he had ever met, and Mrs Thatcher was not among the exceptions. He praised her personal kindness and claimed that, contrary to the prevalent story, she was actually an excellent listener who relished a good-natured argument. 'No one can deny her incredible achievements,' he enthused. The nearest approach to criticism was a phrase that applies to every human being, let alone a Prime Minister of nine years' standing: 'No doubt she has made mistakes . . .'[2]

There was little scope in that for sensational headlines. So Brian Walden was dispatched to interview Willie, in the hope that he might be indiscreet. The seasoned inquisitor – himself a greater admirer of Mrs Thatcher than Willie had ever been – secured an admission that their political partnership had never blossomed into a private friendship; indeed, Willie said that he had avoided social encounters with the Thatchers. At least this ensured that the serialisation was talked about. But there was no direct contradiction of the book, where Willie had written that he and Mrs Thatcher had 'varying backgrounds, interests and thus reactions. As a result we had never been close personal friends before we were brought together in this particular political relationship'. Being Willie, he had found it unnecessary to add that they were not exactly bosom buddies *after* the partnership began.[3]

The fuss about the serialisation only deepened the puzzle of why Willie had decided to write the book in the first place. Some prominent people enjoy an exercise that keeps them occupied in the first few months of retirement. But during his career Willie had always tried to avoid looking back, and it was strange that he should break the habit so conclusively as soon as he had signed off the last of his red dispatch-boxes. He was never going to compete with Jean-Jacques Rousseau in the ranks of confessional autobiographers; few people have been less susceptible to self-examination or brooding over inner demons. In private conversation he could be terribly indiscreet. But Willie liked to be liked – a legacy, no doubt, of his lonely childhood – and he was most reluctant to cause fresh offence to those who had crossed swords with him.

Willie had taken some trouble over his memoirs, even asking Churchill's official biographer Martin Gilbert for advice. But in commissioning the present book he was tacitly admitting that he had made a mistake in writing about himself. After more than one enjoyable lunch, he persuaded Ian Aitken to take on the job. It was something Willie had obviously thought about very carefully. One of his many interesting contradictions was the fact that although he was a staunch party loyalist, he would probably have been happier presiding over a coalition government than a Cabinet full of Conservatives. Certainly throughout his career he had far more trouble from right-wing journalists than from socialists. In making his choice he must have known that the end product would be critical of his part in the Thatcher years; but probably he expected that this would be more interesting than unquestioning admiration. The most important factor, though, was that author and subject had always got on well, whatever their political differences. In fact, it was almost the opposite of Willie's relationship with Mrs Thatcher, at least as he had described it to Brian Walden.

We have tried to live up to Willie's expectations in the following pages. He is not the easiest subject for a biography. While most front-rank politicians of his generation have left behind an invaluable trail of documents, he preferred to transact business through conversation rather than by committing his thoughts to paper. Again, this is an important biographical fact; but it doesn't help very much in the reconstruction of his career. Thankfully, he did bequeath a large troupe of friends and colleagues, without whom this book would have been impossible to write. And in a series of memorable interviews he revealed much that he omitted from the memoirs, before the onset of illness put an end to the exercise.

In those conversations, Willie was true to his nature in shedding light on his attitude to 'Thatcherism' more through evasion than words. He was quite ready to criticise the Major Government. But only under great pressure did he agree that he might have done more to curb Mrs Thatcher's radicalism. The contrast can only be explained by trying to appreciate the nature of Willie's loyalty and his approach to political questions. As Mrs Thatcher's Deputy, he set himself the task of ensuring that the Conservative Party stuck together through all difficulties. So his usual reaction to policy ideas at that time was 'How can we sell this to the troops?' After John Major succeeded Mrs Thatcher in 1990 he was no longer involved in day-to-day decision-making. He was detached enough to ask, 'What on earth are they up to now?' (or, as he said despairingly during the government's darkest days, 'Has it really come to this?'). At the same time, he wished Major well and still hoped that he could help in some way. It was an uncomfortable position for him, and his choice of Ian Aitken as biographer didn't help. During one working lunch at Bucks' (one of his favourite clubs), Willie was complaining about the latest political disasters when Major came in with the Chief Whip, Alistair Goodlad. Willie looked flustered and went over to talk to the Prime Minister, who apparently asked what he was doing having lunch with an opponent of the government.[4]

Willie valued loyalty above any other quality. In a relatively short speech, delivered in 1982, he used the word seventeen times.[5] For some members of the Conservative Party, the Thatcher Governments were a serious trial as they tested various loyalties – to individuals, to party and to country. Willie could not escape the pain of these conflicts, but his career ensured that he placed peculiar emphasis on loyalty to leaders. During the Second World War he had worked best as a deputy, smoothing the feelings that had been ruffled by his rather brusque commanding officer. He deployed the same skills as Chief Whip to Edward Heath. It was loyalty that conditioned his behaviour in the twelve months after February 1974 – the devastating period which explains the rest of his career as a front-rank politician.

In February of that year Heath called an election in the midst of an economic crisis and a miners' strike, which had forced the government to introduce a three-day working week. At that time Willie was Employment Secretary. His efforts to resolve the strike were hampered by colleagues who wanted a decisive confrontation with the over-mighty unions. Willie was strongly opposed to a general election, not least because it would endanger the fragile settlement he had recently negotiated as Secretary of State for Northern Ireland. He ended up getting the worst of both worlds; he prevented a snap election, which the Conservatives might have won, but the speculation scuppered any chance of a settlement with the miners, so he acquiesced in the February contest, which his party lost.

After the election Heath made Willie Chairman of the party. It was probably his most unhappy period in politics; he was still exhausted after his efforts in

Ulster, and he was bruised by the arguments over the election. Worse still, many of his colleagues suspected that he was merely waiting to take over from Heath – an eventuality that he deplored, because although he thought he could be a reasonable Prime Minister, he knew that he would struggle as Opposition leader. When the Conservatives lost a second election, in October 1974, he was the strong favourite to take over from Heath. But even if he had wanted the post, now that Labour was in power his sense of loyalty meant that he could not challenge the man who had made him Party Chairman. When Mrs Thatcher stood and forced Heath's resignation, Willie felt that he had to stand; but he was unfairly lumbered with the label of the man who had feared to strike.

When Mrs Thatcher became leader it was natural for Willie to try to forge a partnership with someone very different from himself. Unlike the 'wets', who tended to behave as if the leadership election had been a temporary aberration, Willie regarded it as a regrettable fact that had to be dealt with. At the outset it seems that he underestimated the strength of Mrs Thatcher's convictions – or rather, he never supposed that she would stick to dogmatic policies even in the face of clear evidence that they had failed. As it turned out, he had become the prisoner of Mrs Thatcher's crusading style; if he refused to plot while he was Party Chairman, he was most unlikely to do so as Deputy Leader. After the Conservatives won the 1979 general election there was a further, more practical objection. Having led the party to victory, Mrs Thatcher was idolised by many ordinary Conservatives. His 'wet' critics deplored Willie's refusal to back them as another manifestation of 'Wobbly Willie', but even they accepted that there was little chance of changing the policies of the first Thatcher Government.

Willie deplored soaring unemployment, and as Home Secretary he was more directly embroiled in the consequences than any of the 'wets'. He was justly proud of his refusal to introduce draconian laws after the widespread rioting of 1981. Since they were also essentially negative, it is tempting to overlook his other achievements – notably his defence of public-service broadcasting against a Prime Minister whose interpretation of political bias was dictated by her own ferocious prejudices. It can certainly be argued that Willie was too timid in his attempts to restrain Mrs Thatcher and her first Chancellor, Sir Geoffrey Howe. His defence was that unless he used his influence selectively, he would never get his way on anything. Logically it seemed to follow that his influence would be strongest if he never used it at all. But in economic arguments he was constrained by his acknowledged ignorance of theory. Instead he took as his guiding principle the idea that governments inevitably fall when the Treasury cannot prevail in the key battles. His support for Howe infuriated the 'wets', but once again it can be argued that the real damage had been done by the 1975 leadership election. At least Willie had managed to prevent the appointment of Mrs Thatcher's 'guru', Sir Keith Joseph, as Shadow Chancellor after that contest; he was not to know that Howe would prove equally doctrinaire, as well as being far more durable.

As a minister without departmental responsibilities, after 1983 Willie acted as chairman of numerous government committees. As a skilful committee man he had the perfect opportunity to make a difference, particularly in areas of secondary interest to Mrs Thatcher. A regular theme in the interviews conducted for this book was that Willie did put a stop to many dubious ideas. His former colleagues found it difficult to recall specific instances, but that is probably the way Willie would have wanted it. His very presence, apparently, was enough to prevent some hare-brained policies coming to Cabinet, or even to sub-committees; ministers, including Mrs Thatcher herself, developed the habit of guessing in advance the objections he would raise and dropping any plans that 'would not wash with Willie'. Few politicians in post-war Britain can have exercised so much unspoken authority. The biggest blot on Willie's record, though, was the Poll Tax. It seems that he never liked the idea, but when he reported that Scottish ratepayers were on the verge of rebellion against the old system of local government finance, he made an important contribution to the most notorious policy disaster of the Thatcher years.

The greatest tribute to Willie's stature is the tendency of so many of Mrs Thatcher's ministers to trace her downfall to his enforced decision to leave the Cabinet. But while we believe that Willie's critics have exaggerated his shortcomings as a potential brake on the 'Thatcher Revolution', the same is also true of those who regard his absence as the key factor in the Prime Minister's departure. Given the strength of emotion involved, he could not have defused the personality clashes that undermined the government; and as we have seen, he failed over the Poll Tax.

But in one sense Willie Whitelaw really was irreplaceable – not just to Mrs Thatcher, but to public life in Britain as a whole. It is going too far to say that 'Every Prime Minister needs a Willie'; but they fare far worse without a source of sound, independent judgement. And the unusual mould which made Willie has not turned out any replicas. Of the representatives of his class who remain politically active, a few are too obviously calculating; the rest are too sadly buffoonish. There are still plenty of 'nature's gentlemen' from more humble homes, but the few who choose politics as a career invariably lose something of their charm in the upward struggle. Willie did not always strike the correct balance, but for the most part he carried off his act. Superficially he seemed stupid; but when one realised that he was nowhere near as stupid as he looked, there was a tendency to over-compensate and to regard him as an infallible operator. The truth was that he had in abundance that form of intelligence which cannot be measured by first-class degrees, or even by dazzling displays at the dispatch-box. His political judgement sometimes failed him, but in this sense he easily outclassed his contemporaries. He was also a first-rate judge of character. He once said, 'If you look very firmly and straight at anybody who comes to talk to you and look straight at their eyes, will they look at yours? If they won't, then you know you're on very bad ground.' It was a simple test, but it rarely misled him. He fostered the careers of many valuable public servants under a party leader whose own favourites tended to be subjected to ideological screening.[6] And few politicians have earned such loyalty or affection from their staff. Bearing his own burdens lightly and always considerate to others, Willie was a favourite with almost everyone who served in his various departments. He was both larger and louder than life; in good times and bad his colleagues would know that he was around when they heard the words 'Splendid! Simply splendid!' echoing around their office walls.

Willie had a remarkable rapport with people, regardless of their background. After his retirement, and the fall of the Berlin Wall, he visited Prague as a tourist. He was spotted by a group of British sightseers in the open carriage of a train. 'There's old Willie!' they cried. Shortly afterwards the holidaymakers caught sight of him again and renewed their greeting. Once he was playing in a golf tournament in his home town of Nairn, on a course that adjoined a caravan site. The news soon spread that Willie was playing, and when he drove from the tee nearest the site a large crowd of spectators had gathered to cheer him on. It was usually easy to detect Willie's presence on a golf course; his voice echoed around every hole. Everyone knew him as 'Willie' – even greenkeepers who habitually addressed members in formal terms. It seemed natural for us to depart from usual practice and follow suit throughout this book. In early drafts we found that we only used his surname when he was doing something we disagreed with.[7]

There was, in short, something rather 'splendid' about Willie Whitelaw. At the time of his death not even the staunchest Conservative could say the same of the party he had served for nearly half a century. It was his misfortune, and not his fault, that he spent half of that period under uncongenial leadership. He would have been elated if his Northern Ireland settlement had been given a chance; he would have loved to have reduced the prison population; and he wished that he could have done something to prevent the mass unemployment that blighted so many lives during the Thatcher years. But his domestic life was extremely happy, and when he died he was sincerely mourned across and beyond the political parties. Had he known of the lot that awaited him, the shy boy playing on the beach at Nairn would have felt that he had taken full advantage of the life that was denied to his father.

CHAPTER I

AN ORPHAN OF THE GREAT WAR

At two o'clock on the morning of 20 February 1852 the British troopship HMS *Birkenhead* struck rocks close to the South African shore. Of 638 passengers, more than two-thirds were lost when the vessel sank. The news reached London in April, and for some days it dominated the newspaper columns. Initial anger provoked a search for scapegoats, focusing on the Captain, who had apparently sailed too close to shore in an attempt to save time. Then correspondents began to produce more constructive suggestions for the future, including appeals for the provision of lifebelts to every passenger, for closer attention to ship design and for the use of public funds rather than private charity to compensate the bereaved.

After the anger and the wise reflections came an outpouring of sentimentality. The wrecking of the *Birkenhead* was a tale of heroism — as one paper put it, 'an historic landmark in the annals of British courage and coolness'. Most of the servicemen aboard had stayed with the ship until it foundered; every woman and child was saved. Of all the selfless feats that were recorded, none was more impressive than the conduct of Alexander Russell, an eighteen-year-old ensign with the 74th Highlanders. As one newspaper reported:

> This young officer was ordered into a boat crammed with women and children, after it had been launched from the sinking vessel. Some sailors under his command rowed it well away from the doomed 'Birkenhead', and he sat in the bows directing them, while hundreds of living and dead bodies floated round. And — most frightful of all — dim shadowy shapes moved about in the deep, sharks, which kept seizing their prey and darting off, telling of the awful fate awaiting the drowning, besides the angry waves.

Russell noticed that close beside him in the lifeboat was a woman with a child. The woman was moaning, because her husband was missing:

> Suddenly a drowning trooper's head rose out of the water beside the boat, and his voice called out for help! 'Oh, save him – save him', cried the woman, 'it's my husband' – and even as she said it a surging wave carried the man close to the side of the boat, and showed also a dreaded shark not far away from him!
>
> Alexander Russell looked at the man, at the shark, and then at the mother and child. But there was not room for even one more man in the boat: such extra weight would jeopardise all!
>
> The young officer of the 74th Highlanders, fresh from Glenalmond School, stood up, took one last look at the woman, and exclaimed, 'I'll save him!' With this he jumped overboard, seized the drowning man, who was dragged into the boat by willing hands, but – no one saw the Hero again – they only saw that awful shadowy form rise near him in the swirling waters . . .

It was the perfect Victorian death – an aquatic anticipation of Gordon at Khartoum. The event was commemorated in an epic painting, 'The Death of Ensign Russell', and celebrated in 'prose and verse, in sermons and in speeches'.[1] Oddly, though, Alexander Russell's great-nephew, Viscount Whitelaw of Penrith, chose not to mention the incident in his autobiography (published in 1989). This was in keeping with a general reticence on the subject of his ancestry. While most political memoirs include tidings of every forebear, however distant and unremarkable, Whitelaw's book reveals little more about his background than a loving tribute to his mother Winifred (née Russell), a warm acknowledgement of his grandfather (also a William) and the revelation that although he cried when he was old enough to understand that his father had died, 'I had a short memory and I soon put this tragedy behind me.'[2]

Even if the grief of the infant Whitelaw was as fleeting as he suggested, as an adult his father was often in his thoughts. In a 1983 speech delivered to the new generation at Glenalmond School – which his father had attended, following in the path of Alexander Russell – he confessed that 'I still feel keenly that I never knew my father, a loss in one's life which can never be replaced'.[3] Presumably he felt that it would be bad form to write at length about his closest personal relationships in his memoirs, and that the faux pas would have been compounded by a prolonged dissertation on his wider family connections. This would have been typical of the man, and of the political approach that he epitomised.

By the time of his death on 1 July 1999 – and, indeed, long before he was awarded his hereditary title – Lord Whitelaw was widely regarded as almost the last representative of the 'patrician' style in British politics. The patrician ideal rests on the assumption that a privileged background implies a duty of service to the public. Whatever their academic or professional qualifications, men of property saw themselves as the natural rulers of British society. Accustomed to command, and enjoying respect from others without stooping to demand it, they had no reason to exploit positions of power for personal enrichment or the satisfaction of their egos. Representatives of 'the landed interest' could be trusted to govern for the general good, because they had most to fear (and to lose) from social disorder. As in the case of Alexander Russell, when the time came for self-sacrifice, they would step forward and perform their duty without flinching.

This theoretical justification for the patrician style has rarely been stated without challenge, even in Queen Anne's reign when legislation was passed restricting the right to sit in the Commons to substantial landowners. In 1792 the former Prime Minister Lord Lansdowne suggested that there could not be 'a more corrupt, ignorant, and tyrannical assembly' than one made up exclusively of such plutocrats.[4] Almost 200 years later, when Old Etonian Douglas Hurd contested the leadership of the Conservative Party, his (relatively) privileged background was seen as a serious handicap. The landed gentlemen who once dominated the House of Commons had been replaced by career politicians. In 1988 Willie Whitelaw noted his regret at the passing of his own kind, 'because they provided a backbone. They had no interest in advancement for themselves. They didn't in the main want to be ministers, they wanted to continue their work in their own counties . . . in their own constituencies.' In one of his last interviews he expanded on the theme. 'Society has changed. It's a shame. I liked things as they were. People were more gracious then.' At the same time, he felt that it was 'a gross over-simplification' to accuse patricians of excessive 'moral softness'; there was nothing wrong in feeling sympathy for their less fortunate contemporaries, provided that this compassion was 'accompanied by an inner toughness where necessary and justified'. Willie himself felt at ease with people from all levels of society and convinced them that he understood their concerns. His own sense of public duty was most unusual in the latter part of the twentieth century, and it might even be said that the 'Last of the Patricians' embodied the ideal better than most of his forerunners.[5]

For all Lord Whitelaw's reticence on the subject of his ancestors, family background was a crucial factor in the making of any 'patrician', and no account of his career in public life could be complete without some exploration of his origins. There were four outstanding features in Willie's background – industry, landed property, politics and war. Of these, the last had the most immediate impact on his life. Although the influence of the landed gentleman was already in decline, the fatal blow for the patrician outlook in Britain was the First World War, which ended the lives of so many promising young men from landed families and sapped the morale of the survivors. As David Cannadine has noted, 'Not since the Wars of the Roses had so many patricians died so suddenly and so violently.'[6] The Whitelaw family was not unusual in being almost wiped out by the conflict. In 1919 Willie's father – yet another William – weakened by wounds and the effects of poisonous gas, succumbed to pneumonia. At least he had married and produced an heir. His two brothers, who died in battle, had not had time to do so.

The First World War also interrupted the genealogical researches of one of Willie's more distant relatives, H. Vincent Whitelaw, whose health was broken by a spell under arms in Libya. However, he survived to complete a book on his family, which was published in 1928. He believed that his surname – meaning 'White hill' – was derived from an estate about four miles east of Haddington in East Lothian. Early spellings varied – there were also 'Wytelowes' and 'Quhitelaws'. An early Quhitelaw, Archibald (died 1498), was a clergyman who became tutor to two Scottish kings, served as an ambassador to England, Spain and France, held several high offices within the Church and was Secretary of State under James III of Scotland. He was noted for his learning, but must also have been a discreet and skilful negotiator. Other members of the family were as loyal as Archibald, even if they lacked his standards of political judgement. A sixteenth-century Sir Patrick Whitelaw was a devoted servant to Mary, Queen of Scots, and shared her captivity in England; he had taken his loyalty to the lengths of assisting his ally, the Earl of Bothwell, in the murder of Mary's unwanted husband Lord Darnley. Another Whitelaw, John, was hanged in 1683 for his part in the Covenantors' rebellion, while one of his brothers died on board ship having been deported for the same offence. Earlier in that century Jenny Geddes, a Whitelaw relative, protested against Charles I's religious policy by throwing a stool at the Archbishop of Edinburgh during a service in St Giles' Cathedral. Even these dissident Whitelaws could square their behaviour with the family tradition of loyal service to a powerful master; before his execution John Whitelaw declared that allegiance to the Lord meant that 'we should deny ourselves, and take up our cross and follow him'.[7]

The inquisitive H. Vincent Whitelaw was unable to trace the precise connection between these noteworthy members of the family and the branch which in the nineteenth century owned estates in Lanarkshire and Dumbartonshire. But he was confident that these Whitelaws were a junior offshoot of the original family. The first notable representative of this branch, a James Whitelaw, was sent to America as a land-agent and joined the rebel side in the War of Independence, rising to the rank of General and subsequently holding government office in the state of Vermont. The main property,

Gartshore, built on land rich in coal reserves about ten miles from Glasgow, was purchased in the mid-nineteenth century by Willie's great-grandfather, Alexander Whitelaw. In 1860 Alexander became a partner in the great steel-making firm, William Baird & Co., to which he was connected by marriage. According to Willie, he was regarded as a kind-hearted employer, while exercising in his personal life the classic 'Victorian value' of thrift. He combined a highly successful business career with the chairmanship of the Glasgow School Board, and in his last years he persevered with his public service despite chronic ill health.[8]

Alexander's eldest son (another Alexander, born in 1862) inherited Gartshore in 1879, and eight years later replaced the existing house with a more ambitious structure. He had married Benjamin Disraeli's niece Dorothy in 1886, but he died without issue in 1938. By then a family dispute had led to an arrangement that compensated his second brother Graeme in return for relinquishing his claims on the property. A third brother, Willie's paternal grandfather, was the new heir. This William Whitelaw already possessed land, at Nairn in the far north-east of Scotland, and in Kirknewton, Midlothian. But he was too dynamic to lapse into becoming an idle rentier. He was successively Chairman of the Highland Railway and of the London and North Eastern Railway Company (LNER); in addition, he became a Director of the Bank of Scotland and 'probably the most prominent lay Scottish Presbyterian of his generation'. His remarkable business career followed a flirtation with politics, in emulation of his father, who had represented the City of Glasgow in the Commons. In 1892 (at the age of twenty-four) Willie's grandfather won the City of Perth for the Conservatives – the first representative of his party to win there, as Willie later recorded with pride. The main issue at the election had been the Liberal policy of Home Rule for Ireland, and Whitelaw, an outspoken supporter of the Union, dedicated his own victory to 'the men of Ulster'. But he was defeated in the next general election (1895) and after another unsuccessful attempt (at a by-election in Banffshire in 1907) his wife persuaded him to turn his back on the ungrateful electorate. During his brief spell at Westminster he had vigorously upheld constituency interests, but he also hounded Home Office ministers (notably the future Prime Minister, Asquith) on overcrowding in prisons throughout Scotland. Demonstrating a balanced approach of which his grandson would have approved, he also advocated improved working conditions for prison officers. He made himself popular within his party by ridiculing slipshod opponents; in his last parliamentary speech he claimed that the Liberal MP for East Aberdeenshire 'had been stupid enough to make one of the silliest charges ever made in the House of Commons'. As an orator William Whitelaw was certainly a vast improvement on his father Alexander, who had been 'sadly lacking in the power of coherent expression'. In a significant compliment, Disraeli had asked the latter to deliver his maiden speech in reply to the Queen's Speech of February 1875, but Alexander's delivery was so poor that his fellow MPs had roared 'Here! Here!' only twice – when he apologised for detaining the House for too long, and when he sat down. Reporting to Queen Victoria, even Disraeli had to admit that the Member for Glasgow 'unfortunately spoke in the language of his country, and, so, soon lost the House', although the substance of his remarks had been 'sensible and acute'.[9]

In his memoir Viscount Whitelaw mentioned his grandfather's political foray, and the Disraeli connection (which did not help great-uncle Alexander, who stood for Parliament unsuccessfully on more than one occasion). Yet he overlooked the more successful career of his mother's maternal grandfather, Henry Baillie of Redcastle, MP for Inverness-shire from 1840 to 1868 and briefly President of the Board of Trade. Baillie was a close friend of Disraeli's; when in 1835 the latter seemed likely to have to fight a duel with the Irish MP Daniel O'Connell, he asked Baillie to act as his second.[10] Later Baillie was associated with Disraeli's radical 'Young England' grouping, and shared their antipathy to the rising middle classes; 'the old aristocracy and the working classes engrossed his attention'. However, like Viscount Whitelaw he 'attached very little importance to pedigrees', although he must have known that one of his distant ancestors (Sir William de Balliol) married the daughter of William Wallace.[11] His own wife was a daughter of the sixth Viscount Strangford, who had represented Britain at the Congress of Verona in 1821 and was later appointed Ambassador to Russia.

Strangford was a romantic figure, a published poet who provoked one of Byron's less inspired couplets in *English Bards and Scotch Reviewers* (1809):

> Hibernian Strangford, with thine eyes of blue,
> And boasted locks of red or auburn hue.

Although Strangford was some years older than Disraeli, he was an astute talent-spotter and another early friend of the future Prime Minister. His son George Smythe became a leader of 'Young England', and was the model for the eponymous hero of Disraeli's novel *Coningsby*. After Smythe's early death in 1857, Disraeli eulogised 'a man of brilliant gifts, of dazzling wit, of infinite culture, and of fascinating manners'. Smythe fully shared Young England's exalted notion of patrician duties, and deplored what he regarded as a decline in his own class over the preceding century.[12] He felt that money had been elevated over manners – a typical complaint for an impecunious aristocrat. Like so many who feature on Whitelaw's family tree, he also suffered for his loyalty, feeling that he had betrayed his friends when he accepted junior office under Sir Robert Peel. His career, according to Lord Lyttleton, was 'a splendid failure', but at least he earned some repute by taking part in the last duel fought on English soil (in 1852).[13] A more orthodox blood-relative of Viscount Whitelaw was his maternal grandfather Frank Russell – a brother of the brave Alexander of the *Birkenhead*. For a short time he was MP for Cheltenham, after a distinguished military career that included service in the Zulu War and a period as British military attaché in Berlin.[14]

In their more mundane dealings, the Whitelaws and their relatives epitomised the boasted virtues of the period – hard-working, God-fearing, devoted to their local community, to Scotland and to the United Kingdom as a whole. In his reaction to the death of his father, the infant Willie Whitelaw showed that he had inherited the stoicism of his ancestors, which was fully shared by his mother. Winnie Whitelaw had been devastated by the events of 1914–19 – if her experience were not poignant enough, her husband died on Valentine's Day of the latter year – and although she was widowed at only twenty-five, she never considered remarriage. But her recovery was helped by the presence of a living memento from her marriage. The first of many scrapbooks kept throughout her son's life contains numerous photographs of the chubby little boy, together with tables of weights during the first six months of his life and a meticulous record of various 'firsts' in his development. Born in Edinburgh at 2 a.m. on 28 June 1918, the child who would later tower over most of his contemporaries in the House of Commons weighed in at 6 lb 12 oz. He was christened William Stephen Ian Whitelaw. In the first scrapbook entries he is called Ian – the name his mother preferred because she feared that 'William' might be abbreviated by schoolfellows to 'Willie'. Her misgivings were only too well founded; the transition from 'Ian' to 'William/Willie' came early.

The recorded rites of passage in the scrapbook include momentous events such as Willie's introduction to travel by rail (aged two months), the first smile, the first and second teeth, and the entry 'Shortened, 3 Nov 1918', which recorded his liberation from the dress-like garment he had worn in his first months. His first faltering steps were noted in December 1919. There follow the usual snaps of young Willie looking angelic, if a little lonely, on a beach near his mother's home; a record of his first salmon catch (10 lb); and several equestrian photographs. Willie was remembered as a fearless, if slightly inelegant, rider to hounds, who would tackle stone walls when more cautious companions flinched. Princess Alice, Duchess of Gloucester, recalled 'a small plump boy on an even plumper pony'. Willie's hunting book records his enthusiasm. After one escapade in his seventeenth year he scribbled, 'Starlight went marvellously and she really is a topping mare. A day to be remembered all my life!!!!!' But his hunting passion was short-lived compared to his shooting career, which began in his early teens. Over eleven days during the 1933 season he and his companions slaughtered more than 500 birds. His appraisal of his own marksmanship was typically modest; in December 1935 he reported that the sport had been good, because everyone 'except me' had been 'very good shots'.[15]

Willie certainly was not deprived of love and adoration in his early years, verifying the letter (if not the sarcastic spirit) of another Byron couplet: 'An only son left with an only mother/is brought up much more wisely than another.'[16] But despite all the evidence of the maternal love lavished on the child, psychologists would agree with his own admission that being deprived of a father's influence was central to his later development. One lively historian has even produced a book to illustrate the regrettable long-term results that can follow the loss of at least one parent in early life; a surprising number of these unfortunate children have ended up trying to compensate by becoming Prime Ministers.[17] But the adult Willie Whitelaw remained convinced that there was no necessary disadvantage for a child in being brought up by a single parent. He demonstrated this belief in 1993 when Peter Lilley, then John Major's Secretary of State for Social Services, appeared to be trying to blame rising crime, moral decline and many other national misfortunes on the explosion in the number of single mothers. To their embarrassment, Lady Thatcher's former Deputy reminded Lilley and his Cabinet colleagues that he himself had been the product of a one-parent family.

Lilley could have replied that young Willie and his widowed mother constituted an unusual one-parent family. This was partly because of the strong character of Whitelaw's mother – a vast improvement on Mrs Byron – and partly because of the circumstances of the grandfather who took over the duties of surrogate father, albeit from a distance. Winnie Whitelaw was a redoubtable woman, who advised her son against becoming a big fish in a small pond, but satisfied herself with legendary status in the Nairn area where she served for many years as a councillor both at town and county level, paying particular attention to housing and roads. During the time when she was Convenor of the Roads Committee she was involved in a minor car accident at a junction. When she claimed that the driver of the other vehicle should have given way, it was pointed out that the road markings on the spot suggested otherwise. But Winnie Whitelaw was not someone who could easily admit that she was wrong. After her death, her son took delight in relating that the road markings were changed within days of the accident.[18] Her combination of dynamism, charm and stubbornness fitted her for national politics. In her seventies she told one interviewer that she would have stood for Parliament, had this seemed a realistic option when she was younger; however, she was scornful of 'this women's lib nonsense that everyone is talking about nowadays'. Proud of her nationality – although a doughty opponent of the Scottish independence movement – she rebuked anyone who mistook her son for an Englishman. Many years later, when an expert appraised a sample of Willie's handwriting, his judgement reflected the decisive influence of Winifred Whitelaw on her son's character: 'independent, honest, good judgement; needs to know he is appreciated'. Willie also owed his impressive speaking voice to his mother. His later parliamentary colleague Jack Page recalled a public meeting in the Highlands, at which he denounced the moral depravity of a novel that his wife had bought at an airport. Winnie rose and boomed, 'I agree with everything Mr Page has said and consider this pornography is disgraceful – but would he like to give me the name of the book?'[19]

Despite his love for his mother, Willie knew that she had to be handled carefully and occasionally her eccentricities were awkward for him. When he was in his mid-thirties he invited a friend to stay with him at Winnie's house. At dinner on the first day the friend noticed that while the others took wine at regular intervals, he was given only iced water. Having only just met Mrs Whitelaw, he kept quiet about this, but when they retired for liqueurs Willie came to his rescue. 'In a voice even louder than usual,' he shouted, 'Mummy, Robert is not an alcoholic.' After this reassurance the drinks were shared equally.[20]

Willie's admiration for his paternal grandfather was unequivocal. As he told James Margach in 1970, 'I am proud when any elderly person who remembers my grandfather when he was one of the leading speakers at the General Assembly of the Church of Scotland tells me that in my speech, appearance and style I am completely like him.' His grandfather was also generous. During the First World War, for example, he was visited by the wife of a Highland Railway employee whose health had been undermined by extra work imposed during the conflict. He had been forced to quit his job, and the company had refused any special payments for his time of hardship. The family's savings were nearly gone. The wife had been born in Nairn and decided to visit the company's Chairman at his home. As soon as he heard the story, William Whitelaw ordered that the ex-employee should be kept on the books.[21]

The fact that Willie shared his name with his grandfather could also be an advantage. Even those employees who had not met William Whitelaw senior knew of their Chairman, who had a locomotive named after him. On one occasion in his late teens, when Willie booked a train ticket, the staff assumed that he must be *the* William Whitelaw, and a complimentary bottle of good whisky was left in his compartment. Young Willie thought it best to enjoy the fruits of the mistake rather than pointing it out. More directly, William Whitelaw ensured that his daughter-in-law and his grandchild would want for nothing. He gave them his substantial house, Monkland, overlooking the sea near Nairn, paid the fees for Willie's expensive education, yet seems to have interfered remarkably little in the upbringing of his grandson. His only attempt came quite late in Willie's boyhood, when he tried to persuade Winifred to send the child to the same Scottish public school, Glenalmond, that his own father had attended (he himself was an alumnus of Harrow School). The formidable Winnie Whitelaw had different plans. It is a testament to her determination and to the strength of her personality – even her son admitted much later that he was a little frightened of her – that she eventually got her way.[22]

After receiving some lessons from 'an awe-inspiring' lady, in Nairn, Willie had briefly attended a local boys' school. In his memoirs he merely recorded that at this establishment he was 'bullied and learnt little'; in fact he was removed from the school when some boys made him swallow a stone. He was diverted to a run-down English prep school in Wokingham, which later became the highly thought-of Ludgrove. The shy and somewhat gawky child hated the place, which provided him with further evidence that small boys can be (and frequently are) appallingly nasty to each other, and especially so to companions who are already lonely and unhappy. Years later he wrote that the main unifying factor for the school's pupils and staff was hatred of its headmaster, a man who seems to have found a special pleasure in beating his charges with a racket.[23]

Winnie Whitelaw was determined that her son should learn something about the larger pond in which she hoped to see him swim. Even so, one is entitled to wonder why a mother and grandfather who cherished young Willie could have condemned a boy who even dreaded attending parties with other children to such miseries at the tender age of eight. If the mother did not realise from personal experience what could happen to her son at public school (and Willie himself records how distressed she was when she sent him off to his distant destination for the first time), the grandfather must have known. Presumably they saw it as a salutary test of character, and their faith in the boy was not misplaced. Whatever his feelings at the time about being sent away from home, Willie came to see Britain's public schools as a great blessing, maintaining that they provided not only 'a very sound education but something deeper in life too, an opportunity for friendship which is built up more closely, I believe, in a boarding school than it is elsewhere'.[24]

When Willie was twelve years old Mrs Whitelaw decided that she wanted her boy to go to Winchester, apparently because a couple who were close friends already had a son there.[25] But the rather second-rate prep school expressed the opinion that Willie was not up to passing the (notoriously difficult) entrance examination. Reassured by this information, Willie's grandfather indulged his daughter-in-law's fantasy and agreed that the boy should be allowed to sit the Winchester exam. To the astonishment of everyone except Mrs Whitelaw, Willie passed. As a result, in September 1931 he became a pupil at a school that is regarded as a nursery for Oxbridge dons, unflappable diplomats, noted military men like Lord Wavell, Civil Service permanent secretaries, numerous judges, high-minded politicians like Stafford Cripps and Hugh Gaitskell, and aggressive eggheads like Richard Crossman. Its public reputation is divided between the opinion voiced by Aneurin Bevan when he described Gaitskell as a 'dessicated calculating machine' and the one encapsulated by its own famous motto, 'Manners Maketh Man'. Inmates of rival public schools regarded Wykehamists as 'smug and dedicated bores'. Ironically, given that Crossman went on to produce one of the most indiscreet accounts of British government, his schoolfellows were reputed to be reserved even by public-school standards, adept at concealing their thoughts and well versed in deflecting probing questions with replies 'that came as close as possible to accuracy without actually telling the truth'.[26]

Willie's own affability was so far from the stereotypical style of his school that Harold Macmillan would later joke that he was 'a Wykehamist masquerading as an Etonian'. His rather casual attitude to schoolwork was as unusual as his easy social manner. One of Willie's teachers, Donald McLachlan, became a journalist and wrote a profile of his former pupil for the *Evening Standard* in 1967, when Whitelaw was the Opposition Chief Whip. McLachlan took a typically Wykehamist view of Whitelaw, who, he remembered, had certainly not been spoiled by 'premature intellectualism'. The young Willie, he declared, was 'the last boy among those I taught at Winchester for whom I would have predicted a successful political career . . . His ambition in life at that time was to excel at golf.' Not that McLachlan was trying to be disparaging; on the contrary, he was clearly impressed as well as surprised by Willie's emergence as a shrewd politician. At least the future Chief Whip was a Prefect in his House ('Hoppers', based in a building called 'Sunnysides'); in his future career his bark was always worse than his bite, and his instinctive leniency was supported at school by the fact that in his House prefects were rarely called upon to administer beatings.[27] Willie made no pretence of having been an outstanding scholar at Winchester, but on the other hand he did not take kindly to the widespread assumption that he was a duffer. He seems to have been really bad only at mathematics, which unfortunately was a compulsory subject for the School Certificate examinations. His maths teacher realistically concluded that his memory – which was excellent – might get him through. So he insisted that Willie should learn by heart all the necessary formulae and that he answer all the examination questions that related to them before attempting any of the others. Willie followed this advice and emerged from the examination in July 1934 with a credit. He was equally successful in scripture, English, history, French and Latin.

Half a century after his departure, Willie received the highest honour Winchester can offer, when he was received *Ad Portas*. He was greatly moved by the award, conferred on him during the wardenship of one of his closest friends, Lord Aldington, who as Toby Low had been head boy during Willie's second year at the school. The only snag was that part of Willie's speech of acceptance had to be recited in Latin, and he had forgotten almost everything he had been taught of this language. Fortunately a classical scholar in the Cabinet Office helped out, and with hindsight Willie felt that his speech passed off without obvious errors.[28] In the short passages that he was allowed to deliver in his native tongue, he revealed the depth of his feeling for Winchester, and contradicted the critics of his old school. 'Experience of life and people,' he said, 'has confirmed my view of some lasting values of a Wykehamist education. The lack of arrogance and pomposity are in themselves great virtues.' And he added, 'In my personal experience, Wykehamists especially are taught not only the need for work, but also equally important, how to work.' The value of hard work, and the importance of loyalty to family and institutions, were 'solid foundations in a changing world. Cling to them,' he told his audience. 'They will not let you down.'

At a school that valued physical exercise as highly as intellectual endeavour, Willie was positively hostile to athletics and only moderately interested in football (appropriately for one of his size, he often played in goal). He was not even very keen on cricket, despite the fact that he showed some ability. Like his grandfather and father, he represented Nairn County as a schoolboy; he also played for Winchester's Second Eleven. At his best he was a forceful batsman; the report of one match enthused that he 'went for the runs from the start'.[29] But his real passion was reserved for golf, something that his famously eccentric housemaster, Major Malcolm 'Bobber' Robertson, tried in vain to correct by pushing young Willie into activities such as cross-country running, birdwatching and butterfly collecting. Willie records in his autobiography that Robertson persuaded him to enter for a cross-country race, which he managed to finish at the cost of being violently sick at the finishing line. The 'Bobber' was delighted, awarding the boy full marks for effort. Presumably it was a stimulus of a different kind that later inspired Willie to emulate the Marquess of Exeter and race round the Great Court of Trinity College. It was almost midnight, and Willie had taken part in a 'very convivial' dinner-party at the invitation of the then Master of Trinity, 'Rab' Butler. At the time Willie was Secretary of State for Northern Ireland, in his mid-fifties, unfit and over-stressed. But witnesses were impressed by his speed; 'he easily led the pack, followed a pace or two behind by his detective and bodyguard'.[30]

When showing his wife around his old school in the 1980s, Willie exaggerated the hardships of his life at the time, claiming that there had been no water closets while he was at Winchester (he repeated this allegation in his memoirs, to the consternation of friends).[31] But his positive remarks at the *Ad Portas* ceremony reflected his genuine nostalgia for his later schooldays. Although at first he seemed shy, Willie blossomed at Winchester, to the extent that in his final year he took the initiative of arranging golf matches against other schools. He has left a vivid account of his introduction to this game. When he was four years old his mother (like her late husband, a golf addict) sent him for lessons to the Nairn professional, a Mr Nelson. At first Nelson would only allow young Whitelaw to swish at pine cones. After a few weeks of this 'unrewarding' exercise Willie protested to his mother. 'I don't want to go today,' he yelled, 'I hate Mr Nelson. I hate fir cones. I hate golf!' The true motivation behind these remarks registered with Mrs Whitelaw. At the start of the next lesson Nelson produced some golf balls. Willie recorded that his first 'real' attempt was successful, and that this induced a lifelong obsession, which at first was fostered by his loneliness: after all, this was one game that a child could practise even if he had no friends.[32] Easy access to a championship course, and the presence there of other gifted youngsters such as the later Walker Cup player David Blair, meant that Willie would almost certainly have been ensnared, even if the first shot had been 'topped' along the ground.

Willie continued to play regularly at both of his schools, and at fifteen competed in the British Boys' Championship. Like Blair, he won the Nairn Under-16 Cup, in 1933 progressed as far as the fifth round of the Boys' Championship held at the demanding Carnoustie course, and was named as a reserve for the 1935 Scottish Boys' side. But his real breakthrough came in 1937, when he reached the semi-finals of a tournament held at Lossiemouth. In July of the same year he competed in the Scottish Amateur Championship, and in the first round produced the best score (74) of those who competed at the Barassie club. This was only one stroke behind the overall leader, who played at a different course. After the second round Willie had slipped to five shots off the lead, but this still ensured that he was high among the qualifiers for the match-play stage. He was beaten in the second round, but his exploits had been prominently reported even in the national newspapers, which at that time devoted many column-inches to amateur golf. The features that would one day become among the best-known in public life are unmistakable in early photographs of Willie in action: the plaintive eyes and heavy brows, contrasting with the strong jaw, seemed a perfect accompaniment to a character that was at the same time stubborn and sensitive.[33]

When Willie went up to Trinity College in 1937 he applied himself to the task of winning a golfing 'blue'. The only distraction was the insistence of his grandfather, who was still paying the bills, that he must get a degree of some sort. With this in mind, the winter terms were devoted to golf while the summer was reserved for academic work. This strategy succeeded, to the extent that Willie not only got his blue in 1938 (by which time he was playing off a 'scratch' handicap) and was elected Captain of the university golf club the following year, but also achieved a part-one third in law – a subject he did not relish.

The standard of golf at Cambridge was particularly high at this time, and matches were regularly reported. The accounts provide useful insights into Willie's character, as well as his physical attributes. After a match in 1938 one good judge gave his views: 'Whitelaw, big and loose of limb and with a wide straddle, is not an elegant player, but he is a very sound, good and powerful one.' On the Nairn course, indeed, he was renowned as the only man to have driven the ball from the seventh tee onto the beach – a carry of 250 yards (he was so wayward, though, that at various times he sent his ball onto the beach at each of the first seven holes). Yet he was also capable of more subtle touches. His bunker-play was particularly adroit, and in a magazine article Henry Cotton (who helped with golf tuition at Cambridge) used a picture of him escaping from a sand-trap to illustrate the proper technique. Cotton thought that Willie 'had good hands but tended to be too much of a swinger and not enough of a hitter' – an interesting observation on such a prodigious striker of the ball. However, Willie was prone to the kind of temperamental display which years later would become very familiar to his political colleagues. In his seventies the impact of blade on ball would usually prompt the exclamation 'By Jove!', and the occasional 'Damn!' But these were no more than typical exclamations of the mature golfer, chastened by experience. In his youth he was the victim of unrealistic expectations, reinforced by a mother who (to his dismay) insisted on watching him compete and hated to see him lose. In one game he was all square with his opponent on the last tee, and took an iron club for safety. All the spectators heard Winnie's response, although she was probably trying to keep it to herself: 'No guts!' Willie lost the hole and the match. In another match he took exception to one of the spectators – a clergyman, who was praying for his opponent. After he had lost a match narrowly to Dai Rees, *The Times* reporter thought that he 'seemed a little sad' – presumably this was a tactful understatement of his emotional symptoms. On another occasion he played thirteen out of fourteen holes in six under-fours; on this form, it was reported, he 'might have overwhelmed anyone'. But he could be 'overwhelmed' himself, by nerves. His excellent opening round at the 1937 Scottish Amateur Championship would have been even better had he not taken three putts on each of the last two greens; at the final hole he contrived to miss the target from eighteen inches.[34]

Apart from his golf, Willie was also a regular poker player at Trinity;

fittingly for one who was later renowned as one of the shrewdest of all political operators, he was a formidable opponent although the stakes were never very high.[35] Despite the allure of these activities, he put in enough academic effort to secure a second in history when he sat the final part of his degree in the summer of 1939. That date tells one a great deal about Willie's university career. It encompassed the Munich agreement between Hitler and Neville Chamberlain, and was dominated from start to finish by mounting fears of war. Cambridge supplied a stream of anti-Fascist recruits to the Soviet cause, which many regarded as the only hope of successful resistance to the German, Italian and Spanish dictators. Willie himself took no interest in undergraduate politics; his attitude had been the same at Winchester, although the 'Bobber' had evidently been anxious to introduce his charges to political figures and on one occasion invited his most controversial former pupil – Oswald Mosley – to lunch with them.

Donald McLachlan suggested that Willie had been discouraged from political engagement by his disillusioned grandfather, which would have shown a surprising degree of sensitivity in the older man; Perth had been a safe Liberal seat, and he had only upset the trend in 1892 because a short-lived squabble produced two Liberal candidates in that year. In any case it seems that William Whitelaw was working along the grain of Willie's own inclinations at the time.[36] Indeed, he never attended a meeting of the Union Society, which he could have sneaked into without any fear that his grandfather would find out. But Willie was not immune to the fatalistic atmosphere created by the apparent inevitability of war; it was obvious to everyone that he and his contemporaries were going have to fight, when it came. Against this background, it is hardly surprising that many undergraduates found academic work increasingly pointless. Willie's sole venture into politics reflects this mood, for he admits to having joined a group of apolitical hearties who picketed a meeting addressed by Winston Churchill. The purpose of the meeting was to demonstrate that Cambridge rejected the Oxford Union's notorious vote against fighting for King and country, and Willie and his fellows appointed themselves to keep out any student who refused to make a patriotic declaration before they crossed the threshold. The vote was won, though whether from the persuasive powers of Churchill's oratory or the intimidatory influence of the picket line is unclear. Certainly a doorstep encounter with the 6-foot 4-inch Willie Whitelaw ('big, loose of limb') must have concentrated a few minds, though it could hardly be called democratic.[37]

A more practical demonstration of commitment to King and country had already been made when Willie, responding to the general atmosphere of foreboding, decided to join the university's Officer Training Corps. It turned out to be a good move, since it enabled him to become a regular rather than a temporary officer in the Scots Guards, thanks to a brief attachment with the regiment immediately after he had taken his degree in the summer of 1939. When war finally came, on Sunday 3 September 1939, Willie was immediately offered a regular commission. It was time to put aside childish things – even the treasured golf clubs – and attend to the more serious matter of defeating Hitler. By the time that had been accomplished, six years later, Willie was the holder of a Military Cross, wore the single crown of a Guards major and was the battle-seasoned second-in-command of a tank battalion. He had also acquired three of the most important qualifications for the career in politics that was to follow. First, he had had what Conservatives like to call 'a good war' – a crucial help in securing selection as a Tory candidate in a winnable seat in the immediate post-war years. Second, exposure to a wider environment fostered his social conscience – a concern for others, which he seems to have felt from his early days. Finally, as the deputy to his battalion commander, he had built on an existing sense of the overriding importance of loyalty, which carried over from war into peace.

CHAPTER 2

'NEVER LOOK BACK . . .'

Some of Willie's Cambridge contemporaries – especially those who joined the Territorial Army – found themselves in France very soon after enlistment and were exposed to Hitler's blitzkrieg in the summer of 1940. This was not the case for Whitelaw's unit. Like tens of thousands of other would-be warriors, Willie and his fellow Scots Guardsmen spent the greater part of the war in a succession of encampments within the United Kingdom, engaged in what was often euphemistically called 'training'. At first this activity was directed to the defence of Britain from the gradually diminishing threat of invasion from the continent of Europe. Later it became a preparation for the cross-Channel invasion that everyone knew would be essential if the total defeat of Nazi Germany was to be achieved.

As Willie conceded, the initial part of this training seemed to be directed towards fighting a repeat performance of the Great War of 1914–18. There was much digging of trenches and gas-mask drill, combined with the endless square-bashing at which Guards regiments are expected to excel, even in wartime. After Willie's period in the army was over, he told the House of Commons that a boy who joins up 'wants a smart uniform and the opportunity to show it off, and to show off the smartness which he has gained through drill'. At the Guards depot at Pirbright in Surrey he and his colleagues were given ample opportunity to acquire this 'smartness'; even if he did not appreciate it at the time, he came to recognise its value in later years when he concluded that 'the smartest units are always the best fighting units'.[1] The long months of drill were followed by Willie's dispatch, as a fully qualified subaltern, to join a Scots Guards detachment detailed to defend the Croydon aerodrome (where Neville Chamberlain returned from Munich with the famous piece of paper bearing Hitler's signed promise of peace in exchange for a slice of Czechoslovakia). Willie's small Guards detachment was commanded by a so-called 'retread' –

a recycled First World War captain who spent most of his evenings in town, attending a perpetual round of parties. According to Willie, he would return from these outings next morning in a sour mood and would then reprimand his two subalterns for idleness.[2]

The standard punishment for this crime was an order to spend the whole night tramping round all the sentry posts on the airfield perimeter. At the suggestion of the sergeant of the guard – who would have had to accompany Willie on his long march, even though he was not included in the captain's accusation of idleness – Willie decided to make his rounds in a little Morris Eight that he then owned, rather than on foot. Though the car broke down en route, and had to be push-started by the sentries, Willie got back to the guardroom before the captain returned from town at his customary 4 a.m. To the muffled hilarity of the entire unit, Willie was complimented on performing a good night's work.

But the Croydon assignment was only a temporary halt on Willie's journey. With the capriciousness familiar to all ex-servicemen, the army decided to make the profoundly unmechanical Lt Whitelaw a transport officer. In this capacity he was sent to join the 3rd Battalion of his regiment at Loughton, Essex, where they saw out the remainder of the London blitz without damage or casualties. Then came the decision to withdraw the 3rd Battalion from its traditional infantry role and turn it into a tank unit, with the original purpose of attaching it to the Guards Armoured Division. With a further flash of inspiration, the army then chose Willie as the battalion's technical adjutant. As he cheerfully recorded, his method of performing this challenging job was to walk round the lines of vehicles with a stick, with which he would bang on the armour plate, shouting 'Repairs going all right?' Willie was already appreciated for his shrewdness, generosity and ebullience – his 'warm and genuine humanity', as the Battalion's popular padre, George Reid, put it many years later – and the squaddies saw to it that he did not make too much of an ass of himself.[3]

Willie's technical prowess was illustrated in an anecdote that he omitted from his memoirs – possibly because by that time the tale had been told so often, and with so many variations, that he could no longer be certain of the true sequence of events. During a course for technical adjutants held at Bovington in Dorset he encountered Brian Johnston, then a lieutenant in the Grenadier Guards and later a much-loved cricket commentator. Along with an older officer, Gerald Upjohn (who was already a distinguished barrister and became a High Court judge after the war), they were ordered by an instructor to reassemble engines from which every nut and bolt had been extracted. Before the exercise they had been warned that the engines were much harder to put back together than to take apart, and that the officer in charge usually checked for any signs of cheating. All three men managed to put together working machines, but Johnston turned to Willie and asked, 'How many bolts have you got left?'

'A pocketful,' Willie admitted. 'So have I,' said Johnston mournfully. As the supervising officer bore down on the incompetent pair, Willie and Johnston sneaked the incriminating bolts into Upjohn's clothing. For some reason the officer ordered the unsuspecting Upjohn to turn out his pockets. At this point Willie and Johnston owned up to their prank, but the trio were all described as being 'unsound under pressure' in their end-of-course reports. In another version, related by William Douglas-Home who was an amused witness, Willie and Johnston were not so honourable. After being unmasked, Upjohn was left to finish the job on his own while the real culprits retired for a celebratory drink.[4]

The switch to tanks involved a move by the battalion to the historic nursery of the British Army, Salisbury Plain. This was towards the end of 1942, and the training continued with a mounting sense of frustration until July 1944, a few weeks after D-Day. After four tedious years of preparation, during which Willie's battalion had become as much a band of brothers as any fighting unit, they were about to carry out the task for which they had been thrown together. It was to be traumatic for all of them. In the space of approximately five minutes of what was later to be known as the Battle of Caumont, Willie was to see many of his friends literally blown to pieces or, worse still, burned to death inside their tanks.

To follow what happened at Caumont, and what led up to it, it is first necessary to explain the peculiar status of Willie's battalion of Churchill tanks. It had been incorporated in the specially formed 6th Guards Armoured Brigade. As one of Willie's closest colleagues has written, it was natural that the British 'should seek to form an armoured division from among their "elite" troops'. The 6th (which later split from the Guards Armoured Division and became the Guards Tank Brigade) was 'elite' in more ways than one; among other notables, it contained 'a future Lord Chamberlain, the man who would become Moderator of the Church of Scotland, the future chairman of United Biscuits and five lord lieutenants'.[5] But the unit had a bad start, in that it came close to disbandment shortly before D-Day in order to be subjected to the military equivalent of asset-stripping on behalf of other formations. The brigade was saved only by the direct intervention in April 1944 of the Prime Minister, Winston Churchill. In the same month the men were given their first clear hint that their 'phoney war' was coming to an end, with the cancellation of privilege leave and the imposition of censorship on outgoing mail. They moved south, and paraded for what the regimental history describes as 'a deeply moving service before battle' at Canterbury Cathedral on 30 May. The service was conducted by the Dean of the Cathedral, Dr Hewlett Johnson, better known at the time as 'the Red Dean' because of his slavish support for the Soviet Union and its murderous dictator, Joseph Stalin. But the sermon was preached by the then Archbishop of Canterbury, William Temple, and among those who heard it was a young Guards officer who was later to become Archbishop himself. This was Lt Robert Runcie, a mess-colleague of Willie's in the 3rd Battalion, who became his close and lifelong friend.

A few weeks later, just after the D-Day landings, the 6th Brigade participated in some spectacular tank exercises in a part of the Kent countryside that was held to be very similar to the so-called 'Bocage' country in Normandy – tiny enclosed fields divided by thick hedges and narrow, sunken lanes – over which the British tanks would have to fight. The exercise was officially regarded as a great success, and was extremely useful in acclimatising the tank drivers to what was to come (unfortunately this experience was denied to the infantry, who in battle were supposed to follow in the wake of the tanks). It was also, according to the battalion's historian, exceedingly expensive in claims for compensation from local farmers whose fields, hedges and ditches had been damaged.

A further word has to be said about the Churchill tank with which Willie's battalion was equipped. One of them stands in a corner of the central lobby of the Imperial War Museum in south London, while in the diagonally opposite corner stands an example of the kind of armoured vehicle that Willie and his friends faced on Caumont Ridge in July 1944 – the German Tiger tank. The Churchill, though not exactly beautiful, looks positively cuddly in comparison to the vast and menacing Tiger, whose huge 88mm gun points directly across the exhibition hall at the more lightly armed Churchill. But it was not only in firepower that the Tiger outstripped the Churchill. It was significantly faster – not all that difficult an achievement, since the Churchill was a notoriously slow vehicle. On the other hand, the Tiger was designed for speed in open country like the Russian steppes – the natural terrain for large-scale tank warfare. The Churchill, by contrast, turned out to be well suited to the bumpy, up-and-down nature of the Normandy Bocage, and to close cooperation with infantry in such surroundings.

But these discoveries lay in the future for Willie. Eventually, six weeks after D-Day, the order came through to leave Kent and head for Gosport for embarkation. The battalion set out for France on 20 July, and after a rough crossing was unloaded on Jig Beach, half a mile east of the famous artificial harbour at Arromanches. The troops assembled in an orchard outside Esquay, two miles east of Bayeux. But there had been a hitch: the Tank Landing Ship in which 'S' Squadron – the one commanded by Lt Whitelaw – had left Gosport along with the rest had not arrived at the beach. Thanks to the compulsory radio silence, no one knew whether 'S' Squadron had perished or simply turned back. There was much anxiety in the battalion.

What had happened was that high winds and rough weather in the Channel had caused eight of 'S' Squadron's tanks to break loose from the chains, and there was absolute mayhem as the heavy vehicles crashed backwards and forwards with every heave of the deck. It turned out that this was because the vessel was extremely old and its chains seriously weakened by rust. Willie and his men – many of whom were seasick – tried desperately to secure the runaway tanks in the blacked-out hold. It proved a hopeless as well as an extremely dangerous task. In the end the skipper of the vessel decided to heave to, switch on the lights, in spite of the danger from U-boats, and do a temporary job of re-attaching the chains before putting back to Gosport for repairs. Fortunately the damage turned out to be relatively minor, new chains were fixed and the voyage was resumed in calm weather. Willie and his comrades eventually arrived, feeling weak and exhausted after fifty hours cooped up in their rusty tub. Their belated arrival in the orchard occupied by the rest of the battalion was greeted with general rejoicing.

They were to stay there for the best part of a week, paying social calls on other units and sampling 'the products of the countryside'. Since the most famous of these were cider and calvados, one can assume that the sampling resulted in a marked improvement in morale. More serious, however, was the discovery of the abandoned wrecks of tanks lost during the initial D-Day landings. After inspecting them with some apprehension, it was decided that it would be prudent to weld extra armour onto the vulnerable Churchills.

The order to move came at 7 p.m. on 28 July. Two hours later the battalion arrived at Ste Honorine-le-Ducy, just three miles behind the British front line on the ridge of Caumont l'Evente to the east, where they were to take part next day in Operation 'Bluecoat'. The aim was to break through the hinge in the German line near the Bois du Homme at the extreme end of the ridge. But the broader intention was to tie up the German armour so as to keep it away from the American sector to the west of Caen, where the main Allied attack was to be launched. At the time, General Montgomery was under criticism from the Americans for the failure of his British and Canadian troops to make a breakthrough, in spite of repeated and costly attempts. Eventually Operation Bluecoat was advanced by three days to prevent the transfer of two German Panzer divisions to the American sector, thereby making sure that the Americans would be facing infantry unsupported by armour. As a result of this urgency 'there was little time for reconnaissance or very detailed planning'. No fewer than three British corps were to take part in the operation. They included the 15th Scottish Division, to which the 6th Guards Tank Brigade belonged, and it was their task to make the initial breakthrough on the ridge and to enable the Guards Armoured Division, with faster tanks, to drive through and complete the job. Therefore the operation's overall success depended on the performance of Willie's untried battalion.[6]

They arrived at the assembly area next morning, after a sleepless night on the road. Their orders were to support the infantry of the Argyll and Sutherland Highlanders, who were to lead the attack through the fields, hedges and ditches of the Bocage country. The German infantry – six battalions, plus a battalion of self-propelled guns from the 2nd Panzer Division – were well dug in across this ideal defensive country, but had not expected to face tanks in such surroundings. In his typically low-key account of the battle, Willie remarks that they had reckoned without the magnificent cross-country qualities of the Churchill tank. Eighteen of them, each manned by five men, constituted 'S' Squadron under Willie's command.[7]

They set off at 7.30 a.m. on 30 July, to face a baptism of fire for which they had been preparing for more than four wearisome years. In a characteristic remark many years later, Willie recalled that he had not been afraid of being shot, 'because, if they shoot you dead, you can't do anything about it'. But the prospect of action was doubly awesome for him, because this was the moment when he discovered the fundamental challenge of leadership – namely, the need to inspire confidence in others when you feel anything but confident yourself. It was a relief when they began to move up the ridge, breasted the top and started the descent into the maze of hedges, fields and orchards – countryside that one officer compared to a giant waffle. Crossing such terrain would have been slow and difficult even without an enemy. Under fire, it became necessary to subject each new field to a quick inspection to make sure that it was free from Nazi tanks or anti-tank guns. As they proceeded, Willie's gunners sprayed every hedge with bullets more or less at random. But in spite of this, they scarcely saw a single German soldier, either dead or alive, throughout the advance. This seems to have been a common but distinctly eerie experience among men whose war was fought inside armour-plated boxes.

But unlike the infantry, at least the men in tanks were protected from the hail of answering small arms fire that eventully brought the Argylls to a halt. Just as the advance faltered, however, Willie's tank hit a mine. It was clambering up yet another embankment topped by a hedge, lost one of its tracks and thus became useless as a command vehicle. Willie records in his memoirs that, under German fire, he covered the distance from his own crippled tank to an undamaged one at a speed that would have astonished his old housemaster at Winchester.[8] He was no sooner inside the new tank when he received orders that, because the attack was falling behind schedule, his squadron and its neighbour should leave the Argylls behind and crash on alone. They did so, and by 12.15 they were so far ahead of their infantry that they were ordered to halt. But it proved impossible for the Argylls to catch up, the tank advance was resumed, and in the event the infantry did not rejoin their armour until several hours later. By mid-afternoon the two leading squadrons of the battalion, headed by Willie's, were stuck on an exposed ridge four miles inside enemy territory, without anti-tank guns or infantry support. Though the squadron's right flank was secure, it was highly vulnerable on the left.

The natural expectation was that any German counter-attack would come from the south, so the tanks remained hull down on the northern slope of the ridge, in textbook fashion. As Willie admitted, greater experience of war would have told them that, without infantry support, they were now in serious danger. But at that moment Willie was ordered to attend a meeting at battalion HQ in a nearby orchard. He travelled there in an unarmoured scout car, but while they were conferring the whole group was alarmed to hear an oubreak of heavy firing from the direction in which his squadron lay. He and the popular battalion second-in-command, Sydney Cuthbert, rushed back to see what was going on – Cuthbert in his tank and Willie in his harder-to-spot scout car. As they hurried along, Willie records that he witnessed something so horrifying that his senses were 'completely dulled'.[9] The turret of Cuthbert's tank suddenly lifted right off the hull and landed on the ground, leaving the tank blazing like a furnace. Willie was so astonished that it did not at first occur to him that the tank must have had a direct hit from a very big armour-piercing shell. After a quick look at the fearful scene, in which five men had been incinerated, he returned to his squadron to find two more tanks in flames and his scout car's wireless operator reporting that he could get no answer from any of the others.

'S' Squadron had had the misfortune to be the first British unit to encounter three of the awsome new German JAGD Panther tanks, armed with an extra-long high-velocity 88mm gun. The presence of these monsters was a mystery – there were only twelve of them on the entire Western Front. While the much more lightly armed Churchills sat and waited to be attacked from the south, the first devastating salvoes from the JAGDs emerged from a wood on the squadron's left-rear. In theory, the wood should have been safely in the hands of the infantry. But they were still struggling through the bullet-swept fields of the Bocage.

German shells knocked out all three of the tanks in one troop of the squadron. Then two of the German tanks emerged from the wood and, covered by a third, lumbered towards the remainder of the squadron. They drove straight through the British position, blasting eight more tanks one by one, at point-blank range. They then slithered away down the ridge to the south, with one of the German commanders clearly visible in his turret. One of those who witnessed the carnage recalls that the man was laughing uproariously.[10] The only consolation for Willie's men was that two of the JAGDs were later found abandoned, one of them having been hit in the track.

But it was not much consolation. At the final count, the battalion had lost twelve tanks, its second-in-command had been killed together with twenty-one others and two of Willie's troop commanders had been wounded, along with eighteen other guardsmen. The whole episode had lasted no more than five minutes. In spite of this, Willie, who took Cuthbert's place as second-in-command of the battalion, reorganised the remainder of his squadron and stayed on the ridge preparing for further trouble. The respect he had already won within the unit, and his apparent calmness during the crisis, proved invaluable in rallying his shocked comrades. At 7.30 p.m., twelve hours after Willie and his men had set out, the infantry arrived with their vital anti-tank guns. 'S' Squadron was ordered to withdraw for refuelling – both for the tanks and for the men.

It had been an atrocious introduction to the realities of war, for it was (as the regimental historian remarked) at once glorious, tragic and exceptional. It was glorious because before the fatal ambush, this untried battalion had effectively destroyed an entire German division and achieved the crucial breakthrough required of Operation Bluecoat. Vital ground and a strategically important road had been captured from the retreating Germans. It was tragic because of the heavy losses incurred by the battalion in general, and Willie's squadron in particular. It was exceptional because these losses represented one-third of all the fatal casualties suffered by the battalion throughout the entire campaign up to the end of the war. All but four of those who were killed were in Willie's squadron; the dead included Captain Charles Grey, another product of Winchester, who had been the youngest member of the House of Commons when he was elected MP for Berwick-upon-Tweed (his death left a vacancy that was briefly filled by Sir William Beveridge).

The praise attracted by the success of the operation could not make up for the pain. As Willie wrote later, 'Then as now, I would gladly have given up all the glory in return for the lives of my friends and colleagues. Nor could I ever get away from that awful "if only" feeling. If only I had guarded the rear more effectively . . .'[11] He never forgot those appalling five minutes, and considered that they changed his entire attitude to life and to his fellow human beings. His self-criticism, of course, was far too severe; even if he had been in a position to give the necessary orders, he could not have known the extent of the danger to his squadron. But the true depth of his emotion is indicated by the fact that in his scrapbook of the war years he pasted photographs of his doomed comrades, alive and smiling, above pictures of their makeshift graves in those foreign fields. He had regarded 'S' Squadron, in whose training he had played a central role, as something like an extended family. Willie wrote to the widows and parents of all the young men who died, and he continued to keep in touch with them.

In his memoirs Willie recorded that Caumont taught him that in life 'One must always look forward, never back.'[12] But this advice could not protect him from the searing memory of battle. The suffering he witnessed was almost certainly the single most important influence in his subsequent political life. It is a fact that most of those who adopted the 'tooth and claw' free-market philosophy associated with Margaret Thatcher were too young to have served in the war. But it would be misleading to apply to Willie the clichéd view that many well-to-do young men came back from the war full of good intentions because they had suddenly realised that the ordinary soldier was a human being, much like themselves. Certainly Willie was deeply affected by the comradeship that can spring up when men from varying backgrounds face danger together. But his life in Nairn had not been sheltered; instead of holding themselves aloof from the less fortunate inhabitants, he and his mother had been part of the community as a whole. It seems that participation in the drama of war, in which shared moments of humour could be turned to tragedy without warning, confirmed an existing conviction that life was too short to be consumed by emnity, whether petty or on the grand scale. Like all members of his class, Willie could hardly be unaware of distinctions in rank, but wherever possible he would take people as he found them, try to live in harmony with those he met and defuse tensions between others.

Almost a year after Caumont, when the 3rd Battalion had ceased to be a tank unit and was rejoining the Guards Division in the army of occupation in the Rhineland, it was inspected by the famous General Sir Miles Dempsey, the commander of the 2nd Army. In his address, he told them that he would always think of them as the tank unit that achieved the breakthrough at Caumont. 'After that, I considered that victory was only a matter of time,' he said. For Willie, however, there were certain immediate personal benefits that flowed from those terrible few minutes. Far from being held responsible for the losses suffered by his unit, he was awarded an immediate Military Cross for his part in the action – probably one of the quickest MCs ever awarded in the field. Although the account in his memoirs plays down his heroism – to the extent that the reader is almost invited to feel that he won the medal by accident – the citation stressed not only his achievement in rallying his troops, but the efficiency with which he had organised the original advance. His battlefield promotion to second-in-command of the battalion, in succession to Major Cuthbert, was made permanent. This appointment meant that Willie could develop that most characteristic quality of his professional life, both as a soldier and as a politician: his ability to comfort the aggrieved and encourage the disappointed. This was a vital quality at the time, because the battalion commander, a Colonel Dunbar, was an excellent soldier but a hard man, a weak diplomatist and a poor communicator with his underlings. Above all, he could never bring himself to say 'Well done', or anything appreciative at all, no matter how great the achievement. Robert Runcie, a fearless soldier who was to win an MC himself later in the campaign, remembered that when Willie became Number Two to Dunbar, he took it upon himself to be the person who went round smoothing the ruffled feathers, saying 'There, there' to men who had been offended and phrases like 'He loves you really' to those who felt they had been unjustly insulted or abused. This, Runcie insisted, became a crucial part of Willie's function as the war progressed. In Runcie's opinion, it was a valuable trial run for his subsequent role as Margaret Thatcher's Deputy Prime Minister.[13]

But being second-in-command, rather than a squadron commander, also meant that the rest of Willie's war was less traumatic. One reason was that the Churchill tanks, which had been such a success in the tight, close-up fighting in Normandy, proved far too slow for the rapid advance that followed the breakthrough. As a result, they tended to be kept in reserve – although in Holland they were engaged in combat for twenty-four successive days, were the first British tank unit to cross the German Siegfried line and were heavily involved in the Battle of Winnekendonk shortly after the Arnhem disaster.

There were lighter moments to relieve the pain of men who had lost close friends with such sudden violence. For example, a fortnight after Caumont they were entertained by a concert party, with a cast that included George Formby. In quiet times there was also scope for improvised entertainments. 'Killer' Runcie was to the fore in these activities. One one occasion, apparently during the unit's time in Germany, a camp dance was proposed. Someone pointed out that the event might be more entertaining if there were some women in attendance. Runcie intervened to say that, if they would provide him with the necessary transport, he would guarantee to deliver the girls. A couple of two-and-a-half tonners were laid on, though with considerable scepticism, and everyone was astounded when the future Primate of All England drove into camp a few hours later with two lorryloads of giggling women.[14]

The battalion crossed the Rhine on 25 March 1945, two days after Field Marshal Montgomery had arrived in person to present Willie with his Military Cross. In the spring of 1944 Montgomery had been infuriated by Churchill's decision to keep the 6th Tank Brigade in existence; now he had changed his mind. There were still dangers to be faced, and losses were being incurred from enemy fire or from accidents. On one occasion during the advance across Europe Willie's scout car attracted attention as he arrived at some farm buildings for consultations with members of his battalion and American paratroopers. His friend Charles Farrell remembered that because of the German shelling, the discussions had to be conducted under a wooden table. But he also recalled Willie's words of greeting before the shelling started: 'Simply splendid! Simply splendid!', accompanied by 'a circular wave with the hand held stiffly from the wrist'. His comrades were already familiar with a form of greeting that would be seen and heard many times during Willie's political career, even in the most unlikely circumstances.[15]

Major Whitelaw was on temporary leave when his comrades entered Germany. But he was back in time for the 5 May Armistice. He celebrated the news of Hitler's death with a cigar – the only time, surprisingly, that he had ever succumbed to tobacco throughout his career in uniform. Even this was in fulfilment of a promise he had made, which was enforced by comrades who burst in on him early in the morning, brandishing the cigar. In conformity with his pledge he appeared at breakfast smoking, but detested the taste and never exposed himself to it again.[16]

For Willie, there were three final formative experiences to be undergone before the business of active soldiering came to an end. The first and most searing of these was a visit to the notorious death camp at Belsen. With characteristic generosity, Willie wrote that the surrounding countryside through which he approached the camp gave no sign of the appalling horrors inside it, and that it was therefore quite conceivable that the local inhabitants had been unaware of the full truth of what was being done there. But the total degradation of human life that he witnessed at Belsen became a permanent fixture in his memory. Like the trauma of Caumont Ridge, it almost certainly contributed to his instinctive support for the ideal of European cooperation, which he consistently regarded as crucial to the establishment of peace and reconciliation between Germany and her former enemies and victims.[17]

The second significant experience was the process of accepting the unconditional surrender of the German military machine, in which Willie had a walk-on part. He was ordered to take the surrender of a small coastal town in Schleswig-Holstein called Lütjenburg. On arrival, he and his party of Guards officers in their threadbare battle dress and scuffed boots were comprehensively upstaged by their German opposite numbers, who turned out in carefully pressed uniforms complete with immaculate breeches and gleaming field-boots. Given his view that smartness was inseparable from military efficiency, it must have been an unnerving encounter for Willie. He records that the senior German officer saluted, and said in perfect English, 'I surrender Lütjenburg to you, and with it all responsibilities.' Willie did not immediately appreciate what that word 'responsibilities' entailed – until he realised that the town was bursting with refugees, many of whom had fled from the advancing Russians. It was his dismal job to evict many of these desperate people from their temporary homes in order to provide billets for his own troops. 'At that moment there was little pleasure in victory,' he recorded.[18]

In August 1945 Willie left his old unit and was sent as a staff officer to join the 1st Guards Brigade in Palestine. Originally the brigade had been earmarked for the task of invading the Japanese mainland, but they were spared what would have been a dangerous and bloody engagement by the dropping of atomic bombs at Hiroshima and Nagasaki. In Palestine, however, Willie had a third formative experience. The brigade took on a role with which Willie was to become all too familiar in Northern Ireland – counter-terrorism. He records that he and his colleagues at the sharp end of the affair were often scathingly critical of the orders they received from the politicians back home in London; for example, they were detailed to search houses for arms, well aware that the insurgents had advance warning and would have hidden their stockpiles. Later, as the Cabinet's first Northern Ireland Secretary, Willie was acutely conscious that the men charged with carrying out his orders were almost certainly equally critical of him, and for much the same reasons. Perhaps here, too, he was over-sensitive. Now that the full horror of Hitler's persecution had been revealed, the task of suppressing those who were fighting for a Jewish homeland was unlikely to be relished by any British soldier. In his memoirs Willie records that his colleagues felt 'considerable sympathy for the Jews', and clearly he shared that view. Presumably this explains why he does not record his reaction to such terrorist atrocities as the destruction of the King David Hotel, which took place while he was still in Palestine and underlay a general antipathy in his unit towards the British Foreign Secretary Ernest Bevin, who 'never understood the driving force of Jewish nationalism' and could be 'monumentally insensitive in the handling of Jewish grievances'. During his military career Willie had also recognised that soldiers could suffer from the wrong-headed orders of their immediate superiors. Years later he revealed that on one occasion he had been ordered to make a particular disposition of his men. He seemed to agree, but as soon as the messenger left he gave quite different instructions. When someone suggested that they should obey the original order, Willie lost his temper: 'What! Do you want to get us all bloody well killed!'[19]

Two other events took place during Willie's period as a soldier. The first and most important of these was his marriage to Celia Sprot, a childhood friend who also came from a distinguished Scottish family. Willie remembered that he first met Celia when, at the age of eight, he was dragged to a children's tea party and was trounced in a game of 'Racing Demon'. Although he had an excuse for losing to Celia, who was his senior by eighteen months, he 'went home feeling miserable and rather frightened of the family'. But the two mothers were old friends, and it seems quite probable that Winnie secretly hoped, and perhaps even actively planned, for the marriage. In any event, it was she who informed her son, during his long and tedious sojourn on Salisbury Plain in 1942, that his intimidating holiday playmate was now serving in the Auxilliary Territorial Service (ATS) and was attending a course not far away in the New Forest. Dutifully Willie invited her to dinner in Salisbury. The event was a triumphant success, for they fell in love over the dinner table, at what Willie called 'renewed sight'.[20] They were married in St Giles' Cathedral in Edinburgh on 6 February 1943; Charles Farrell was best man. On the day Willie was sporting a moustache, but this adornment proved to be an early casualty of the marriage.

The vow to love and honour each other until death did them part must have seemed grimly immediate at the time, with the certainty of an eventual invasion of Europe looming over the newly-weds. Almost certainly Willie's decision to marry and start a family at that perilous moment, rather than waiting for peace, was influenced by the fate of his own father, and his determination to continue his line whatever might befall him. In fact, the marriage lasted well beyond their golden wedding anniversary, and everyone who saw them together appreciated that it was not just a warm and loving personal relationship, but also the central pillar of Willie's subsequent career. Whitelaw himself, in an early example of those delightful 'Willie-isms' that were to become his trademark, put the matter succinctly. He told one bemused journalist, 'She is much more than she says she isn't, if you follow me.'[21] Celia originally believed she was marrying a professional soldier. She only discovered much later that she had become the life-support system of a politician, but she adapted perfectly to the new role.

That change of occupation from regular soldier to upwardly mobile politician only became possible because of a second event – Willie's inheritance, on the death of his grandfather in January 1946, of the mansion at Gartshore, plus the substantial estates that surrounded it. At the time Willie was still serving in Palestine (where for the second time in his career he earned a mention in dispatches). It was clear both to him and to the family that it would not be possible to combine soldiering with running a large agricultural estate in Scotland; and Willie was also missing his wife and two young children, Susan (born in 1944) and Carol (1946). He returned from Palestine in October 1946, and after a few more months serving at the Pirbright Guards Depot he resigned his commission. But this was by no means the end of his connection with the Guards. Even when he was at his most active on the political scene he would attend reunions with the surviving members of the 'happy family' with whom he had spent the most dramatic period of his life. He had forged with the Guards another of those crucial ties of loyalty that he always prized so highly. It was no surprise that he chose the Guards' Chapel on Birdcage Walk in London as the venue for his memorial service.

CHAPTER 3

A GENTLEMAN IN POLITICS

After leaving the army Willie returned to his family to begin learning the entirely new trade of estate management. Happily, he had the help of John Park, a wise estate manager whose value to the Whitelaw fortunes extended well beyond the agricultural sphere. Perhaps his greatest service was to warn his new employer that he would sooner or later be invited to become a member of Lloyd's, the London insurance market. 'Don't on any account do it,' said Park. Willie took this excellent advice to heart, and thereby saved himself from the appalling financial losses – in some cases amounting to total ruin – that engulfed several of his colleagues on the Conservative benches during the 1990s.[1]

In retirement Willie revealed that his interest in politics had begun while he was in the army, but the idea of running for Parliament does not seem to have occurred to him until he had been settled at Gartshore for a couple of years. He did not join the Conservative Party until 1948, although he was an enthusiastic supporter of the Nairn MP, Churchill's Chief Whip James Stuart (who also had won an MC, in the First World War). True to the best standards of his class, Willie engaged in good works in the locality and returned with relish to golf. In August 1949 he won the Nairn Open, in succession to his friendly rival David Blair. As a local paper recorded, with this victory he 'realised one of his earliest sporting ambitions'. It was a popular result, and Willie was recognised as a worthy champion because of his 'crisp iron shots' and 'his extraordinarily long driving'. He was less successful in four assaults on the British Amateur Championship, between 1950 and 1954. In 1951, for example, he was crushed six and five by an American amateur in the third round; on this occasion it seems that he was reconciled to being outclassed by a better-prepared opponent, because despite his ill-fortune on the course he was described as 'smiling Whitelaw, a former Cambridge Blue and now a week-end golfer'. But even if other distractions prevented him from devoting as much time as he would have wished to playing, his status within the game was such that he was chosen as a selector for Britain's Walker Cup team for the 1953 contest against America, and he served on the Championship and Rules Committees of golf's governing body, the Royal and Ancient based at St Andrews, which he had joined before the war.[2]

Willie's sporting responsibilities represented only one element of what soon became an extensive CV. His attractions as an office-holder went far beyond his personal warmth; he was also widely respected for his shrewd decision-making under pressure. By 1955 he had become Deputy Lieutenant of Dumbartonshire, a member of the Queen's Bodyguard for Scotland and a Director of the Royal Highland and Agricultural Society. He was also a senior Freemason – although unlike the other distinctions, this information was not advertised in his election material. It was almost inevitable that at some point this affable, comfortably-off country gentleman with a solid military record and strong family connections within the party would be approached by the Conservatives to stand for Parliament. Willie's highly developed sense of duty made it equally likely that he would accept the challenge. As his old Winchester tutor Donald McLachlan put it, 'He simply felt that anyone who had been as lucky as he had owed something to others to adjust the balance.' Typically, when reflecting on his decision to stand, Willie himself merely wrote, 'I thought it would be fun to gain political experience.'[3]

The call came towards the end of the Attlee Government's first term. The seat for which he was invited to stand was East Dumbartonshire, which included not only the well-to-do Glasgow dormitories of Bearsden and Milngavie – and Kirkintilloch, where Gartshore stood – but also several mining villages. With an electorate of more than 57,000, it was one of the most populous constituencies in Scotland. At its heart was the solidly socialist shipbuilding community of Clydebank, and the famous 'Red Clydesider' of the inter-war years, Davy Kirkwood, was the sitting Labour MP. John Park was a leading official within the Conservative constituency party, and he helped to persuade Willie to put himself forward. There was little chance of unseating Kirkwood – he had represented the area since 1922 – so there was no rush to secure the Tory nomination. Indeed, Willie was the only applicant. When he made his first important public speech, to the 1949 Scottish Unionist conference at Perth, he confessed to feeling 'desperately nervous'. With characteristic self-deprecation, he claimed that it must have been painful to listen to any of his early efforts, because they were laboriously chiselled out from the party literature supplied by Conservative Central Office. But the Perth speech gave him the opportunity to square loyalty to the official party line with his instinctive approach to contemporary issues; it was delivered in support of the Conservatives' 'progressive' new policy document, *The Industrial Charter*.[4]

Willie's inexperience was a serious handicap for someone contesting a class-conscious constituency, many of whose inhabitants prided themselves on their capacity for robust repartee and remorseless iconoclasm. Glaswegian music-hall audiences were renowned among professional comedians as the ultimate test of nerve. It must have been even worse for a neophyte Conservative candidate with a marked English public-school accent, a background that placed him firmly in the 'bosses' camp, and a political programme alien to most of the people he was addressing. He made no secret of his support for free enterprise, calling for a reversal of Labour's nationalisations wherever appropriate, and he declared in his election literature that the trade unions should 'be kept free from purely political considerations'. Communism, he felt, was a 'wicked and anti-Christian tyranny'. But like his grandfather, who had seen state ownership as the best solution to the plight of the railways,[5] Willie was far from being a doctrinaire opponent of nationalisation. While he advocated lower taxation, he expressed himself 'delighted' that the Conservatives had endorsed the goal of full employment, applauded 'our Social Services which have been built up by all political parties especially in the past 30 years', and welcomed the new National Health Service (although he thought that it should not provide 'luxury' items such as wigs, and argued that foreign visitors should be denied access to free treatment). He also supported 'decentralisation of authority and responsibility in the handling of our Scottish affairs', only reserving his position on any 'far-reaching steps' until he was 'quite clear about the financial and other vital problems involved'.

The most spectacular outburst of heckling during the campaign was directed not at Willie himself but at an (unnamed) MP who came to speak on his behalf. Willie records that at this meeting – attended by more than 800 people – someone interrupted the guest with the single word 'Liar!' The visiting dignitary stopped and unwisely demanded to know who had levelled this dreadful accusation.

'I did, and I'll say it again – Liar!' shouted the same voice.

To the dismay of the platform party, the speaker replied huffily, 'If you say that again I shall sit down and speak no more.'

Soon afterwards, the same voice shouted 'Liar!' and the speaker duly sat down.

Turning to Willie, he said, 'I shall go now, and leave this rabble to you.' With that, he left the platform, to the noisy derision of the audience.

When his own turn came, Willie decided that he would be characteristically conciliatory, but would speak so fast that the opportunity for interruptions would be minimised. This seems to have worked, for the original heckler accosted him afterwards to say, 'Well done, laddy – you'll do fine.'[6]

At another meeting, though, Willie may have overdone the conciliation.

After being badly mauled by one heckler, he felt that he could not afford to be seen to bear a grudge. So when the man approached him in the street afterwards, just as he was about to drive off to his next meeting, Willie offered him a seat in the car. The man accepted the lift – and duly persevered with his barracking at the next event. In those days before the probing television interview, this sort of verbal jousting was an appropriate test of a candidate's mettle. But one veteran of Clydeside contests was reported at the time to have complained that the art of heckling was already in decline. 'It's no' whit it used to be,' he lamented, 'the young 'uns don't know the first thing about it.'[7]

Willie felt that for the most part he only encountered good-humoured and occasionally witty heckling. The tone of the campaign, he thought, had been established by his Labour opponent who, according to Willie's friend James Stuart, had now mellowed into 'a good patriot and citizen'; he ended up in the House of Lords.[8] Willie always remained grateful to Kirkwood for teaching him by example how to behave towards a political adversary; the disappearance from the Commons of genuine representatives of the working class, like Kirkwood, was another development that he noted with regret in his final years. Perhaps his feeling of nostalgia for this first outing was fostered by the fact that he did surprisingly well. In 1945 Kirkwood had enjoyed a majority of more than 7,500. Against Willie in 1950 he won by fewer than 5,000 votes. This was a symptom of a nationwide swing against the Labour Government, which cut Clement Attlee's majority to six, compared with 147 previously. The 1945 general election had reduced Tory representation north of the border from forty-three to twenty-nine; after the contest of 23 February 1950 there were thirty-two Scottish Conservative MPs.

An early return to the hustings was probable, so Willie was invited by the East Dumbartonshire Unionists to stay on as their candidate in the hope that one more heave might wipe out Labour's shrinking majority. This had begun to look a realistic possibility, partly because the seventy-eight-year-old Kirkwood had announced that he would not be fighting the seat again, and partly because the local Labour Party had chosen a Welshman, Cyril Bence, as his successor. At least Bence could claim to be continuing the tradition of impassioned Celtic oratory, although he had lived for many years in Birmingham. But any hopes that the neutralisation of Kirkwood's personal support would be sufficient to deliver the seat to Willie were dashed when the election was called, even earlier than expected, for 25 October 1951. The hopeful candidate was reported as saying that the overall election result 'would depend on the situation in the country at the time of the polling'. Even by Willie's standards of impeccable common sense, this seemed to be a statement of the obvious. But if by 'the situation in the country' he meant the perceived impact of government policies, he was too sanguine. Although the public was growing tired of wartime restrictions on consumption, which had to be maintained while industry concentrated on the export market, this was the notorious 'Whose Finger on the Trigger?' election. The *Daily Mirror* tried to portray Churchill as a warmonger, in an attempt to exploit fears among voters who were digesting the implications of the atomic bomb and conflict in Korea. Willie believed that this slur on his leader proved sufficiently potent to hold down the eventual Conservative majority at Westminster to just sixteen seats.

Major Whitelaw himself did not play down his 'warmongering' past; he campaigned in his military greatcoat, and made no changes to a vocal style reminiscent of the parade ground. 'Mr Whitelaw has a voice that requires no megaphone to aid it,' one local reporter suggested. 'Of the three candidates he is by far the most picturesque, towering as he does to [a] giant's height.' Obviously Willie was growing accustomed to this new kind of campaigning: his organisation was efficient, particularly in securing postal votes, and he was regarded as 'a ready speaker without notes', although he had 'a disconcerting habit of running the end of his sentences, just as he might hurry a doubtful putt on the golf course'. Possibly this was a clever tactical device to evade hecklers. In any case, it seems that by now he had won something more than grudging respect from his opponents. 'You may not agree with his politics, but you've got to admit that he's a real gentleman' was the verdict of an elderly woman after she had heckled Willie at one meeting.[9]

Unfortunately for Willie, his chances of converting sufficient numbers in a constituency with such ingrained loyalties were no greater than they would have been had he exhibited the attitudes and charisma of Colonel Blimp. Up to the day of the election he gave the impression of feeling 'soberly confident', but his support did not increase as he had hoped. Although he managed a further dent in Labour's majority, this was still well over 3,000 when the votes were counted.

But the Tories were back in office, even if Major Whitelaw was not among them. Moreover, he had now been bitten by the political bug. Bowing gracefully out of Dumbartonshire, he told his contacts within the party that he would like a more winnable seat next time. Unfortunately no sitting members in Scotland had announced their intention of stepping down. This may have been frustrating to the newly ambitious Willie, but it turned out to be a blessing in disguise. Had he secured a Scottish seat in 1950 or 1951, Willie would probably have been condemned to serve a substantial part of his ministerial career in the Scottish Office, almost certainly ending up as Secretary of State for Scotland.[10] This would not have attracted him very much, despite his deep affection for the country of his birth and his many friends in the Scottish establishment. Already his horizons had broadened. So when an old friend and wartime comrade, Charles Graham, suggested in 1954 that Willie should put himself forward for the 'safe' seat of Penrith and the Border, just across the line in north-west England, he agreed. Graham's support (and that of his mother, Lady Graham) was crucial within the local party; the family had been 'long famous in the history of the border', and an ancestor, Sir James Graham, had played a key role in the passage of the 1832 Reform Act, before accepting the post of Home Secretary under Peel.[11] Apparently no one foresaw any conflict of interest in the fact that, as High Sheriff of Cumberland, Charles Graham was also the Returning Officer for Penrith and the Border. By July 1954, Willie had been formally selected as the prospective Conservative candidate, after making much of the fact that he had family links with the area through his paternal grandfather and that his great-aunt lived in the constituency.

How Willie's selection was (literally) fixed is an instructive lesson in how such matters could be dealt with in a Conservative Party still wedded to patrician values, even if its leaders had recognised the need to recruit candidates who were more representative of the population as a whole. The chairman of the local Conservative Association was a gentleman called Colonel (later Sir) Timothy Fetherstonehaugh. As a retired soldier he naturally favoured a former major with an MC from the Brigade of Guards, and the fact that Willie was now a farmer increased his appeal to the chairman of a predominantly agricultural constituency. In May 1954 Fetherstonehaugh confided to Conservative Central Office his fear that the National Farmers' Union might put up an independent candidate, thus enticing away many natural Conservative voters.[12] He had not enjoyed the smoothest relationship with the sitting MP, Donald Scott, who was variously reported in the press as having decided to stand aside (in his early fifties) on health, personal, business or family grounds. According to one astute and sympathetic judge, Scott enjoyed 'all the requisite ability' to succeed in politics and was 'an excellent speaker'; unfortunately he was 'serious and dull', apparently lacking in personality.[13]

Having decided that the very different Willie was the ideal replacement, Fetherstonehaugh was faced with the irksome ritual of a selection process. As he breezily informed John Hare (later Lord Blakenham), the Central Office official responsible for the selection of candidates, he looked back with nostalgia to 'the nice undemocratic days such as existed when my father was chairman of the old constituency'. But in decadent post-war England some semblance of a contest was necessary; there were three other people on the shortlist for the selection meeting. So the colonel rang up Willie's rivals and informed them that the local members would expect them to make a speech of at least half an hour, preferably on some complex subject like housing policy. Then he telephoned Whitelaw and said, 'Keep it short, Willie – ten minutes at the most. Oh, and stay clear of any policy issues.'

One of the three hopefuls declined the engagement at lunchtime, after being told that he would be expected to devote considerable time to the constituency, if selected. Willie's two remaining opponents stayed to deliver their lengthy disquisitions and bored the audience rigid, exactly as the colonel had intended. Then Willie bounded in, charmed them for ten minutes, without straying far beyond general expressions of solidarity with the farming community, then sat down amid universal relief. One member who was present as the representative of the Young Conservatives remembered vividly what followed. As soon as Willie had left the room, Colonel Fetherstonehaugh said, 'Well, I don't think there's much doubt about that, is there? It's got to be Whitelaw. Any objections?' The Young Conservative felt a slight stirring of democratic outrage against this monstrous high-handedness. But he was not yet out of his teens, and everyone else in the room seemed to be saying things like 'Absolutely' and 'No doubt at all', so he kept his feelings to himself. The colonel then declared Willie to be the winner, without pausing to take a vote, and he was invited back into the room to enthusiastic applause. The disingenuous chairman reported to Central Office that 'The decision was unanimous, on a show of hands, much to my surprise, as I'd expected a difficult meeting to have to deal with.' He showed more of his own hand when he added, 'Between you and me and the door post, I think we'll have a better chap in these parts now than there's been for years'.[14]

Probably Willie would have won without the chairman's assistance. If Scott felt aggrieved about losing the seat he did not show it in public; possibly his feelings were assuaged by advance knowledge of the knighthood he was awarded soon after his retirement. Willie made numerous friendly references to his predecessor, and at his adoption meeting Scott raised a laugh by saying that the invitation to give a speech was 'like being asked to act as best man to another man who is marrying my wife'.[15]

Willie now inherited a seat that was virtually unlosable (although he continued to suffer from nerves at every count until his retirement nearly thirty years later). Apart from the small town of Penrith, the constituency stretched from the Scottish border down to the fringes of the Lake District and up to the windswept Pennines. Agriculture and tourism were the main economic activities, but there were a few industrial concerns on the west coast. There were 160 separate polling stations, scores of tiny villages and countless isolated farmhouses. The electors were certainly different from the heckling Clydesiders; instead of excessive volubility, this time the problem for Willie was taciturnity. In September 1953 one Conservative official had reported that 'By nature the people are parochial and sometimes very difficult.'[16] Willie himself recalled that at one election meeting, attended by about a dozen people ('all men sitting silently with their caps on'), his audience made no response at all from the moment he walked in to his expression of good wishes to them all on his departure.[17]

While awaiting the approaching election, Willie and Celia set out to win the idiosyncratic hearts and minds of his new constituents, not with policy ideas but with a pack of cards. The couple attended several village-hall whist drives, and Willie always insisted that this simple tactic introduced him directly to more people than any number of public meetings could have done.[18] At first he was disconcerted, as the card-playing fraternity seemed to extend their suspicion of strangers even to their leisure activities. But gradually Willie sensed that he had established a rapport, and learned to appreciate his constituents as much as they warmed to him. Public meetings had to wait until the start of the actual election campaign, when he addressed an average of five village meetings a night, feeling that if he missed a trip even to the most remote hamlet he would create a mood of resentment. Thus two days before the election Willie was quizzed on the cost of living by eleven denizens of Mungrisdale. Such were the contrasts in this constituency that half an hour later he addressed a 500-strong rally in Penrith. Had he been inclined to exploit it, his booming voice offered labour-saving opportunities. During the 1964 election he turned up with his loudspeaker at the village of Great Salkeld, only to find that the inhabitants had heard the whole of his speech an hour and a half earlier when he had shouted his way through Little Salkeld, just across the river.[19]

Willie's 1955 campaign was remarkable only for the discomfort of continuous travelling over obscure roads. On the stump with the candidate, a local reporter gained an impression of 'sustained speed'. Even so, Willie could not quite keep up with a hectic schedule of six meetings on the night in question. The reporter noted that, in spite of the delays, there were never fewer than twenty people in those audiences. At High Hesket, indeed, there seemed to be a bumper turn-out, judging by the number of cars outside the local school. Unfortunately the great majority of these motorists had turned up to watch a football match. During the meeting itself Willie gave an early glimpse of his tactical skills, as well as his lifelong preference for conciliation over confrontation. One questioner asked whether it were not time to introduce legislation to outlaw strikes. The candidate began by denouncing recent industrial disruption, but proceeded to praise many trade-union leaders as 'great patriots' and argued that the best way to solve the problem of industrial relations was to strengthen their influence over their members.[20]

For the most part, Willie's task in this campaign was to applaud the government (Anthony Eden had recently replaced Churchill as Prime Minister) and to insist that farmers ought to be left alone to conduct their businesses as they knew best. He encountered few hecklers, and his most troublesome moments came when he was asked pointed questions by Conservatives whose ideas were more extreme than his own. One elderly lady at Ivegill repeatedly pressed him on the subject of purchase taxes that increased the cost of goods affecting the lives of women, such as washing machines. Willie replied rather lamely that 'he would not like to get into an argument on that subject with his wife present'. The most interesting feature of the election was the candidature of a fifty-eight-year-old Carlisle farmer, William Brownrigg, whose dislike of the London-based government was such that he demanded Home Rule for Cumberland. He was not a single-issue candidate, however; he also urged that cock-fighting should be legalised, and that mole-catchers deserved better wages. But even this intervention came as no surprise to the locals, since Brownrigg had stood in the 1951 contest, amassing just over a hundred votes.[21]

The election was duly won, both in Cumberland and in the country at large (although East Dumbartonshire again failed to succumb to the Tory tide; Bence held on by just over a thousand votes). The frantic itinerary in Penrith and the Border had been kept up right to the end; Celia and Winnie Whitelaw accompanied the candidate on a 100-mile dash on the eve of polling, and visited nearly fifty villages the following morning. Just after midday on 27 June 1955, Charles Graham announced at the Penrith Drill Hall that his friend Willie Whitelaw had secured the seat with a record majority (despite a moderate turn-out) of 13,672. The victor was warmly congratulated by his Labour and Liberal opponents, who accepted that it had been a hard-fought but good-natured contest. The only discordant note was struck by Brownrigg. His support had increased by more than 200 since 1951, but the case for an independent homeland was endorsed by only 368 of his fellow Cumbrians. The local press reported that the vanquished separatist 'mounted the rostrum to speak but after he had begun to speak inaudibly the Returning Officer said he was not allowed to make a political speech at that moment and Mr Brownrigg left the platform'. Willie's recollection was more dramatic. He wrote that after the count, Brownrigg had loudly accused him of having filched 'bundles and bundles' of his votes and had squared up for what he called 'the real fight' with his bulky opponent. When prudence persuaded him to switch his aggressive attentions towards Graham, he was escorted from the platform by a policeman. It was not the end of Brownrigg's political career; he resurfaced as an Independent Conservative in Carlisle in 1964, when he added to his usual prospectus the idea that the lakeland hills should be flattened by a nuclear device to reduce rainfall in the area.[22]

After a victory tour of the villages, Willie celebrated his win in style with a boat-party on Lake Ullswater for 250 supporters and friends. His family now faced not one but two major domestic upheavals. The first was the search for somewhere to live in London when Parliament was sitting; they rented a flat in Marsham Street, just a brisk walk away from the Commons. The second was the move from Gartshire to Cumberland. The latter was the greater wrench of the two, for the Whitelaws had been happy in the vast stone mansion they had inherited from Willie's grandfather. It was far too big and grotesquely expensive to heat. They tried at first to sell it, but without success. Then it was offered to Glasgow Corporation as a possible home for the Burrell art and craft collection, but was judged too distant from the city centre. So, with great regret, they decided that it should be demolished rather than allow it to crumble into ruin.

The house that the Whitelaws chose became a much-loved base for them both over almost half a century. At the time of the election 'Ennim', in the parish of Dacre two miles west of Penrith, was owned by a Conservative family and, by chance, it had been the venue for the first of the many fêtes that Willie attended with Celia after his selection as Conservative candidate. Once the result was known, a deal was struck and the family took up residence in July 1955. The house, set in a total of fifteen acres of land, dated back at least to the 1640s, although over the centuries various residents had made alterations. The Whitelaws continued this trend, but the building retained its original character. The main feature was a spacious drawing-room, with a large bay window overlooking a lawn to one side of the house. The situation was very private – the house was set back some distance from the road – but with Penrith close by it was certainly not isolated. It was the perfect home for a prosperous gentleman farmer: solid, rather than showy, but very comfortable (after suitable modernisations) for a young and growing family. Willie and Celia now had four daughters; the births of Mary (1947) and Pamela (1951) were both welcomed by their grandmother with the exclamation 'Not *another* girl!' Perhaps it was a concession to her frustration that Pamela was given Winifred as her second name. Obviously Willie had been anxious for a son, but despite all of the demands on his time, his use of his family in his election literature reflected a rich reality far more than was the case for many of his Conservative colleagues, even then.

Willie was determined to keep up his farming activities, and bought the neighbouring Mount Pleasant farm, where he continued to breed pedigree cattle. The pattern of his future life looked set. At the age of thirty-seven he had every reason to look back on his career with pride; certainly he had made the most of his advantaged background. Perhaps there were more glamorous figures among the newly elected Conservative MPs but it was already recognised that Willie possessed other rare qualities, which were likely to take him far in politics.

CHAPTER 4

IN AND OUT OF OFFICE

'Just like a new boy going to school' was how Willie remembered his feelings on attending the House of Commons for the first time.[1] At least the 'new boy' was sure of a warm greeting from several existing pupils, in contrast to his great-grandfather Alexander Whitelaw, who had always been regarded as a misfit. The Deputy Speaker of the Commons, Charlie MacAndrew, was a golfing chum, and Willie could also rely on advice from Sir Fergus Graham, the MP for Darlington and father of his friend Charles. James Stuart, the Secretary of State for Scotland, was not as close to Anthony Eden as he had been to Churchill, but few people could match his knowledge of the House. Even without these contacts, the new MP would have adapted easily to his new surroundings. His constituents were already remarking on his approachability, and they quickly exchanged 'Major Whitelaw' for 'Willie' – the name he used when signing all his letters.[2]

As someone who had always suffered from nerves before speaking in public, Willie was unlikely to relish the prospect of his maiden speech. But he quickly pushed himself through what he described as an 'ordeal', catching the Speaker's eye for the first time on 27 October 1955 during a debate on a tax-raising package, which became known as the 'pots and pans Budget'. Convention demanded that he should steer clear of partisan comments, and make some warm references to his constituency, but all of this came naturally to Willie. His speech focused on the problems of rural life, and echoed some of the complaints he had heard during his election tours. More than 3,000 homes in the Lakeland area had no electricity, he reported, and many isolated farms lacked telephones. Country people made a crucial contribution to the economic health of the nation, and for that reason alone they deserved better treatment; in addition, 'no class of people could be more loyal to their country and to the land in which they work'. In short, they were a 'priceless asset' to Britain.[3]

It was a workmanlike speech, rather than a specimen of sparkling oratory. But it was warmly received on the Conservative benches, even though passages could be interpreted as mild rebukes of the Chancellor, 'Rab' Butler. Messages of congratulation were passed to the relieved Willie by several friends, including Bill Deedes and the President of the Board of Trade, Peter Thorneycroft. Unsurprisingly, his audience had found no difficulty in hearing this inaugural effort. The next speaker, by chance, was Cyril Bence, the victor of the 1951 contest at East Dumbartonshire. Bence remembered that the fight had been 'carried out with every courtesy by the Hon. Gentleman'. Contradicting Willie's own self-deprecating comments, Bence was struck by the newcomer's 'supreme confidence', and claimed that he could not recall 'a more eloquent or ably delivered maiden speech'. This, perhaps, was taking cross-party goodwill a little too far. But Bence compensated for his friendly gesture by excoriating the government in the remainder of his speech.

Willie's next notable intervention, on 6 February 1956, introduced him to a more robust form of parliamentary debate. Welcoming a bill designed to promote the safety of agricultural workers, he claimed that 'The Conservative Party has always shown interest in the health and welfare of all those who work, wherever it may be'. At worst this was only a slight exaggeration; certainly the paternalist tradition that Willie represented had always been strong within the party. But the speaker who followed him, Labour's Fred Willey, chastised him for his 'flamboyant inaccuracies'. Perhaps by this time Willie had been identified by the Opposition as a worthwhile target, because he had just climbed the first rung of the ministerial ladder, only eight months after his arrival in the Commons.

If Willie's selection for Penrith and the Border had been engineered by well-placed friends, his promotion of February 1956 was the result of a family connection. The MP for Henley, John Hay, had just resigned as Parliamentary Private Secretary (PPS) to Peter Thorneycroft, who was Willie's second cousin. By coincidence, Thorneycroft's junior minister at the Board of Trade was Toby Low, who had been at Winchester with Willie. The position of PPS is unpaid, and the holder is not an official member of the government. Individual ministers normally have a free hand in making these appointments. No objection was raised when Thorneycroft suggested that his relative should replace Hay; nepotism was to become a bigger issue the following year, when James Stuart used the fact that he was Harold Macmillan's brother-in-law as an excuse to resign from a Cabinet that already numbered too many of the Prime Minister's extended family.[4] The position at the Board of Trade gave Willie valuable insights into the life of a minister – and the chance further to extend his contacts, since the main requirement of the job was to spend long hours in the House gauging the mood among backbenchers. It also allowed him to continue to speak on subjects outside the remit of the department. After his appointment he spoke on local topics such as hill farming and the state of the roads in Cumberland, but he also showed himself to be a strong advocate of capital punishment by seconding a hostile motion during the debates instigated by Labour's Sydney Silverman, the leading abolitionist in the Commons.

Churchill's peacetime administration had been uneventful – a time of relative social harmony, which would be remembered with affection by future Conservative politicians, notably John Major. But trouble rapidly engulfed Anthony Eden's premiership. Willie's recorded views on the Suez crisis, which culminated in an invasion of Egypt by British and French forces in early November 1956, leave room for speculation. At first he was bellicose, endorsing Eden's determination to punish President Nasser for having nationalised the Suez Canal Company. But he began to sympathise with the government's critics when he learned that the RAF had started to bomb Egypt while the invasion force was more than six days' sailing from its destination, unable to make secure a speedy victory. This incompetent military strategy had been dictated by the politicians, who could not allow the fleet to leave port, while keeping up a pretence of impartial negotiations. Evidently Willie remembered his own experiences in the Middle East, when political interference had prevented soldiers from doing an efficient job.[5]

In retirement, Willie would recall the parliamentary clashes over Suez with horror, tempered with nostalgia for a time when outbursts were based on real emotion, rather than the synthetic anger which, he felt, disfigured later parliamentary rows. But if his own account is an accurate reflection of his feelings at the time, he was almost entirely lacking in the moral considerations that inflamed the contending factions in the House. In his memoirs he wrote as if the Suez adventure might have been a mistake – but emphatically not a crime. With hindsight, he sympathised with the view that Britain's ignominious withdrawal was based on short-term thinking, 'and if only the British action had had sufficient support to enable our troops to reach the end of the canal, the Middle East problem would probably be much easier to solve today'. Given Britain's post-war status – and the issues at stake in the Middle East – this assessment was a surprising departure from Willie's usual realism. He only criticised British policy on the grounds that 'international cooperation had not been assured before action was taken'. For others, British policy at the time was morally abhorrent precisely because a degree of 'international cooperation' *had* been secured – through the duplicitous diplomacy which resulted in the plan for Britain and France to pose as peace-makers between Egypt and Israel.

Convoluted as it was, Willie's retrospective view of the Suez crisis provides a fascinating insight into the approach to serious controversies that he developed during his later career as a whip. He admitted that when the great majority of his party – including himself – voted 'for going in and then for coming out', it was behaving in a manner that was not 'honourable, or in any way logical'.[6] The task of a whip, however, is to put aside all such objections and ensure that, somehow, the dishonourable and illogical policy gains parliamentary approval without producing disastrous splits in the ranks. The Chief Whip at the time, Edward Heath, performed this feat in 1956 despite his own serious reservations about the government line, and thus won Willie's lasting admiration. It was vital for the Chief Whip at least to understand the various viewpoints within the party, however unrealistic they might be. In writing about the episode more than thirty years after the position of the diehard Suez Group had been exposed as an irrational spasm in response to the loss of Britain's empire, Willie tackled the subject as if there were still outraged feelings to mollify, and much to be said for every conceivable point of view. It was his way of suggesting to the reader that, had he been in Heath's place, he might almost have emulated his performance.

Clearly Willie did feel at the outset that the Suez intervention was justified and had every chance of success. But it seems likely that he changed his mind only in part because of the tactical blunders. The main factor in his thinking was US opposition, which exposed Britain's new dependent status and induced an economic crisis. Whether or not it was 'honourable' for Willie to revise his thinking in response to a new awareness of world realities, it was certainly not 'illogical'. While a substantial section of the party was enraged by America's action, and more than a hundred backbenchers signed a motion of protest, Willie himself was deeply embarrassed by the government's blunder and greatly relieved when the storm blew itself out after Eden's resignation in January 1957.

Neither of the main candidates for the succession, the Chancellor Harold Macmillan and the Lord Privy Seal, Rab Butler, had covered himself with glory during Suez. Willie had no role in the informal process that resulted in the elevation of Macmillan, and he felt no strong preference for either man. In the domestic field both stood for continuity with the social paternalism of Churchill and Eden. There was, though, a personal bonus for Willie when Macmillan moved from Number 11 to Number 10 Downing Street. Thorneycroft, who had impressed the new Prime Minister with a robust parliamentary defence of the Suez adventure after it ended in failure, was nominated to succeed Macmillan as Chancellor, thus ensuring new prominence for his PPS. It was reported that Willie had 'quickly become one of the most popular Members in the House', and that a job which would acquaint him with the workings of the Treasury would be 'another step forward in a Parliamentary career which has already shown great promise'.[7]

Within twelve months that promising career had encountered its first setback. On 6 January 1958, after a protracted struggle over the level of public spending, Thorneycroft resigned along with his junior ministers, Enoch Powell and Nigel Birch. The previous July Macmillan had warned about the economic outlook, in a speech that included a line later wrongly quoted as evidence of his complacency: 'Let us be frank about it, most of our people have never had it so good'. Actually he was warning against the consumerist mood which had swept a public anxious to forget the immediate post-war days of austerity. In September a run on the pound, partly inspired by fears of inflation, led Thorneycroft to raise bank rate to 7 per cent – the highest level since 1921. Departing from his habitual pragmatism under the influence of Powell, the Chancellor had been converted to the doctrine that would later become notorious as 'monetarism'. He told the Cabinet that the inflationary problem could only be tackled if the money supply was restricted.

The 'September measures' also included a reduction in public-sector investment, and an announcement that more swingeing cuts in government spending would follow. But while Macmillan had agreed with Thorneycroft that overall spending should be cut in real terms, when ministers presented their demands for the annual expenditure review, the total envisaged turned out to be £276 million above the level for the current year. Ministers offered a compromise, reducing their demands by more than £100 million. But in the ensuing discussions it became clear that, rather than setting his sights on a particular figure, Thorneycroft was making an ideological attack on the welfare state. Powell had decided that the most effective deflationary cut would be to deprive up to five million mothers of their family allowances, and while the Chancellor indicated that he would be satisfied with something less than this, he was determined that the welfare budget should be targeted for significant savings. Together with Powell and Birch, he declared his intention of resigning if this position was rejected, but at the crucial Cabinet meeting held on Sunday 5 January 1958 Macmillan argued that the projected assault on welfare spending would be 'contrary to the traditions of the Conservative Party'.[8] So the whole Treasury team departed, dragging the Chancellor's PPS with them.

Economic theory was not Willie's strongest suit, then or later. But Thorneycroft certainly confided in him, and he quickly grasped the implications of the dispute. In a characteristic passage in his memoirs he claimed that he regarded the issue of principle as probably sufficient to justify the resignations. On the other hand, he expressed doubts concerning the 'political wisdom' of the Treasury ministers. Accurately deconstructed, this sentence means that in politics wisdom is rarely the same as abstract principle, and should always take precedence over it. This was a rule that guided Willie's conduct throughout his political career, and for him 'political wisdom' meant that one should never resign or rock the party boat, unless the provocation was impossible to bear. In his memoirs there is only a delicate hint that he was unhappy with Thorneycroft's decision, but he argued forcefully against it at the time. A few days after the resignations he made a public declaration of support for the Prime Minister, adding characteristically, 'It is often said that silence is golden and I have decided to follow that wise saying.' He also wrote a highly sympathetic letter to Powell, concluding with the thought that 'Assuredly the battle for courageous handling of our national finances will be won *in the end* and that will be your reward.' But his true feelings about the issue at stake – a 'principle' that ran counter to his own paternalist instincts – are suggested by the fact that in retirement he dated his antipathy to Powell back to January 1958, rather than to the 'Rivers of Blood' controversy ten years later.[9] By contrast, if his admiration for Thorneycroft was shaken by the crisis, the damage was short-lived.

Willie's temporary banishment from the centre of government activity gave him the opportunity to supplement his political apprenticeship by immersing himself in business on the periphery. His services were in demand on Conservative backbench committees, and he became secretary of the groups concerned with horticulture and transport. He was also elected joint secretary of the 1922 Committee, the influential mouthpiece of backbench opinion. Having stalled on the ministerial ladder, Willie was presented with an alternative career path, more congenial to most Conservatives from his landed background. He seemed an excellent long-term candidate for succession to the chairmanship of the 1922, currently held by the formidable John Morrison. This post would allow him a significant voice within the party, while leaving him free from the full-time pressures of departmental business.

But Willie's stints at the Board of Trade and at the Treasury had convinced party managers that he was as able as he was affable. His conduct over Thorneycroft's resignation had also shown that he was loyal to the party. Ministerial talent was not so plentiful on the Tory benches that the government could afford to let a promising and popular young MP flourish on the outside track. Thorneycroft himself was brought back into the fold in 1960, but Willie's recall came even sooner. The *Daily Telegraph* had reported in August 1958 that he was regarded as one of six 'horses to follow' on the Tory backbenches; the list included two others who went on to fill high offices, Sir Keith Joseph and Geoffrey Rippon.[10] Five months later Willie was invited by the then Chief Whip, Ted Heath, to become an unpaid Assistant Whip. Being a PPS or a junior whip are, in the Conservative Party, the two most reliable conduits to ministerial office. As a mere PPS, Willie had been required to sit immediately behind his minister on the Treasury bench. Now, as an Assistant Whip, he could sit on the front bench for the first time, albeit only in the absence of his Chief. Willie could hardly have guessed it, but he was to remain on either the government or the Opposition front benches in the Commons until he transferred to the House of Lords thirty years later.

During his three years as a junior whip, Willie absorbed the subtle and sometimes devious skills involved in being one of the government's so-called 'business managers'. Contrary to the public perception, this is not exclusively a matter of twisting arms in order to persuade reluctant MPs to vote for things they don't want. The job also entails keeping one's eyes and ears open, picking up the gossip, swapping intelligence with journalists, Commons clerks and the like, and even assessing the effectiveness of junior ministers at the dispatch-box, so as to report back to 'the Chief'. It is therefore a gregarious job, and one ideally suited to someone of Willie's temperament. It is also an invaluable education in the mysteries of the often murky backstairs deals which oil the legislative wheels of all governments. Among the most important lessons to be learned is the absolute necessity of keeping your word once a deal has been struck. Willie learned it well. He was a popular whip, both with MPs and journalists, and a frequent visitor to the Smoking Room. It was noticed, though, that he soon developed 'the disconcerting habit of never looking at the person with whom he was talking but over their shoulder, as if someone rather more important or interesting was standing just behind or approaching round the corner'. More likely, on these occasions he would be putting his senses to maximum use and trying to concentrate on everything going on around him. Later, as Chief Whip, Willie would deny that he kept a 'difficult customers' file, containing information on anyone (whether sober or otherwise) who was overheard making disloyal comments. But MPs could assume that, like most whips, Willie had picked up some knowledge of their personal peccadilloes. The nature of the whip's job meant that no MP could be entirely sure that his secrets were safe; but Willie could be trusted more than most.[11]

There was also a special kind of camaraderie in a Tory whips' office, which had much in common with a junior officers' mess or a very exclusive gentlemen's club. For a start, there were no women. Also, a copious supply of alcohol was kept in the cupboard, and not just for dispensing to visitors. During late-night sittings, the atmosphere in the large open-plan room occupied by the less senior whips could become boisterous. Masculine jokes were repeated with schoolboy relish, bets were laid on almost anything, and there was a sense of participating in some kind of jolly adolescent conspiracy. Only a profoundly gloomy personality could fail to enjoy it, especially since the prospect of preferment was an ever-present stimulus (it is not only ambitious young naval officers who take the view that 'where there's death, there's hope'). Moreover, the appointment gave Willie the opportunity to seal a friendship with Ted

Heath that was to last many years, to the great benefit of both. The atmosphere was not quite so cheery in the whips' office after the 1959 election, when Heath moved on to become a Cabinet minister and was replaced by the bad-tempered Martin Redmayne. But even the boredom of long hours spent in the Smoking Room could be turned to amusement. One evening in 1961, as Willie and his friend and fellow whip Robin Chichester-Clark surveyed the occupants of the room, they asked each other if they would have any of them as weekend guests. Chichester-Clark remembers that having run through the ranks of the living, they could only agree on the Labour radical Nye Bevan – who was beyond the reach of any invitation, having died the previous year.[12]

As a government whip, Willie was unable to speak in debates – a deprivation which he could certainly live with. In November 1958 he had made what proved to be his last contribution for nearly four years. At least this debate, on a package of measures designed to help small farmers, offered him the chance to deliver another tribute to an occupation that provided 'the backbone of our country'. Earlier he had also drawn on his agricultural experience when supporting the bill that introduced life peerages. For once he had made a misjudgement, which had provoked an intervention from Bevan, one of the most formidable Commons performers of this or any other era. Willie had agreed that appointed life peers could add to the expertise of the upper chamber, but claimed that there was still a place in the Lords for those who had inherited their seats. There was every reason to expect that the hereditary peers would retain most of the qualities of their ancestors, even if they held titles that were originally granted in recognition of services which had been performed centuries ago. Bevan dissented from this view in a series of interventions, and Willie tried to respond by alluding to Bevan's own practice as a pig-breeder. Surely, he argued, Bevan would mate his sows with the best-bred boars, in the confident expectation that the offspring would inherit the qualities of their sire? This illustration might have brought nods of approval from a meeting of Cumberland farmers, but it only served up an irresistible pun to Bevan. There were plenty of 'bores' in the Lords already, he suggested. Willie recovered from his slip, and closed with the characteristic reflection that 'In constitutional matters it is always right to walk before attempting to run'. It was a perfect expression of a Conservative outlook – worlds apart from the dogmatic theorising that had led to Thorneycroft's resignation only six weeks before this debate.[13]

Despite the Treasury resignations – breezily dismissed by Macmillan as 'a little local difficulty' – the Conservative Party's fortunes recovered and, when Willie first joined the whips' office in December 1958, Gallup found the government neck-and-neck with Labour. With an election approaching, the MP for Penrith and the Border had less reason for concern than most of his colleagues. He could not remind his constituents of his existence by winning headlines through parliamentary speeches, but he continued to make his presence felt in other respects. In April 1958 a visiting official from Central Office had reported from a 'well-organised and efficiently conducted meeting' of local members, noting that Willie had delivered 'an excellent address'.[14] A wider audience was reached in March 1959, when the BBC asked Willie to represent his party in the television programme *Who Goes Home?*, an early prototype of *Question Time*. This was his first prolonged appearance on television, and local interest was increased by the fact that his Labour opponent was Fred Peart, the MP for Workington. The audience contained a number of vociferous Labour supporters, whose interventions were unlikely to cow the veteran of two East Dumbartonshire elections. Willie was congratulated on his performance by many of his friends, including an old wartime comrade who was impressed by 'the guardsman-like manner in which you answered the various questions'.[15]

By the time of the general election, in October 1959, more than half of the voters approved of the government's record and the Conservatives had edged ahead in the polls. The confidence of Willie's supporters was indicated by the compilation in advance of a detailed itinerary for the victory tour. But Willie himself took nothing for granted, covering more than 1,000 miles in five days of campaigning after his adoption meeting. He told his supporters that the government's performance proved that 'our Conservative party stands for one nation as a whole and not for any single section of the community'. Full employment meant that greater prosperity was being shared by the overwhelming majority of the population. Although more needed to be done to improve amenities in his constituency, some of his own efforts had been rewarded. For example, at a meeting at High Hesket he was applauded for having helped to push through a scheme that ensured supplies of clean water. In reply, Whitelaw produced another early 'Willie-ism': 'We continue to put more and more baths and toilets into our houses and we must make sure there is plenty of water behind us.'[16]

It is often said that this was the first election conducted primarily on television, but even so Willie claimed that his meetings had been very well attended. True, only five people heard him at the Cumwhinton hall, but almost 4,000 attended his final rally at the Penrith Drill Hall and audiences tended to be more enthusiastic than they had been in 1955. According to Willie's private notes, Suez – the issue which at one time had seemed certain to condemn the Conservatives to long-term Opposition – was mentioned only twice in more than a hundred meetings. Even by Willie's standards, the 1959 election in Penrith and the Border was a good-natured affair. The cry of Home Rule for Cumberland was not heard this time round, since Mr Brownrigg declined the poll. After the count, which saw Willie returned with a record vote of 23,551 and a majority of more than 14,000, the Labour candidate acknowledged that it was a bad day for his own party, but that 'if one had to be beaten it was a pleasure to be beaten by someone like Mr Whitelaw'. The victory tour could proceed as planned.[17]

In March 1961 Willie moved another rung up the parliamentary ladder, taking a promotion within the whips' office which gave him, for the first time, a paid appointment, adding £2,000 to his parliamentary salary. The task was not too onerous, since the government now had a comfortable majority of 100. But after the summer of that year the Conservatives began to lag behind in the polls, and Macmillan grew jittery. In July 1962 the Prime Minister tried to restore some credibility to his increasingly lacklustre government by sacking seven members of the Cabinet, including his Chancellor, Selwyn Lloyd. This desperate move, which was all-too-obviously intended to save his own skin, caused the cartoonist Vicky to call the Prime Minister 'Mac the Knife', after the slightly sinister hero of Brecht's *Threepenny Opera*, which was conveniently showing in London at the time. The sackings also generated two of the better political jokes of the decade. Jeremy Thorpe, who later became leader of the Liberal Party, remarked, 'Greater love hath no man than this, that he lay down his friends for his life.' And Harold Wilson, the future Labour leader, fell into the habit of referring to the event as 'The night Macmillan sacked half his cabinet – the wrong half, as it turned out'. The ministerial massacre not only made Macmillan seven unnecessary enemies; it also ended his reputation for unflappability. The whole 'never had it so good' edifice would collapse little more than a year later.

But there were beneficiaries as well as victims, and Willie was one of them, as the reshuffle opened up vacancies in the junior ranks. According to Willie himself, he was not at first considered for one of these posts, but the Minister for Labour, John Hare, 'didn't want the person offered to him; they were so desperate to find someone that they stuffed my name in'.[18] So Willie became Parliamentary Secretary to a department that might well have been called the Ministry of Beer and Sandwiches, since one of its principal functions was to help resolve industrial disputes. Like Willie, Hare was a master of conciliation – which meant that he was ideal for the job, as it was then conceived. Beer and sandwiches later fell out of favour within the Conservative Party, but by British post-war standards the Macmillan Government was successful in restraining wage inflation and avoiding industrial troubles.

Throughout this period of apprenticeship, Willie revealed an unwavering commitment to the kind of patrician Conservatism associated with Macmillan and his de facto deputy, Rab Butler. In a speech at Manchester in 1961 Willie went so far as to urge the imposition of a new tax on company profits to balance the restraints on wages being proposed by the newly established National

Economic Development Council (NEDC). At the Ministry of Labour, his work involved highly interventionist legislation such as the Industrial Training Bill and the Offices, Shops and Railway Premises Bill – a measure designed to extend health-and-safety protection to white-collar workers. Taking legislation through the Commons could be a gruelling process. The Offices and Shops Bill was debated intensively over thirteen sessions between November 1962 and February 1963, and Willie had to follow the proceedings with great care, making instant responses on behalf of the government to anything that might suddenly be proposed by any of the twenty-nine members of the cross-party committee. Cooperation between members of the same party had to be carried out by means of covert signalling, which could produce moments of levity. On one of these occasions the Conservative MP Graham Page said that he had prepared two speeches on an amendment, one for use if Willie nodded his head and the other if he shook it. 'What happens if I do nothing at all?' Willie inquired. Apart from this new burden, he also took his share of the parliamentary questions addressed to his minister. At Willie's first appearance in his new role, the Conservative MP Nicholas Ridley remarked on the contrast with the life of a whip, congratulating him on 'emerging from his chrysallis of silence'.[19]

One of the present authors first set eyes on Willie at about this time, and the impression was unfavourable. The 1962 Conservative Party Conference in Llandudno was dominated by Macmillan's ill-fated application for membership of the European Common Market. Willie had already made up his mind on this subject; as early as 1956, while he was still PPS to Thorneycroft at the pro-European Board of Trade, he had spoken out in favour of membership. In 1962 the boardwalk outside the Llandudno conference hall was festooned with 'Yes' and 'No' posters erected by what would nowadays be called the Euro-enthusiasts and the Euro-sceptics. But inside the hall another big issue was industrial relations. Normal practice at these unedifying occasions is that the closing speech from the platform is made by the minister, while his parliamentary team sits beside him, leading the applause at appropriate moments. But on the night before the debate, John Hare was detained at the ministry in St James's Square by urgent talks concerning a potentially damaging strike. So Willie was deputed to deliver his text instead, and must have spent most of the night learning his piece, for he was word-perfect by next morning. But just before the debate began, Hare arrived on the platform to deliver his speech after all. Not only were Willie's famous oyster eyes more than usually sorrowful; to the delight of the press table, his lips appeared to move in time with his chief throughout the performance. At least one witness decided that Willie Whitelaw wasn't very bright.[20]

Others made the same mistake. Labour's Bill Rodgers, later a founder-member of the SDP, recalled that he thought of Willie 'as a slightly laughable, Bertie Wooster figure' when he served with him on a committee at about this time. But he soon realised 'that behind the slightly muddling style, there was a great deal of substance'.[21] Journalists found that their first impressions were contradicted by Westminster gossip. Willie's qualities were appreciated on all sides of the House, and in the government as well as on the backbenches. When Hare left his post in October 1963 he thanked Willie for having been 'a tower of strength and a joy to work with'. 'You will go far,' he added, hoping that Willie would stay at the Ministry of Labour for a little longer because he clearly had so much to contribute (curiously, when Willie did finally leave the ministry after his party's defeat in the 1964 general election, Hare's successor, Jo Godber, also chose to describe him as 'a tower of strength' in his valedictory letter). The friendship with Hare lasted until the latter's death in 1982. At the same time Willie was building an enviable reputation among civil servants as a congenial and courteous boss, and exchanged very friendly letters with many of his officials when he left the ministry. These personal touches came naturally to him, and it did him no harm to have so many admirers in Pall Mall clubs speaking highly of his charm and his administrative abilities. He was also improving as a parliamentary performer. He delivered a long and well-received winding-up speech for the second reading of the Offices and Shops Bill in November 1962, closing with the claim that the measure represented 'yet another social advance promoted by a Conservative Government'. When the bill was finally passed four months later, the *Manchester Guardian* reported that Willie had 'surprised Labour members by his reasonableness and by the knowledge shown of his brief'. His demeanour, it was felt, 'suggested that he was the happiest and most sanguine member of the Government'.[22]

Very few Conservative MPs felt happy or sanguine during 1963. Previously public dissatisfaction had lacked a specific focus, but now everything seemed to be going wrong for the government. The year began disastrously, with General de Gaulle's veto of Britain's application to join the EEC. The government had already been damaged by the Vassall spy scandal, and in March the House first learned of rumours concerning the Secretary of State for Defence, John Profumo. Although Macmillan hoped to lead his party into the next general election, he was struck down by illness and resigned just before the conference of October 1963. Willie, who played very little part in the crisis precipitated by the resignation, this time backed Rab Butler for the succession. But he was certainly among the heaving mob of MPs, party officials and journalists who surged up and down the lobby of Blackpool's Imperial Hotel during the amazing three days that followed the bombshell.

The announcement was brought to Blackpool by the then Foreign Secretary, Lord Home, who helped to compose Macmillan's message and read it to an astounded assembly from the platform. At that stage, Butler and Lord Hailsham were universally regarded as the only serious contenders, on the basis of their popularity with the parliamentary party and the wider electorate. But in those pre-democratic times, the decision was not entrusted to any kind of ballot – not even a semi-democratic one confined to Tory MPs. The winner was held to 'emerge' from the private deliberations of a shadowy group of party grandees, which was later dubbed 'the Magic Circle' by Iain Macleod in a devastating article in the *Spectator*. A key figure within the circle was Willie's old boss, the Chief Whip Martin Redmayne.

It was Redmayne's job to 'gather the voices' of Commons backbenchers and lesser ministers so that the Lord Chancellor, Viscount Dilhorne, and assorted other party nabobs could make an 'informed' but wholly unaccountable decision about who was best qualified to succeed Macmillan. Armed with Redmayne's gleanings, their choice eventually fell on a fourteenth earl instead of the acknowledged architect of the post-war Conservative Party, Rab Butler; or Hailsham, who as Chairman in 1959 had done much to secure a third consecutive electoral victory for the party. Dilhorne interrogated most of the members of the Cabinet. Redmayne approached the backbenchers and junior ministers, including Willie, who declared himself for Butler. Then the Chief Whip followed up with what Willie regarded at the time as an extraordinary question – whether he would support Lord Home if he were to become 'available'. Willie replied that he felt sure Home would be an excellent leader and Prime Minister, but he could hardly be expected to renounce his peerage and come back to the Commons as PM.[23] Presumably this equivocal response would have been reported as further evidence of a groundswell of support for Home; the party's canvassers apparently interpreted anything short of an uncompromising preference for another candidate as a vote for Home.

When Home duly 'emerged' there was a brief drama during which Macleod and the rehabilitated rebel Enoch Powell refused to serve under him and declared for Butler. In Macleod's opinion, Butler had only to make the same declaration and Home's position would have become untenable, even under the prevailing procedures. With a substantial section of the Cabinet, including the Deputy Prime Minister, against him, Home would have been forced to advise the Queen that he was unable to form a viable government. However Butler refused to wield the dagger, and Home duly took possession of Number 10. Though Willie had been urged to join the anti-Home boycott (by, among others, Rab's wife Mollie), his already well-developed concept of party loyalty left him in no doubt about where his duty lay. So he soldiered on in his lowly ministerial job.

For Willie, the main incident of note between the fall of Macmillan and the end of thirteen years of Tory rule in October 1964 was his leadership of a parliamentary delegation to the Soviet Union. Willie greatly enjoyed his fortnight of meetings, factory tours and sightseeing, but most of all he relished the hospitality, and returned home with caviar and vodka in his briefcase. In their report the delegates noted with some amusement the impact of rigid Soviet economic planning – 'after a while one begins to look for it at the ballet or the circus,'[24] they wrote. Although many of the people they spoke to were keen to learn about Britain and readily admitted that their own country was deficient in many ways, there were troubling suggestions of a paranoid state apparatus. After one local tour they invited the three married officials who accompanied them to bring their partners along for dinner. At first the officials were happy to accept, but later all three came up with different, but equally unconvincing, reasons why their partners could not attend. Willie emerged from his first exposure to life in a communist state with great affection for the people, and no feelings of antipathy for a system which, for all its inefficiencies, seemed to bring concrete benefits to the ordinary worker.

Back in Parliament, a less happy memory for Willie was an uncharacteristic blunder during a debate on a private member's bill designed to facilitate the amalgamation of trade unions. Willie's enthusiasm for a measure that enjoyed cross-party support was such that he failed to notice a group of Conservative backbenchers urging him to wind up, because the time allotted to the bill's second reading was running out. When he finally realised what had happened it was too late, and he was reported to have sat down in 'red-faced confusion'. The Speaker ruled that the minister had inadvertently 'talked out' the bill, which had to be reintroduced.

The general election of October 1964 was another unpleasant experience for Willie. With such a large majority in his own constituency he had no reason to fear defeat, but the national prospect was gloomy and it was difficult for him to find the adrenaline necessary for campaigning. The only conceivable incentive was to try to break his personal record for votes, but even this was a remote possibility since he had come under criticism after two local railways were condemned to closure in the Beeching Report. In private Willie had tried to save the lines, one of which (Carlisle to Silloth) had been constructed by his grandfather (partly because he thought that Silloth was an ideal location for golf). But to reveal in public that he had fought and failed would have been to make an admission of impotence. Constituents were unlikely to understand that a member of the government could fail to defend his home patch, and to make things worse Willie's ministerial status had debarred him from airing his grievances in Parliament. But despite a couple of difficult meetings during the campaign he was still a popular figure; even a local Liberal who wrote urging him to step down, to allow her favoured candidate a free run against Labour, found herself addressing her letter 'Dear Willie'. His majority fell, but only by around 3,500; his vote still comfortably exceeded the combined support for his opponents. The only awkward moment came when it seemed that the votes announced for each candidate added up to a couple of hundred fewer than the official turn-out. It took some time to resolve the matter, and during the protracted inquiry Willie was heard to exclaim, 'Anybody can have the missing votes; let's go away for some lunch.'[25]

Labour duly won the election – though by a wafer-thin majority of only three. Even before the poll it had been reported that Redmayne was likely to be replaced as Conservative Chief Whip. Home was a man who knew something about loyalty, and especially the vital importance of a reliable Chief Whip to a leader with formidable enemies on his own side – Home had, after all, been PPS to Neville Chamberlain when he was replaced by Churchill as Prime Minister in 1940. So, for Home, the ultra-loyal Whitelaw was the obvious choice to succeed Redmayne. He had been tipped for the post since his previous stint in the whips' office, and his relationship with the new leader had been cemented when he spoke on Home's behalf at the Kinross and West Perthshire by-election that enabled him to rejoin the Commons after renouncing his peerage. Now Home showed his confidence in Willie's feel for the mood of the House by asking him, within a few days of his appointment, for advice on how to stay in touch with backbench opinion. For his own part, Willie felt that he might not be ideally suited to his new job: 'I am a somewhat more talkative character perhaps than I ought to be,' he confessed.[26] From the point of view of debating on the floor of the House, he was now reabsorbed by 'the chrysallis of silence'. For the next six years his only recorded remarks in the Commons were formal requests at the end of Opposition-sponsored debates 'that the Question be now put', and the occasional pithy observation from a sedentary position during the more controversial passages of a speech from the Labour benches. But he stepped into the top ranks of his party, making it almost certain that the Cabinet lay ahead.

CHAPTER 5

'A TOWER OF STRENGTH'

There is a popular notion that psychiatrists fall into one or other of two categories: the 'there there, better soon' variety, or the 'pull yourself together, man' school. Much the same can be said of Chief Whips, who rely either on the stick or the carrot. Willie belonged very clearly to the carrot category. Martin Redmayne, on the other hand, believed not so much in the stick as in the bludgeon. He had won an alarming reputation as a disciplinarian while wearing the red tabs of a staff officer during the war. As Chief Whip he had exercised the same methods on the Tory backbenchers. A typical demonstration of the Redmayne technique happened during a dangerous Tory revolt against a bill to abolish Resale Price Maintenance (RPM) – a radical measure that was adopted by Ted Heath during his stint as President of the Board of Trade, after Home had succeeded Macmillan. Many backbenchers saw Heath's bill as a charter for the supermarket chains, and therefore the beginning of the end for small shopkeepers – a group of people who were in those days regarded as unwavering Conservative voters.

During the committee stage of this bill, the rebels managed to cut the government majority to a single vote. There was panic in the whips' office, and Redmayne began calling in the rebels one by one to receive a dressing-down and a warning of dire consequences if they continued to defy the party line. One of these reprobates passed a reporter on his way into the chief's room, saying cheerfully, 'I'm for it.' Six or seven minutes later he emerged again, brick-red in the face, his teeth tightly clenched and tears of rage squeezing out from under his eyelids.

'Well?' he was asked.

'I've never been spoken to like that in my life – not even at school,' said the MP. 'The bastard.'[1] Ironically, Redmayne privately sympathised with the rebels and made regular pleas for the Prime Minister to drop the legislation.

Since Heath was clearly the most dynamic force within the government, the martinet Chief Whip was undermining his own future prospects at the same time that he was bullying backbenchers.

Redmayne – who, at fifty-three, could have expected many more years in a senior front-bench position – was extremely reluctant to depart, and his mood did not brighten when he learned that Willie was to be his successor. Willie seems to have made it obvious that he did not agree with Redmayne's methods of man-management. In turn, Redmayne probably felt that Willie was far too conciliatory, and thus unfitted for the job of Chief Whip either in government or in Opposition. Several party grandees were brought in to persuade Redmayne to go quietly, and he was offered a baronetcy to soften the blow. He left in November 1964, after a rather awkward interlude in which Willie served as his deputy. Redmayne stayed on the front bench, but only in the relatively humble role of spokesman on the Post Office. In 1966 he lost his seat in the Commons.

Willie would have been well prepared for his new task even without his brief spell as Deputy Chief Whip; he had been a close student of Heath's methods, and could rely on advice from James Stuart, who acted as his mentor at this time. During this second stint in the whip's office he forged a lasting friendship with Francis Pym, the MP for Cambridgeshire, who later became Willie's own deputy and then his successor. Pym's career to date had closely mirrored that of his chief, and in the coming years they would continue to run along parallel lines. The product of a landed family, Pym had joined the army fresh from Cambridge and won the Military Cross in a distinguished spell under arms. Like Willie he had fought in a tank, albeit in the very different terrain of North Africa. He had also seen close comrades burned to death, and his own vehicle was hit on several occasions. First elected at a by-election in 1961, Pym had been recruited almost immediately to the whips' office and shared Willie's view that Redmayne's militaristic style was outdated. In addition to his own remarkable ability to mollify opponents and persuade waverers, Pym brought considerable quiet charm to the office and helped to make it a very pleasant place in which to work over the coming years.[2]

Although his party had been deprived of office, Willie was now a significant figure. In government, the Chief Whip is surrounded by Cabinet ministers who are running major spending departments, and he also works alongside the Leader of the House, who has ultimate responsibility for the smooth passage of government business. In Opposition, however, the Chief Whip is at least as powerful as any front-bench spokesman (although the holder of the office is not formally a member of the Shadow Cabinet), and does not have to defer to anyone beneath the party leader. Moreover, in Willie's case he was taking charge of the day-to-day opposition to a government with a cliff-hanging majority of three.

Every division in the Commons held out the possibility of a government defeat. The Conservative press expected ministers to be harried at least as strongly as Attlee's government had been when it held a similar fragile parliamentary majority in 1950–1. When it became clear that Home did not greatly relish wrecking tactics, and was not actively trying to bring down the government every night, some Tory commentators and MPs grew restive. For obvious reasons, the Opposition Chief Whip was also implicated. Willie was sharply attacked at a meeting of the 1922 Committee for being too ready to cooperate with the hated enemy. Feelings were running so high that one MP urged Willie to withdraw from the system of 'pairing', which enables government members to be absent from Westminster, provided that an Opposition MP also abstains from voting. The end of this arrangement would have forced even seriously ill Labour MPs to attend the Commons, in order to be certificated as being present by Opposition whips ('nodded through'). Willie was opposed to such a drastic step. Of course, on crucial votes there had to be a three-line whip (meaning that 'pairing' was suspended), and he entered into the macabre spirit of these occasions. Once an ambulance drew up in New Palace Yard, and Willie inspected the vehicle to check that its occupant was a still-extant Labour MP. As usual, the Whitelaw whisper was too powerful to be confined to his closest lieutenants: 'I think this one's already dead, but I'll give him the benefit of the doubt. Nod him through.'[3]

A good Chief Whip needs contrasting (if not contradictory) personal qualities. He or she has to rouse his own troops for battle, while maintaining friendly relations with the enemy. Constructive consultations over parliamentary business, the composition of committees and other matters, such as the award of life peerages, are a crucial part of the Chief Whip's daily routine. As Willie himself remarked at this time, in 'a mature democracy it is essential that battle is waged according to some rules. Otherwise chaos would result. Now the maintenance of these rules must in the long run rest on the common sense and trust of what are frequently described as "the usual channels".' To this end, Willie always taught new whips that pledges given to one's opponents should be sacrosanct.[4] He was understandably sensitive if anyone suggested that he had acted unfairly; and on these occasions the bond between rival Chief Whips could prove stronger than party ties. After the Commonwealth Secretary, Arthur Bottomley, had accused him in the House of having disregarded the pairing system in a vote on the government's controversial legislation to re-nationalise the steel industry, Willie told a reporter that he regarded the imputation as 'a direct personal reflection on my honour'. His opposite number, Labour's Edward Short, signed a statement deploring Bottomley's outburst.[5]

Criticism of Willie from his own side intensified during the early debates on Labour's 1965 budget. He decided that it was time to take action. In collaboration with Heath (who was taking the lead for his party in the debates on the Finance Bill), he staged a highly entertaining 'ambush' on the bill in the early hours of the morning of 7 July, inflicting three defeats before the government whips could bring in enough troops to halt the rout. As is often the case at Westminster, the performance had elements of a schoolboy prank, albeit one that demanded the meticulous planning of a covert wartime operation. Once the scheme had been hatched, only selected Tory MPs were entrusted with the secret; the last Opposition speaker in the debate, William Clark, was passed a note while he was on his feet, telling him to keep on talking until he received further instructions. Willie and several of his colleagues had ostentatiously left the Commons flourishing their umbrellas and briefcases, and noisily bidding the policemen good night, to lull the Labour whips into the belief that they were admitting defeat and heading home. To reinforce that impression, Willie let it be known that he had relaxed the instruction for the night to a two-line whip. Some Labour MPs felt that something was up; but having searched every cupboard in Westminster, they relaxed. The departing conspirators had sneaked into the St Stephen's Club in nearby Queen Anne's Gate where, amid much alcohol-induced hilarity, they waited for a phone call telling them that the division had been called. When the signal came, at 1 a.m., they streamed back across Parliament Square and into the 'No' lobby. Here the plan almost came unstuck; the ambush depended on speed and the square soon became jammed with the onrushing Tory traffic. Willie himself almost missed the division, sprinting into the House at the last moment.[6]

Ludicrous scenes ensued, as the frantic government whips phoned round every Labour MP and minister, ordering them back to Westminster. One of the sleepy reinforcements, Alice Bacon, ran all the way up Victoria Street in her nightdress and a pair of wellington boots – probably the only time that anyone has ever entered the 'Aye' lobby in a frilly nightie. Willie subsequently insisted that the ploy had fallen within the rules of the game, since neither he nor any other Tory whip had actually told a lie to anyone; for the government's business managers it was all the more vexing because they knew that they had been outwitted by an honest tactic. Willie felt that for whips the first rule should be: 'we should never take credit ourselves but always give it to the troops'. He had also taken to repeating a piece of advice he had been given by his friend Edward Boyle: 'Nothing in politics is ever as good or bad as it first appears'. But in his euphoria on this occasion he told the *Sunday Times* that 'it was a brilliant success, brilliant', and he was reported to be 'walking around the Palace of Westminster looking like the cat who swallowed the cream'. The victories raised backbench morale without precipitating a general election, which the

Conservatives would have been likely to lose despite a recent (and short-lived) resurgence in the polls. Most important of all, from Willie's point of view, the escapade relieved some of the pressure on his leader.[7]

The incident must have seemed surreal to anyone unfamiliar with the arcane practices of the House. But it rattled Harold Wilson, who denounced it as a game of 'Cowboys and Indians'. During Prime Minister's Question Time two days later a petulant Wilson accused Willie of falling asleep on the Opposition front bench. But the most serious repercussions fell on Labour's ailing backbenchers. During July, Short had to order the attendance, at one time or another, of five MPs who were judged by their doctors to be in mortal danger. This caused understandable anger in the Labour ranks, and Willie himself decided to speak out. 'You don't effectively beat a government by accident of sickness or health,' he said. 'You beat it because some of its members decide they won't support it any more. It would need very few.' Adverse press comment helped him to persuade those within the party who wanted to keep up the guerrilla tactics. In November 1965 a private agreement was struck between the two Chief Whips to allow 'pairing' for MPs whose lives might be at risk if they were dragged from their sickbeds.[8]

Whatever the short-term justifications for Willie's ambush, it could not quell for long speculation about the party leadership. Far more than Willie himself, Home was a figure from another age, prone to being photographed in the eccentric garb adopted for grouse-shooting, and instinctively inclined to a form of self-deprecation that bordered on parody. It was not, for instance, Wilson who said that Home's grasp of economics was so sketchy that he required a box of matches to help him add up. That devastating quip came from Sir Alec himself, in a fit of self-mockery which even he must have regretted. When Home was not laughing at himself, the newly founded satirical magazine *Private Eye* did the job for him. Much of the criticism aimed at Home was exaggerated; the party, after all, had only narrowly lost in 1964, despite its unpromising prospects. But while his friends argued that in private no one could be more charming than Home, these qualities did not translate to television, which was becoming increasingly important. Willie himself thought that the cameras should soon be allowed into the Commons – at least after an experimental period of sound-only broadcasts – and since Home rarely mastered Wilson in their exchanges at the dispatch-box, this innovation would have made matters worse.[9]

In February 1965 Home wrote to thank Willie for his support during what he referred to as a ' "Leadership" drama'. Rumours of discontent had reached the press, and presumably after consultations with his Chief Whip, Home had felt secure enough to dismiss the number of malcontents as 'infinitesimal'.[10] But the muttering on the Tory benches mounted steadily until Home's position became the subject of serious concern in the Opposition whips' office. Matters were not improved by the behaviour of Ted Heath, who had sprung to prominence as the chief negotiator in Macmillan's doomed attempt to get Britain into the Common Market and whose reputation had been consolidated by his performance during the Finance Bill debates. It was felt by Home's supporters that Heath was behind the rumbles of discontent, but most likely this was an independent initiative on the part of Heath's admirers. At worst, the pretender himself left room for speculation through his silences. One journalist was invited to lunch at Heath's elegant rooms in the Albany, Piccadilly. He had expected to find himself one of a number of guests, but arrived to discover that the meal was to be 'à deux'. Mr Heath was apparently anxious to demonstrate a magnificent new stereo record player, with two vast loudspeakers that dominated the room. After lunch, at which music was the main subject under discussion, Heath and his guest sat on either side of an oriel window overlooking Savile Row listening to a rather noisy recording. As it progressed, the journalist decided that it was now or never if he was to raise the big issue. So he drew breath and yelled above the din, 'If there were a leadership contest now I think you'd probably win it!' The music turned pianissimo just at that moment, then rose to fortissimo again. Heath remained silent until there was another quiet passage. 'You may be right,' he growled. And that was that. A day or two later the journalist learned that his *Guardian* colleague Peter Jenkins had undergone a similar experience.[11]

At first, Willie was irritated by what was seen as Heath's attempts to draw attention to his qualifications for the leadership. Heath's successes over the Finance Bill drew extravagant praise from the Conservative press, which began to contrast his performance with that of his nominal chief. Before long, this was translating itself into louder demands at Westminster for Home's resignation, and his replacement by someone more capable of standing up to Wilson. The pressure on Home was increased by two significant developments. The first was the loss in March of a key by-election in the Scottish borders, not far from Home's substantial estates near Coldstream. A twenty-six-year-old Liberal, David Steel, snatched Roxburgh, Selkirk and Peebles from the Conservatives, and his victory was immediately hailed as a vote of no confidence in Home's leadership. As a Borders MP himself, Willie was particularly struck by this ominous development. The second incident was the publication by Home of a new set of rules designed to ensure that future Tory leaders would be chosen by a direct ballot of Conservative MPs rather than by a secretive group of party grandees. The rules were drawn up by a small committee, which Home – still smarting from the criticism of the way he himself had secured the leadership – had set up soon after the 1964 election defeat. With the principle of election at last established, there was clearly a temptation among the newly enfranchised MPs to try out the system.

During the summer of 1965 MPs and the press fed each other's frenzy with rumours of plots and counter-plots matched by public declarations of undying loyalty, culminating in a formal statement from Home that he definitely would not be quitting before the end of the year. This was intended to head off the possibility that Wilson might call a snap election in the middle of a Tory leadership contest. The ploy was neatly trumped by the wily Wilson – then at the height of his political skill – with an announcement that he would not be calling an election until 1966 at the earliest. The message this conveyed to Tory MPs was that they could now get on with the assassination of Alec Home without fear of interruption. Indeed, rather than a political murder, it was beginning to seem more like a mercy-killing. Home had to be goaded by his Chief Whip into speaking during a debate on Vietnam, and even then he was unimpressive on what was his special subject. Observers noticed that he looked 'visibly jaded, his skin pallid and tauter than ever'. 'It's just cruelty – he can't go on,' one backbencher told Willie. This was a marked contrast from the Home of October 1963; at that time one MP had noticed that he had a gleam in his eye that was out of keeping with his pose of 'reluctant' leadership candidate.[12]

Loyal as ever, Willie stuck by his incumbent leader until the last moment. He was reinforced in his preference for the status quo by advice from old friends like James Stuart and Earl Swinton. But he was irritated by Home's tendency to ask too many colleagues for their advice. This could only increase speculation instead of dampening it down, as Willie would have preferred. Eventually a group of backbenchers called on the executive of the 1922 Committee to allow a debate over the leadership. Their demand was headed off only when the committee's chairman, Sir William Anstruther-Grey – like Willie, a Scotsman, a Guardsman and a recipient of the Military Cross – promised to convey the feelings of backbenchers to Sir Alec. But the envoy was a devoted Home supporter, and he contrived to translate the critical spirit of the 1922 Committee into a message of reassurance. At this point Willie decided that it was his duty to tell Home the unqualified truth about the collapse of his support within the party. At the time friends noticed how distracted he seemed. He visited Home along with the Party Chairman Edward du Cann, who reported on grass-roots opinion. Home said that he was inclined to step down, and would only be dissuaded if Willie could assure him that this would be against the best interests of the party. In all honesty Willie could not do this. He sensibly argued that if Home stood down before the demand became overwhelming, his reputation would be enhanced; if not, his departure would seem like a humiliating capitulation to his opponents. After a few days' reflection – and further talks to overcome his reluctance – Home accepted that he must go. He announced his resignation at a full meeting of the 1922 Committee on 22 July 1965, with Willie sitting at his side.[13]

The meeting, in Room 14 on the Committee Corridor of the Commons, remained a vivid memory for those who attended – and for the journalists waiting outside. They listened in increasing excitement to the growls, cheers and, eventually, the banging of desk tops, which are part of the 'customary practices' on such occasions. Then the door burst open and the backbenchers started to stream out. One or two were tearful; some were obviously triumphant; others were livid. When one Knight of the Shires was asked what had happened, he snarled, 'The rotters' eleven has won.'[14]

In the end Home stepped down with dignity and a characteristic lack of fuss. Willie, on the other hand, was tormented by feelings of guilt about his role in the toppling of a decent and generous friend, brooding over the accuracy of his advice, just as he had questioned his decisions after the Battle of Caumont. He need not have worried. Westminster-watchers at the time were convinced that he had no alternative if the party was to recover in the medium term. And as far as Home himself was concerned, instead of blaming his Chief Whip, he expressed his gratitude. Three days after the meeting he wrote:

> My Dear Willie,
>   No one can ever have had a stauncher friend and counsellor in time of trial. I asked you to tell me the truth, the most difficult of all requests, and that helped me to make the decision which I am convinced in my heart was right. Thank you for such complete and loyal help. Friendship like yours makes up for all.

A fortnight later Lady Home also wrote, in response to an emotional letter from Willie:

> I really don't want to intrude the Douglas-Homes into your life again just as your holiday is beginning . . . but (a) I think you are much too nice to have forgotten all about us, and (b) of course I must answer your letter. It was wonderful of you to write so much to me. I really loved your letter. My dear, I don't think one can quite see it all in perspective yet, but it is a crazy world when Alec's good points seem to have been the fatal ones . . . I remember telling you one day in Whitehall last year that whenever you thought it right for him to go he would be quite content; and so he is – but I hideously underestimated how much he'd mind. How dumb can you be? Alec has never stopped telling me how wonderful and supportive and helpful you have been and we will never stop being grateful.

Willie, by contrast, never stopped feeling guilty. Even in his memoirs he could not bring himself to reveal the nature of the advice he gave Home, recording only his racked emotions and concluding, characteristically, 'In the end perhaps the outcome turned out for the best.' In private conversation he revealed far more of his pivotal role, but continued to praise Home for the timing of his decision.[15]

Three candidates put themselves forward to fill the vacancy. Heath and Reginald Maudling were the heavyweight contenders; the third, Enoch Powell, was standing merely to put down a marker for the future. The main contest was a straight clash of personalities; there was little difference on policy between Heath and Maudling, and both represented Willie's own brand of pragmatic Conservatism. Heath, the abrasive scholarship boy, contrasted sharply with Maudling, the brilliant amateur, who was regarded as being perhaps just a little too laid-back. Maudling had been Home's Chancellor, and had almost delivered him victory on the back of a pre-election boom which left Wilson an unenviable economic legacy. Heath, on the other hand, was the only Opposition front-bencher who had laid effective gloves on both Wilson and the Labour Chancellor, James Callaghan.

Maudling entered the race as marginal favourite. But Heath was soon outclassing him in the campaign. A couple of days before the first ballot, one of the present authors filed a news story which claimed that Maudling's hitherto stationary bandwagon was beginning to roll. If so, it was rolling onto its side. Opinions are divided as to whether the Maudling campaign was hamstrung by complacency, but Heath's team certainly struck observers at the time as being more energetic. When the votes were counted, Heath was leading, with 150 to Maudling's 133 and Powell's disappointing fifteen. But Heath's majority fell short of the tally required under the Home rules, which demanded that an outright winner should have at least a 15 per cent margin over the runner-up. Theoretically, then, Maudling could have prolonged the process and forced a second ballot. But a gentleman's agreement had already been reached, under which the losing candidate, even in a close contest, would immediately concede. Maudling gracefully stuck to the bargain, although he was shattered by the outcome. His public conduct provided a model for other defeated candidates to follow as the Conservative Party grew accustomed to democratic practices.[16]

Willie himself remained studiously neutral in public, and imposed the same restraint on his junior whips. Since he obviously hoped to work with the winner, it was only sensible for him to keep his cards close to his chest during the course of a close contest – leaving aside the impropriety of such a powerful figure as the party Chief Whip acting as a dedicated partisan for one side or the other. After the vote he informed Maudling that he had voted for Heath, and was amused to discover that the canvassers for both main candidates had confidently expected his support. In fact he had quietly confided to his friend Robin Chichester-Clark, who was working for Heath, where his true loyalty lay. Apparently Willie's alleged 'defection' from the Maudling camp came as a shock to the defeated candidate, but probably this was more a product of Maudling's over-confidence than of anything Willie had said. According to the Labour politician and diarist Woodrow Wyatt, even in retirement Willie was inclined to think that Heath bore the main responsibility for Home's precipitate departure, and that he had made a mistake in acting so soon after the 1964 election. But it was quite logical for Willie to vote for Heath in 1965, while deploring the fact that an election was being held at all.[17]

Almost the first act of the new leader was to confirm Willie in his post. This was scarcely surprising, since there had been widespread admiration for his past performance, with more than one newspaper describing him as the great discovery on the Opposition front bench under Home. It was the beginning of a new chapter in what was a surprisingly close relationship between two men who might not have been expected to get on particularly well. Though they both believed in state intervention in the economy, and both had become committed Europeans as a direct result of their wartime experience in the army, they were very different characters. The journalist Patrick Cosgrave, an early biographer of Margaret Thatcher, once claimed that all politicians are either warriors or healers – his heroine being a notable 'warrior'.[18] On this basis Heath belongs in the same category as Thatcher – albeit in a rather different cause – while his Chief Whip was clearly a healer. By contrast with the gregarious Whitelaw, Heath was notoriously taciturn unless he found the company sufficiently interesting. But it was the contrast between their characters that brought them together. Sympathetic observers would say that they had complementary strengths, while in future years enemies could claim that they suffered from complementary defects as Conservatives – Heath because he over-estimated the human capacity for rationality, Willie because he put too much faith in the ability to bring bitter opponents together over a friendly drink. In fact Willie thought that a Chief Whip should always emphasise characteristics that complemented those of the existing party leader. With Heath he tried to be 'slow and calm and opposed to fast action'; if Maudling had been elected instead, he would have been 'just the opposite'.[19] By nature he preferred acting as a brake rather than an accelerator, so this may explain why he preferred Heath to Maudling when deciding on his vote at the leadership election. Lord Carrington, who witnessed both relationships at close quarters, felt that Willie's service to Heath was even greater than his subsequent contribution under Mrs Thatcher. He has written that Willie was as good a Chief Whip as the Conservative Party has ever had. Heath had lacked experience when he took over, Carrington added, and 'Whitelaw's moral and political support was decisive in establishing his authority'.[20]

Willie's admiration for Heath had come close to hero-worship at the time of Suez. Years later he still marvelled at Heath's ability to conceal his own views at a time when all around were losing their heads. In the whips' office Heath had impressed him with 'the extent of his attention to detail, the way he takes tremendous pains to think through every problem and listen to the views of his Whips'; he was a truly 'inspiring' Chief. Willie even thought the prolonged silences that infuriated journalists could be interpreted as masterful tactical ploys. 'Silences are practical actions,' Willie told one of Heath's biographers, 'well planned, and they are always happening. Silence is a means of getting the other person to produce more and more of his views so that you know them without getting committed yourself.' By the end of 1974 most Conservative backbenchers were taking a less charitable view of Heath's refusal to indulge in small-talk; to his own subsequent regret, Willie was too ready to assume that they still shared his own respect for the party leader.[21]

Heath was only two years older than Willie; but he had joined the Commons five years earlier, and the latter clearly regarded him as his superior. Years later, Willie said that 'in my experience of government, life without friends would be bleak, even unbearable'.[22] It was another attitude that seems dated at the beginning of the twenty-first century, when rumours of rifts among the residents of Numbers 10, 11 and 12 Downing Street are commonplaces of political commentary. But there can be no doubt that Heath was one of those in Willie's mind when he spoke. After Heath had become Prime Minister, Willie explained their relationship in more folksy terms: 'If he told me tomorrow that I was to become ambassador to Iceland I should go straight off to Iceland . . . I trust his judgement absolutely. It's not because he has charm, because he hasn't any charm. It's not because he's easy to work with, because he isn't easy to work with. I don't know what it is – it's a mystery to me. I only know that I trust him more than I've ever trusted anybody.'[23] Rarely can a Chief Whip have described a more ideal relationship with his leader, and Willie worked hard to reassure any backbenchers who expressed doubts about the new leader. Occasionally Willie's protective feelings prompted him to reveal more than his usual tact would have dictated. For example, before Heath delivered a crucial speech to the 1967 party conference, Willie told a reporter that 'the party is overwhelmingly anxious for Ted to be a success'. By that time Heath had been leader for more than two years, and most observers would have felt that he had already held the office long enough to prove himself.[24]

One of Willie's first duties was to advise on the formation of Heath's Shadow Cabinet. The new leader rightly valued his lieutenant's judgement of individuals. James Prior recalled that during one of the meetings at this time it was proposed that there should be at least one female member – the 'statutory woman', as Prior described this role. (Privately one of Willie's friends was even more dismissive, telling him that although it was 'nonsense' to have to accommodate a woman they would have to find a place for someone 'who is not 70 or hopeless'.) A profound silence followed, and then the name of Margaret Thatcher was mentioned. Heath reported Willie's view that she was by far the most able among the rather small sample of her sex who had battled through to the Commons. But Willie also warned that 'once she's there we'll never get rid of her'. 'So we both think it's got to be Mervyn Pike,' Heath concluded. Miss Pike, who was briefly a junior Home Office minister in 1963–4, was scarcely better known then than she is now.[25]

When Parliament reassembled that October, Heath's standing as the newly elected leader of the Opposition came under almost immediate criticism. He had won the party's first 'democratic' leadership contest because he was seen as the kind of aggressive parliamentary bruiser who would stand up to the triumphalism of Harold Wilson, and might even score a few points at Prime Minister's Question Time. But the reality of these twice-weekly jousts – that the Prime Minister of the day, bolstered by all the resources of the Civil Service, had an overwhelming advantage over his or her adversary – immediately reasserted itself. Contrary to expectations, Ted Heath did not seem to have improved greatly on Alec Home. The disappointment was intense, and was compounded by a growing sense of guilt about the treatment Home had endured.

Had Heath been better at tackling Wilson at the dispatch-box, it might have distracted some attention from other developments that endangered discipline within the parliamentary party. The return to Westminster coincided almost exactly with the illegal unilateral declaration of independence (UDI) by Ian Smith, the Prime Minister of Rhodesia (now Zimbabwe). Smith's repeated threats of UDI had already dominated that autumn's Conservative Conference, and Wilson had made a ministerial broadcast which was clearly timed to upstage the Tory gathering. But UDI, when it finally came on 11 November 1965, deepened the divisions among Conservatives. In spite of the Suez fiasco – or, perhaps, because of it – the Conservative Party still incorporated a substantial 'Imperial' faction, which favoured not only apartheid in South Africa but also white-supremacist Rhodesia. The right-wing Monday Club strongly sympathised with UDI. On the other hand, the party's left wing, led by people like Iain Macleod, backed the most stringent sanctions against what they regarded as an act of rebellion against the Crown. Heath and Willie struggled to hold the two groups together through a cobbled-up compromise, which stopped a long way short of endorsing the United Nations' demand for rigorous sanctions.

At Willie's request, Edward Short agreed that the first parliamentary debate on Rhodesia after UDI should not be followed by a vote. It was a costless concession on the government's part; during the debate the Conservative divisions were clear enough anyway. For a few weeks the Heath-Whitelaw compromise held, but only because Wilson had not yet committed himself to imposing the oil sanctions demanded by the UN. It was obvious that if the Prime Minister sought Parliament's approval of an embargo, the Opposition split would open up again. The expected announcement came on 17 December 1965, and the necessary Order in Council was debated in the Commons three days later.[26]

Willie himself admitted that (just like his own position over Suez) the attempt to stave off a split was neither particularly 'honourable' nor 'logical'.[27] Nevertheless, he personally attended a succession of backbench meetings in the hope of persuading his flock to abstain on the vote along with the Shadow Cabinet; he also held private talks with individual rebels. Nigel Fisher, a senior advocate of sanctions against the Smith regime, considered that despite the pressure the Chief Whip was 'patient, understanding and tolerant' when they discussed the likelihood of a serious rebellion. But Willie was not always so polite in dealing with potential rebels. It was no secret that 'his language to erring MPs would often be picturesque, even crudely Anglo-Saxon'. A younger MP retained a clear memory of his confrontation with an apoplectic Chief Whip on this occasion. Faced with an obdurate refusal to promise not to make trouble, Willie 'completely lost control, he shook with anger, and bellowed'.[28]

Demonstrations of this kind became familiar to Willie's colleagues over the next three decades; within his family his outbursts were affectionately known as 'Daddy's stampers'. After Willie's death, Lord Denham described the rages as an 'endearing memory'; they 'lasted approximately a minute and a half, and were followed by a totally unnecessary and abject apology'. On one occasion, at least, an explosion nearly landed Willie in serious trouble. Noticing the left-wing Labour MP Joan Lester apparently berating his friend Robin Chichester-Clark, Willie screamed, 'Pay no attention to that redheaded socialist bitch!' News of the altercation spread, and some Labour MPs wanted to raise it in the House. But Willie's anger had died away with his words, and he immediately felt sorry and ashamed. He wrote an apologetic letter, and peace was restored. His feelings on that occasion must have been particularly strong: normally when he was moved to anger in female company he would say 'I'm terribly sorry, but . . .' before expressing his feelings.[29]

Over the course of the sanctions crisis Willie racked up quite a few 'stampers'. To him it seemed irresponsibly self-indulgent for left-wing Tories to wish to follow their consciences when the government was bound to win the vote anyway. They were only making their own leaders look weak and – perhaps – stirring up trouble for themselves in their home constituencies. If they abstained, he argued, they would expose the Monday Clubbers as the main source of indiscipline within the party. Despite Willie's efforts, the best he could manage was to secure promises from both sides that they would abstain, provided that their opponents followed suit. This was a fragile arrangement, since it was obvious that it would break down if even a handful of mavericks defied the whips and entered either lobby. During the debate the pent-up feelings of both left and right spilled over; in the vote fifty Tory supporters of UDI and thirty-one from the pro-sanctions group broke ranks. As Short recalled, 'our Members were content to sit back and watch the Opposition in turmoil'; what might have seemed a personal humiliation for the Prime Minister was transformed by the Conservative rebels into a tactical parliamentary triumph.[30] The government won a majority of 228.

That night Willie boarded the sleeper for his long journey up north 'in a state of misery', as usual blaming himself for what was an unavoidable débâcle. He could expect that so long as the Rhodesian problem persisted, it would damage his own party more than the government, and before the winter was over he was again called into action, delivering 'a dramatic appeal for unity' at a meeting of the 1922 Committee over a new vote on sanctions. This time his anger was mainly directed at the right, whom he accused of acting with 'criminal irresponsibility'. But individuals on the left could still annoy him. For example, when Humphry Berkeley told him that he had been holding private discussions with Wilson on sanctions, Willie immediately accused him of disloyalty. If Berkeley is to be believed, he weathered the storm in some style, replying that he would not tolerate being spoken to in that manner by 'a party functionary'. Willie was taken aback and muttered an apology. Although Berkeley sat for Lancaster, a north-western constituency close to Penrith and the Border, Willie was relieved when this truculent MP lost his seat in the 1966 general election. Eventually he left the party altogether. But even in the heat of battle Willie drew a clear distinction between irreconcilables, like Berkeley, and others who might return to the fold, whether from the right or the left. One young MP had been startled when the Chief Whip tried to shout him into submission before the sanctions vote, but he stuck to his intention of voting with the right. When they met again in the lobby a few moments later he knew that Willie had noticed his disobedience, but instead of firing a volley of recrimination, the Chief Whip merely muttered that it had been a terrible day for the party, as if no one in particular was responsible.[31]

Wilson's adroit tactics over Rhodesia were mirrored by his decision to call a general election at the best moment for his party. In January 1966 Labour won a by-election at Hull North, despite an exceptional effort by the Conservatives who drafted in a large campaign team, including nine front-benchers.[32] The national poll was called for 31 March. Despite Heath's repeated (and accurate) warnings that the British economy was facing a crisis, the Conservatives were always expected to lose heavily. Willie himself feared that Labour might win anything up to a 150-seat majority. Since he was now a senior figure in the party, he found that there was less time for fighting his own seat, but Celia proved a more than capable deputy and his majority fell only to 8,901. Overall the Conservatives held just 253 seats after the election, leaving Labour with an overall majority of ninety-six. Peter Thorneycroft was among more than fifty defeated Tory MPs.[33]

The only consolation for Willie was that, as in 1964, his leader was not held personally responsible for the disappointing result. Against the fact that he no longer had to worry about pressure from below, for more aggressive parliamentary tactics to topple the government, had to be set the strong like-lihood that morale would slump on the denuded Conservative backbenches. One way in which Willie tried to limit discontent was by finding jobs for those whose talents were under-utilised, and spotting promising newcomers at an early stage. This was an aspect of the Chief Whip's job that always gave Willie great pleasure, and he used his influence to promote colleagues on the basis of character (and background) rather than ideological considerations. On the day after Heath replaced Home, for example, Jim Prior (first elected in 1959) had been summoned to the leader's room in the House of Commons to be told that 'Willie says you have to be my Parliamentary Private Secretary'. At least in part this appointment was influenced by Willie's knowledge of Prior's interests in farming. Similarly, John Biffen (elected at a 1961 by-election) believes that Willie was responsible for his first promotion to a junior Shadow post; an only child, like Willie himself, Biffen had been brought up in rural Somerset.[34] And like all good fathers, Willie fussed over emerging bad habits in his favourites. On one occasion his parliamentary neighbour Michael Jopling was summoned back from a cross-party visit to Malta for an unimportant vote. Subsequently he learned that the Chief Whip had decided that he was becoming too much of 'a tripper'.[35]

Proof of the respect that Willie had earned on both sides of the House came in the New Year's Honours List for 1967, in which he was named as a Privy Councillor. For an Opposition Chief Whip this was by no means an automatic accolade, and it was awarded at Wilson's instigation. At this time Willie was enjoying particularly warm relations with Labour's business-managers, John Silkin and Richard Crossman, respectively Chief Whip and Leader of the Commons after July 1966. According to Crossman (another alumnus of Winchester), Willie and Silkin got on 'uncommonly well personally'. Crossman's incomparable diary reveals his own high opinion of the Tory Chief Whip, who quickly gauged his character and ended up treating him rather like a wayward pupil. In March 1967, for example, Crossman blurted out his problems to Willie, saying that he had just endured 'a pretty awful eight weeks'. Willie expressed sympathy, and confided that the same period had been even worse for him. This apparent candour revived Crossman's spirits, although on reflection he couldn't think of any reason for Willie to feel downcast at that time. The conversation had actually been a prime example of Willie's man-management; it had begun with Crossman complaining about the recent behaviour of the Opposition towards him, which was greeted with an immediate and disarming apology. Crossman was an irascible character, and for Willie to transform his original irritation into gratitude in the course of a brief chat was a remarkable feat, even by his standards. A few days later Crossman recorded that Willie had evaluated his performance as Leader of the House, telling him that he lacked the 'small-talk' which would enable him to satisfy his audience while giving away nothing of importance. Ironically, this was precisely the tactic that Willie himself used in his dealings with Crossman, but instead of resenting the advice the latter was grateful for it.[36]

Crossman seems to have convinced himself that Willie was a more supportive friend than most of his own parliamentary colleagues. Even when he suspected that Willie was responsible for the damaging leakage to the press of the news that the Cabinet was split on his cherished bill to reform the House of Lords, he bore no grudge.[37] When in March 1969 Willie confided that his party would impose a three-line whip for a crucial vote on the bill – thus effectively pronouncing its doom – he managed to mollify the crestfallen Crossman by claiming that he agreed with the principle behind the proposal.[38] This, of course, did not mean that he wanted the government to push it through. Whatever his personal feelings, Willie had to report the backbench mood to Heath, and a substantial number of his colleagues were deeply unhappy about a measure that attacked the hereditary principle and greatly increased the Prime Minister's powers of patronage. From a narrow party perspective there was advantage to be gained in allowing Labour to use up valuable parliamentary time in endless debates on the bill, so Willie made no attempt to restrain MPs who wanted to engage in 'filibustering' tactics. Peter Carrington, who led for the Tories in the Lords, was unhappy at the lack of support for a measure which he, too, warmly approved. But subsequently he accepted that Willie had been right.[39]

However much he might hobnob with government business managers, no one who watched the Chief Whip in operation could doubt where his true loyalties lay. Heath himself believed that Willie was indispensable. In September 1967 the leader stayed with the Whitelaws at Ennim. It was a jolly occasion; according to one story, the Tory leader persuaded Willie to participate in the sack race at a fête; the burly Chief Whip failed to complete the course. Probably this was a diplomatic visit. Heath had just chosen Anthony Barber as Party Chairman in succession to Edward du Cann, despite a widespread feeling that Willie would have been perfect for the job. In fact Barber worked very closely with the Chief Whip; every Tuesday at 10 a.m. the pair met Heath at the latter's flat for informal discussions.⁴⁰ At the end of the year Heath sent a handwritten note to Willie, telling him, 'No one ever had a better Chief Whip, in or out of office – and I speak from some experience!' Deploying the phrase that seemed to occur to every boss Willie ever served, he described his colleague as 'a tower of strength', and could only hope that 'in some way not yet foreseen' 1968 would give him the chance to show how grateful he was.⁴¹

The year did bring unforeseen events, but not of the kind for which Heath was hoping. The crisis over Rhodesian sanctions had already proved the capacity of racial questions to damage the Conservative Party, but an even more spectacular row was brewing. Many Kenyan Asians who had retained British citizenship under the terms of the 1962 Commonwealth Immigrants Act had asserted their rights to settle in the country. Strong feelings were aired at the 1967 Conservative Party Conference, and Labour decided that it should take action in view of the (wildly exaggerated) number of immigrants likely to move to Britain. In February 1968 an emergency bill was introduced to close what Enoch Powell and Duncan Sandys had condemned as a loophole in the original legislation; the alleged 'flood' of up to 300,000 Kenyan Asians would be reduced to a trickle. The bill passed easily, and the fourteen Conservatives (led by Macleod) who refused their support presented only a minor problem to Willie, since thirty-five Labour MPs followed suit. But there was a hint of further trouble in the fact that two more members of the Shadow Cabinet, Robert Carr and Sir Edward Boyle, voted for the bill only on the understanding that they would be free to support promised legislation on race relations, which Labour had offered as a sop to liberal opinion.

The Shadow Cabinet agreed a compromise on the Race Relations Bill in the face of Willie's concern that a hostile backbench motion might bring about a three-way split on similar lines to the ugly Rhodesian episode. A Reasoned Amendment was drawn up, which explained why the party could not support the bill even though it deplored 'racial discord'. To Willie's relief, Powell agreed to be a member of the sub-committee that drafted the amendment; it would be enforced only by a two-line whip. But he was already worried (as he confided to Earl Swinton whose son had married his daughter Susan) 'that the Tory Party is so emotional now about anything to do with race'.⁴² His misgivings were confirmed when he was telephoned by Quintin Hogg three days before the second reading, scheduled for 23 April. Hogg asked him to watch the television news for coverage of a speech that Powell had just given in Wolverhampton. Apparently believing that the party's official policy allowed him to give full voice to his feelings, Powell had conjured a nightmarish vision in which the 'black man would have the whip hand' in Britain; he also spoke of 'wide-grinning piccaninnies', and ended with a classical allusion to 'the River

Tiber foaming with much blood'.[43] As Willie pointed out in his memoirs, Powell's 'lurid language' was certain to exacerbate tensions in the country. For him, though, the likely repercussions within the Conservative Party were a more pressing concern. He felt that Powell ought to have consulted him before making the speech – and if not him, then certainly Hogg (who was the Home Affairs spokesman) and the party leader. This aspect of the affair left Willie 'totally outraged. Frankly, I knew then that I could never bring myself fully to trust him again.' Years later he went even further, claiming that Powell had drafted the offending speech before he agreed to the Reasoned Amendment.[44]

Heath asked Willie to come down to London to discuss the situation. He spent most of April 21 (a Sunday) at his leader's Albany flat. It soon became obvious that several senior figures, including Macleod, Boyle, Carr and Hogg, would resign if Powell were not sacked. But Willie later told Robert Shepherd, the biographer of both Powell and Macleod, that Heath's anger was the greatest. Clearly the speech had caused genuine offence and alarm at the likely consequences; but Powell had already proved to be less than fully reliable when speaking directly on his allotted portfolio of Defence. For some, the grievances were long-standing. In his memoir Willie claims that until this point relations with Powell were good; indeed, the latter remembered more than one occasion when he agreed to tone down speeches in response to appeals from the agitated Chief Whip. But Willie had not forgotten the Thorneycroft resignation of 1958 and it would be difficult to imagine two politicians whose characters could have been more different. Willie heartily agreed with his leader's decision to sack Powell, and greatly admired his decisive handling of the crisis. For his own part, once the sacking had been agreed, he acted as firmly as his leader had done. Ironically for someone who had just referred to a person in his own constituency whose only 'lifeline' against hostile immigrants was a telephone, Powell had put a block on the newly installed device in his own Wolverhampton house. Willie was deputed to contact him through the local Conservative agent. Heath remembered that when the agent seemed reluctant to ask Powell to find a telephone, 'he was firmly told to get on with it' by the Chief Whip.[45]

As so often with Willie, his memoir emphasises the tactical damage caused by Powell's speech rather than his personal reaction, though he did recount with obvious relish the fact that Edward Boyle, who abstained in the vote on his own party's Reasoned Amendment, escaped disciplinary action.[46] Boyle himself later described how Willie had helped to defuse right-wing resentment of his views. Feeling vulnerable in his Birmingham constituency, which contained a significant immigrant community, Boyle had been photographed in a Sikh temple, wearing suitable attire. This gesture only stimulated further complaints against him within the parliamentary party. Willie accosted Boyle in the packed Commons' Smoking Room. 'Oh, Edward,' he boomed, 'that picture of you in the paper, I haven't seen anything so funny in years – I laughed till the tears ran down my cheeks.' Once again, his action here was determined by his personal feelings towards an individual rather than ideological concerns. While Willie firmly believed that all British citizens should be treated equally, his own centre-right views on immigration were revealed in a free vote of February 1969, when he joined Powell, Home and Margaret Thatcher in supporting stricter controls.47

Powell's dismissal did not resolve the difficulties within the Shadow Cabinet as the Race Relations Bill proceeded through the Commons. At a meeting in June, Willie reported that 'people felt very strongly' about race and that 'there was a feeling that the Party had been going too far Right on too many issues'. Heath betrayed his irritation, complaining that the party was bound to shift to the right if the left continued to make trouble for the leadership.48 For the time, though, the problems were restricted to the wing that continued to behave as if Britain was an imperial power, rather than the middle-ranking European state it had become. Before the third reading of the Race Relations Bill, the Shadow Cabinet agreed that the party should abstain, Willie arguing that this would be the best way to avoid another split. But the decision provoked an angry deputation from the 1922 Committee. In collusion with Silkin, Willie delayed the vote until 4.30 on the following morning (a Friday) in the hope that would-be rebels might leave for their beds (or their constituencies for the weekend) before the division was called. Forty-four right-wingers (including Powell) decided to resist fatigue and vote against the bill. To make matters worse for Willie, when Quintin Hogg tried to explain his party's position he was repeatedly heckled by the right, and his attempted self-defence only increased what he described as an 'unmannerly' chorus of abuse. His opponents claimed that Hogg's contribution was 'convoluted, silly and eventually rude'. Willie was reported as sitting 'grim, white-faced and silent' a few feet away on the front bench.49

Powell was not the only Conservative to bring trouble to Willie in 1968, but by comparison the case of Dame Irene Ward was a light-hearted interlude. Dame Irene, the MP for Tynemouth, was a legendary figure who had first entered Parliament in 1931. Once she had questioned the First Lord of the Admiralty about a shortage of uniforms for the WRNS. When the unfortunate minister pleaded that priority had to be given to naval uniforms, she cried, 'Is the minister saying that Wrens' skirts have to be held up to satisfy the needs of sailors?' During the 1966–70 Parliament, Dame Irene was a regular visitor to the Chief Whip's room. On one occasion, when she had been rehearsing her various complaints for longer than usual, she detected that Willie's attention was wandering. 'Are you listening, Willie?' she asked. 'No, I'm not,' the Chief Whip replied. She was never slow to bring her grievances to the attention of the

House. During the debates on the Transport Bill in May 1968 she announced her intention of making a demonstration against Labour's heavy-handed action in curtailing debate. Willie called her in. Knowing that there was no chance of stopping her, he told her that he wouldn't object if she went ahead with her plan of standing in front of the Mace in defiance of parliamentary etiquette. His only proviso was that when he felt she had made her point, he would wink at her from his front-bench seat as a signal for her to clear off. When the demonstration passed off as planned, Willie thought it was like a scene from a farcical silent film. Dame Irene had made her point and was duly 'named' by the Speaker for her temerity. But as Crossman lamented, her suspension from the House made her 'the heroine of the day'. At least she had not actually picked up the Mace and brandished it – a more spectacular version of the protest later adopted by Michael Heseltine, much to Willie's displeasure.[50]

As the Parliament drew towards its close, Conservative fortunes fluctuated. In November 1969 Willie told the newspaper proprietor (and fellow Wykehamist) Cecil King that he felt confident of victory at the next election. The Opposition had been buffeted by controversy, but the Labour Government had been racked by economic problems, George Brown's National Plan was in ruins and in June 1969 Wilson abandoned the tough industrial relations proposals contained in Barbara Castle's White Paper, *In Place of Strife*. The government had been behind in the polls since March 1967; at times they had trailed the Tories by almost thirty points. But when Willie made his bold prediction to Cecil King the gap had narrowed, and by the time the Shadow Cabinet gathered at Selsdon Park Hotel early in 1970 to deliberate on its proposals for the coming election, it was down to single figures. By May Labour was ahead, and Wilson decided to seize the moment by calling a general election for 18 June.[51]

Heath himself was deeply depressed by his party's decline. His speech writer Michael Wolff noticed that Willie's whips were 'going about with faces as long as a wet week' and Jim Prior was asked to tell the Chief to galvanise them. Willie was almost as unhappy as Heath. Having observed Wilson at close quarters for so long, he had become adept at forecasting his adversary's moves, and he was able to predict the election date well in advance. But this was scant consolation for him. It now looked as though the hard grind since 1964 was set to continue for the foreseeable future. Five more years as Opposition Chief Whip was an unappetising prospect. After three consecutive election defeats those Tory MPs who struggled back to Westminster were likely to be in an ugly mood; and Bob Mellish, the new Labour Chief Whip, was nowhere near as emollient as Silkin had been. In December 1969, with tempers frayed after a snap vote cunningly called by Wilson to expose Tory divisions over capital punishment, Mellish accused his opposite number of 'barbaric conduct' over the well-worn issue of pairing arrangements. Willie was outraged, since he had met Mellish before the vote and had thought there was no cause for disagreement. In his reply he deplored Mellish's 'hysterical statements'. There was no prospect that this relationship would improve if the two men found themselves in the same posts after polling day.[52]

Whatever the outcome of the election, it was far from certain that Willie would be Conservative Chief Whip for much longer. He was quite sincere when he told Cecil King that Heath 'would be a superb prime minister'. Even so, he had not been an unqualified success as leader of the Opposition, and King was keen to speculate about the future. For example, what would happen if the next Conservative Government proved to be a failure? Willie felt that he would not be considered for the leadership himself, because he was relatively unknown outside the Commons; in any case he had always seen his role as that of a servant to the existing leader. It was a prophetic conversation. Perhaps Willie's job had kept him out of the public eye. But he was well known to the colleagues who would choose a new leader, should a vacancy arise; and, if he ever moved to a departmental role, whether as minister or shadow, his physique and his character – 'eupeptic and high-coloured, cheerful and good-tempered' – were sure to register with the world outside Westminster. But the question remained: whatever others might think of him, could Willie ever shake off the feeling that he was one of nature's deputies?[53]

CHAPTER 6

'MUD – FILTHY MUD'

Penrith and the Border was safe regardless of the overall election result in 1970, but Willie was determined to meet as many constituents as possible. He and Ceilia would canvass villages together, Willie greeting 'old friends and new with a cheery wave or handshake' while Celia distributed window stickers and spoke to anyone who might have evaded her energetic husband. One local reporter reflected that 'To see them electioneering in the villages is to see true team work and to see how they are received by party workers and opponents alike shows the power of establishing a reputation for integrity and friendliness'.[1]

As Chief Whip, Willie had broader concerns. When he was in the North he kept up regular telephone communication with his leader. But he was responsible for the party's election broadcasts, and this meant that he had to spend the middle of each week in London. Many years later he claimed that this campaign 'broke new ground in the use of television in this country to project a political party, its Leader and its policies', and he felt that the Conservative propaganda exercises of 1979 had not been as innovative as some commentators assumed. At the time he was more doubtful, wondering whether the 1970 broadcasts might have smacked too much of 'slick salesmanship', and feeling that the campaign itself could have featured more positive messages. But the Conservative strategy, masterminded by Geoffrey Tucker from Central Office, was certainly well planned. The first meetings of the so-called 'Thursday group', which discussed the format and content of the broadcasts, had been held in the summer of 1968. Tucker had not known Willie before the group was formed, but after the election he wrote to him saying that he felt they had been friends for a long time and expressing his hope that 'the history books would record' the fact that 'Without your trust and support and understanding we could not have done what we did'.[2]

Research had shown what seems obvious today — that the traditional, straight-to-camera lectures by front-bench spokesmen were unappealing. Willie had an informal focus-group of his own, and noticed that his daughters lost concentration when Wilson addressed the nation in this fashion.[3] So the Conservatives produced programmes which aped the style of ITN's *News at Ten*, interspersed with 'advertisements' driving home the message that Labour's economic policies had failed. Fortunately the Tories could call on two MPs with extensive experience as TV presenters — Geoffrey Johnson-Smith and the former Olympic runner and ITN newscaster, Chris Chataway. Bryan Forbes directed their final broadcast, a flattering portrait of Heath emphasising the breadth of his interests. This was an inspired idea of Tucker's, the culmination of his persistent campaign to soften the leader's image. Other innovations included a theme tune that accompanied Heath's broadcasts and public appearances. Despite Heath's own musical background, this foretaste of future campaigns was judged by two journalists covering the campaign to sound 'like a cross between the Forsyte Saga theme and the opening of a travelogue'.[4] If he was consulted, Willie could not have been much help; although he liked music his taste was rather unadventurous, and when he appeared on *Desert Island Discs* he included 'Run Rabbit, Run' among his selection.

Like Tucker, Iain Macleod believed that the 1970 election would be decided on 'shopping-basket' issues, and the Conservatives argued that under Labour prices were rising while wages had stagnated. Although the Chancellor Roy Jenkins had stabilised the economy, Wilson was highly vulnerable to attack since the humiliating 1967 devaluation of sterling. Although he recognised the importance of economic issues, Willie was keen to broaden the scope of his party's appeal. In his own campaign speeches he tried to exploit industrial relations, contrasting his party's tough proposals with Wilson's climbdown over *In Place of Strife*. But however warmly his message was received in the Cumberland villages, Willie remained deeply pessimistic about the national picture. While colleagues in more marginal seats were able to detect on the doorstep a swing towards the Tories, he felt that his own constituency was exceptional and was greatly worried — to the point of obsession, it seems — by the opinion polls. When the Party Chairman Tony Barber contacted him on 12 May with the news that Gallup had placed Labour more than 7 per cent ahead, he had spluttered: 'Good God . . . What? . . . Do you mean it?' Worse was to follow. On Saturday 13 June an NOP poll revealed a Labour lead of 12.4 per cent. Willie felt 'total dismay' at this news. Fortunately for the Conservatives, a printers' strike ensured that the finding was not widely publicised; and the next day's Gallup poll suggested a deficit of only 2.5 per cent. Willie felt that this was over-optimistic (although Jim Prior remembered him yelling the news down the phone). Only in the last week of the campaign did Willie tentatively suggest that the Conservatives might win after all. 'So you've decided to climb on the bandwagon at last!' Heath retorted. Yet Willie had spent much of the previous Parliament whistling to keep up his leader's spirits, and probably his optimistic forecast was another example of this. On the morning of polling day an ORC poll put the Conservatives marginally ahead, but although he made the most of this in a new round of 'frantic' telephone calls, Willie felt sure it was just another 'rogue' poll. Journalists attending Wilson's eve-of-poll meeting in Liverpool were stunned when the news filtered through to them. Unlike Willie, they quickly realised the real significance of the finding.[5]

Senior Tories were so pessimistic about their chances in 1970 that they spent much of their time contemplating the likely repercussions of what would have been a third consecutive defeat. Heath's position would be untenable, and it was quite possible that MPs might turn in their desperation to the alternative candidate who promised the most radical break from the post-war leadership. Enoch Powell attracted almost as much media attention as Heath during the election campaign, and made a speech that was trailed as a leadership bid on the last Saturday before polling. Some thought that Heath and his team over-reacted to the situation – one senior aide went so far as to describe a Powell speech as an example of 'real fascism' – but the threat of a major upheaval within the party was obvious. Willie had to recruit a deputation of senior colleagues to talk Heath out of withdrawing his routine letter of support for Powell as a Conservative candidate, an action that would have been tantamount to expelling him from the party. At the same time, he tried in press conferences to steer the subject away from Powell. His own view was typically phlegmatic; as he put it later, 'The great thing you have to do with someone like Enoch in your party is to keep your nerve.' If he remained within the fold, Powell would probably win the Tories as many votes as he lost, but to drive him out would guarantee a big drop in support in key Midlands seats.[6]

This was a demonstration of the same pragmatic outlook that had led Willie quietly to explore the possibility of a rapprochement between Heath and Powell in the months before the election. If anything, Willie's personal antipathy for Powell increased over the years, and occasionally he found it difficult to follow his own counsel about 'keeping your nerve'. In 1978, when the issue of immigration once again threatened to open a split in the Tory party, he replied to one of Powell's supporters, repeating familiar allegations about the latter's recruitment of staff from the New Commonwealth when he had been Minister of Health. When Willie's letter was passed on to him, Powell retorted, 'I know you better than to be surprised by the enclosed', and brusquely refuted the allegations. After Powell had lost the Down South seat that he held as an Ulster Unionist from October 1974 to 1987, Margaret

Thatcher was keen to offer him an hereditary peerage (the only kind he was willing to consider). Like Willie himself, Powell had no male heir, so the title would have lapsed on his death. Yet although he had only just received a similar honour himself, Willie is alleged to have been among the 'senior colleagues' of the Prime Minister who opposed the award. Presumably he felt that the House of Lords was already difficult enough to manage without bringing Powell in on the wave of publicity that would have followed such a mark of approval from Downing Street.[7]

But in 1970 the decision to endorse Powell as a Conservative candidate meant that he would be available to challenge for the party leadership after a defeat, and the pessimists knew that contingency plans were urgently required. A series of meetings were arranged, without Heath's knowledge. Willie is unlikely to have been the instigator, but it seems that he was involved in discussions from an early stage, along with Alec Home and Reginald Maudling. According to one (admittedly hostile) source, after supervising the filming of the party's final broadcast four days before the election, Willie 'made his excuses and left' instead of accepting Heath's invitation to accompany him to the Albany for talks. The following day Heath instructed Willie to fly down to London 'when we have won'. At the time, Willie was privately forecasting that his party would lose by fifty seats. The situation was highly embarrassing, but the conspirators agreed that a unifying figure would have to be annointed as quickly as possible after the defeat, in order to stop a Powell bandwagon in its tracks. As in 1963 Home seemed best suited to this role, but true to his previous form he initially expressed reluctance. Even so, he agreed that Willie should visit his home at the Hirsel in the Borders on the day after the defeat; Maudling would join them later. At least Willie would not be the one to break bad news to his leader, as he had done to Home in 1965. Lord Carrington attended Heath's count at Bexley, and discussed the leadership question before the news of the surprise victory came through. Although he has denied any knowledge of plans being laid elsewhere, this would have demanded unusual reticence from Willie and Home, his close friends.[8]

Fortunately for Willie, the damage-limitation exercise was never activated, and readers of the respective memoirs of the would-be regicides were denied the story of how they had prepared for the worst. The general belief that Labour would win belied the widespread feeling that the government had not lived up to the expectations aroused by Wilson back in 1964. In adopting a statesman-like pose for the 1970 campaign, the Prime Minister had left himself vulnerable to unexpected setbacks. Just before the election bad unemployment figures (which Macleod had anticipated), strikes and the adverse balance of payments apparently bore out Heath's warnings on the economy; the national mood may also have been affected when West Germany came from behind to beat the England football team in the World Cup quarter-final. In April Willie had proved a better judge of sporting prospects, guessing that the election would be delayed until October because Wilson would want to avoid tying his own fortunes to those of the national team, which was defending the trophy. In the same interview Willie had confessed that he did not know how his own party would fare in the election, but he did predict that the winning side would be left with a thirty-seat majority. On election night his mathematics proved uncannily accurate, and the victorious Conservatives emulated the German comeback.[9]

At 3 a.m. Willie rang Heath with his congratulations. Both men struggled for words to describe their feelings.[10] Heath regarded the outcome as a personal vindication, a triumph of principle and persistence over opportunism and carping critics. This verdict was reflected in many of the letters that Willie received from old friends.[11] While some of his colleagues remained sceptical – 'Now our troubles begin' was Reggie Maudling's lugubrious reaction to the result – the new Prime Minister eagerly embarked on the task of creating the 'Better Tomorrow' promised by the Conservative manifesto. Instead of driving over to see Home after his own count at Penrith (his majority increased to 13,544), Willie did fly down to London after all, to advise on the formation of the new government. Thus began what he subsequently called 'the most exciting day of my life'. Unsurprisingly, the violent conflict of emotions that he had experienced before the election took their toll. After working into the evening at 10 Downing Street, Heath suggested a break for a light supper. When David ('Sandy') Isserlis, Wilson's Principal Private Secretary, announced that there was no food in the house, he was told to find some sandwiches. Twenty minutes later Isserlis reappeared, shouting, 'Grub's up!' Willie was enraged by service that fell a long way short of the standards at his favourite London club, Bucks'. Heath remembered him saying, 'How can anyone behave like that? He must be sacked at once', and that Willie was still shaking as he tackled his sandwiches. Isserlis had only just been appointed to his position by Wilson, and had previously served under Charles Hill and Quintin Hogg in Conservative ministries. But he was indeed replaced, by Robert Armstrong, who shared Heath's love of music and quickly established a close partnership with the new Prime Minister.[12]

The other witness to Willie's short-lived 'paroxysms of fury' on this occasion was Francis Pym, formerly his deputy and now his successor as Chief Whip. As had been predicted, Willie himself became Lord President of the Council and Leader of the House of Commons. The Presidency of the Council dates back to medieval times, and entails direct dealings with the monarch. But it is an almost wholly ceremonial position, and although some have ridiculed the main ceremony – the swearing-in of new members of the Privy Council – this was unlikely to trouble a traditionalist like Willie. He came to admire the

Queen's judgement, finding that unlike most of his parliamentary colleagues she was too astute and well informed to fall for any bluster. His main difficulty lay in fending off her numerous corgi dogs without committing a fearful breach of protocol. Years later, while flying up to Balmoral, Willie advised Kenneth Clarke to steer the beasts away with a foot while no one was looking: 'The little buggers nip,' he warned.[13]

The Leadership of the House of Commons demands skills similar to those of a good Chief Whip. The ideal for a Leader, as Willie told one of his successors, is not to be noticed. The overriding duty is to see that the government's legislative business gets through the Commons with minimal fuss. In this capacity, Willie was the first minister to speak after MPs had been sworn in for the 1970 Parliament (in what would look like a surreal coincidence by the time that Parliament was dissolved, the first two questions he fielded were on the coal industry and Northern Ireland).[14] Above all, the Leader of the House must combine considerable subtlety with an ability to command the trust of MPs on all sides. This necessarily involves close liaison with the government Chief Whip, but also a great deal of consultation with the Opposition front bench and the Speaker. The Leader is also supposed to have an obligation to the whole House to ensure that legislation is adequately debated and that the rights of backbenchers are respected. In addition, lacking departmental responsibilities of his own, Willie was the natural choice to chair government committees, and to attend many others. Another, less formal task was to take a broad survey of government activity and spot likely trouble ahead. A colleague had already drawn a mischievous comparison between Willie's rise and Stalin's path to power in Soviet Russia; a more hostile observer noted in 1972 that he was free 'to stick his thumb into almost every Tory pie'. But this was not such a boon as Willie's critic implied; it made him the ideal person to defend government policy in speeches outside the House, whenever any of his colleagues was having difficulty getting the message across. This was no sinecure. On a visit to Strathclyde University, for example, Willie was shouted down by students protesting against the government's policy on industrial relations.[15]

For Willie, the burdens of office were greater still. Although Maudling was ranked second in the Cabinet and was thus the unofficial 'Deputy Prime Minister', his relations with Heath were never warm and, at least until March 1972, Willie was regarded as the real second-in-command. Accompanied by the new Foreign Secretary, Sir Alec Douglas-Home, he had arrived early at Number 10 on Saturday 20 June, Heath's first full day in office. His status as the Prime Minister's right-hand man was emphasised by the fact that while Sir Alec left fairly quickly, Willie stayed on, and after the first batch of new ministers had been told of their appointments he went off for lunch with Heath. As a result, Willie was the recipient of some of the bright-red paint which a young female demonstrator hurled at the new Prime Minister on his return. To an eye-witness Willie's reaction towards his assailant seemed to be one of pity rather than anger; obviously a shower of paint was more acceptable than the casual serving of sandwiches.[16]

Willie also attended Heath's first post-election party for lobby journalists on 20 July, when a far more serious blow fell in Downing Street. The new Chancellor of the Exchequer, Iain Macleod, was killed by a heart-attack. The party ended with both host and guests unaware of the disaster that had taken place just on the other side of the wall, and the press did not learn about it until an hour or so later. As soon as they heard the news, Heath and Willie hurried through the connecting door to Number 11 to comfort Macleod's widow. Macleod's death deprived the government of its most able communicator, and the loss threw a shadow over Willie's own victory party of 24 July held in the Carlisle Market Hall and attended by more than a thousand people. He paid tribute to Macleod, having arrived straight from the funeral at Gargrave, near Skipton. The Chancellor had only been able to make one speech in his new office, and had obviously been in discomfort as he delivered it. At the end of the debate he had told Willie that he needed abdominal surgery; his inability properly to rest after the ensuing operation had brought about his death.

As he praised Macleod's courage, Willie had good reason to reflect on the stresses of office. The previous day he had been present on the government front bench for twelve hours, returning to his London home (the Whitelaws had just purchased a house on Clabon Mews in Chelsea) in time for a hasty breakfast before catching the train to Yorkshire with Cabinet colleagues. The long hours were not unusual for someone who had been a key party manager for so long, but this sitting had featured a dramatic interruption. A man in the public gallery had suddenly yelled, 'How do you like this?' and had flung two cannisters of CS gas into the Chamber. One of them landed near the dispatch-box on the government side, but Willie was not seriously affected by the fumes. The Speaker, Dr Horace King, was less fortunate; the air-conditioning system sent the gas in his direction, and he was taken away in a state of near-collapse. Another victim was the left-wing Labour MP Tom Swain, who later explained that he had inhaled too much gas because he had feared for Willie's safety and had been groping towards him in the smoke and confusion. Inter-party strife was already bitter and would get worse over the course of the Parliament, but the incident provided further proof that Willie inspired cross-bench affection, as well as evidence that Britain's body politic was deeply troubled during these years.

Golf always provided a welcome respite from political pressures, and many of Willie's happiest memories came from the summer of 1970. In May 1969 the Royal and Ancient had bestowed on him 'the ultimate honour in golf' by choosing him as its Captain for the coming year.[17] In September 1969 he had faced the traditional ordeal of driving off the first tee at St Andrews in the presence of club members and other interested spectators. In theory, the incoming Captain has the most enviable of golfing tasks; he only needs to play one shot (regardless of its quality) in order to 'win' the medal first presented to the club in 1838 by Queen Adelaide, the widow of William IV. But the ceremony allows ample scope for public humiliation in front of hundreds of people, many of whom are half-hoping that the R&A Captain will prove to be no more skilful than the average, fallible golfer. Willie was acutely aware of the fate of the then Prince of Wales (the future Edward VIII), who had somehow contrived to hit the ball between his own legs when performing his shot in 1922. Although other Captains had found it impossible to keep their heads still in the approved fashion, no one had yet hooked the ball out of bounds; but Willie's combination of strength and inaccuracy made this a plausible outcome. His anxiety was increased by the early start — 8 a.m — by which time he was unlikely to have made a full recovery from any revelries of the previous evening. In the event his ball travelled low and left, but to his relief at least it was airborne for a while and it stayed in play. Two hours later Willie teed off again, and promptly sliced his shot well out of bounds. At least this would have pleased the constituent who had written to Willie alleging that his MP was neglectful of local issues. 'And now I hear that you are to be President of the Royal & Ancient,' he complained. 'I hope that you lose your balls.'[18]

In April 1970 the Whitelaws had visited Augusta, Georgia, to watch the season's first major championship, the US Masters. Willie regarded the trip as 'an enormous treat', and although he did not have the chance to play at Augusta, he did manage a respectable round at the magnificent Pine Valley course in Philadelphia.[19] The general election interfered with some of his duties as Captain, and he had to miss the British Amateur Championship. By that time, though, he had fully justified the faith of those who had thought it proper to appoint such a busy politician to a key role in the golfing hierarchy. He felt there was very little wrong with the administration of the game, and saw his main task as simply ensuring that he bequeathed an equally rosy inheritance to his successor. But although he conceded in his memoirs that the role was little more than that of a 'ceremonial figurehead', he did have ideas for improvements, suggesting for example that there should be more nine-hole courses to compensate for the shortage of suitable land. One of his most prominent successors, Michael Bonallack, considered that 'In this ambassadorial role no one could have achieved more for the Club or for golf', and he presided over a succession of dinners and functions. Willie had become Captain in a year of high hopes for British golf, since Tony Jacklin had won the British Open in 1969. To Willie's disappointment there was no repeat in July 1970, but there was some consolation when he presented the British Open trophy to the world's greatest player, Jack Nicklaus, who overcame his fellow American Doug Sanders in a dramatic eighteen-hole playoff at St Andrews. Given his own vulnerability under pressure, the R&A Captain had good reason to sympathise with Sanders, who would have avoided the playoff had he not fluffed a tiny putt on the last green of the final round.[20]

When Willie himself took part in a well-publicised game during these years there was no need for extra holes. At the end of September 1973 Heath recruited him to partner the Japanese Foreign Secretary in a four-ball against the golf-loving Prime Minister, Kakuei Tanaka. Before the game (which took place at the gale-lashed St George's course in Sandwich) Willie was warned not to watch Tanaka too closely because he had developed the habit of making surreptitious adjustments to the position of his ball. Whether or not this tactic was deployed, it was reported that the Prime Minister and his partner won the match easily. On the way back to the clubhouse the participants climbed into a buggy. Willie politely offered Tanaka the driver's seat, and with equal good breeding the Japanese premier suggested that Willie could do the honours. It then transpired that neither of them had any idea how to operate the machine. So Willie clambered into a rear seat, almost causing the buggy to topple over. Although he must have enjoyed the distraction from his duties in Northern Ireland, he suffered a further setback after the game when he discovered that, unlike the other British participants who were presented with useful high-tech gadgets by their courteous guests, he had been honoured with the gift of a cumbersome Japanese statue, which Celia hated on sight.[21]

Heath's honeymoon with the media proved short-lived and already there were clear signs of the kind of trouble that Maudling had expected within days of the Tories taking office. A state of emergency – the first of many – was declared on 16 July in response to a dock strike. But it was felt that Heath had performed well in his Commons exchanges with Wilson, while Willie was praised for being 'at once firm and authoritative as Leader of the House and at the same time ready to listen to the reasonable requests of Back-Bench MPs on both sides'. He was quoted as telling a friend, 'I never expected to get as far as I have in British politics and I have no ambition to go any further.' But he had been mentioned as a possible successor to Heath, had the election been lost, and it was now assumed that he, rather than Maudling, would take over at Number 10 should the Prime Minister topple from his yacht *Morning Cloud*.[22]

Over the whole of the 1969–70 parliamentary session Willie was recorded by Hansard as having uttered only two words: a shout of 'Sit down!' during a row when a Labour MP had accused Conservatives of being drunk in the Chamber.[23] But after becoming Leader of the House he spoke as frequently as any of his colleagues, taking questions on Parliamentary Business every Thursday and often contributing to debates. When he made his first major speech, during the debate on the Queen's Speech in July, he admitted that it was 'a moment of truth', before suggesting that he might have featured in the official record quite regularly in the past if it had included even a fraction of his noisy commentary during other people's speeches. Willie explained his approach to his new job. 'Our predecessors have handed down to us a parliamentary tradition that is the envy of the world,' he said, and although he would not shrink from necessary reforms of procedure, he certainly would not rush into change for change's sake. In particular, while there were proposals for an overhaul of the committee system, the floor of the House was 'the place where true debate should take place'. He hoped to encourage better attendance. It was a perfect illustration of the moderate Conservatism that Willie had upheld throughout his political career:

> In as far as we are all involved in politics because we want to serve our country and its people, so we belong to particular political parties because we believe that policies based on their principles will be best for Britain's future . . . We on this side know that the Conservative Party has behind it a fine tradition of service to our country over generations. This Conservative Government will uphold those traditions as they face the future. We shall not be swayed by sectional interests. We shall govern in what we believe to be the best interests of all the people.[24]

It was an excellent start, mirrored in Willie's performances during Business Questions, where he generally followed his own advice to Crossman and said as much as possible while giving away the bare minimum of useful information. In the early days of the government, Willie was acclaimed as 'the politicians' politician, the resident professional' – an ironic accolade given that he was also the Cabinet's 'most genuinely amateur member'. But the prolonged absence from the dispatch-box was hardly likely to have increased his confidence. As Barbara Castle put it, 'The most endearing quality about the right hon. Gentleman is that he loves to be loved'. Given the government's generally poor public image, and the exaggerated sense of outrage expressed by Labour MPs in response to many of its measures, no senior minister could take continuing popularity for granted. Willie had decided that the best way to disarm his critics was to adopt an exaggerated line in self-parody. In future years he would master this technique, which enabled him to escape from many tight spots. But between July 1970 and March 1972 the image of a bumbling, well-meaning simpleton was not applied selectively enough. There were two unfortunate by-products. Some media commentators concluded that, despite his disclaimers, Willie was trying to make himself agreeable to all in advance of a bid for the top job. The sour 'Crossbencher' column in the *Sunday Express* denounced Willie's 'happy habit of repeating a colleague's last sentence as if it were the most profound thing he has ever heard', and speculated that he 'makes himself so pleasant because he really has just one true friend in politics. Himself.' At the same time, while his personal popularity undoubtedly increased – and even Labour members were prepared to admit that his reputation had been boosted – his manner in debate was bound to provoke long-term doubts about his real leadership qualities among those who speculated about the succession to Heath.[25]

A typical example of Willie's method came in December 1971, when a Labour MP pointed out some of the possible drawbacks that might arise from televising Commons' debates. Willie suspected that opposition to such a change was based on fear of public exposure rather than any solid principle. But he did not help his own cause when he jeered, 'I am sure that there is a very subtle point behind that [question], but I am afraid that my simple brain has not perceived it.' There were other instances when the 'simple brain' really did seem to confuse itself in an attempt to keep up the pose. For example, in November 1971 Willie expressed amazement that anyone should think that the Solicitor-General, his fellow Wykehamist Sir Geoffrey Howe, was a 'sinister' figure. Labour's Russell Kerr shouted out that Howe was 'thick'. Willie replied that 'if one is thick one is usually not sinister', which seemed to imply that his colleague could only be defended against one allegation by accepting another that was even more wounding. Laughter from the Opposition benches enticed Willie further into the hole he had dug for himself: 'I can understand that the House may think that I am thick, but if they do think I am thick, they will not think that I am sinister.' Alan Watkins had identified Willie as one of only three Cabinet ministers who could boast of a sense of humour, and by tradition some knock-about passages were allowed in the closing speech of an adjournment debate. But the levity seemed out of place on this occasion, since Labour had chosen to discuss the growing problem of unemployment.

Later in the same speech Willie tried to rally his own MPs by quoting against the Opposition an excerpt from a 1967 debate, in which the then Chancellor James Callaghan seemed to be advocating higher unemployment. 'On these occasions,' Willie continued triumphantly, 'the right hon. Gentleman the Leader of the Opposition likes to say, "Read on", so I will read on. He always asks for reading on and now he is going to get it. He did not ask for that just now but I am going to give it to him.' Possibly Willie was playing for time, while frantically searching for the punch-line on the Hansard page in front of him. If so he was out of luck; far from being killer quotes, the next few lines he read out seemed irrelevant to the debate. Fortunately a Labour member rescued him from further recitals by complaining that 'The subject is being treated as a pantomime'. But at the conclusion of his speech an explosion of anger betrayed Willie's frustration at the travails of the government and the tactics of the Opposition. Having earlier referred to the 'good temper' of the debate and having hoped that he himself had shown 'moderation', he suddenly bellowed, 'It is the most amazing effrontery for right hon. and hon. Members opposite to talk of coherent strategy. They have been ever since the Session began slinging mud — filthy mud — amongst themselves.' The following day Labour MPs put down two motions censuring Willie's conduct. Opposition members could soon forget the incident and pass on to new targets, but it made a lasting enemy of the *Daily Mail*'s Andrew Alexander, who had been watching from the Press Gallery.[26]

These verbal infelicities came towards the end of Willie's stint as Lord President, by which time the government as a whole had suffered further setbacks. It was predictable enough that Labour would be 'flinging mud' from the outset, but there were also problems closer to home. The leading authority on the subject, Philip Norton, has written that while unrest within the Conservative Party began 'quietly' in 1970–1, 'the 1971–72 session witnessed an unprecedented — and, in respect of a number of issues, unexpected — degree of intra-party dissent within the Conservative Party in post-war history'. As his own fiercest critic, Willie had reason to feel dissatisfied with himself. His first difficulty had arisen over the choice of a new Speaker to replace Horace King in January 1971. The former Cabinet minister John Boyd-Carpenter was keen to take the post, and at first Willie made encouraging noises, reassuring him that another possible candidate, Selwyn Lloyd, would be bought off with a different job and advising that in the meantime Boyd-Carpenter should refrain from making controversial speeches. When it emerged that Lloyd was not interested in the other offer (which turned out to be the Ambassadorship to the United States), Willie had to prepare Boyd-Carpenter for a disappointment, because Lloyd apparently enjoyed the overwhelming support both of the government and of the Shadow Cabinet. Feeling that his honour had been compromised by his early assurances, Willie told Boyd-Carpenter that he would have to resign from the government if Lloyd won. Boyd-Carpenter clearly saw this as an over-reaction, and took it as a sign of 'the pressures to which [Willie] was exposed'. But at the end of December Boyd-Carpenter did withdraw, and Lloyd was duly elected although fifty-five MPs continued to oppose him. Many backbenchers felt aggrieved that a deal had been stitched up without proper consultation, and Boyd-Carpenter received private assurances that in reality the Shadow Cabinet had been bitterly divided — Crossman was among those who had argued against Lloyd. Willie was accused of having promised MPs a proper say while privately encouraging journalists to assume that there was unanimous front-bench support for Lloyd. Before Lloyd won and was dragged into the Speaker's Chair as custom demanded, Labour's Willie Hamilton claimed that 'this House is riddled with pretence and hypocrisy'. The response to the criticisms was a 'Willie-ism' out of the top drawer: 'I did not actually hear myself say that I would be most anxious to consult anybody on this matter . . . I only think that I am entitled to say what I thought I said.'[27]

An even more serious challenge to Willie's authority arose over his handling of the government's key Industrial Relations Act. In the run-up to the 1970 election he had been at his most prescient when discussing this issue. In July 1969 Cecil King reported him as saying that Wilson's climbdown over *In Place of Strife* had been a serious blow to the Conservatives; like King himself, Willie thought this would 'encourage the hotheads in the trades union movement and make the unions that much harder to deal with when the time comes'. This begs the question of why he had not persuaded Heath and Iain Macleod that the Conservatives should offer full parliamentary support over *In Place of Strife* – a statesman-like stance that would have carried few risks for the party. This seems to be one master-stroke that he entirely overlooked, and if so it proved to be a fateful slip. A few months later he divulged his ideas for dealing with the problem, but this added up to a rather desperate strategy: 'when the Tories do take over their first task will be to overhaul the emergency powers and to look for an occasion to take on the trades unions and put them in their place'. In April 1971 it was reported that he expected a general strike, and was ready 'to fight one to the bitter end'. Such comments seem ironic alongside Alan Watkins' belief at the time that Heath considered Willie 'much too conciliatory' to take over the Department of Employment (the old Ministry of Labour). In the event, far from confronting the unions, the Heath government was accused by its supporters of having caved in over the dock dispute and later over the first miners' strike for almost half a century, which broke out in January 1972. Its only 'victory' came in a postal workers' strike, but significantly this involved one of the more moderate unions. According to Douglas Hurd, Willie used to groan when the cliché 'light at the end of the tunnel' first appeared in the press during a dispute: from that moment on he knew that the government would have no alternative but to meet union demands.[28]

The government had hoped that the Industrial Relations Act would restore order in the workplace by strengthening 'responsible' unions. Unfortunately its provisions could only be accepted by unions that were 'responsible' in the first place; and, Willie argued, the great majority were noticeably lacking in this quality when the Conservatives came to office. As if to ensure a hostile reponse, there was minimal consultation before the bill was published. It ran to 160 pages, and even the Employment Secretary Robert Carr later confessed that he never grasped its full complexity.[29]

In practice the law was always likely to be controversial, but Willie must have expected serious trouble getting it onto the statute book in the first place. After the government had fallen and sections of the press were hailing Willie as the man who had been proved right on every subject, it was said that he had been 'very unhappy' about the legislation; presumably this reflected his tactical traumas more than the principle at stake, which he broadly accepted. The bill differed sufficiently from *In Place of Strife* for Barbara Castle to repair her reputation among union leaders by throwing herself into vehement opposition, and in addition to her oratory there were numerous devices available to Labour MPs who wanted to obstruct its passage through the Commons.

By 21 January 1971 the government had concluded that debate on the bill was taking up more parliamentary time than was justified, even for a measure of such far-reaching importance. It fell to Willie to announce the introduction of a 'guillotine' motion. In those days the procedure, which is nowadays the rule rather than the exception, was unusual enough to attract criticism even on minor matters. On this occasion Willie was interrupted by cries of 'Fascist' and 'dictator' from the Labour benches. *The Times* reported that he ended Business Questions 'roaring like a stag at bay'; twenty-five times the newly elected Speaker Lloyd had to intervene to restore order. It was again alleged that there had been inadequate consultation through the 'usual channels' – perhaps, as with the unions, the government had felt that discussions with Opposition business managers would be a waste of time. Later Willie was attacked by Castle for delivering 'the scantiest, flimsiest and most dishonest argument for an arbitrary action that I think anyone has ever listened to in a guillotine debate'. A group of about forty Labour MPs (described by Lloyd as 'some of the rowdier elements', and including the young Neil Kinnock) prevented Robert Carr from speaking by standing in front of the Mace. Lloyd handled the situation well, and was rewarded by one Oppostion front-bencher with the accusation that he was 'nothing but a government stooge'. Only the Speaker heard this remark, so he could take no direct action against the offender. But afterwards Lloyd drew up a list of phrases that he would not tolerate, including 'bloody hypocrite' and 'bloody twister'. These were difficult times in which to be Speaker – or, for that matter, Leader of the House.[30]

Ultimately the government decided to compromise on the Industrial Relations Bill by allowing more time for debate. Willie's reputation had been damaged by the affair, argued the *Sunday Express*; it had been 'handled with all the finesse of a trigger-happy myopic in an ill-lit abattoir'. In the end, after more slices by the guillotine, further demonstrations from Labour MPs, several all-night sittings and one session that featured a record fifty-seven separate divisions spread over eleven hours, the measure reached the statute book in time for the 1971 summer recess. But within a year trade union opposition (and employers' misgivings) had rendered the act unworkable. Before the government left office Willie would have personal reasons for wishing that it had been dropped.[31]

Unfortunately for Willie his problems with the Industrial Relations Act were matched by difficulties over a measure that was even more important in Heath's eyes – the legislation required before Britain could sign up to the Treaty of Rome and thus (in the geographically perplexing but apparently irresistible phrase) 'go into Europe'. Negotiations in Brussels were completed by Geoffrey Rippon in June 1971, after the French had withdrawn the opposition that had led to de Gaulle's famous vetoes in 1963 and 1967. The next step was parliamentary approval for the principle of EEC membership, and Willie joined Pym in persuading Heath to delay the vote until after the summer recess. Polls suggested that as few as a quarter of voters had supported EEC membership at the start of 1971. In response the government began a concerted campaign of persuasion, which by the end of the year had virtually redressed the balance. Willie (as the minister responsible for information) took a leading role in what opponents felt was an illicit use of taxpayers' money. His own positive views had not changed since the war. In particular, he argued that those who opposed the diminution of British 'sovereignty' were 'on a false track' because both the Germans and the French had continued to fight hard for their national interests after joining the Community. Privately he was dismissive of people within his own constituency 'who were worried about "sovereignty", whatever that meant'. Such people, he thought, believed 'that blacks began at Calais'. Even so, his 1970 address to the voters of Penrith and the Border took account of genuine economic concerns among the local farming community. 'If I am re-elected,' he wrote, 'I will not make up my mind on the question of joining until the terms are known and until I have had an opportunity to discuss them fully in the Constituency.' Similarly, the official party line was to 'negotiate – no more, no less'.[32]

Pym and Willie were confronted with the problem of deciding whether or not to allow a free vote for Conservative MPs after a six-day debate on the principle of membership in October 1971. It was hoped that before that date potential dissidents would have had their minds concentrated by an overwhelming vote in favour at the party conference. Nevertheless, Pym judged that feelings among the 'anti-marketeers' were running so high that they would defy any sort of coercion; indeed, the imposition of a three-line whip might act as an additional provocation. On the other hand, if the government allowed a free vote, it would pressurise Labour into following suit. Wilson himself had led the 1967 bid for membership, and his present opposition to the precise terms secured by Rippon was regarded by many Labour MPs, including the Deputy Leader Roy Jenkins, as a piece of brazen opportunism even by Wilson's standards. It was felt that the Conservatives might win more comfortably if they announced a free vote well in advance of October. In June 1971 Willie told a young Labour pro-marketeer, David Owen, that he was already supporting Pym's arguments in Cabinet, adding that once the vote of principle had been won, the government would have to reimpose the whip for future divisions.[33]

Against Pym's view, Home, Carrington and Maudling argued that the government would look half-hearted in the eyes of its potential European partners if there was a free vote. Heath himself was sympathetic to this view. In the end Pym and Willie prevailed at a meeting only three days before the debate. His extensive circle of contacts had enabled Willie to pick up vital cross-party intelligence; for example, on the day that the government published its White Paper (7 July) the former Labour Foreign Secretary, Patrick Gordon-Walker visited him and predicted that around fifty MPs from his party could be trusted to support EEC membership in crucial divisions. When the vote came, the government enjoyed a larger majority than expected, and although Owen thought that the decision on a free vote had come too late, it was an additional bonus for Willie that this eleventh-hour move fully exposed Labour's divisions. Gordon-Walker had underrated the courage of his colleagues. Eighty-seven Opposition MPs, including Jenkins, Roy Hattersley and John Smith, defied their party whip – sixty-nine supporting the government and eighteen abstaining – while only thirty-nine Conservatives (led by Powell) voted against the motion. Heath's victory by 112 votes appeared to be a great triumph – in January 1971 Willie had suggested that a majority of seventy would be 'all right'. But the Conservatives had been 'free' more on paper than in practice (private pressure was brought to bear against potential dissidents) and it was far from certain that the outcome would be repeated when the Commons considered ratification of the Treaty.[34]

There was uproar in the House when the bill for ratification turned out to contain only twelve clauses. Anti-marketeers regarded this as another attempt to curtail debate, and certainly the brevity of the bill contrasted sharply with the voluminous documentation delivered to MPs beforehand. 'A lawyer's conjuring trick' was Michael Foot's dismissive verdict. As government information officer, Willie took the full brunt of the criticism. But the bill had been drafted by Sir Geoffrey Howe; the fact that the government emerged undefeated from a total of 104 divisions owed most to the skilful management of Pym and his team of whips,[35] and to the calculations of the Labour dissidents, who combined to juggle with the parliamentary arithmetic to ensure that even when some of the government's supporters failed to turn up for one key vote, there was still a majority in favour of membership. On the decisive second reading of 17 February 1972 there was a majority of eight, with fifteen anti-market Tories voting with Labour and five abstaining. Heath had called a meeting with his internal opponents, and warned them that defeat would prompt a general election. After he repeated this threat during the debate, Wilson made what some judged to be a sneering response. This provided an excuse for many of the Tory rebels of October 1971 to return to the fold. The bill became law in October 1972.[36]

In the short term the European battle played itself out to the benefit of the Tories, and indeed to the extent that it fostered the formation of the Social Democratic Party (SDP), which broke away from Labour in 1981, the repercussions continued to benefit the party for many years. Heath's internal opponents also seemed to have been worsted; Enoch Powell, at one time a strong supporter of EEC membership, had become a tireless critic in and out of Parliament. But Heath and his closest supporters, including Willie, also incurred comparable damage. The long-term failure of the considerable propaganda effort on behalf of the European policy was marked by the fact that, even at the beginning of the twenty-first century, the so-called 'Eurosceptics' were still habitually speaking of their opposition to 'going into Europe', as if Britain had never joined the EEC. The parliamentary manoeuvres of 1971–2 gave them ammunition to deny the decisive nature of the voting – despite the fact that the 112-vote margin of October 1971 had reflected the true opinion of MPs far more closely than any 'whipped' vote ever does – and even the result of the 1975 referendum failed to convince them, because by that time membership could be presented as a *fait accompli*. Although Heath had made it no secret that he considered the EEC to have a political as well as an economic dimension, this message seemed not to have penetrated as far as his much-quoted pledge before the 1970 election that Britain would not be committed without the 'full-hearted consent' of its people. There was no sign of this level of support in the opinion polls; and in some quarters the leading figures in the Heath Government would never be forgiven for what was stigmatised as a victory for sharp practice.

Willie's term as Leader of the House was also marked by more esoteric problems concerning procedure and Commons housekeeping. Business Questions were occasionally surreal, when a blood-curdling attack from Wilson over the timetable or content of a bill would be followed by a request that room should be found within the Palace of Westminster for table-tennis facilities. In one of his last performances in this role, Willie was confronted by a complaint about the number of mice at Westminster, followed by a demand that the buildings should be policed by an equivalent army of cats.[37]

For Willie, the main problem concerning parliamentary procedure was a hangover from the previous government. His predecessor but one, Dick Crossman, had set out to create a network of all-party select committees to monitor the activities of Whitehall departments. The idea was that ordinary backbenchers asking questions and making speeches in the Commons chamber were inadequately equipped to do this job as individuals. What they needed, Crossman argued, was the back-up of professional advisers, and the opportunity to summon ministers and officials for more intensive examination than was provided by the daily knockabout of Question Time. Crossman had made a start with this plan, but before he had a chance to complete it he was replaced as Leader of the House by the cautious Fred Peart. When Willie took over from Peart, several new committees existed on a trial basis, but the most dramatic change had been in the overall number of sittings: 629 in 1969 compared to just 240 in 1964. This was not good enough for the reformers; as the Tory MP Ian Gilmour pointed out, 'A strengthening of the committee system should not be confused with a mere extension of it'.[38]

In Opposition Willie seemed to side with those who wanted something similar to the powerful committees of the US Congress, apparently seeing reform on these lines as a way of introducing television cameras into the House in easy stages. In office he proved far more wary, on this and other plans for the 'modernisation' of the political process. The creation of American-style committees at Westminster, Willie insisted, would denude the chamber of the Commons, undermine its debates and speed up the trend towards a slapstick Question Time. His change of mind probably arose after consultations with Whitehall departments; certainly his arguments echoed those of civil servants who had no desire for more effective scrutiny from MPs. The result, following on from a 1969 report by the Commons' Procedure Committee and a consultative Green Paper published in October 1970, was a far less ambitious new system. The main innovation was the replacement of the existing Estimates Committee with a more powerful Expenditure Committee. There would also be a number of specialised sub-committees. At first there were six of these, reflecting broad subject-areas (such as Employment and Social Services) rather than precise departmental remits. This could be seen as a victory for Whitehall self-interest. But while the old Estimates Committee could only suggest ways in which government policies might be carried out more economically, the Expenditure Committee could evaluate the policies themselves. The first Chairman, Edward du Cann, supported this important initiative, which had been recommended in the 1969 Procedure Committee report. In private Willie was highly critical of du Cann, believing that despite his background he had a limited grasp of finance and was generally a poor administrator. Whatever popularity he enjoyed within the party, he claimed, du Cann owed to his ability to be 'all things to all men' – precisely the trait that enemies disliked in Willie himself. But like any good deputy, Willie was prepared to share the animosities of his leader. There had been ill-feeling between Heath and du Cann since the early 1960s, when they both served at the Board of Trade.[39]

Willie's proposals were generally welcomed; Crossman was among those who expressed approval. But in the event du Cann was disappointed by the performance of the Expenditure Committee, which he thought was still under-staffed and suffered from a lack of strategic thinking among its members. A more serious problem was a lack of motivation among MPs, who were not so keen on holding the executive to account as their seventeenth-century counterparts had been. In 1971 Willie allocated two parliamentary days to the government's White Paper on Expenditure, but the debate failed to run its full course due to a lack of speakers. While Willie had considered that the balance of power between Parliament and the executive was just about right, by 1978 du Cann felt compelled to argue in a Private Members' Bill that independent scrutiny of government decisions had become increasingly inadequate. The following year Norman St John Stevas became Leader of the House in the first Thatcher Government, and proved a far more energetic reformer than Willie had been, introducing a new system of twelve specialist Select Committees. In retirement Willie described these changes as 'a bore', which probably sums up his attitude back in 1970.[40]

Whatever his shortcomings as a reformer, Willie was deeply concerned about Parliament's reputation. In February 1969 he had agreed with Cecil King's view that 'parliamentary government is dying all over Europe'. At a Press Gallery lunch in July 1971, while reviewing his first year in office, he noted that MPs were now 'in general younger, worked harder, were at Westminster for longer hours and had far more resources than their predecessors . . . I believe that these developments, which are anyway inevitable, are in fact good for both Parliament and the country.' This upbeat message was clearly inspired by the fact that a committee under the chairmanship of Lord Boyle was about to recommend a significant pay rise for MPs; as Leader of the House, Willie was the nearest thing MPs had to a union boss, and he was keen to soften up public opinion in advance of the increase. He may have believed what he said at that time, but the changes in the composition of the House that he identified in 1971 were precisely those that he bemoaned towards the end of his life.

Perhaps more telling were the pessimistic sections of Willie's speech to the Press Gallery. He thought that attendance in the House was deplorable, and he had no doubt that standards of oratory had declined: 'more and more people sit there with their prepared speeches'. Yet he was no champion of backbenchers' rights, and he actively discouraged Private Members' Bills. Under the Wilson Government the scope for such bills had been increased; notable reforms (including David Steel's Abortion Act) had been introduced by this method.

By contrast Willie cut back the number of available days, from sixteen to twelve – despite promising in his first speech as Lord President that there would be no change in the time available. Possibly this was against his inclinations and in response to pressures on the government's own time; equally Willie might have felt that the eclipse of the Private Member, however regrettable, was 'anyway inevitable'.[41]

Debating standards might have been declining, but Willie could not question the passionate commitment of some MPs. In March 1972 the Labour backbencher Dennis Skinner accused Willie of having given him false assurances about the procedure to be adopted on the European Communities Bill. It turned out that Skinner had telephoned the Leader of the House at 1.30 a.m., and in those circumstances an innocent misunderstanding could easily have arisen. After several demands from Speaker Lloyd that he withdraw the unparliamentary word 'liar', Skinner apologised. But Lloyd's worst moment came on 31 January 1972, during a statement by the Home Secretary Reginald Maudling. On the previous day in Londonderry thirteen people had been shot dead by British troops in what immediately became known as 'Bloody Sunday'. Bernadette Devlin, the nationalist MP for Mid-Ulster, interrupted Maudling several times to accuse him of lying. Finally she described him as a 'murdering hypocrite'. This certainly fell outside Lloyd's list of permitted phrases – indeed, so far outside that the Speaker thought it best to feign deafness. Eventually the diminutive Devlin rushed across the Chamber and physically assaulted Maudling, who remained impassive at the time and did not see fit to mention the sensational incident in his memoirs. Alec Home, sitting beside him, tried to fend off the assault by flapping his handkerchief. Some thought that Devlin had seated herself on the Opposition front bench below the gangway with this purpose in mind, before Maudling had even begun his statement; but to someone who was actually present in Derry it was highly provoking to hear Maudling accept the need for an 'independent' inquiry only after reading out the army's version of events, as if this were established fact. Even so, many MPs were deeply concerned that the authority of the Speaker had been jeopardised. Willie and Pym went to see Lloyd afterwards to make clear their disquiet, losing sight of the fact that Devlin's violence could hardly be compared with the carnage in Derry that had inspired it. And worse had happened in the Chamber when the affairs of Ireland were being discussed; in 1912 Winston Churchill had been struck on the head by a book thrown by a Unionist MP, while the Prime Minister, Asquith, was directly accused of treason.[42]

Less than two months after the attack, Maudling was withdrawn from the line of fire. On 24 March 1972 Willie Whitelaw became the first British Secretary of State for Northern Ireland.

CHAPTER 7

'WILLIE WHITEWASH'

Late in the evening of 19 February 1972 the political scientist David Butler noticed a familiar figure walking alone up Constitution Hill. Willie Whitelaw had been made a Fellow of Butler's Oxford college, Nuffield, back in 1966. Since then he had given regular interviews that provided Butler and his colleagues with helpful insights into his own thinking and the state of his party. When Butler stopped his car he had no reason to expect a protracted conversation; busy Cabinet ministers rarely spare time for an interview without an appointment, and Willie looked 'extremely exhausted'. But he was obviously preoccupied and in the mood for a talk.

Willie began by saying that the Cabinet had met between eight and eleven that evening. The main subject had been the miners' pay dispute, the effects of which were graphically reinforced by the fact that the Cabinet Room was being lit by candles. The miners enjoyed widespread public sympathy and backed their case with an unprecedented level of picketing. A generous settlement had been offered after a hasty inquiry chaired by Lord Wilberforce, but it seemed that the National Union of Miners (NUM) might reject it. 'We looked absolutely into the abyss,' Willie revealed. The implications were appalling – troops would have to be deployed to safeguard power supplies, and there was every chance that Heath would have to call a general election. The issue was still unresolved as Willie and Butler were speaking; an NUM delegation tried to prise out more concessions until a deal was finally struck at one o'clock the following morning. This was bad enough – far removed from the 'Better Tomorrow' that voters had been promised in June 1970. But there were other problems in the background. A week earlier Heath's Political Secretary Douglas Hurd had recorded in his diary, 'The Government [is] now wandering vainly over the battlefield looking for someone to surrender to – and being massacred all the time.' At least Willie was relaxed about party divisions on Europe, feeling that Labour's pro-marketeers in the Commons would prove reliable and would ensure a victory for the government. 'But,' he continued, 'of course there is Ireland. That can't do anything but get worse. It is those impossible unionists. They won't see reason and I fear it may come to Direct Rule.'[1]

In some respects the crisis in Northern Ireland resembled the European issue. Among the general public on the British mainland, indifference and ignorance were equally common; of those who cared, very few were open-minded. And in each case the underlying issue had been troubling policy-makers throughout the history of the modern British state. 'The Irish Question' was so intractable because bitter feelings could still be aroused by the events of the seventeenth century. Each side had a lengthy list of heroes and villains – Cromwell, William of Orange, Wolfe Tone, Daniel O'Connell, Charles Parnell, Roger Casement, Edward Carson, and so on – whose names could provoke cheers or abuse whether or not their deeds and motivations were remembered with much precision. The Government of Ireland Act of 1920 had at least insulated the Westminster Parliament from Northern Ireland; although the province elected twelve MPs (normally members of the Unionist Party, associated with the Conservatives), until the late 1960s the situation occupied the House for an average of only two hours per year. Certain issues, notably defence, were reserved for Westminster, but beyond this mainland politicians left the legislators of Northern Ireland to themselves, and their counterparts in Belfast rarely commented on developments in London.

But the settlement was never likely to produce more than an interim solution; indeed, since the borders of the Six Counties had been designed to ensure an overall Protestant majority, partition was itself an obvious source of future trouble. It created that nightmare scenario for democratic theorists – a sizeable minority population that seemed fated to perpetual political impotence. As a further guarantee of their dominance, Protestant leaders had 'gerrymandered' their constituencies. The parliament, based at Stormont Castle, was regarded as a private debating-chamber for the majority population; very few Catholics had ever held office of any kind in an institution that was summed up by the erection in front of the building of an imposing statue of Carson, the great unionist lawyer and rabble-rouser. Securing a majority in Stormont was never very difficult for unionists, but more creativity was required to win local elections. In 1966 there were twelve Protestants to eight Catholics on Londonderry Borough Council. Yet among the Derry electorate Catholics outnumbered Protestants in a similar ratio. The Catholic population tended to be fairly concentrated anyway, in areas like the Bogside; the rest of the trick depended on a careful demographic study to ensure that most of the 'mixed' seats produced a narrow victory for Protestant candidates. In turn, control of local government led to further grievances. Discrimination in council housing was commonplace. Fermanagh County Council employed 370 people, of whom 332 were Protestant, and not one of the top positions was held by a Catholic. Private employers also seemed confident that Protestants were far more promising workers than their Catholic neighbours. Although cultural differences were now at least as important as religion in fuelling ill-feeling between the communities, there were still some Protestants who 'thought of the Pope as a personal and inveterate enemy, who spent all his time scheming to get his hands on the Belfast shipyards'. It was therefore considered prudent to keep his agents out; in the early 1970s more than 95 per cent of the 10,000 shipyard employees were Protestants.[2]

'The Troubles' had never gone away, although by the mid-1960s the Irish Republican Army (IRA) was fairly inactive and had begun to explore the possibility of forging links with the Protestant working class. But by the end of the decade there had been a change of mood. Inspired by civil-rights movements abroad, students had begun to kick against the widespread discrimination. One of their number, Bernadette Devlin, was elected to the Westminster Parliament. A new alignment of existing nationalist groups, the Social Democratic and Labour Party (SDLP), was founded to press for peaceful change. At the same time, divisions opened within the Protestant community, between those who accepted the need for compromise and others (such as the Reverend Ian Paisley) who regarded any move towards real accommodation as a pitiful 'surrender'. The unionist population had good reason to feel vulnerable. While the British had pushed through the union in the first place because of the need to guard an exposed flank during the Napoleonic Wars, in the post-war era of atomic weapons only fanatical nationalists could imagine that Northern Ireland represented a 'strategic interest' worth defending at a heavy cost. For the British, the Ulster 'statelet' had become a nuisance rather than a necessity, and those who adhered to the existing system could no longer depend on unquestioning support from across the Irish Sea. Within the ruling Unionist Party resistance to concessions and demands for rigorous action against nationalists forced the resignation of the moderate Prime Minister, Terence O'Neill, in April 1969; his replacement, James Chichester-Clark, left office for similar reasons two years later. Significantly, O'Neill and Chichester-Clark were relatives who had both belonged to Guards' regiments and attended Eton. The old ruling class of Ulster was being shouldered aside by those who had risen from the ranks of the people whose views they claimed to represent; despite their own commitment to peaceful change, they were paying the price for the inertia of previous leaders such as Lord Brookeborough, who had refused to countenance reform over nearly twenty years as Prime Minister.

When the Conservatives took office in 1970 the situation was deteriorating.

Labour's Home Secretary, James Callaghan, had acted energetically in response to disturbances that accompanied the civil rights campaign. The Protestant-dominated Royal Ulster Constabulary (RUC) was disarmed, and a new part-time Ulster Defence Regiment (UDR) was established under a British commander to replace the notorious 'B' Specials. Catholics were encouraged to enlist, with some success (at first). Meanwhile British troops were dispatched to take over certain duties from the RUC. Initially the soldiers were welcomed by most Catholics. But elements within the minority population still felt they would be vulnerable without a protective force of their own. Some Catholic enclaves in Derry and Belfast were now considered to be 'no-go areas' for soldiers and police. In January 1970 the Provisional IRA (Provos), a new and more militant organisation committed to a united Ireland, split off from the old 'Officials'. On the Protestant side, the Ulster Volunteer Force (UVF) had started to murder Catholics back in 1966. O'Neill had been horrified by the first attacks, but there was some delay before he proscribed the organisation – and no one was charged with membership until 1973. In the month before the 1970 general election the deposed O'Neill thought that all-out civil war was 'inevitable'. The honeymoon period of the British Army had ended. On 2 April CS gas was used against Catholic demonstrators in Belfast's Ballymurphy housing estate.[3]

The Heath Cabinet's sensitivity on Northern Ireland was signalled at its first meetings. The initial draft of the Queen's Speech (drawn up under Willie's supervision) had referred to the need to promote 'equality and freedom from discrimination', as if the British Government were directly responsible for such matters. This was revised, so that the published version stressed the need to 'support the Northern Ireland Government' in its efforts to secure 'peace and harmony'. Maudling was urged to visit the province as soon as possible, and at the second Cabinet meeting it was agreed that the army should be reinforced. But early signs on the ground were unpromising. Maudling made his visit, on 30 June 1970, after a weekend of gun battles between the Provisionals and Protestant marchers, resulting in several deaths. At the beginning of July a weekend curfew was imposed on the Catholic Lower Falls area of Belfast, and house-to-house searches were conducted in a high-handed manner which suggested that the whole area was regarded as enemy territory. The action was the best way of turning a supposition into a fact; it convinced many nationalists that the Conservatives were determined to suppress any opposition to the unionists, their traditional allies. This impression was reinforced when two leading unionist politicians were given a tour of the Falls on the back of an army Land-Rover. Four Catholics were killed over that weekend. The Lower Falls curfew was probably the most serious of several decisions after the election of the Heath Government which gave a significant boost to Provisional IRA recruitment.[4]

Back in Whitehall, the Cabinet Secretary Burke Trend emphasised the gravity of the situation. Things could remain much as they were, with Northern Ireland 'stabilised only by the presence of British troops and trembling on the edge of disaster but never quite tipping over'. 'The resultant burden on ourselves,' Trend thought, 'would be so intolerable if it were maintained indefinitely that we ought not to contemplate it if it can be avoided.' Yet to 'wash our hands of the whole business' was no solution, either. The only realistic option, Trend felt, was a radical re-examination of the 1921 settlement. Ministers should contemplate the suspension of the Stormont parliament, and since the Governor of Northern Ireland lacked the political training necessary to pursue a new initiative, Trend's argument clearly foreshadowed the appointment, for the first time, of a Cabinet minister with special responsibility for Northern Ireland. This job was unlikely to suit Maudling, who had made a poor impression on his first visit. An army source thought that 'He seemed amazed by the ghastly situation', and as he flew back to London he had muttered, 'For God's sake bring me a large scotch. What a bloody awful country.' In his final Cabinet memorandum on the subject he complained that the people of Northern Ireland suffered from 'a death wish'.[5]

As Leader of the House of Commons, Willie was usually anxious not to disclose too much about his private feelings, or those of his Cabinet colleagues. But he made an exception of Northern Ireland. At the end of an adjournment debate in August 1971 he expressed the government's determination to root out terrorism, whatever its source, and to ensure that people in all the communities of Northern Ireland could conduct their business in peace. Later he explained in typical style that 'sometimes the Leader of the House has an opportunity to make clear the sort of feelings he is entitled to have. People sometimes feel that inside this large frame nothing else exists at all, and therefore it is reasonable to point out . . . that perhaps there is something up above and down below.' His listeners did not know that the Cabinet had just granted permission for the Stormont administration to introduce internment without trial for terrorist suspects – a decision that had first been discussed by ministers on 22 July, but which Maudling was considering as early as February.[6]

In August 1971 there was no suggestion that Willie would ever become deeply involved in the affairs of Northern Ireland. He was not asked to attend the relevant Cabinet committee until November, and talks with the new Prime Minister Brian Faulkner were conducted by Heath, Maudling, Home and Carrington, the Defence Secretary. The situation had been grave enough in August, but between the introduction of internment and the end of 1971 there were 144 murders, and 1972 opened with 'Bloody Sunday'. In response demonstrators burned down the British Embassy in Dublin, as the Irish police looked on; the Official IRA detonated a bomb at the Parachute Regiment's barracks in Aldershot, killing five kitchen staff, one gardnener and a Catholic padre.

Even before the conflict spilled onto the British mainland, Heath had begun to prepare the ground for a radical departure, having consulted all the relevant papers in the government archive. On Friday 4 February he discussed several options with Faulkner, including the idea that republican-dominated areas of Ulster, such as the Bogside and Creggan in Derry, should be ceded to the South. Something like this would be floated by Margaret Thatcher in 1985, but it made no more sense then than it did in 1972.[7] Faulkner pointed out that it would leave unsolved the problem of 200,000 Catholics in Belfast. Other initiatives were canvassed, during what the British ministers clearly saw as a chance to test the limits of unionist tolerance.

Maudling took a full part in these talks, although he had just echoed hard-line unionist language by telling the 1922 Committee that the most common suggestions for a new departure would represent a 'surrender' on the part of the authorities at Westminster and Stormont. For some months Faulkner had felt that Maudling was being sidelined; although he was present at Chequers in September 1971 when Heath met Faulkner and the Irish Taoiseach Jack Lynch, the Home Secretary had been excluded from the main discussions and was forced to ask civil servants to keep him informed of any progress. Later he had revealed far too much of his hand when he confessed that the IRA could 'not be defeated, not completely eliminated, but have their violence reduced to an acceptable level'. Clearly a new, more dynamic figure would be needed if the British Government chose to follow Trend's advice and embark on a new settlement.[8]

In his memoirs Willie claims that the first clear intimation of a transfer to Northern Ireland came when he was sounded out on the subject by Heath's Principal Private Secretary, Robert Armstrong, on the day before he accepted the appointment. There is evidence, though, that he had known what was coming for some time, and Maudling claimed to have spoken to Willie about it with Heath's authority. In private conversation Willie had confided that he was worried about Maudling's likely response if he took over responsibility for the province (although Heath was probably closer to the mark when he speculated that Maudling 'was rather glad to get rid of it'). Since Maudling would be forced to resign from the government less than four months later (for his part in the Poulson corruption scandal), the timing was equally fortuitous for Heath. Certainly others had identified Willie much earlier as the right man for a post that was seen as a necessity. Back in September 1971 Cecil King had suggested his name to a senior civil servant, who had replied that Willie would be 'very acceptable' at Northern Ireland – or, for that matter, in any other government department. The unnamed civil servant thought that Willie was 'the only man who, when he speaks on something on which he feels strongly, has the personal authority to silence opposition'. As King's published diary shows, Willie was also well informed on Northern Ireland – at least compared to the average Westminster observer – even though he had only visited the province twice, on social occasions.

To King's surprise, the new Secretary of State turned up for lunch before his appointment was officially confirmed, and as usual was quite prepared to divulge his thinking. Naturally after this the opportunities for meetings were fewer, but even so the biographer can only regret King's decision to publish the first volume of his indiscreet diaries in November 1972. Since King had his own very strong – and eccentric – views on Northern Ireland, his accounts are open to serious challenge; but even if his memories were occasionally selective, it seems that the senior politicians and civil servants who were summoned to his table were rarely misquoted. Some people continued to gossip with King over lunch, presumably in the hope of winning greater publicity for their opinions. Willie had been warned in advance that King was unreliable, and he was apoplectic when the book was published: 'I suppose the man must have had a tape-recorder under the table whenever we met,' he spluttered. Although he felt that he could not break off relations entirely, he became far more guarded. Fortunately the second volume of King's diary did not appear until after the fall of the Heath Government, but the publication of some frank remarks must still have been embarrassing to Willie. For example, in January 1971 he had assented to King's characterisation of his government's policy as no more than 'a wish that Ireland and the Irish should go away and get lost'.[9]

Whether or not Willie had much prior notice of his appointment, he was present on 14 March 1972 when the British Cabinet took the key decision to remove responsibility for law and order from the Stormont government. Ministers still hoped that Faulkner might stay in office, but this was a remote possibility after a step that would reduce his status to that of 'chairman of a county council'. Direct Rule from Westminster would be the inevitable consequence of his resignation. For the first time Willie was invited to join talks with Faulkner just over a week later, on 22 March. The nine-hour negotiations took their predictable course, although Faulkner agreed to stay on until the machinery of Direct Rule was in place. On his return to Stormont he was cheered by a crowd of around 100,000 as he told them, 'we understand the resentment that you feel . . . We have tremendous power. Our power is the power of our numbers; our power is the justice of our cause; our power is the responsibility of our conduct . . . Let us show the world that, so far as we are concerned, violence and intimidation are out.' Standing beside him was

William Craig, the former Stormont Home Affairs minister. Craig had recently founded the Vanguard Movement, which held a rally for 60,000 supporters in Belfast's Ormeau Park on 18 March. Craig had personally inspected several hundred men in uniform and hinted at the need to 'liquidate the enemy'. Although he was more erratic than truly sinister, even Faulkner had felt that 'comparisons with Nazi-style rallies could hardly be avoided'. Perhaps there was a place for 'violence and intimidation' after all. Craig had chosen to demonstrate his power more peacefully, calling for a two-day general strike. But even this protest was backed by the threat of violence; any Protestant who felt disinclined to obey ran the risk of victimisation. Very few were foolhardy enough to work on those two days, and power supplies were drastically curtailed.[10]

Some observers thought that Brian Faulkner resembled Heath, in so far as both men seemed to be technocrats who owed their political prominence to an aptitude for tough decision-making. The likeness did exist, but their relationship was uneasy from the beginning, and those who saw the parallels omitted one crucial factor: their different perspectives. Where their emotions were disengaged, both were essentially problem-solvers; but while Heath regarded the Protestant ascendancy in Ulster as a problem, Faulkner felt an emotional commitment which matched Heath's passionate views on Europe. His bias was reinforced by an unusual degree of preoccupation with Stormont politics (and his own position in particular) rather than the real situation in the housing estates of Belfast and Derry. As a result, although his courage was remarkable by any standard, only in the context of Ulster politics could he be regarded as a moderate. His memoirs (published after his death in a riding accident in 1977) give the impression that the troubles in Northern Ireland had been provoked by lawless Catholics, and that apart from a few over-enthusiastic souls like Paisley and Craig, the majority population had behaved impeccably in the face of incessant provocation. It was true that the majority of unionists were anxious for a just and peaceful settlement; but Faulkner forgot to say the same about their nationalist opponents.

Faulkner's protestations that the decision to suspend Stormont came out of the blue are unconvincing; he was certainly given advance warning by Robin Chichester-Clark, an impeccable source. Willie's subsequent acknowledgement that more could have been done to prepare the ground was obviously influenced by hindsight; in March 1972 he shared the general mistrust of the unionist leader. But Faulkner did have grounds for interpreting Direct Rule as a personal betrayal. He thought that he had established a good rapport with Heath, and as recently as 3 March the latter had sent a telegram dismissing rumours about a change as 'pure speculation'. Beyond Faulkner's obvious resentment at the implication that he was incapable of governing, many other unionists detested what they saw as a craven concession to the violence of the Provisionals. Comparisons were drawn between Heath's decisions and the strategy of Neville Chamberlain at the time of Munich. Naturally this interpretation of events was shared by many of the Provos themselves. The suspension of Stormont had been an important goal for republicans, whose theory dictated that unionist politicians were merely stooges for the real enemy, the English – the 'colonial' power that Wolfe Tone had denounced back in 1791 as 'the never-failing source of our political evils'. While Faulkner genuinely thought that Provo activity was at a low level 'due to the progress of the security forces' and the dwindling calibre of Provo recruits, the Provos themselves 'felt we were very close to victory'. One senior figure claimed that 'the IRA was in the best state it had been for fifty years in terms of men, ammunition and equipment and morale'. Gerry Adams remembered the fall of Stormont as the cue for 'complete and utter jubilation' among nationalists and republicans.[11]

The assumption that terrorism had secured the suspension of Stormont was perhaps the most important background factor throughout Willie's time in Northern Ireland.[12] Of course, in all conflicts of this kind impressions mean far more than reality. But in the imposition of Direct Rule, Provo violence was only one of many factors.

Certainly the Provos were active in the months before Direct Rule. On 4 March 1972 a bomb in Belfast's Abercorn restaurant caused two deaths and injuries to more than a hundred others. Five days later four Provo volunteers were killed when their own bomb exploded prematurely, and ambiguous warnings led to the deaths of seven civilians in a car-bomb attack on Donegall Street. But the relevant 'violence' to consider was that of the security forces, not the Provo campaign. Apart from anything else, 'Bloody Sunday' was a public relations disaster for the British Government. It could only be expected that the incident would further swell the ranks of the Provos. In America sympathisers to the nationalist cause, such as Senator Edward Kennedy, were already making political capital out of the Troubles; any embarrassment he could cause the British Government would be supplemented by fund-raising efforts on the part of expatriate Irishmen in the United States. More importantly, the incineration of the British Embassy in Dublin was a catastrophe at a time when both governments were hoping to become EEC partners. Even if the Stormont government had been truly autonomous, there would have been a strong temptation for Westminster to take formal powers in a situation to which it had already committed so many troops. As the slight mix-up over the 1970 Queen's Speech had shown, it was easy enough for British ministers to talk as if they already ran the province. One commentator has accurately described the position before March 1972 as one of 'direct rule by proxy'. Contingency plans for cutting out the unionist middlemen had been in Whitehall files for many months, and on a visit to the province in June 1970 Alec Home had carefully explained that Stormont would be suspended if it was judged to be making the law-and-order situation worse rather than better.[13]

But there was another element of violence in the equation. When Willie had spoken of 'those impossible unionists' back in February, it seems most likely that he was responding to the emergence of the Vanguard Movement, which Craig had established less than a week earlier. His remark that the situation could only deteriorate was well founded. Craig seemed to be setting himself up as a figure in the mould of Carson, whose threats of mass insurrection had been the main factor in producing the ill-fated compromise of 1921. It seemed quite possible that British troops would soon be faced with the ultimate nightmare – a war against two well-armed and fanatical guerrilla organisations. If the British Army was withdrawn, the inevitable result would be intolerable bloodshed; yet on present trends this looked likely to happen anyway, and as the dominant player the British Government was sure to be blamed. The Cabinet's only viable option was to remove the ambiguity in its relationship with Northern Ireland and seek a political breakthrough. In hindsight, the biggest surprise is that the move was delayed so long after Bloody Sunday. Heath had accepted the inevitability of Direct Rule by the end of February, but he was hampered by splits within the Cabinet, and a meeting of 7 March had ended in deadlock. The most outspoken opponent of Direct Rule, surprisingly, was Lord Home, who wanted the British to withdraw completely and accept the inevitability of a united Ireland. In the end, though, agreement on a middle course was unanimous.[14]

The illusion that Direct Rule was a reward for republican violence was not universally shared on the unionist side. Indeed, the suspension of Stormont could be welcomed as a step towards the full integration of Northern Ireland within the United Kingdom, which was the ultimate goal for some, including (at this time) Ian Paisley. Yet the associated belief that Willie was arriving in Belfast as a symbol of appeasement suited almost everyone on the unionist side. Whether explicit or unspoken, it acted as a challenge for him to provide concrete evidence that he was no pushover for the Provos. In fact, as the Provos noted, the British had tried to make Direct Rule more palatable to unionists by reaffirming that there would be no easing up in the battle against terrorism, and that a united Ireland would never be established against the wishes of the majority. To this end, it was proposed to hold a referendum on the border, which in the circumstances of 1972 could have only one result. It was clearly hoped that world opinion would soften, once the 'statelet' of Northern Ireland had been granted this democratic endorsement. The proposed referendum should have been viewed as an important concession to unionists, since the

1970 Conservative manifesto had included a pledge to retain the border unless Stormont voted to abolish it; and, as the Northern Irish had every reason to remember, it is easier to bribe or coerce an assembly than to affect the votes of a people. There was no question – at least for the foreseeable future – of including the population of the South in the electorate for the referendum. The idea that plebicites in the North would be held at regular intervals suggested that British ministers wanted to keep open the possibility of reunification in the future, but if the unionists were right in thinking that life was intolerable in the impoverished 'priest-ridden' South, they could have no reason to fear a defeat.

The initial unionist response to Direct Rule demonstrated a point that Maudling had never quite grasped. In his memoirs he wrote that 'if you make some concessions in a situation like this they are almost always too little and too late'. This conviction induced the defeatism which, rather than any constitutional laziness, underlay Maudling's failure. But if anything his analysis was too optimistic.[15] It was not that the politics of the trade-off – so familiar to Westminster practitioners – were mistimed: rather, in themselves they were inappropriate. In Northern Ireland politics was a zero-sum game. Politicians on both sides tended to overlook any concessions to themselves, and to resent even token attempts to compensate their opponents.

The choice of Willie Whitelaw as the first Secretary of State for Northern Ireland seemed obvious to Westminster observers, because he so clearly excelled at the game he had played there since 1955. In one important respect the faith was well founded. Without the ability to put people at their ease, no minister could hope to get anywhere in Northern Ireland, and few MPs could rival Willie's reputation for affability. The fact that Willie came from roughly the same social class as the Stormont politicians who had failed might have seemed a drawback; but a 'gentleman' from the mainland was always more likely to win respect than a home-grown specimen. Even so, hundreds of hours of friendly discussions could never be enough to overcome centuries of hatred; and however easily Willie might win the trust of the leaders he consulted, their followers would always be watching for the first hint of a 'sell-out'. So the choice of Willie was what a logician might call a 'category mistake'; it was like selecting a cricket captain on the strength of an excellent performance in the FA Cup. This was a country where (as one of his successors reminded him years later) people habitually greeted visiting ministers with apologies for the miserable weather, apparently oblivious to the more serious problems about which they really could do something. Willie would have to learn a new set of rules, and instead of being an asset, his years of experience at Westminster would be dangerously misleading. When Cecil King wrote in June 1972 that Willie was 'having his introduction to real politics', his choice of words was somewhat eccentric. Politics in Ulster could scarcely be 'real' when even Lady Brookeborough, the ageing widow of a former Stormont premier, could refuse to shake hands with the Secretary of State, at the start of a meeting that she had herself requested. Even so, King was right in thinking that Willie had been thrown in at the deep end.[16]

The final irony was that almost everyone with an intimate knowledge of the terrain was automatically disqualified. In the spring of 1972 any MPs who really knew what was going on were bound to be suspected of nursing a raging commitment to one side or the other. Willie and Heath were immediately confronted with this problem. They wanted their mutual friend, the Unionist MP Robin Chichester-Clark, to take office as a junior minister in Northern Ireland. For a normal Whitehall department it would have made perfect sense to appoint a congenial colleague who had been the relevant Shadow spokesman; but in the context of Northern Ireland it merely showed how much Heath and Willie had to learn. Despite his long front-bench service, Chichester-Clark was discredited in the eyes of many unionists, who had recently removed his brother from office for being too conciliatory; he was equally unlikely to find warm admirers among hard-line nationalists. He politely declined the offer. But Heath had promised him a place in the government at some point, and in April 1972 he accepted a junior post at Employment. His reward was the passage of a no-confidence motion by his constituency party in Londonderry. Vanguard accused him of treason, and his house was picketed. At least the extreme unionists did not parade in front of his house with an empty coffin; they had reserved this treat for his brother James.[17]

Internment was the last, but by no means the least, of the problems that Willie faced in his new office. According to Ian Paisley, Willie confided that he had opposed the policy, and regretted it more than any other decision of the Heath Government. He was not alone in his misgivings; senior British soldiers were also deeply unhappy, and even Heath himself had grave doubts. That he allowed himself to be convinced is a sign that he had lost track of political events in Ulster. The previous month the SDLP had walked out of Stormont after failing to secure an independent inquiry into the shooting of two unarmed Catholics. Cooperation from moderate nationalists was crucial, and internment was calculated to alienate them further. Yet Faulkner could argue that the policy had worked between 1956 and 1962. At that time it had been introduced simultaneously by the South, and it was unlikely that this would happen again. Nevertheless, Faulkner convinced Heath that it was worth a try.[18]

Faulkner later recorded his belief that his security measures 'were, by the end of 1971, beginning to pay off and would, if consistently and firmly applied over the succeeding months, have resulted in the virtual defeat of the IRA by the end of 1972'. Yet of the 172 people who met violent deaths in Northern Ireland during 1971, only twenty-eight had been killed by the time that the raids were launched across the province in the early hours of 9 August. Like Claude Rains in *Casablanca*, the security forces 'lifted' the 'usual suspects' instead of the real ones. Some Provos were apprehended, but most escaped across the border as soon as they noticed an unusual build-up of troops. Their intelligence network proved far better than that of the RUC's Special Branch. Most of those arrested were merely republican sympathisers. The Provo leader Sean MacStiofáin later recorded his amazement at the list of those who were taken; it included civil rights activists who were outspoken critics of violence in any form, 'members of the Gaelic Athletic Association, people arrested instead of their relatives, and people we had never heard of at all'. He estimated that fewer than sixty had real connections to the Provos. Faulkner's assessment was more sanguine, but even so within forty-eight hours he had released almost a hundred men out of the 337 who had been arrested. MacStiofáin does not even bother to record that no Protestants had been thought dangerous enough to pick up, but at the time this fact must have deeply impressed any Catholic who had continued to believe that the British Army was a neutral force.[19]

By the time of Direct Rule the number of detainees had risen again, to around 700, and this number included a fair proportion of bona fide terrorists. But the Catholic community was understandably scornful when Faulkner claimed that internment was designed to relieve them of 'the shadow of fear'. Certainly it had not relieved them from the shadows of gunmen. In the four days after internment twenty-two people were killed in clashes between the Provos still at large, 'loyalist' gangs and the army. Several thousand Catholics left their homes and fled to the South. Faulkner dismissed this mass emigration as a republican publicity-stunt; perhaps he felt that the loyalist gangs who were burning Catholics out of their homes really consisted of yet more unapprehended Provos, rather than Protestant militants. It was also possible to accuse the Provos of spreading false rumours that internees were being ill-treated, but the Irish Government took them seriously – with good reason – and instituted proceedings against the British at the European Court of Human Rights in Strasburg. The case became a running sore in relations between the two states. Maudling had set up an inquiry into the allegations; he had also instructed Lord Widgery to investigate the events of Bloody Sunday.[20]

Heath formally asked Willie to take up the challenge of Northern Ireland in the early hours of the morning of 24 March 1972. Remembering the advice given to him years before by Charlie MacAndrew, he accepted the post without even asking for time to discuss the prospect with his wife. He knew that, despite all the likely dangers and inconveniences to come, he would have Celia's full support. Had the need arisen he would have made the winding-down of internment a condition of his acceptance, but the Cabinet had already agreed that the policy was a disaster. Instead, Willie's single stipulation was that he should have an aircraft at his disposal at all times.[21]

For the time being he was only Secretary of State designate; he could not be given the seals of office from the Queen until the passage of legislation establishing Direct Rule. But this would be a formality, and the Commons could be told without delay. As Heath announced the appointment, Willie sat beside him on the front bench. It was reported that while Heath looked 'tense and strained', Willie shed some tears as he heard the tributes paid to him by other speakers. Almost all of his correspondents over the next few days agreed that it was not exactly a time for congratulation, but that he was the only man whose qualities gave any hope of success. Richard Crossman was one of the rare exceptions; he expected that Willie would be relieved to escape from 'the squabbles and points of procedure of the House in order to take on an exhilarating – and possibly – an historic responsibility'. While he thought that Willie had been a good Leader, his own memory was of a task 'which nags and gets one down'. Another former Labour minister, Dick Marsh, had recently reported that Willie was 'browned off' because his present job was only meaningful in the eyes of Westminster insiders. Willie might have regretted losing his magnificent room in the Cabinet Office, from which he could look down on Guardsmen going through their drill on Horse Guards Parade, but there were other aspects of the job that he was glad to leave behind. It was a thankless task having to explain government policy to an increasingly unsympathetic public. He even had difficulty within his close family; plans for the reorganisation of local government included the absorption of Nairn into a Highland regional authority, and he had to confess that his mother had protested violently against this.[22]

Having never before headed a major government department, Willie had suddenly become something more than a Prime Minister; his powers were most frequently compared in the press to those of a viceroy (the well-qualified Lord Mountbatten, who wrote to him at this time, made the same point). He was given a free hand in choosing his junior ministers. After Chichester-Clark's refusal, Lord Windlesham and Paul Channon became Ministers of State, with David Howell as Parliamentary Under-Secretary. Willie also hand-picked his press secretary. Knowing that this would be a crucial role, he selected the former industrial correspondent of the *Daily Mail*, Keith McDowall. A tough, witty and abrasive character with cropped hair, McDowall was often mistaken for a soldier or a plain-clothes policeman when he accompanied his boss around the province. Initially he was in two minds about accepting such a hazardous position, but his doubts were dispelled during his first meeting with his prospective boss. 'People are going to ask why I am employing a Labour man like you,' Willie lamented. McDowall found himself offering the assurance that he was not a member of the party; although he made no secret of his political preferences, he pointed out that he had been properly recruited as a temporary civil servant and had no intention of abusing the position he had been offered. Willie never mentioned the matter again.[23]

Willie's performance during his first press conference in his new job had emphasised the need for a shrewd operator at his elbow. On the day after Heath's announcement he had flown to Aldergrove Airport outside Belfast, where he met the media. True to Irish custom, local journalists bombarded him with historical questions. It was an awkward baptism for someone who believed in the necessity of focusing on the future, and since the whole point of the exercise was to introduce Willie to the province at the first opportunity, his inquisitors should have expected the new Secretary of State to be imperfectly briefed. He became, in turn, bewildered and then irritated by this treatment. So after a series of similar questions he replied, in a tone of slightly pained dignity, 'I always feel it is quite wrong to prejudge the past.' One of the most celebrated of all 'Willie-isms', this remark – however nonsensical it might have seemed to a pedant – contained the usual kernel of penetrating insight. Yet it was still the comment of an outsider. When McDowall joined the team he decided there would be no further airport conferences. He also felt that Willie needed to brush up on his technique for television interviews, since he could expect constant exposure from now on, after so many years of relative obscurity. Before his next important round of interviews Willie was subjected to a rigorous dress-rehearsal, and his performances quickly improved.

Before Willie met any of Northern Ireland's politicians, his diplomatic skills had been called into play. He did not speak in the Commons after Heath's announcement, but on the same day he delivered a conciliatory address to Harrow Conservatives. According to *The Times*, he said that 'he understood all the feelings that existed. He wanted to make a contribution to peace and understanding'. He offered a tribute to Faulkner, hoping that he would reconsider his decision to resign. But the task Willie had accepted was vital, since 'We have a duty to the people of the United Kingdom to preserve law and order'. Anyone doubting the need for a commitment of men and *matériel* in Ulster should realise that this was not a far-away country, but one whose problems were 'on our doorstep'. Under difficult circumstances the British Army was carrying out its role with 'efficiency and understanding'. Yet 'the solution will not be found by military means alone. It will only be found in the hearts and minds of men and women.'[24]

Willie had already established a good relationship with the army commander, General Tuzo, but his praise for the army was directed towards the troops on the ground who faced the greatest dangers. And there were other servants of the state to consider. The 15,000-strong Civil Service in Northern Ireland remained in being, but it was reinforced by Whitehall officials (mainly drawn from the Home Office), and instead of reporting to eight separate Stormont ministers, as before, it was now under the direct authority of the Secretary of State. The experienced William Nield was transferred from a post in the Cabinet Office to act as Permanent Secretary. The transition went ahead smoothly, thanks largely (in Willie's view) to his senior officials, Nield, Philip Woodfield (based in Belfast) and Neil Cairncross (London). But Willie certainly played his own part in easing what could have been a difficult process. There had been considerable friction between the Northern Ireland Civil Service (NICS) and the Home Office in the months leading up to Direct Rule. During his first meeting with the Northern Irish officials Willie admitted that he had no strong desire to be in the province himself and would understand if others were even more discontented with his presence. But Parliament had decided to suspend Stormont, so as 'members of the British nation' they should all buckle down to the task they had been set. If any of them felt that it was too much to ask, they should resign as quickly as possible. This typically direct approach worked well; there were no resignations. Later Willie reflected that the best civil servants had been 'delighted at the takeover; the second best were pleased; the duds were shocked'. Even the best, though, were 'quite irrational at the prospect of being absorbed by the Republic'.[25]

There was a more relaxed meeting on Willie's first evening at Stormont. Lord Windlesham remembers that at 9.30 p.m. he was about to retire after an exhausting day when the telephone rang and he was summoned to a dinner for about twenty of the key officials and junior ministers. Willie used this opportunity to give his colleagues a pep-talk: 'Well, here we are. We've arrived. Who can tell what will happen. We'll do our best. When we are together, as we often will be, we will dine together, lunch together. However awful things are outside, however many bombs go off, when we're together in private we're going to enjoy ourselves. One house rule – no long faces. That won't make anything better.'

This set the tone throughout Willie's stay. Windlesham was not alone in feeling that the atmosphere was similar to that of an officers' mess, and that Willie played a crucial role in keeping everyone cheerful, even under the most depressing circumstances. Certainly his laughter was louder, and more frequent, than that of his colleagues. Sometimes the 'humour' could only be explained by the atmosphere of near-hysteria that surrounded a group of people under constant pressure, but some of the anecdotes would be funny even to those excluded from the 'in' jokes. On one occasion Willie agreed to listen to an obscure citizen who claimed that he had vital 'confidential' information to impart. When he was alone with the Secretary of State, this person said that he would take the additional precaution of speaking in French. After he had spoken uninterrupted for a quarter of an hour Willie gave him a knowing smile, and his satisfied visitor left the room. Willie never knew what the message contained, because he had lost even the limited grasp of French that his Winchester schooling had given him; but a month later his visitor wrote thanking him for taking the action he had suggested. Perhaps the best incident of these years happened back in Whitehall. During a Cabinet meeting a message was passed to Willie telling him to contact his officials at Stormont as a matter of urgency. He made his excuses and left the room. Seconds later ministers heard a terrific bellowing; they could hear every word of Willie's side of the conversation. When he returned Heath said, 'We don't mind you talking to Belfast during a Cabinet meeting, but next time would you mind using the telephone?'[26]

From his army days Willie had learned that a small gesture could go a long way. Within weeks of his appointment he amazed his senior officials by announcing that he had taken advantage of a trip to London to telephone each of their wives, to apologise for the disruption that government business had caused to their Easter holidays. Ken Bloomfield, a senior civil servant who had been based in Northern Ireland, remembered Willie as:

> the heart and soul of the new system . . . It was to be one of the great pleasures of my life to enjoy the company, and, I hope, the confidence of that large, emotional, sometimes irascible, apparently spontaneous but infinitely cunning man. His big personality lit up any room, and we were soon to become familiar with his booming cries of 'Wonderful, wonderful! . . . Splendid, splendid!' as he made his way through the hallway of [Stormont] Castle to the office he had inherited from Brian Faulkner, while his private secretaries staggered under a load of red despatch boxes.[27]

Willie had always been adept at winning loyalty from his colleagues, but he faced a new and even more difficult challenge in establishing friendly relations with the Governor, Lord Grey of Naunton. A New Zealander by birth, Grey was an experienced colonial hand, having served previously in Africa. Faulkner had regarded him as 'a new kind of governor', who followed events closely and offered advice without showing any preference for particular parties. But while some unionists respected the office as well as the man, even Faulkner doubted that the post of Governor 'filled any indispensable constitutional function'. The role of the Queen's representative was further undermined by Willie's appointment, but obviously while Grey remained in place he would have to be handled sensitively.[28]

The treatment of Grey in Willie's memoirs is a case-study in tact. He relates that on their first encounter Grey handed him a copy of the The Times, which was forecasting that his post was about to be abolished. This could hardly have been a surprise to Willie, but he records that he was 'greatly shaken'. He pleaded with Grey to stay on in the Governor's residence, Hillsborough Castle, because his advice would be invaluable. 'Thus started a friendship that meant a lot to me.' Several more tributes appear on succeeding pages of Willie's book. In fact one would assume from the bare record that Grey was far more important in Willie's life than Nield, Woodfield, Bloomfield or McDowall.[29]

Willie's gratitude for the hospitality of Lord and Lady Grey was genuine. Even that was slightly awkward, though. He could hardly refuse the Governor's invitation to stay at Hillsborough, but the symbolism was unfortunate at a time when relations with the nationalist community depended on a move away from memories of the 'colonial' past. At the same time, it is difficult to plan the abolition of a post when one is the guest of the present incumbent. Willie had discussed this inevitable step before leaving for Belfast, remarking that Hillsborough could be turned into an agreeable mess for the Northern Ireland Office (NIO) team, complete with its tennis court and extensive gardens. Grey's invitation persuaded him to defer such plans. But everything about the exisiting set-up at Hillsborough irritated him. It was forty-five minutes away from Stormont; meals were served at fixed times, which was hardly ideal for someone with Willie's hectic timetable; the food was frugal in quantity and dismal in quality. The Governor was not even king of his own castle; that role was played by a formidable butler. Willie was obliged to make small-talk at the beginning and end of tiring days, and he was immune to Grey's charm, which to someone who appreciated informality could seem like stiffness. For instance, during the first weekend Grey insisted that Willie should accompany him to worship at the local Presbyterian church. Obviously this would go down badly with the Catholic community, and the potential hazards to life were even greater than the risks to reputation, because the Governor had decided to follow a tradition of walking back to the castle along the public highway. This experiment was never repeated, but there could be no escape from Grey's attempts to influence Willie's thinking. At breakfast every morning the Governor made a point of flourishing that day's edition of the strongly pro-unionist Belfast Newsletter. This did nothing to convince the Secretary of State that he should look more favourably on 'those impossible unionists', and made him more anxious to rid himself of the turbulent diplomat.[30]

At times Willie thought that Grey might be trying to provoke him into a quarrel, which would at least clarify the situation. But he kept the peace, helping to mollify the Governor by ensuring that he saw copies of Cabinet minutes, which had previously been withheld from him. Only after a decent interval of more than a year was the anachronistic post abolished. In the meantime Willie had quickly joined his officials in one wing of a large, old-fashioned hotel, only ten minutes from Stormont. In an ideal world this would not have been called the *Culloden* – in honour of the battle (fought only a few miles from Willie's childhood home) in which the 'Butcher' Duke of Cumberland had slaughtered the army of the Catholic Bonnie Prince Charlie. But at least the food was satisfactory, the drink was plentiful and the occupants could go straight up to their rooms after a hard day at the office. The obvious drawback was that the hotel presented a tempting target for terrorists, and protecting a hotel that remained open for ordinary business was a nightmare for the security forces. By modern standards the response was inadequate. Among the measures that were taken, residents were informed of seven different routes by which they could travel to Stormont, and were told to vary these as much as possible to keep would-be assassins guessing. At least this was a great improvement on Hillsborough, from which there were only two possible routes to Stormont.[31]

Direct Rule demanded further changes, which added strain to what was already a crowded timetable for the government's business managers back in London. Legislation concerning Northern Ireland, which would have been debated at Stormont, was now dealt with at Westminster in the form of Orders in Council, which required the approval of both houses. For the remainder of the Heath Government the amount of parliamentary time devoted to Northern Ireland was exceeded by the business of just three other departments; and while the Labour leadership invariably offered either support or neutrality, Willie knew that his measures were likely to encounter opposition from MPs on all sides with their various viewpoints. The Commons debate on the measure that introduced Direct Rule, the Northern Ireland (Temporary Provisions) Bill, extended over three days, including an all-night sitting at Committee Stage on 29 March. Opposition support meant that defeat was never a possibility, but Francis Pym monitored the situation closely and during the Committee Stage Willie deployed all his persuasive charm, at one time being spotted 'in a friendly huddle' with Paisley and Merlyn Rees, the Labour spokesman. He had also felt it necessary to attend the Conservative home affairs committee when it held a crowded meeting on the subject. Despite his presence there was some outspoken criticism of Direct Rule, and on the crucial second reading nine Tories joined the unionists in opposing the bill. The only consolation for the government was that those who took their stand to the extent of adverse voting tended to be those (like Powell) who were already habitual rebels. A more serious threat was that unionist MPs had sufficient numbers to endanger the government majority on other legislation passing through Parliament, but there was no concerted attempt to exploit this advantage.[32]

Willie was well accustomed to parliamentary skirmishes, but his new job also brought physical dangers. He had greater personal protection than any previous minister, and the fact that his routine was conducted within an extended triangle (London–Belfast–Penrith) made life even more complicated for himself and his security team. Less than a month after accepting this formidable challenge he was already sounding weary as he discussed his daily itinerary. The previous week had begun at Ennim, where he always tried to spend at least one day relaxing. He had flown directly to Belfast on the Monday morning, and on Tuesday night he had voted in the Commons. The next morning it was back to Belfast, then he returned to London for a Cabinet meeting on Thursday morning. On the Friday he had flown to Yorkshire to deliver a speech. His various duties meant that no two weeks would ever be exactly the same, but on average he travelled from England to Northern Ireland four times. On a typical day he would rise in his London flat at seven-thirty, bolt down his breakfast by about eight, then leave for the airport. By nine he would be airborne, in the six-seater Hawker Siddeley plane that had been reserved for him. The journey to Belfast took just under an hour. Then he flew by helicopter to Stormont. At 10.20 a.m., five minutes after his arrival, he was ready for his first meeting. Usually he would begin by discussing the present situation with his civil servants and any junior ministers in attendance, but often he would have to meet politicians or other representatives of the community. And since he had stressed that his door was always open – even to those who spoke in French – he was rarely freed from these engagements before seven. Then there would be a reception to attend, or a dinner at Hillsborough.

As Willie mournfully reflected, he had no time at all for golf and although he was constantly meeting people, it was impossible for him to develop anything resembling a private social life while he was in Belfast. One day he remembered being in his helicopter for about ten hours, on visits to eight towns. Even when it seemed outwardly peaceful at his destination, trouble could always erupt. On an early visit to Derry he arrived to see crowds of people doing their shopping. He walked over to one group, stuck out his hand and boomed, 'Nice to meet you – I'm Willie Whitelaw.' During the conversation a man in a flat cap observed, 'You're a nice enough feller, but we've yet to find out if you've got anything in yer head.' Willie must have been reminded of the old days on Clydeside, when political antagonists could exchange unpleasantries without resorting to gunfire. But when he went into an army post he was advised to keep his head down to avoid being shot. The veteran of Caumont was not afraid; he was sleeping well, as usual. The only effects he had noticed were that he found himself listening to the news more carefully than before – although he now hated the radio – and was not always sure which day of the week it was. His only response to his experience in Derry was 'It's perfectly absurd'. But that word could apply with equal justice to his present style of life, and he admitted that eventually it would be too much for him.[33]

To add to the physical disorientation, Willie had entered the twilight world of British politics, along with his junior ministers. He insisted that at least one of the team must be in Northern Ireland at all times, in case emergency decisions were required of someone on the spot. This was problematic when attendance was needed at Westminster for close divisions; David Howell remembers having to fly back specifically to vote on four occasions in one hectic week. On his arrival for one division, Conservative colleagues asked him where he had been. When he enlightened them they promptly changed the subject. At least this was an improvement on the attitude expressed by a senior Tory backbencher within the hearing of one of the present authors. During a debate on Northern Ireland he strayed into Westminster's Strangers' Bar long enough to declare, 'The man who flew the plane to Nagasaki went in the wrong direction. He should have gone to Belfast.'[34]

Although the Stormont parliament was no longer sitting, it had not been dissolved. At Maudling's suggestion it stood prorogued for a year, after which time the Westminster Parliament would decide whether or not to renew Direct Rule. In theory, then, Willie might be asked to serve in his new post for only twelve months. But few people imagined that a solution could be found in Northern Ireland so quickly. A Future Policy Committee of civil servants was set up in Whitehall, and decided at its early meetings that the best possible outcome would be for Northern Ireland to become independent within a federal Europe – a proposition that would not be practicable for some years, notwithstanding Heath's passionate commitment to 'Europe'. Although Willie expressed cautious optimism when he reported back to the Cabinet for the first time, he felt at the outset that the chances of a negotiated settlement were minimal; it would probably be necessary to impose a solution. Cecil King agreed, feeling at this time that 'Whitelaw will have to be very tough indeed. The Government has the money and the machine-guns, and will have to tell all and sundry they mean, if necessary, to use both.' In one of their last conversations Willie told King that he had been dismayed by what he had discovered about the Stormont regime; he now realised the full extent of discrimination against Catholics, and thought that Protestant politicians had lined their own pockets. King later commented that the Conservatives had only themselves to blame: 'They learn of the bias, bigotry, corruption and intimidation widely practised. This was all known to anyone interested, but Conservatives in the past did not want to know. Now they control the administration at Stormont, they have access to the whole sorry story.'[35]

Willie had more advance knowledge of the 'sorry story' than most of his colleagues, and his genuine surprise on encountering a situation in Northern Ireland comparable to 'the Augean stables' proves how difficult it could be for people to make the transition from the relatively peaceful party squabbles at Westminster. An early foretaste of the troubles he would encounter came when the *Belfast Newsletter* claimed that he was a closet Catholic. When he told an experienced official that the story must be contradicted at once, he was told, 'You will find in this community that that is easier said than done.' It was particularly galling, since he had been careful to choose a balanced team of junior ministers (Windlesham came from an Irish Catholic background, and as a member of the Guinness family Channon had obvious connections with Ireland). Given Willie's own origins in a Scottish Presbyterian family – and his fiercely unionist grandfather – a rumoured connection with extreme unionism was more predictable. But when MI5 combed through his life-history it found nothing more damning than membership of various Freemason's lodges. For Willie, as for many other representatives of his class, freemasonry was an obligation; for one of his outlook it could hardly be a passion. MI5 saw no reason to question his appointment, and the contradictory stories soon died away.[36]

For the incoming Secretary of State there were two pressing issues that required decisions before he could hope to progress on a long-term strategy. One of these was whether or not to maintain a ban on marches, which had been introduced at the time of internment. Lifting the ban was an even-handed measure; in the short term it would allow Catholics to commemorate the ill-starred 1916 Easter Rising, and civil rights demonstrations (such as Bloody Sunday's march in Derry) would now be legal. At the same time Protestants would be free to don their bowler hats and sashes to commemorate the military prowess of William of Orange in a series of triumphalist marches beginning in July. These rituals were particularly difficult for outsiders to comprehend – even for someone like Willie, who came from a country which for hundreds of years had burned a Catholic in effigy every 5 November. Ken Bloomfield gave Willie a helpful background briefing on one of the most contentious marches, the Apprentice Boys' parade, held in Derry on 12 August. 'They are not apprentices,' Bloomfield reported, 'they are not boys, and for the most part they do not come from Derry.' Willie decided to lift the ban on 27 April. He could, though, still forbid parades and demonstrations that looked likely to provoke disorder, and soon he was poring over advance notification for a whole series of events, which would be piped along by musical outfits like 'The No Surrender Flute Band'.[37]

Willie's first important task had been the more complex job of examining the cases of those who had been interned since August 1971. Several factors came into play here. He was committed to the phasing out of internment, and immediate releases would be a useful conciliatory gesture. If it proved that a significant number had been detained due to faulty intelligence, they ought to be released immediately. On the other hand, the Protestant community would be further alienated if it was felt that Willie erred on the side of leniency, and if any internees returned to violence there would be furious recriminations. And the army, which had obeyed orders while viewing the whole operation with distaste, would be dismayed if the policy was suddenly reversed. Finally, much as he disliked internment, Willie realised that its existence was a bargaining chip with republican terrorists. He had used his Harrow speech to promise that 'The same day violence ends, internment will end'. It would be a serious mistake to throw away this card in the absence of a reciprocal gesture from the Provos. So, despite his private feelings, he affirmed that more people would be interned without trial if the security considerations seemed to justify such action.[38]

In his conversation with David Butler on Constitution Hill, Willie had voiced his frustration that 'We have absolutely no control over the business of internment. We don't know who is interned and we cannot get explanations out of Stormont for why they are interned.' Now that he was on the spot he was scandalised when he reviewed the documentation that was supposed to justify previous arrests. Faulkner claimed that he had 'used quite stringent conditions for the evidence required', asking for detailed explanations in each case. But according to Willie, the 'evidence' usually amounted to no more than hearsay, and there was very little even of that. He later revealed that one of the local officials involved in drawing up the list of suspects had a reputation for sectarian bigotry; he was quietly 'retired' on a good pension to avoid an outcry from the Protestant community. But the slipshod work had left Willie with an ironic problem. If the grounds for keeping anyone in detention were slender, so was the documentary justification for releasing specific individuals. In an ideal world everyone should be let out while the security forces conducted proper investigations; but Willie's appreciation of practical politics meant that his hands were tied. The cynical approach turned out to be his only realistic option. It was agreed that a figure of about seventy releases would be about right, although a round number would look too contrived. Eventually Willie plumped for seventy-four, in two batches. Despite his caution, worries that some terrorist outrage would be blamed on a newly-released internee proved well founded. After an explosion in Lurgan, Willie was given 'a very rough reception' during a visit to the town, although on investigation the story that the device had been planted by someone he had released 'was found to be wholly false'. Unfortunately this comforting conclusion was inapplicable in one well-publicised case. During an early visit to Newry, Willie's car had been punched and kicked by republican demonstrators; a woman in the mob screamed, 'Now you know what it's like to be hated.' Later Willie spent twenty minutes talking to a deputation of women, one of whom revealed that her husband had been interned. As a politician who wanted to be loved, Willie was shaken by the angry shouts and they produced an ill-advised, impulsive gesture. He promised to make inquiries about the husband, who was speedily released. As soon as he was free he rejoined the Provos.[39]

Undeterred by outbursts of unionist anger, Willie decided that he should offer further concessions to nationalist feeling. There would be an amnesty for around 300 people convicted for their involvement in demonstrations during the time of the marching ban (the people concerned included Bernadette Devlin and the SDLP leader Gerry Fitt). Under the Stormont regime released internees had been required to promise that 'for the remainder of my life, I will not join or assist any illegal organisation, nor engage in any violence, nor counsel nor encourage others so to do'. A more futile oath could scarcely be imagined; only those who accepted the legitimacy of Stormont would consider sticking to it, and by definition these would be the internees who should never have been arrested in the first place. The fact that this obvious point had been missed by the old regime betrayed its lack of contact with reality; it was one absurdity that Willie could deal with immediately. In addition, detainees would no longer be held in the prison ship HMS *Maidstone*, moored in the eastern part of Belfast harbour close to unionist enclaves. One former inmate, Gerry Adams, recalled it as 'a terrible, dismal place', floating in its own sewage. Pictures of this vessel in the overseas press were unlikely to generate a wave of sympathy for a regime that cared so little for its image, and more than a hundred prisoners had gone on hunger-strike to underline the point. Adams wrily noted that the quality of the food on offer improved considerably in response to the strike. He was the last man to leave the ship when it was decommissioned.[40]

By the end of April 1972 Willie had some reason to feel satisfied with his early moves. Direct Rule had been imposed without too much resistance from the unionists, a start had been made in winding down internment, and other grievances had been addressed. He was coming under pressure to deal with the Catholic 'no-go' areas, but so far he had resisted on the grounds that action might involve unacceptable civilian casualties. Personally he had made a strong impression, and he could take heart from the fact that the predictable hostility he had inspired from the irreconcilables on both sides was tempered with respect. To the unionists the tag 'Willie Whitewash' quickly proved irresistible, but there seemed to be a grudging acceptance that the majority population should at least give him a chance. Later in the year one 'militant loyalist' told the *Guardian*'s Simon Hoggart, 'Make no mistake, that Mr Whitelaw is only waiting to sell us out to [Dublin]. He's nothing more than a traitor. Mind you, he's a grand wee fellow when all's said.'

At first relations with Brian Faulkner were frosty; on one occasion when he was watching the ex-premier on television Willie was observed to be mouthing oaths. But a working relationship was gradually established, despite the fact that as a resolute teetotaller Faulkner was invulnerable to the usual lubricants of amity. For the republicans, Sean MacStiofáin could not conceal his irritation as the media hailed Willie as some kind of 'miracle man'. In a revealing passage of his memoirs MacStiofáin recalled:

> the cult of personality carefully built up around William Whitelaw was designed to win him the support of the women, particularly the better-off ones, in the Catholic communities . . . He went out of his way to be polite and said that everybody should stop talking about what was past and build a new Northern Ireland. He made great use of television. It was not his policies that a certain sector of his audience considered, but his personality. The less political grasp such viewers had of what he was talking about, the more they told each other that he was a nice, patient man.[41]

Given the circumstances, and the respective positions of MacStiofáin and Willie, it was a remarkable backhanded compliment.[43]

In March there was a brief Provo ceasefire, but on 6 April the leadership announced that it would keep fighting unless the British Government agreed to three conditions: confinement of troops to their barracks, the complete abolition of Stormont and an amnesty for 'political prisoners'. Obviously Willie could not agree to such terms, but it was a chink of light in the darkness since it represented a modification of more stringent conditions announced in September 1971. Less militant nationalists, including the representatives of the SDLP, were now prepared to talk. Willie's task had seemed impossible at first, but after the initial charm offensive it seemed realistic to plan for a peaceful future.

CHAPTER 8

BAD DAY AT CHEYNE WALK

Stormont Castle lay in the Hollywood Hills overlooking Belfast. Through the French windows of the cramped room he used as a private office, Willie had an extensive view of the city. It was an uncomfortable vantage point. Bad enough before Direct Rule, the security situation was now getting worse. At no time during his spell in Northern Ireland could he look out over the city without expecting to see a plume of smoke; it was even possible to hear the larger detonations. During 1972 as a whole, around 1,500 bombs exploded; another 500 were made safe. There were 10,000 shootings – up from fewer than 2,000 in 1971. Just under 500 people were killed, and 5,000 injured. Belfast had no monopoly, but the great majority of these violent incidents took place within a few miles of Stormont.

Obviously the situation bore no resemblance to the world's major trouble-spots, like Vietnam, and some commentators noted that the casualties resulting from road accidents in the province were comparable to the toll taken by terrorists even in the worst years. Yet the restoration of peace was essential if the United Kingdom was to repair its reputation as a well-governed polity, and to justify its continued presence at the top table of world powers. May 1972 was a particularly bad month. One journalist, visiting Belfast for the first time in six months, wrote of 'a profoundly depressing experience'. While the scenes looked terrible enough to television viewers on the mainland:

Only in Northern Ireland itself can one fully comprehend the shattering effect of the escalation of violence: the wrecked buildings, the talks behind sandbagged windows; the routine frisking when entering hotels; the disruption of ordinary life – three times while writing this I have been warned of a bomb scare and asked to leave my room; the deserted city centre at night. The fear, above all of another explosion or burst of fire.[1]

In addition to the frequent bombings, there had been a surge in sectarian killings. The majority of these – about two-thirds of the total – were perpetrated by Protestant paramilitaries, who usually chose their Catholic victims at random and sometimes subjected them to ritual torture before ending their misery. Meanwhile the Provos bragged about their 'successes' against military targets, but it was difficult to distinguish their view that all soldiers were legitimate prey from the morality of those 'loyalists' who regarded every Catholic as subhuman. When civilians were killed or maimed by Provo bombs, that organisation was usually ready to excuse such 'mistakes'. But at least it was slightly more competent in its deadly missions than the Official IRA, which followed up the Aldershot atrocity by 'executing' William Best, a young Catholic soldier home on leave from service in Germany. It soon emerged that, far from being an unquestioning instrument of the colonial power, Best had often whiled away his periods of leave alongside other Catholic youths in Derry, throwing stones at army patrols.

Willie had known that he would have to steel himself to carry on his work despite daily tidings of death and mayhem, but the accelerating toll was an early test of nerve. His strategy was to continue releasing internees in the hope that this would win the trust of the majority of Catholics, who opposed violence and found a natural political home in the SDLP. On this hopeful scenario, with moderate nationalists bound in to negotiations, the Provos would lose support; and once republican terrorists were isolated, they might come to terms, as men of violence like Michael Collins had done in the past. But if they refused to talk, Willie's Achilles heel would be exposed. It would be difficult to resist calls for a military crackdown against a weakened but unrelenting foe. Yet actions on the scale of the Falls Road curfew and the introduction of internment were only likely to reactivate wavering Provo sympathisers; and the all-out military offensive sought by right-wing Tories would expose Britain to worldwide condemnation, possibly leading to the imposition of UN troops. The other weakness of the strategy was that the attempt to isolate the hard men on the nationalist side dictated concessions that would tend to polarise opinion among unionists. O'Neill and Chichester-Clark had already fallen because British policy left them vulnerable to diehard unionists. Faulkner's flirtation with Craig suggested that he had no intention of suffering the same fate, but this was always an uneasy alliance and it soon dissolved. When Willie had indicated to Cecil King that he saw Ian Paisley as the future leader of Northern Ireland, he was forecasting that moderates of any kind could reach no more than an interim settlement, and that real peace would come only when war-weariness forced the extremists to hammer out a deal. But this presupposed that violence and intemperate rhetoric could eventually be translated into tough but practical talking. From the outset, Willie knew that all of his options were based on wishful thinking.[2]

There was nothing at all to offer the unionists, beyond a misty vision of a distant, prosperous and peaceful future if only they could learn to accept their Catholic neighbours as equals. Although David Howell worked assiduously to keep hope alive on the economic front, Willie must have realised that regular announcements of investment were unlikely to carry much conviction, particularly when infrastructural developments like motorways could easily be sabotaged by terrorists. It was like offering jam in a month to an audience that had already lost its taste-buds. Meanwhile he carried through a commitment made at the time of Direct Rule, setting up an Advisory Commission composed of moderates from all sides. The commission operated exactly on the lines foreshadowed in March – it discussed forthcoming legislation without having any power to change it, and at its weekly meetings the current security situation would be reviewed. On paper it looked like another opportunity to foster a feeling of trust, but by definition the moderate members could not speak for the violent factions. Even they disagreed violently at times of particular tension, and at almost every meeting Catholic representatives reported incidents which suggested that the army and the RUC were prejudiced against the minority population.

Nevertheless, many unionists disliked the commission as another sign that Willie wanted to 'appease' the nationalist community. But before the end of May there were signs that events might lend support to Willie's cautious strategy. The killing of William Best provoked such a sense of outrage among Derry Catholics that a thousand people marched in protest. In response the Official IRA announced a ceasefire, which proved to be permanent. The SDLP's John Hume, who warmly approved of Willie's strategy, appealed for a total cessation of hostilities. Meanwhile the Provo Council had announced a ceasefire in March, but this had only been a ploy to show the British that theirs was a disciplined organisation. Now rumours reached Willie of divisions within the council, as some members began to contemplate a negotiated peace.

The nightmare for Willie was the possibilty that, just as the republican furnace began to cool, so pressure among the unionists would boil over. Incensed by the lack of action against Catholic no-go areas, the UDA began to construct its own barricades. Hundreds of uniformed men supervised this work, verifying Faulkner's hint that if it came to a confrontation the numbers really were on the unionist side. One legacy of the unjust past was that many of these men carried arms quite legally; Protestant magistrates had been happy to grant licences to their co-religionists. Although he had explained why a move against the Catholic areas was not in contemplation, Willie had stressed that new barricades could not be tolerated. The soldiers went in, and although they came under attack there were few serious skirmishes. Even so, it was a grave development. *The Times* reported that 'For many Protestants the Westminster initiative probably died' when the army moved against the barricades. Without a trace of irony, its reporters went on to claim that the so-called 'loyalists' now thought 'that the Government has one law for Protestants and another for the IRA'. They did not add that at last the majority population was beginning to feel what life had been like for Catholics under the old Stormont regime.[3]

At this time Willie felt that he could afford to make light of such incidents, telling *Guardian* reporters that on one particularly cold evening some impatient UDA men had asked the army to hurry up and relieve them by taking away their barricades. But in the same interview he complained that no one was allowing him time to put together a workable plan, and the threat of Protestant barricades was a clear indication that patience was running out. The more constructive approach of the SDLP presented an opportunity. Hume was able to confirm that some members of the Provo high command really were inclining towards a ceasefire. On 13 June an audacious Provo press conference was held in 'Free Derry', the area enclosed by Catholic barricades. The show of bravado, presumably, was intended to compensate for the fact that the Provos had relaxed their terms for a cessation. Previously they had demanded the release of all internees, an amnesty and the confinement of British troops to their barracks. Now MacStiofáin announced that there would be a seven-day ceasefire if the army stopped its arrests, searches and other forms of 'harassment'.[4]

Heath and Willie considered that the offer 'had come at the wrong moment and at too short notice'; it was rejected. But the press conference represented a major breakthrough, because it suggested that Hume's sources were reliable. At least the Provos were serious about talking, and by dropping the end of internment as one of their preconditions they gave the SDLP a pretext to enter fully into the process. Willie discussed further steps with Hume and his colleague Paddy Devlin two days after the Provo announcement. He suggested that internment could be brought to an end if the ceasefire held for just two weeks. The SDLP leaders drew attention to immediate Provo demands, concerning several prisoners in Crumlin Road jail. These convicted terrorists were currently on hunger-strike in support of their claim to be regarded as 'political prisoners'. Willie agreed to consider this issue.[5]

Politically, Direct Rule had been followed by two sterile months. Now the pace began to quicken, as Hume and Devlin embarked on their own version of Henry Kissinger's 'shuttle diplomacy'. The SDLP itself was in a delicate position; if the Provos plumped for peace, the party would no longer enjoy its near-monopoly of constitutional politics on the nationalist side. Nevertheless, its leaders reported back to Provo representatives in Derry before meeting Willie again in Belfast. According to Willie, Hume and Devlin argued that the talks would stall without some concession, and Willie felt that he should comply, not least because this would boost the credibility of his new allies as intermediaries. Accordingly he granted 'special category status' to the hunger-strikers. In his memoirs he stressed that in the short term this measure affected only 'eight Republicans and forty Loyalist prisoners'. In hindsight, though, he thought it was a serious blunder, and most observers have agreed with him. But in its true context the decision looks entirely justified. Obviously the whole peace process was a gamble, but it made little sense to scupper it at the outset. The main critics at the time, predictably, were hardline unionists who resented the implication that the republicans were 'prisoners of war'; yet they were precisely the same people who wanted the British Army to crack down on the Catholic population as if there really was a war going on. The obvious difficulty was that prisoners of all kinds tended to demand the new status, which allowed them to wear their own clothes and enjoy other privileges. By September 1974 well over half of all prisoners in Northern Ireland fell into the 'special' category. But as Willie himself noted, at the time it 'seemed a fairly innocuous concession', and although it did indeed cause his successors 'considerable trouble', if the gamble had come off there would have been no need for any successors.[6]

Willie had no illusions about the nature of the conflict in Northern Ireland. At an early stage he had given reassurances to the army that informants would continue to be paid, and he had no qualms about the (unpublicised) presence of SAS operatives in the province. Clearly the security forces had to improve their intelligence networks; the fiasco over internment proved that. More problematic for Willie was the question of how much intelligence to release to the public.

On the same day in May 1972 that the British Army was firing rubber bullets at Protestants over the barricades, two young Catholics were shot in the Ballymurphy area. Local Catholics reported that the shots came from a nearby Protestant estate, 'but the Army said that this was impossible'.[7] A few days later Willie assured the Commons that a full investigation had found no reason to blame Protestant extremists for a car bomb that exploded outside Kelly's Bar, in a Catholic area of Belfast whose residents included the family of a young republican activist, Gerry Adams. The army had claimed that the bomb was delivered by two Provo members who had suddenly been overcome by thirst and left their device unattended outside the pub. Since the car bomb was a recent Provo innovation, there seemed to be superficial justification for this version of events. Yet the army knew that the car had been hijacked on the Shankill Road, a hardline Protestant area where only 'loyalists' could operate in safety. As the wounded were being ferried to hospital, Protestant gunmen had opened fire, finally drawing a response from the Provos on the Ballymurphy estate. In turn British paratroopers attacked the Provos. Five civilians and one soldier were killed in the battle; sixty-three people had been injured in the original blast.

The academic commentator Steve Bruce has rightly warned of the dangers of attributing blame for violent incidents in Northern Ireland. Yet the British Army evidently felt no such qualms, even when persuasive circumstantial evidence contradicted its assertions. On careful examination Bruce concludes that the Kelly's Bar bomb was the work of Protestant paramilitaries; the parched Provos were an army invention. He also records the claim of a loyalist activist that soldiers helped him to find a convenient spot from which to shoot Catholics after the explosion; allegedly the soldiers witnessed him making one 'kill', and no attempt was made to arrest him or any of his fellow gunmen.[8]

Allegations of collusion in Northern Ireland between the army and 'loyalist' terrorists have been regularly aired, and this is not the place to discuss them in detail. But in a large body of troops there were bound to be elements who actively sympathised with the unionist cause, and by the nature of things William Best was probably one of a tiny minority of servicemen who favoured the other side. Even those who had no feelings either way about unionism could not behave impartially. The British Army was not trained as a peace-keeping force, and in any case there was no peace to keep in the blackspots of Belfast or Derry. Well-informed observers were amazed that the problem was not very much worse. John Cole, who was reporting on the conflict at the time, could understand that soldiers were 'not too delicate' in their house-to-house searches, since they were regularly 'shot at, stoned and attacked with petrol and nail bombs'. The Provos, rather than the loyalist groups, were killing soldiers on a regular basis; and from the army's point of view the only response was to fight back hard, rather than asking whether or not they were defending a dubious system. The natural instinct of soldiers, indeed, would be to retaliate with far more vigour than the politicians would allow. No wonder Willie was reminded of his own feelings when he had served in Palestine after the war.[9]

But misinformation was possibly even more serious than collusion or undue severity. Typically, whenever murders were reported in the British press, readers would be left in no doubt if there were any grounds at all for blaming the Provos; when Catholics were killed, only their religion would be given, as if responsibility was an open question. Bruce suggests that the impression that the bulk of the violence was committed by the Provos was bound to help the Protestant paramilitaries; and their activities threatened to produce a never-ending stream of 'tit-for-tat', random killings. More importantly, it made life nearly impossible for anyone on the mainland who wanted to comprehend a conflict that was costing the country men and money. Even Simon Winchester of the sceptical *Guardian* newspaper later confessed that he had been used by senior army officers to disseminate inaccurate information.[10] The risk with this strategy was that if the spell ever broke, and the army's version of an event was discredited, then citizens in the rest of the UK would no longer know whom to believe.

On the face of it, Willie himself was equally disadvantaged. But it seems that on his appointment he made a conscious decision always to take the army's word on security matters. Having realised that there was no viable alternative to the present situation, ultimately his choice lay between acceptance of the army's version of events and his own resignation, which would only present someone else with his own unpalatable dilemma. Morale among the troops was difficult to maintain anyway, since opinion polls consistently showed that most people on the mainland wanted the government to abandon the province. Feeling unappreciated in the first place, the troops bitterly resented any press comment that seemed even remotely favourable to the terrorists: 'It seems to me that the IRA have a press they can be proud of,' one officer told Willie. So while ignorance was not exactly bliss, for Willie it was preferable to the alternative. In the meantime he had to hope that political progress would end the troubles and allow him to bring the army home. This view was echoed by an anonymous officer who told a reporter in late May, 'We must be solidly behind anything that might bring peace to this infernal country.' It was a grudging acceptance of Willie's strategy, but at least it was an improvement on the attitude openly voiced by a retiring senior officer who backed up his demand for decisive action against the Catholic no-go areas by saying, 'I have engaged in campaigns against blacks, yellows and slant-eyes. Why should we have one rule for the whites and one for coloureds?'[11]

The relationship between truth and war is always delicate, but never more so than when there is a prospect of peace. While Willie was giving the House of Commons questionable information, he was deciding whether or not to accept the Provo offer of talks. Harold Wilson had already met the Provos and caused a stir by arguing for a fifteen-year 'transition period' to a united Ireland. On 26 May 1972 Willie told Cecil King that he was prepared to meet 'someone who represents the IRA – but someone [I] can be seen talking to'. While the SDLP was acting on its own initiative, Willie could honestly deny that official contact was taking place, but at some point he would have to commit himself. As late as 8 June he was still rebutting allegations that discussions had begun. But after further talks, on 20 June a delegation of Provos and republicans (including Gerry Adams, specially released for the purpose) met British officials for a preparatory exchange of views. It seems that most of the discussion concerned the terms of a preliminary truce and the timetable for a meeting between the Provos and Willie. These topics threatened to expose at the outset the gulf of understanding between the two parties; the

British had already convinced themselves that the Provos regarded ceasefires as nothing more than breathing spaces in which to regroup, while for their part the republicans expected that the British would use the opportunity to gather intelligence. Surprisingly, though, a 'straightforward and businesslike' meeting settled all the procedural points at issue. Adams and his colleagues wanted to meet Willie a week after the ceasefire, while the British held out for a gap of a fortnight. The result was a sensible compromise. Two days later the Provos announced that they would cease operations from midnight on 26 June. The meeting with Willie would take place after ten full days of cessation.[12]

The Cabinet had accepted the principle of contact with the Provos on 15 June – it could hardly refuse, since Willie had already met UDA leaders who had advertised their terrorist credentials by wearing masks. At the following day's meeting of the Cabinet sub-committee on Northern Ireland it was agreed that 'some understanding would have to be reached with the Provisional IRA; no solution seemed possible unless their views were represented'. When Willie told the Cabinet that he 'had reason to believe' there would soon be a ceasefire – and stressed that no hint of his advance notice must leak out – Heath congratulated him warmly. That evening Willie told the people of Northern Ireland that 'the time has come for some straight talking'. He confessed that some people might be grumbling that he seemed to spend more time talking to one side than the other and had made unbalanced concessions. During his broadcast he mentioned another of these – the next local government elections would be held on the basis of proportional representation, which promised to overcome the problem of 'gerrymandered' constituencies. But the unionists were also given the option of an early poll on the border. Above all, he claimed that there was 'a real chance now to draw back from the brink, end the violence, and promote a real and lasting peace'. The speech was generally well recieved; even Ian Paisley's response was positive.[13]

But if a week is a long time in Westminster politics, it is even more protracted in Northern Ireland, and before the meeting took place there were several ominous incidents. In his memoirs Willie recalled that 'so-called "offensive action" continued until the very eve of the ceasefire'; this, he felt, was 'typically callous' on the part of the Provos. Three soldiers were killed by a landmine within hours of the ceasefire announcement, and just a few minutes before midnight on 26 June the Provos murdered a British sergeant in Belfast. One can understand why Willie regarded this cynical act with particular revulsion; yet if the Provos had been privy to his own remarks in Cabinet, they might have been tempted into a more spectacular gesture. When he reported the imminent ceasefire Willie attributed it to the government's strategy, and to the Provos' fear of the UDA. The eleventh-hour murder had been committed to show that the Provos were not suspending operations through weakness, yet clearly Willie needed a lot of convincing that this was not the case. Evidently the security forces shared the same delusion; MacStiofáin claims that a Provo unit intercepted telephone conversations between the army and the RUC, which included confident assertions that 'the IRA was on its last legs and that was why the Republican leadership had offered to talk'.[14] Meanwhile, for their part, the Provos thought that the British had decided to negotiate because they were losing the will to fight on, and were now prepared to look again at extravagant demands that had previously been rejected.

Both the army and the Provos had promised to halt their operations, but there was no moratorium on the UDA. Its members resumed the task of constructing barricades, declaring that some would be permanent. To underline the point, they equipped themselves with pneumatic drills. As Willie notes, this was 'a direct challenge to the Government and to the rule of law'. It called for decisive action; yet he was still opposed to an assault on the republican barricades in 'Free' Derry. Indeed, in Protestant eyes the terms of the ceasefire suggested that the British were prepared to tolerate the Catholic no-go areas indefinitely.[15]

On 3 July Willie was dining with a member of the Northern Ireland Commission when the Commander of Land Forces, General Robert Ford, telephoned from Ainsworth Avenue in Belfast. A permanent barricade there would have trapped several Catholic families, and Willie had turned down a UDA suggestion that once the structure had been erected it might be manned by the army. In the past the security forces had tacitly accepted that their writ could not run through the whole of the province, and had struck deals with paramilitaries on both sides to allow them to 'police' some of their 'own' areas. But the notion that the army should make itself so publicly complicit in the sectarian schemes of the UDA was a non-starter. Even so, at first the army played for time and opened negotiations.

Now Ford had interrupted Willie's meal to tell him that the situation on Ainsworth Avenue was getting out of control. The General asked for permission to fire on the UDA if they advanced on his outnumbered troops. Willie remembered 'feeling very sick' as he considered his options. There was no time to consult with Heath and Carrington; yet his decision could lead to the first major street battle with loyalists. He was presented with the surreal prospect of declaring war on the UDA just when peace seemed possible with the Provos; instead of facing a war on two fronts, the British Army might be asked to switch enemies overnight. In fact, a bloody confrontation with Protestant paramilitaries would have made the talks with the Provos politically impossible. Understandably, after giving Ford his permission to fire if necessary, Willie requested a stiff drink from his host. The pause in communications before Ford told him that the UDA had backed off must have been almost as difficult for Willie to bear as those few minutes at Caumont, which had claimed the lives of so many comrades.

In his memoirs Willie recorded that the incident helped him in his future dealings with Protestant extremists; after Ainsworth Avenue they knew that British patience had definite limits. He decided not to publicise his decision to fire, leaving it to the people involved on both sides to spread the story and draw the appropriate conclusions. Unfortunately this cunning ruse backfired. Rather than viewing the incident as a psychological defeat, the UDA claimed a tactical success, and Catholics were inclined to believe them when they heard rumours that the army had agreed to set up joint patrols with an organisation whose bulletin had recently featured a letter advocating 'ruthless, indiscriminate killing'. One UDA man remembered it as 'our best f****** night. Brilliant!' As the British Army backed down, the men and women behind the barricades celebrated by singing the national anthem. Recruitment to the UDA, already running high, was given a fresh boost. In the days before the secret meeting with Willie, the Provos carried out several murders, but the Protestant paramilitaries more than matched them. The usual problems of attribution apply, but it seems that the UDA chose some of its targets in the hope that it could provoke a breakdown in the ceasefire between the Provos and the army. It might not have been a coincidence that one of the Catholic victims was found dumped on Penrith Street.[16]

The stage was thus set to make the talks with the Provos (in Willie's words) 'a non-event'. To underline the futility of the occasion, in his memoirs the three-hour meeting is dismissed in two curt sentences. Fortunately members of the six-strong republican team have been more forthcoming. MacStiofáin and Adams have described being ferried by bus, helicopter and plane from Derry to RAF Northolt, where they were picked up by two limousines. Their treatment on the outward journey was 'very formal, if not frigid'. It was as if they were visiting dignitaries rather than sworn enemies of the state, who during the helicopter journey had been worried that their own side might misinterpret its manoeuvres and shoot it down. Their destination was 96 Cheyne Walk, Paul Channon's elegant London house. This venue was far from ideal for a clandestine encounter; in retirement Willie suggested that the meeting should have taken place at an airport, and he could not imagine why this idea did not occur to him at the time. Near the one-time Chelsea home of Sir Thomas More, 96 Cheyne Walk might have been fairly isolated in the sixteenth century, but in 1972 it was part of an affluent and heavily populated residential area. It had been chosen at the last minute, and the visitors noticed evidence of hasty preparations. When Willie entered the library where his guests were assembled he seemed flustered, and as they shook hands Adams felt that his palms were sweaty. Possibly Willie had been disconcerted by MacStiofáin's appearance;

later he referred to his 'stark, staring eyes', and privately described the Provo leader as 'mad'.[17]

Willie began by congratulating the delegation on the Provo observance of the ceasefire, and by assuring his visitors that he was a man of his word. The republicans were determined to resist a charm offensive; the offer of a relaxing drink was declined, David O'Connell refused to sit next to Willie, and MacStiofáin records that he was unimpressed by the opening words of goodwill towards the people of Northern Ireland. It sounds as if Willie was basing his conduct on his wartime meeting with German officers at Lütjenburg. If so, that was a mistake, because those soldiers had been well aware that they had lost a war. Invited to speak freely, MacStiofáin rehearsed the familiar demands of his organisation: British troops were to be withdrawn from 'sensitive areas' immediately, and must leave the province before 1 January 1975; there would be an amnesty for all 'political prisoners', and an end to internment; the key demand, however, was for an all-Ireland referendum on the border.

In reply to this last point Willie promised that the Cabinet would examine it 'very carefully', but he reminded MacStiofáin that the terms of the 1949 Ireland Act guaranteed the border unless the majority of the population decided otherwise. The delegation pointed out that no parliament could bind its successors; this seems a reasonable answer given the flexibility of the British constitution, although some observers have taken it as proof that the Provos were politically unsophisticated. There was a more pertinent objection, namely the effect on Eire of the border's disappearance; but it seems that Willie did not raise this point. The mood deteriorated further when Willie asserted that British soldiers would never fire on unarmed civilians; he was forcefully reminded of Bloody Sunday by the twenty-two-year-old Martin McGuinness from Derry. However, it was agreed that there would be a further meeting between the republicans and British officials in a week's time, provided that the ceasefire held. It was even decided that there would be an orderly return to hostilities if things went wrong, with twenty-four hours' notice of a resumption. But Willie warned that if news of the meeting leaked out, 'all bets are off'. For his own part, he kept up the appearance of normality by going straight from Cheyne Walk to Walton Heath Golf Club, where he enjoyed the rare luxury of indulging in his favourite sport, competing in a match against the Press Gallery.

Strangely, both Adams and MacStiofáin merely report the exchange between McGuinness and Willie about unarmed civilians, as if further comment would be spurious. Presumably the delegation regarded Willie's claim as a straightforward lie. One of them later raged that 'Whitelaw is a ruthless bastard. "We can accept the casualties," he said, "we probably lose as many soldiers in accidents in Germany."' In fact Willie had not said anything of the kind;

those words were used by one of his officials, Frank Steele, on the flight back home. Yet the Provos had entered the meeting believing that Willie was the representative of a cold-blooded colonial power, and his emollient manner had done nothing to shift that conviction – despite the fact that at one stage he said, 'The minority in the North have been deprived of their rights. I set myself the task of conquering this.' MacStiofáin wrote later that 'In some ways [Willie] had turned out to be smarter than he appeared to be on television'. Either Willie had appeared to be very stupid indeed, or MacStiofáin had interpreted the remark about unarmed civilians as a piece of calculated provocation rather than evidence of naivety or ignorance. In fact, before the publication of the Widgery Report, Willie had told the Cabinet that he was concerned in case it seemed like a whitewash of the Bloody Sunday paratroopers. Presumably any doubts he might have had were overcome by his respect for Widgery as a distinguished figure in the legal world. Yet Widgery had once served in a regiment that was currently on duty in Northern Ireland. For many Catholics this ruled out the possibility of an impartial inquiry; it seems that for Willie it was a guarantee of open-mindedness.

In the immediate aftermath of the three-hour meeting the delegation was divided. Adams claims that during an adjournment MacStiofáin was exultant, while his own feelings were far less positive. On the British side, Willie himself apparently told his visitors that he was 'depressed' they had proved so inflexible. Frank Steele has said that he was 'appalled at their naivety and lack of understanding of political reality'. Years later even MacStiofáin hinted that his side might have been 'totally unrealistic'. Yet the allegations of naivety surely apply with equal force to the British. They had assumed that the Provos would never negotiate unless they felt they were losing their fight; they failed to realise that the Provos were likely to interpret Willie's willingness to talk as a symptom of the same defeatism. Hence the Provos' anger when Steele said that the British were prepared to accept the present level of casualties indefinitely. Steele felt that instead of continuing with the armed struggle, the Provos should have been trying to convince the unionist community that 'some sort of satisfactory life – jobs, housing and so on', would be secure if partition ended.[18] Yet this implied that militant unionists would be ready to reach 'a sensible agreement' without the threat of violence, and while the British Army was still in Ireland, with its undeniable preference for the majority population. It could even be argued that the Provos understood some crucial 'political realities' better than the British – after all, the British ministers themselves habitually used colourful language when referring to the conduct of the unionists, as if they agreed that no rational deal was possible with such people. On occasions Willie himself found it impossible to control his feelings; after listening to an extremist rant from a group of unionist women he was overcome by one of his 'stampers', banging his fist on the table. After the delegation had hurried away Willie instantly repented and dispatched a civil servant to convey his apologies.

Although reported reactions on the British side may have been affected by subsequent events, Willie was very unhappy after the Cheyne Walk meeting. But his recollection that the Provos had 'simply made impossible demands which I told them the British Government would never concede' is not strictly true, as we have seen. And his account of the subsequent breakdown of the ceasefire is even more questionable. He wrote, 'Two days after the talks the IRA manufactured a pretext for breaking the truce.' In fact the UDA was the main culprit, as Willie revealed when he reported back to the Cabinet. The Provos had been encouraging the rehousing of Catholics who had been intimidated into leaving their previous homes. There were some empty properties on Lenadoon Avenue in West Belfast, but this road connected a Catholic estate with 'loyalist' territory; and the UDA, inflamed by recent events and hoping to celebrate the sacred anniversary of the Boyne with a new victory over the Catholics, 'threatened mayhem' if the rehousing went ahead. When the Catholics tried to reach the houses, the army blocked their path. Obviously a violent confrontation had to be averted, but most reports suggest that the soldiers were unnecessarily provocative, ramming one lorry with a Saracen armoured car. Fighting broke out, and the soldiers were cheered by watching Protestants as they fired rubber bullets and CS gas into the crowd. Provo gunmen were waiting, and fired about 300 rounds at the troops. The ceasefire was over. Later that evening the Provos broke the news of the Cheyne Walk meeting,[19]

To the British and the unionists, the Lenadoon incident was a prime example of Provo cynicism. Brian Faulkner wrote that the republicans were clearly no longer interested in the ceasefire, and had 'staged a confrontation with the Army' in order to look like the injured party, instead of aggressors. Yet no one denies that their leaders made repeated efforts to resolve the situation through secret channels, and that the British were wholly uncooperative. The Provo 'dove' David O'Connell claimed that the incident would never have happened if Willie had been in Belfast. But MacStiofáin recalls that 'Heath could not be contacted at all and Whitelaw was out walking or something in Cumberland'. When Willie was finally tracked down, 'He promised to look into the crisis, but nothing further was heard from him.' Nationalist members of the Northern Ireland Commission were already well aware that a promise from Willie to 'look into' an insoluble problem was usually a diplomatic way of shelving it. But Steele had been a little more revealing when O'Connell warned him that the ceasefire was in danger. His reaction showed that the British were relaxed about a renewal of hostilities.[20]

Certainly there were some Provos who were more than relaxed that the gun had beaten politics. For them violence had become a way of life; as one of them put it, 'Maybe you can't bomb a million Protestants into a united Ireland but you could have good fun trying.'[21] This merely underlines the risk Willie had taken by embarking on talks without being absolutely certain of the strength of various factions within the Provos, and it still leaves open the possibility that attitudes might have been changed if the peace had lasted longer. Cutting through the usual blame-game, there is a straightforward explanation for the breakdown of the ceasefire. The Provos had to be ready for renewed fighting, given the fragility of the situation, but they had no reason to bring matters to a head, with a further meeting with British officials less than a week away (and despite seeking to blame the Provos for the breakdown, Willie makes precisely this point in his memoirs).[22] On the other hand, it seems likely that the British had begun to regret the truce during the meeting at Cheyne Walk. A ceasefire was an essential precondition for talks; and once Willie and his officials formed the view that those talks would lead nowhere the ceasefire seemed a headache rather than a tonic. He had told the republican delegation that it would be very difficult to make progress during the impending Protestant marching season. In fact, the increasing disaffection among the unionist population meant that it would be almost impossible for the army to prevent provocative incidents. Certainly there was no chance that it would risk an all-out confrontation with the loyalist paramilitaries in order to cling to a precarious peace with an enemy who had shown no signs of compromise.

One British official later told a journalist that the British had not really been interested in talks; rather 'It was a case of letting the dog see the rabbit'. If true, this remark would discredit all of the British accounts of the meeting, and their expressions of outrage over the ending of the ceasefire. More likely it was a retrospective attempt to make light of a serious blunder. The only satisfactory conclusion is that it was the Provos who had let the British dog 'see the rabbit', and that Willie had lunged at the creature without anticipating that it might bite. Overheated by the unexpected chance of a breakthrough, he invested too much hope in a single meeting, after inadequate preparations. With hindsight, the British might have convinced themselves that the Provos entered the talks under false pretences, but there was no reason to suppose that the leadership would have budged from the terms that Willie had previously rejected. Presumably Willie hoped that his personal warmth could break the log-jam: that the Provo faction which favoured peace would take the lead, once it became clear they were dealing with a sympathetic and trustworthy man, who had the power to make his decisions stick. Had there been further meetings between the Provos and Willie's officials, covering substantive issues rather than procedure, he would have tempered his expectations. Those who favoured peace — like O'Connell, who regarded Willie as 'the best kind of British gentleman' — tended to be based in Dublin, distant from the front-line fighters whose opinions were always likely to prevail. Given the republican conviction that the negotiations of 1921 had resulted in a 'sell-out' that should never be repeated, it was unlikely that there would be any give and take in the first few meetings; this memory, burned into the Provo psyche, could fade only over a protracted series of talks. Although the Provo breach of confidence meant that Willie could be depicted as a man who was prepared to talk to anyone, this image was not positive enough in the context of Northern Ireland (or, for that matter, at Westminster) for it to justify his gamble. His further point, that the Provos had 'proved that they were intransigent and that it was the British Government who really wanted an end to violence', is not very convincing given the real course of events at Lenadoon.[23]

Ironically, just before the meeting was arranged, the Irish Foreign Minister Garret Fitzgerald had praised Willie for 'refusing to be rushed'. When the Provos breached the secrecy surrounding the talks, Fitzgerald was incensed. He felt that the meeting sent a signal to the Provos that 'if they went on murdering people long enough, Britain would negotiate with them'. The Irish constitution still contained a clause laying claim to the whole of the island, but under no circumstances did the government contemplate the prospect of unity forged through violence; and in the weeks before the meeting senior figures had given clear warnings against any talks with the Provos. In retrospect Fitzgerald felt that his government should have been more vigorous in condemning Wilson's earlier meetings with the Provos. Cecil King, who had warned Willie against clandestine negotiations because the news was bound to leak out, also thought that no one would believe the British claim that Lenadoon had been 'a put-up job by the IRA'. Although the two groups did meet again, from this point on the great majority of entries in King's published diary relating to Willie in Ulster are indexed under 'failure of'.[24]

If Willie had been allowed to act on his immediate impulse after the Provo revelation that talks had taken place, King would have been writing about a new Secretary of State. As Willie recalled in his memoirs:

> I learnt the news on my wireless at home in Cumbria in the early hours of the Monday morning. I knew that I was facing a major storm and my first reaction was that I ought to resign, since I would certainly forfeit any remaining vestige of confidence in the Unionist population of Northern Ireland. Needless to say, even I failed to sleep any more that night . . .[25]

In fact he could not have been surprised; his closing remark at Cheyne Walk about bets being off suggests that he had grown increasingly concerned about the likelihood of a leak as the mood of the meeting deteriorated. Since Willie had held the talks with the full approval of the Cabinet, he must have been aware that his colleagues were unlikely to accept his resignation, because collective responsibility would demand that they should all follow him out of office. Heath and Carrington, at least, were as deeply implicated as Willie in the decision to talk; and the government could not have survived their resignations. But there can be no doubting Willie's sincerity. Regardless of the responsibility felt by others, he knew that his decision had gravely damaged his plain-dealing reputation in the province, and he rightly felt that without his personal authority his job would be far more difficult, if not impossible.

Only the combined efforts of Heath and Lord Grey convinced Willie not to resign immediately. The decisive factor, though, was the general goodwill offered by MPs and the press after Willie had explained his actions in a Commons statement on 10 July. However difficult the circumstances, it was probably a relief for him to plunge back into the atmosphere of Westminster. He held the attention of the House by adopting exactly the right tone for the occasion; he was solemn, yet unapologetic, as he gave a brief summary of events and declared that he was willing to 'soldier on' so long as his services were required. David Wood in *The Times* wrote, 'it is notable that Mr Whitelaw becomes a larger politician as his ordeal intensifies . . . There are times when he has the air of a character in a Greek tragedy as he takes his stand.' Hardly any of the subsequent interventions were critical; one Tory backbencher went so far as to claim that Willie 'deserves the praise of the whole House and the whole country for the courage, patience and skill with which he has attempted to carry out the Government's policies in Northern Ireland'. Willie's reply could not have been bettered: 'I have not succeeded, and if one does not succeed one cannot deserve those kind comments.' He was particularly grateful that Labour refused to take advantage of his embarrassment; Richard Crossman, who disagreed with the government's general approach, nevertheless acclaimed Willie's initiative as an 'heroic enterprise'. When Willie visited Harold Wilson and Merlyn Rees after his statement, tears were shed; Wilson thought that Willie's emotional state had been enhanced by a few drinks, which in the circumstances was hardly surprising.[26]

But the storm could not be expected to dissipate so easily. On the day after Willie's statement a meeting of the Conservative backbench committee on Northern Ireland gave MPs an opportunity to express opinions that would have seemed inflammatory in the Commons chamber. Nicholas Ridley called for the sealing of the border between North and South – a measure that Willie had previously rejected on the grounds of impracticability. Enoch Powell said he disbelieved the government's assurances about the future of Ulster, on the grounds that Heath and his ministers were 'not committed to the Union'.

Peter Tapsell went even further, calling for the imposition of martial law and 'a change in Secretary of State' – '. . . and a new Prime Minister too,' Powell was heard to mutter. Willie was not present at this meeting, but he took the criticisms head-on, saying that if the government changed course 'in three months' time [the hard-liners] would be calling for a new political initiative. And it would be the same one as this.' He also provided a stout defence of his approach on BBC's *Panorama*, and in the Commons a few days later lashed out against Powell, who continued to think that a harsher policy would be the best way to avoid civil war in Ulster. Forgetting for a moment his own advice to keep cool in the face of Powell's provocation, he accused his former colleague of opposing every constructive action he had tried to take.[27]

Willie had learned a valuable lesson; in all of his future negotiations he ensured, as far as possible, that the groundwork had been done in advance. If anything, he emerged from the gravest crisis of his career to date with his reputation enhanced. Serious disorder during the Protestant marches would have renewed the pressure on his position, but they passed off fairly quietly. And other events, terrible enough in themselves, helped to silence Willie's political critics. Although it had begun with a ceasefire, July 1972 turned out to be the worst month of the whole conflict in terms of casualties. Apart from the usual toll of Catholic lives taken by the 'loyalist' paramilitaries, the Provos killed eight soldiers and a policeman within three days of the resumption of hostilities. It also began to copy the loyalist groups and to murder at random. On 21 July twenty-two bombs were planted, many in the centre of Belfast. According to MacStiofáin, these devices were aimed at 'industrial, commercial or economic' targets; the intention was to show the British that the Provos were still in business, despite the fact that Willie had been talking about a ban on traffic from Belfast city centre, declaring the area to be 'bomb-proof'. In his memoirs MacStiofáin claims that adequate telephone warnings were given, but that in several cases these were not acted upon by the British. As a result, nine people were killed and more than a hundred injured. At Oxford Street bus station two Welsh Guardsmen were blown to pieces as they tried to warn bystanders; a woman and a young girl also died. David Howell, who was the minister on duty that day, remembers hearing the repeated thumps and seeing the smoke hanging over the city. Others were left with even more vivid memories, of policeman shovelling human remains into plastic bags. Parts of one body were spread over a thirty-yard area. For the perverse moralists of the Provos there was some consolation in the fact that four of the dead could be classified as 'legitimate targets', but of the five civilians MacStiofáin records that 'our attitude was that it was five too many'. His predictable judgement was that 'the responsibility for the loss of life rested squarely on the British, who had failed to pass on the warnings'.[28]

Matters might not seem so clear-cut for those who consider that anyone who plants a bomb in an area frequented by civilians opens up an obvious risk of killing 'innocent' people (including children, on this occasion and many others); that risk is greatly increased when more than twenty bombs are timed to go off in a small area within a hour. In any case, if the Provos really did think that the British were ruthless, they would have expected them to allow a few fatalities now and again to remind the world that there should be no dealing with (Catholic) terrorists. In this context the fact that three people with connections to the security forces died on what became known as 'Bloody Friday' underlines the ill-judged nature of Steele's remarks about army losses; a state that really is unconcerned about the deaths of a few soldiers will be happy to sacrifice one or two for the sake of a wider propaganda gain. Unfortunately this impression was reinforced by the report that on the evening of 21 July Lord Carrington had told Willie, 'Now we can go into the no-go areas.' Actually, it seems that Willie was the more bellicose; according to a senior civil servant, after Bloody Friday 'he had had enough and was incandescent with rage'.[29]

Whether or not Willie made this automatic connection – between a Provo assault on the population of Belfast, and barricades in Derry which the unionists abhorred as a symbol of nationalist defiance – he would not have been the only one who thought that the Provos had given the British an irresistible pretext to move in. Had they not done so, the 'loyalists' were threatening to take matters into their own hands; and British policy stood on the brink of collapse. Willie reveals in his memoirs that plans were well advanced for action against the no-go areas, and that Bloody Friday 'gave me further propaganda assistance'. In fact he had realised that a mistake had been made in not dealing with the barricades at the time of Direct Rule. He assured Faulkner that 'the Government now realised that the IRA would have to be beaten'.[30] If these were his precise words, stress must have got the better of him; the army and the politicians knew there could be no military solution to the problem of republican terrorism. This point had been underlined when, against his better judgement, Willie had been persuaded to allow an assault on the Provos in the Lenadoon area. Two soldiers were killed in that encounter. In fact, when the first reports of Bloody Friday reached Willie, he was locked in discussions with Heath about the timing of the proposed border poll. While he wanted the necessary legislation to be passed quickly, his colleagues were generally unsympathetic, feeling that the parliamentary timetable was already cluttered enough. Willie felt strongly enough on this issue to contemplate resignation if he was thwarted. In creating a pretext for action against the 'no-go' areas, Bloody Friday made the referendum less urgent; Willie needed to offer a concession to the restive unionists, and, if anything, the clearing of the barricades meant more to them than a border poll whose result was a foregone conclusion.

'Operation Motorman', launched before dawn on Monday 31 July 1972, was a major risk on the part of the British. The possibility of armed confrontation, which had prevented action earlier in the year, might still become a reality, whether or not the British held the moral high ground after Bloody Friday. Even more daunting was the possibility of mute, unarmed resistance by civilians who might choose to obstruct the army. So the preparations had to be meticulous. As usual Willie did nothing to arouse suspicion, spending the weekend in the North of England as usual and even attending a game show in Durham. On the Sunday evening he travelled to Belfast and delivered a carefully rehearsed radio broadcast, explaining the necessity for action, even though this guaranteed that the most wanted Provo activists would have time to escape across the border. Overwhelming force was to be deployed. Thousands of troops – including some Scots Guards – were brought in from all over Europe, equipped with special tanks adapted to act as bulldozers. Willie awaited news at the Lisburn army headquarters; Heath was in contact via a secure radio link. The government had already faced several crises, but this was perhaps the most serious so far; the Prime Minister even ensured that world leaders, including President Nixon, were informed in advance.[31]

There was an agonising period of radio silence from Ford, during which Willie received unofficial reports of violent clashes. But as soon as communications were restored, the General was able to reassure him. There had been minimal resistance in the town where memories of Bloody Sunday were so vivid. The barricades were destroyed, and although two civilians died in later exchanges of fire, Willie hailed an operation that had 'succeeded beyond our wildest dreams'. The press was inclined to share his feelings of relief and exultation.[32]

But what, really, had been achieved? No state can tolerate the existence of pockets of territory in which its laws are flagrantly disobeyed. One expert has noted that the areas reclaimed by 'Motorman' 'were a considerable military asset'. The operation was thus 'a decisive blow against the IRA'; with the barricades down, the British could dream once again of reducing the Provos to a rump. Whatever the situation in the South, they could search unmolested for republican suspects in cities like Belfast and Derry. But since the army had tacitly accepted the authority of the UDA in certain areas of Belfast, the impression remains that Motorman was essentially a political victory, calculated to please the unionists who already held the whip hand in Northern Ireland. While Willie wrote that during Motorman 'I realised what it must have been like for Army Commanders during the war', MacStiofáin's contrasting verdict was that 'The great victory had at last been won, against unresisting civilians'. The Provo leadership had issued instructions for its remaining operatives in the relevant areas to lie low; Gerry Adams was reading a book when he heard the long-expected invasion. He was finally re-arrested a year later. Meanwhile, the well-publicised might of the British Army driving through the Catholic enclaves was likely to act as another incentive for republicans to join the Provos, whatever the damage incurred in the short term.[33]

For Willie, though, there were immediate political payoffs. When he made his next visit to his party's backbench committee on Northern Ireland, the man who had been rudely denounced three weeks earlier was warmly received. Although he must have known that the whips had reported his earlier call for Willie's scalp,[34] Tapsell hailed Motorman as a 'remarkable achievement'. Almost the only criticism of Willie came from an MP who thought that the Secretary of State should be seen in more relaxed surroundings in his public appearances. Willie replied that Celia was making a sterling effort in this respect – in her efforts to meet the people of Northern Ireland she proved to be a sore trial for her bodyguards – but that he felt handicapped because if he made such appearances himself he would be criticised by those who 'thought he should be at his desk all the time'.[35]

Perhaps Willie took this advice too much to heart. A couple of weeks later, having criticised the Secretary of State for taking a holiday, Cecil King recorded his disapproval of a photograph that appeared in the *Sunday Express* of Willie shooting grouse. This mistake was typical (as King put it) of a government 'tone deaf to public relations, however elementary'. Yet Willie badly needed his two-week break. It was probably this short holiday that was remembered by the broadcaster Ludovic Kennedy, whom Willie had first met when they were both children. Kennedy recalled that all the guests agreed beforehand not to mention Northern Ireland, yet as soon as Willie arrived he talked incessantly about it: 'by the time the visit ended we all agreed that we had learnt everything there was to learn about Northern Ireland, and that if Willie had omitted anything, it would not have been for want of trying'.[36]

In common with many of those engaged in the surreal politics of Northern Ireland – though not the teetotaller Brian Faulkner – Willie was drinking heavily. Lord Howell remembers that when Willie would invite him for lunch before making a statement in the Commons, typically a large Martini would begin proceedings, followed by a carafe of claret, then wine with the meal. More dangerous, even to such a robust man, was the quantity of spirits Willie could drink as a matter of routine. The Tory MP Hugh Fraser reported after one meeting that he and Willie had dispatched 'a fantastic number of double whiskys and soda'; this appears to have been a normal day. Willie suffered no short-term damage from this intake; the drink had no outward effect on the performance of his duties, and if anything made him even more affable. Yet he can have gained little refreshment from such a punishing regime, and his weight ballooned to seventeen stone. As he embarked on his holiday, an insider told Cecil King that 'Whitelaw was very hurt by the suspicion and hostility he encountered in Northern Ireland. He is now recovering.' But the stress ensured that the recovery process was far from smooth; in early October John Hume reported a rumour that Willie was about to resign, and warned government officials that he would leave politics himself if this turned out to be true.[37]

However much Willie might try to resist it, one of the main reasons for his stress was the feeling that the security forces were not being entirely honest when they furnished 'official' explanations of events on the streets. Some months after Motorman the head of the Metropolitan Police, Robert Mark, told the *Guardian*'s Alastair Hetherington that Willie had 'seemed in need of talking to somebody. He had been speaking almost too candidly about his problems which were very worrying.' His main problem concerned the RUC, which he knew was in need of reform (one early suggestion was that the force should be softened up in advance of change by sending a message of congratulation on its fiftieth anniversary). But Willie went on to express 'some anxiety' about recent army operations. A thirteen-year-old boy had just been killed in Newry. Apparently Willie accepted that the troops had acted in good faith, and had fired in the direction from which they thought they had come under attack. But Willie observed, perplexingly enough, that 'even if the troops were none the worse for drink they had gone a bit too far in some of the things they had done immediately afterwards'. There are other suggestions of scepticism towards the army. The Cabinet Committee on Northern Ireland certainly chewed over allegations of collaboration on at least one occasion. Cecil King picked up a story that Willie had expressed regret that he had been sent to Northern Ireland 'two years too late'. This seems to tally with the view of some observers that, in addition to the lack of political initiative in the first two years of the Heath Government, the politicians also failed to bring the army under control. One official was more candid in a conversation with the journalist John Simpson: 'Our idiotic army think that this is a war, and that they can win it by shooting down the enemy. Bloody fools: they are as bad as the Yanks in Vietnam.' Finally, despite his claims during the Cheyne Walk meeting, the account of Bloody Sunday in Willie's memoirs is very cautious, relating only that 'the firing started and thirteen people were killed by British troops'. In a book that generally repeats the 'official' explanations this seems guarded; perhaps McGuinness's blunt retort at Cheyne Walk inspired Willie to think again about that crucial incident.[38]

Motorman had been so successful that Willie could once again look forward, even if some incidents from the recent past were too painful to forget. The fact that the Provos were out of the political equation need not prove fatal; indeed, it promised to simplify matters. A few internees could be released now and again to demonstrate goodwill, but it was time to concentrate on the constitutional parties. At the end of Willie's holiday, on 11 August 1972, he invited the leaders of all the old Stormont parties to a conference on the future of the province.

CHAPTER 9

HERO FOR A DAY

In early September 1972 Willie reviewed the situation in Northern Ireland in advance of his new initiative. Judging from recent correspondence the outlook was 'unpromising'. Since July more than 2,000 letters had been received from members of the public; of these, less than 300 directly expressed support for the policy of reconciliation. More than 800 demanded an immediate restoration of Stormont, outnumbering by more than two to one those that accepted the need for some reforms before the parliament sat again. Less than 1 per cent called for a conference on the future; yet this was the policy currently favoured by the Secretary of State.

Willie had few illusions about the prospects for the conference, which was scheduled for the end of September at the Europa Lodge Hotel, near Darlington. He wisely tried in his speeches to dampen expectations. He had told his Cabinet colleagues that it was worth a try, even though some key parties would refuse to take part. Among these was the Democratic Unionist Party (DUP), led by Ian Paisley. Willie had thought the DUP might attend, on the calculation that it would recognise a propaganda advantage. But of all the politicians he encountered in Northern Ireland, Paisley was the furthest removed from the Westminster type (even though he had thought it worthwhile to get himself elected to the Commons). First Paisley demanded an inquiry into a shooting incident between the Ulster Defence Association (UDA) and British soldiers; then, after Willie refused his request, he announced that the DUP would not be represented at Darlington.

Originally Willie had seen Paisley as a person to do business with, but he was quickly disillusioned. Soon after Willie's arrival in the province the DUP leader had asked to see him at Stormont, on some constituency matter. The meeting was amicable, until on his way out Paisley suddenly introduced a new subject. 'The people of Ulster will never forgive you,' he declared, 'if you pull down the statue of Edward Carson.'

Taken aback, Willie spluttered, 'Now look here, why the hell would I want to do a thing like that? I don't care two hoots, but I'm not doing anything of the kind.'

Paisley pointed out of the window at some roadworks near the famous statue of the unionist hero. 'We expect you to do it in the middle of the night,' he said. 'Look, you're already building the roads. But we've had a nice chat. Goodbye.' He told reporters assembled outside that he had warned the Secretary of State against dismantling the statue. When Willie listened to the lunchtime radio news an hour or so later, he heard a report that Paisley's intervention had saved one of Ulster's best-known landmarks from destruction.[1]

This experience meant that Willie was less disappointed than surprised by Paisley's staged boycott of the Darlington talks. On reflection he saw it as a gain rather than a loss; presumably at some stage Paisley would have led a dramatic walk-out, or held regular press conferences denouncing the talks. For others, Paisley's antics were part of a well-established tradition in a province whose voters always appreciated larger-than-life characters, but from Willie's perspective they just seemed like irresponsible posturing. Although in his memoirs he chose to describe Paisley as 'friendly and engaging' when the subject was steered away from politics, his real opinion was closer to that of his friend Lord Carrington, who disappointed Cecil King by describing his hero as 'a bigot of bigots'.[2] After one of their conversations Willie declared that 'he would never talk to that man again', but this resolution proved easier to make than to keep. Just before the end of his time in Northern Ireland, Paisley, who had excluded himself from another round of vital talks, realised that he had made a mistake and demanded to see Willie after a fruitless conversation with Heath. Willie reminded Paisley that he had never been denied when he asked to see the Secretary of State; indeed, he had stormed into Willie's presence on at least seventeen occasions since March 1972. For him boycotts and walk-outs were tactical weapons; it was not Willie's fault when they misfired.

More serious than Paisley's defection was the SDLP's refusal to join the discussions. Recent events had strengthened their hand; their role in arranging the Provo talks underlined their influence in most sections of the nationalist community, and the breakdown of the ceasefire and Motorman had knocked out the Provos as potential rivals in the political process. The SDLP believed that they were strong enough to play hard to get, and not even a direct intervention from Heath could persuade them to turn up. The sticking-point, as before, was internment. After Motorman Willie had brought a temporary halt to releases, but he knew that the SDLP would want some concession. He announced that future decisions on internment would be taken by a non-political tribunal, and timed the restart of releases to coincide with last-ditch talks with the SDLP. But the party's leaders had seen enough of this tactic, which too clearly implied that the remaining internees were being held to form part of future deals. Sensing their new power, they aimed for the best of both worlds; they still boycotted the talks, but they published their own ideas before the meeting was held, in order to influence the agenda. Their action was another example of the rules being changed just as Willie had begun to master the game; their ploy was designed to secure the maximum advantage for themselves once a settlement had been reached, but without their full and open cooperation it would be impossible to reach a settlement in the first place.

In the end, only the Northern Ireland Labour Party, the cross-community Alliance party and the Ulster Unionists sent delegates to Darlington. Faulkner had decided to attend, thinking that at least one leader on his side should show some constructive statesmanship. It was a mixed blessing for Willie that the other main unionist grouping, Vanguard, followed Paisley's example and boycotted the talks. This new evidence of profound divisions within the unionist ranks was welcome in itself, but his whole strategy now depended on Faulkner's ability to keep a grip on his party. Although Darlington turned out to be little more than a public-relations exercise, it established the future marching orders for every British Secretary of State: give enough to the nationalists to keep them at the table, without making life impossible for any unionist leader courageous enough to stay in the process. There were disagreements, mainly over the question of who would control the security forces once Direct Rule was lifted. But after a secret session on the subject one delegate told reporters, 'Today was really Mr Whitelaw's show. He has cleverly picked out the ground of compromise where no one would have thought they existed.' If nothing else, the Darlington talks increased confidence in the Secretary of State.[3]

Since the talks had at least given the impression of movement, Willie followed them up by issuing a Green Paper on future options. Although this disclaimed any intention of dictating a solution, it indicated the government's own preference for a new devolved parliament that would guarantee a significant role for the minority population. The extreme alternatives, of full integration or independence, were presented unfavourably. The commitment to the existing border was reaffirmed, but as usual it was stressed that the British would not block a vote by the people of Northern Ireland to leave the Union. Offering something for all of the constitutional parties, the document was generally well received – the best that Willie could have expected. But in one key respect the muted response from unionists was misleading. The document was literally a 'Green' Paper; it introduced for the first time a reference to an 'Irish Dimension' to the problem, suggesting that the Irish Republic would be involved in a future settlement. To furious anti-Papists like Paisley this idea was anathema, but for the time being senior unionists convinced themselves that the offending phrase was 'meaningless'.[4]

The Green Paper suggested an eminently reasonable framework for a deal, but by now Willie was painfully aware that in Northern Ireland the process would take many months – at best. Before the paper appeared he had faced an audience which, if anything, was even more irrational. On 11 October 1972 he addressed the Conservative Party Conference in Blackpool. He had given light-hearted speeches at both of the previous two annual gatherings; this time it was bound to be very different. Despite Motorman, he knew that some of his critics still regarded him as a traitor. If anything, the lack of any concrete grounds for objection was likely to make the diehard supporters of the Union more angry. And although public awareness of the real issues was no better than it had been at the time of Direct Rule, Heath used his own conference speech to stress the importance of Ulster; it was, he said 'the most terrible problem' the government had to face.[5]

When Willie began to speak the mood was ugly. Two Young Conservatives who had defended the government were interrupted with boos and slow handclapping; those who demanded more vigour in the battle against terrorism, or expressed crude anti-Irish sentiments, were loudly cheered. During these speeches Heath sat impassive on the platform, but as usual Willie was unable to conceal his emotions. His plight was made worse by the fact that the only new piece of information he had to offer – that the border poll would be delayed until the New Year – would be unpopular. But once again he rose to the occasion, delivering what *The Times* hailed as 'in every way the most impressive speech he has made since he entered Westminster politics'. As the *Daily Telegraph* noted, Willie's 'impassioned sincerity about his own position' swayed the honest doubters in the audience. But he reinforced his message by painting the alternatives in lurid colours. At one point he challenged critics of his policy towards the no-go areas to admit 'that they would have preferred, in a position of responsibility, to stand back and not take action to protect the lives of innocent women and children'. There could be no persuading the Powellites; when he said he tried not to allow 'bitterness and hatred to well up in my own heart', he was probably referring to them rather than to the combatants in Ulster. Although the anodyne pro-government motion was passed easily, and Willie won a standing ovation from many of his listeners, there was some heckling during his speech and after the vote the chairman was obliged to admit that support had been less than 'overwhelming'.[6]

Willie was particularly infuriated by the accusation that he was stalling on the border poll, because in private he had been pushing for a quick decision against colleagues who regarded it as irrelevant to the problem. When the referendum was finally held, on 8 March 1973, Willie's stand was vindicated. A boycott by the nationalist community reduced the turn-out to less than 60 per cent, and of these only 1 per cent voted for a united Ireland. After juggling with the figures Faulkner took heart from a result which, he felt, suggested that around a quarter of the Catholic population had defied the boycott and voted for the Union. A more credible verdict would be that, far from validating partition, the poll merely underlined the need for change along the lines Willie was proposing. In his Green Paper he had stressed that any devolved institutions would have to 'enjoy the support and respect of the *overwhelming* majority'. The mass abstentions of March 1973 gave an authoritative rebuff to the 800 people who had written to Willie demanding the immediate return of Stormont in its old guise.7

In the six months between Darlington and the border poll Northern Ireland slipped from the front pages which it had dominated since Bloody Sunday. The murders continued, but at a reduced level; the security forces were at last making headway against the Provos. Willie continued his policy of conciliation; in December 1972, after a concerted attack on his inaction by Catholic members of the Northern Ireland Commission, he announced the establishment of a special task force to investigate sectarian killings; he accepted Lord Diplock's recommendation that trials in terrorist cases should be conducted without juries (to guard against intimidation); and he held further exploratory talks with the various factions. He felt strong enough to ignore Provo suggestions of a new ceasefire. But it was becoming clear that he would need to do more than act as a passive chairman while the interested parties thrashed out a deal. Preparations began for a major statement of British intentions in the form of a White Paper, *Northern Ireland Constitutional Proposals*. This was published on 20 March 1973, less than two weeks after the border poll and almost exactly a year since the imposition of Direct Rule.

Willie went on television to explain his proposals to the people of Northern Ireland. There would be a new legislative body of seventy-eight members, elected by proportional representation. To dispel memories of Stormont, it would be called an assembly rather than a parliament. The assembly would be autonomous in most domestic matters, but elections, the judiciary and the use of emergency powers would be reserved to Westminster. Control of the police and prisons would also be reserved, but only on a temporary basis until the British Government felt that authority could safely be handed back. For the time being the post of Secretary of State would remain, with reduced powers; but the Governor was finally dispatched. The outstanding problem was how the executive of the province would be chosen. Willie had wanted the right to appoint its members after elections had been held, but Heath rejected this idea. The White Paper merely predicted that under proportional representation there could be no chance of single-party dominance – except in the unlikely (but very welcome) event that one party could draw significant support from all sections of the community. Thus the White Paper sought to introduce the idea of meaningful 'power sharing'; it also built on the Green Paper's vague reference to an 'Irish Dimension' by proposing an All-Ireland Council.

The White Paper formed the basis of the Northern Ireland Constitution Act, rushed through the Commons with full cooperation from Labour. While the provisions were congenial to the SDLP, they presented unionists with a clear choice. This was illustrated with merciless logic by Enoch Powell, who pointed out that the principle of power sharing meant that whatever the result of the elections, some positions of authority would be reserved for politicians committed to the eventual destruction of Northern Ireland. For Willie it was a time of stress, even by his own recent standards. One of his officials later quipped that the White Paper was 'too clever by three-quarters', but *The Economist* was closer to the mark when it described the proposed settlement as 'a reasonable constitutional framework which could work reasonably well if it were operated by reasonable people'. For this reason, the journal thought, it was probably doomed in the context of Ulster. But it would have had a much better chance of a widespread welcome if Willie's hands had not been tied by his colleagues. He had wanted to improve the deal for unionists by increasing the representation of Northern Ireland at Westminster to eighteen MPs, from the current twelve. But Heath was now taking a closer interest in the affairs of the province, having made his first visit as Prime Minister in November 1972. He took a tough line with the unionists, reminding them that Westminster provided annual subsidies worth £200 million. This was unlikely to faze politicians who would much rather be poor and Protestant than prosperous and Papist; but it seems that the experience encouraged Heath to imagine that sticks were more likely to produce results than carrots. He overruled Willie in the Cabinet Committee, arguing that there was no justification for more Ulster MPs when the politicians of Northern Ireland were to be given an assembly of their own. In strict logic he had a point, but in the Commons debate Powell presented an alternative logic with icy clarity. Willie's response to Powell was ineffective – unsurprisingly, since for once he actually agreed with Powell.[8]

Fearing the worst, Willie had asked the various parties in Northern Ireland to pause for a few days before giving a considered response to his proposals. Brian Faulkner thought the White Paper 'was one of the most controversial documents ever produced by a British Government'. Yet he had committed himself too far to the constitutional road to draw back now, and he gave it a cautious welcome. This proved too much for Craig, whose Vanguard movement finally defected from the Ulster Unionists and established a party of its own (an early recruit was David Trimble, a law lecturer at Queen's University, Belfast). According to Cecil King, Paisley's initial private reaction was positive, but he soon decided to join Craig in all-out opposition to the measure.[9]

In later years Willie wondered if he had made a mistake in announcing that the assembly elections should be held no earlier than the end of June. He felt that it might have been wiser to take the tide at its full flood, and call a snap poll before Faulkner's position was undermined. This course was urged on him at the time by Labour. Yet the schedule was already demanding enough, since local elections were due on 30 May and Willie felt these should not be postponed. Faulkner remembered this as 'an exhausting time'. Well aware of the strength of feeling within his party, he did his best to defend the White Paper while fighting the two elections and trying to fend off challenges to his leadership. To reassure unionist voters he promised that he would never share power with any party whose *primary* purpose was the destruction of Northern Ireland; later he would claim that this was a *long-term* aim for the SDLP rather than an immediate priority, but this verbal dexterity was not enough to save him from the familiar charges of betrayal and hypocrisy.[10]

The local elections went well for the moderates, but as so often in Northern Ireland the result of the assembly poll (held on 28 June, Willie's fifty-fifth birthday) was tantalisingly inconclusive. Faulkner took his own victory in South Down as a vote of confidence, but Paisley topped the poll in North Antrim. The arithmetic was complicated by the fact that several elected Ulster Unionists had refused to pledge themselves to the principles of the White Paper, and although the official tally for candidates backed by Craig and Paisley was eighteen seats, Cecil King was more accurate when he judged it to be twenty-seven. The SDLP fared better than expected, with nineteen representatives; two days before the poll it had lost one of its prominent members, Paddy Wilson, to loyalist assassins. One serious disappointment for Willie was the performance of the Alliance, which won only eight seats.[11]

Close examination of the results indicated that a majority of the unionist population had voted for candidates opposed to the White Paper. Nevertheless, the outcome provided majority support in the Assembly for Willie's initiative, and it was an additional bonus that, for the first time in a Northern Irish election, no single party had been returned with an overall majority. When Paisley reported to King that the Secretary of State seemed 'thin, white and jittery, and deeply disappointed by the result', his powers of observation must have been affected by wishful thinking. Nevertheless, there had been rumours for some time that Willie was ready for a recall. Back in September 1972 he had told John Cole that the existing arrangements made no sense as a long-term solution, because 'you would kill one Secretary of State a year'. The rumours intensified around the time of the White Paper; King thought that when he made his broadcast Willie 'gave the impression that he will not remain as Northern Ireland Secretary for much longer'. But whatever his feelings about his present job, Willie was determined not to leave it half-finished. Official denials were issued, explaining that although he found the work tiring he had been well aware that this would be the case when he first accepted the responsibility. Yet speculation persisted, and Willie was not always adept at dampening it. Before the assembly election, when asked directly about his future during a radio phone-in, he gave the opaque reply that 'The Prime Minister must decide what he wants me to do, whether he wishes to have me in this job or another job, or in no job at all'. In truth, Willie was impatient for signs that his policy was succeeding, both for the good of the province and for his own health; but not even he could find a tactful way of spelling this out in public. Privately he complained of feeling isolated, even lonely. He told journalists that his inability to intervene had made him feel 'like an eunuch in a harem' during the election campaign.[12]

An obvious source of stress for Willie was the fact that even before the Governor's departure he was called upon to act as if he were both Prime Minister and Head of State of a province that was not recognised by a large proportion of its inhabitants. In Northern Ireland capital punishment had not been abolished, and in the spring of 1973 Willie had to decide whether or not to exercise the prerogative of mercy. He had accepted the suspension of capital punishment on the mainland in 1965, but this seems to have been the result of pragmatism rather than real revulsion. Exposure to the conflict in Northern Ireland presented the dilemma in particularly acute form. The most serious offences, like sectarian murders, seemed to cry out for the harshest punishment; yet 'political' crimes were sure to make martyrs even of the most callous killers. Ironically, given the undue press attention paid to Provo atrocities, Willie's first case of this kind concerned Albert Browne, the Protestant killer of a policeman. A law passed in 1966 had made capital punishment mandatory in such cases. Later Willie recalled that Ian Paisley paid one of his visits and demanded clemency, warning of 'dire consequences' should this 'good Protestant' be executed. In fact, despite Browne's membership of the UDA, the calls for a reprieve came from across the community. So Willie complied, and decided to spare himself further difficulties by introducing the necessary legislation to abolish capital punishment altogether. From this time he was a consistent opponent of the death penalty in all cases. The lesson about creating martyrs hit home; when two hunger-strikers in Crumlin Road jail were close to death in August 1973, he released them without hesitation.[13]

At the end of July the Northern Ireland Assembly opened amid disorderly scenes that would have mortified Selwyn Lloyd – although for the first few months the violence was more verbal than physical. In December the restoration of order required the intervention of the police, not the Speaker. When procedure was not being wrangled over, it was being exploited to create the impression of a pointless talking shop. Even the replacement of a confrontational Westminster-style debating chamber with a more consensual semi-circle did nothing to defuse the tension. Predictably, Paisley was the main culprit here, and thus allayed Willie's fears that the SDLP might be tempted into a tactical alliance with the caustic clergyman.

Willie could view the mayhem in the Assembly with some detachment because the real action was happening in discussions elsewhere. 'Action', perhaps, is not the right word. Over his period in Northern Ireland Willie showed amazing stamina during tedious and repetitive negotiations, but even for him there were limits. When one unionist group came to see him, his officials were alarmed that the Secretary of State allowed his eyes to close and his chin to droop onto his chest. As soon as the delegation began to complain about this, Willie astonished everyone by sitting up and answering all the points that had been raised. His visitors left in good heart, mollified by their courteous reception. When they had gone the civil servants expressed relief at their boss's performance. 'We were terrified that you were fast asleep,' one of them said, 'but you were really listening all the time.' 'Oh no, I wasn't', Willie retorted, 'but I've heard it all so often that I don't need to listen any longer.'[14]

As soon as the Assembly results came through, Willie invited the various party leaders to Stormont, to recycle their arguments yet again. Meanwhile Heath began to discuss the 'Irish Dimension' with his new opposite number in Dublin, Liam Cosgrave. On 17 September Heath startled observers by suggesting that the ultimate solution might be the full integration of Northern Ireland into the United Kingdom. This was one outcome that Willie had always rejected, and the result was a semi-row, which, given that it happened in the presence of the garrulous Paisley, was something more than semi-public. Later Paisley suspected that Heath had really meant integration of the North into a united Ireland, and given the preferences of senior ministers he could easily have been right. Fortunately the whole affair could be dismissed as an aberration, but it was an inauspicious precedent given that Heath was sure to maintain a leading role in negotiations. Willie also talked directly to the Irish Government, with mixed results. He was enraged when the Foreign Minister, Garret Fitzgerald, appeared in Belfast unannounced; since the Irish had decided not to risk holding a referendum on their constitutional claim on the territories of the North, and feelings were already aroused by the idea of a Council of Ireland, it seemed unnecessarily provocative for a senior minister to hold talks in Belfast without official clearance. Fitzgerald was later told that at a press conference for Dublin journalists a senior British civil servant had descended into vulgarity when estimating the chances of his country making any financial contribution to the running of a Council of Ireland; this unprofessional conduct was somewhat ironic, given that at this time the men from Whitehall tended to patronise their Irish counterparts as representatives of a relatively weak and impoverished nation. Willie himself was open to criticism on this score; he could not really understand the Republic without visiting it, but he never did because (as one official put it) 'the unionists would have torn him apart' on his return.[15]

After further preparatory talks the stage was set for the main event. For the most part Willie had met the various parties independently and, given the non-participants, Darlington had been no guide to how a real 'Round Table'conference might go. Formal inter-party talks, featuring the Darlington cast plus an SDLP delegation – but not Paisley, who had now discovered that he could not talk to the SDLP while it supported a rent-and-rates strike – began in the old Cabinet Room at Stormont on 5 October. The proceedings opened with a discussion of the economy – a shrewd choice, since all parties were likely to agree on the need for greater prosperity, and Willie had no more exalted aim at this stage than 'to prevent anyone walking out'. Even so, he had taken the precaution of providing ample supplies of food and drink in case the ice still had not thawed by lunchtime. Looking back on the occasion, Willie felt that these had been timely lubricants. No one walked (or staggered) out. Most importantly, the parties promised to keep the detail of their deliberations from the press. The fact that there were no serious breaches of this rule was a clear indication of the trust that gradually built up between the participants.[16]

From the outset, though, there were disagreements, notably on the question of policing. The SDLP wanted the RUC to be reformed and renamed; then it should be placed under the authority of the Council of Ireland. Faulkner demurred at this, asking whether the SDLP thought that the Irish Government would allow the Garda to come under joint control. Surprisingly Hume made no objection, but Faulkner still thought the proposal was 'totally impracticable'. It was a serious impasse; as the SDLP pointed out, currently only 4 per cent of recruits to the RUC were Catholic. Willie stepped in, suggesting that his officials would prepare a paper and at a future meeting they could all 'discuss whether they could discuss' the police. In other areas progress was satisfactory; all the parties agreed to the principle of the Council of Ireland, although the question remained of whether this would be inter-governmental or drawn from the parliaments of North and South.[17]

After three days of talking Willie left to prepare himself for another Conservative Party Conference. Keeping to the terms he had laid down, he merely told the *Belfast Newsletter* that although he had always been prepared for 'a long slog', he was satisfied with the 'steady progress'. However, the SDLP was growing nervous. On the day after Willie's departure their delegation met Frank Cooper, who had taken over from Nield as Permanent Secretary of the Department. As Cooper reported, they accused him of helping Faulkner to present his case. 'They all got up in unison and said they were not prepared to talk. I told them to sit down,' Cooper noted. 'They did so.' The SDLP had made careful preparations for the talks, and obviously thought that without special favours from the British, Faulkner and his team would have capitulated to their arguments. In fact, although the British were troubled by the weakness of Faulkner's position within his party, Cooper had assisted only to the extent of acting as a sounding-board for the unionist leader and generally trying to keep up his morale.

The SDLP had some reason to feel fidgety, because Faulkner also travelled to Blackpool to speak at the Conservative Conference. Even if some Ulster Unionists now hated the British Government, to the SDLP there could have been no better reminder of the ties which still persisted between that party and the Conservatives. Faulkner was 'warmly applauded' as he claimed that the new constitution promised to bring the people of Ulster 'a stronger Government than ever before'. Significantly, he appealed to Heath not to move Willie from his post until his job was done, and praised the Secretary of State for his 'able mind, understanding personality and his really hard work'. Willie himself had a much easier time than at the previous conference. He denounced the parties which had boycotted the Stormont talks, referring darkly to the limits of British patience and to the growing strength of the domestic 'Troops Out' movement. He compared himself to the British soldier who had recently told him 'it is more difficult to keep your patience in public than it was at the start'. But he won a standing ovation for his peroration: 'the Northern Ireland problem is our responsibility, and we shall not shirk it with dishonour, but shoulder it with honour'.[18]

Willie had consciously addressed himself to four audiences: the Conservatives in the hall, the UK public watching on television, the unionist refuseniks like Paisley and Craig, and those like Faulkner who were committed to the talks. He knew that soon after his return to Belfast he would have to negotiate the make-up of the Executive. Faulkner had staked out his own position; there must be a unionist majority. One possible solution was to change the framework laid down in the Constitution Act, and allow additions to the maximum twelve-man body proposed in that document. This had been suggested to Willie by unionists, but at the conference he ruled out any tinkering with the existing terms.

If Willie had not learned from his experiences in Ulster he might have been tempted to use Faulkner's weakness to press him into further concessions. But the former premier had become indispensable to his plans. Years later Willie reminded the right-wing journalist Peter Utley 'you always told me that I was driving Faulkner too far. My God you were right! But what a fool he was to allow himself to be driven.' Willie was only trying to flatter Utley; at the time he had been well aware of the pressure on the unionist leader, and he never thought it foolish to put the interests of the community above personal concerns. Before the talks were over Faulkner's position was endorsed at a tense meeting of his party's ruling council; in an electorate of nearly 750 he won by only ten votes. Since so many of the hardliners had already deserted his party, this was a clear signal of what was to come. Yet Faulkner took the view that 'one was enough', and soldiered on. The SDLP also showed their mettle, refusing to be provoked into a walk-out by a new campaign of violence by the Protestant paramilitaries, who included the party's headquarters among their targets. Willie responded by naming the Ulster Freedom Fighters and the Red Hand Commando as 'proscribed organisations'; he also instructed the army to step up their investigations into 'loyalist' violence.[19]

The talks proceeded, but progress was punctuated by evidence of entrenched positions. Faulkner wanted to be Chief Executive, and to command a majority of members – seven of the twelve. The SDLP argued that this would be out of proportion to the outcome of the Assembly election, and demanded parity with the unionists (five members each), with the balance of power being held by two Alliance representatives. Wisely, Willie called a halt before the meeting degenerated into a dialogue of the deadlocked. Over the next week he held meetings with each delegation in turn, but even he could not persuade politicians who were acutely sensitive of the need to present their supporters outside with a 'victory'. On Monday 19 November the same arguments were rehearsed, although this time Gerry Fitt drew attention to new rumours that Willie was about to be moved and deplored the impression that the province was far less important than any industrial troubles on the mainland. The meeting was adjourned until the Wednesday.[20]

Willie had regarded the Monday meeting as 'make or break'. He was scheduled to deliver a full report at Westminster on the Thursday, 22 November, so Wednesday really was the last chance. He presented the parties with a draft agreement, covering all of the main issues. The Council of Ireland was to be given restricted powers, and Willie chipped that ball into the long grass by explaining that its precise role would be decided at a forthcoming 'tripartite' conference between the new Executive and representatives of the two national governments. But it was likely that the Council would be more than a consultative body, which meant that the SDLP had won an important concession. The timing of the tripartite conference had been yet another major sticking-point; Faulkner wanted the Executive to be formed before the conference, while the SDLP held out for the opposite timetable. The draft agreement conceded this point to Faulkner.

Skilful as it was, this balancing act seemed unlikely to be repeated on the key question of the make-up of the Executive. After the morning meeting this point was as far from resolution as ever, although an important hazard was crossed when the SDLP reluctantly agreed that the Ulster Constabulary should retain the prefix 'Royal' (Willie felt that removing it would be unnecessarily provocative, and would detract from the real aim of creating a force that enjoyed cross-community support). Even before the morning meeting Willie had telephoned Heath – as the latter put it, 'in a desperate state, to prepare me for the worst'. In his own account Willie would only allow that he had awoken that morning 'in a very depressed mood', and that Heath had sounded equally morose when he heard the discouraging news. But Willie decided on one last throw of the dice. He had no intention of creating more full Executive posts to accommodate everyone, but this still left room for manouevre. He proposed that *non-voting* members could be added to the Executive. This might square the circle, by satisfying the SDLP demand that there should be no overall majority for the unionists on the Executive as a whole, while denying the minority parties the power to veto Faulkner's proposals.[21]

Years later Faulkner recalled the difficulty of explaining the feelings of participants in those talks to anyone who had not been there: 'We were united as people who had come through an ordeal together, pushed closer by the attacks made on us from outside by politicians and terrorists who shared the common objective of wishing to see us fail.' For his part, it had suddenly dawned on the SDLP's Paddy Devlin 'that our unionist opponents were basically a decent bunch of well-meaning men, with a great desire to build something of value for the people of the North'. Amid the tension and the rows there had been moments of levity that lingered in the memory. Willie's personal favourite was Devlin's outburst when thwarted on one issue: 'Mr Chairman, you are a bloody [I think he probably said worse!] Chairman!', to which Willie responded that whatever his faults, he was the best chairman they were likely to get. An hour later, when Devlin got his way on a different subject, he exclaimed, 'Mr Chairman, all our progress is due to your remarkable skill as Chairman.' Willie took this as a prompt 'for lunch and possibly for a drink'.[22]

At one point during the talks Willie told Frank Cooper that this was the pinnacle of his political career.[23] It was certainly true that the atmosphere which developed at Stormont over those weeks presented him with an ideal opportunity to deploy the psychological skills that he had accumulated since his army days. Had the SDLP delegation heard his new idea, free from all the bonds that had enveloped them over arduous negotiating sessions, they would probably have rejected it. Faulkner had not really done well enough in the elections to justify both his effective majority *and* his position as Chief Executive. But the SDLP had been softened up for a deal, and after ten hours of shuffling from room to room, trying to coax the parties into committing themselves, Willie pulled off his final master-stroke.

It was a high-tech version of a trick he must have learned as a boy, when his relatives told stories of Disraeli's brinksmanship at the Congress of Berlin. Everyone knew that Willie would be leaving for London at the close of play on Wednesday; and although the talks had suddenly taken a more positive turn, he decided to allow his helicopter to land outside the castle at a pre-arranged time. In Ulster politics since 1973 the skilful use of deadlines has proved invaluable, but Willie was the first to discover this. When the machine swooped down, minds were concentrated on a quick solution, and although they were still talking when the helicopter made a second sortie an hour later, all the key points had been settled. The final tally on the Executive would be six unionists, four SDLP and one Alliance, supplemented by non-voting members in the proportion 1:2:1. The SDLP was partly compensated by being awarded some choice portfolios, and Gerry Fitt decided that he would act as Faulkner's deputy. The nationalist party could justly feel that things had changed beyond recognition since the days of single-party rule. But with Willie's connivance Faulkner had ensured that unionists enjoyed a preponderance (if not a monopoly) of real power, in the hope that this would mollify disillusioned members of his party. Certainly Garret Fitzgerald thought the SDLP might have asked for more; he sent a note to Devlin, pointing out that John Hume could have demanded the Finance portfolio, which instead went to Faulkner.[24]

Willie had the good sense to keep his feet on the ground; after all, the deal had been thrashed out between practical people who were in short supply outside the negotiations – and it had been hard enough to get even them to see reason. But an emotional man like Willie could not be immune to the mood of 'euphoria' as he emerged from the building to announce the agreement. His personal pride at that moment was fully justified, although Oliver Napier of the Alliance had to prod him into a prominent position for the photographs. In hindsight, Ken Bloomfield acknowledged that the talks had been 'a remarkable triumph for the diplomatic and persuasive powers of Whitelaw'. This was fully recognised when he reported to his Cabinet colleagues, and later when he addressed the Commons. He tried to praise everyone but himself, and made no attempt to minimise the troubles ahead. But the Commons was in a hyperbolic mood, and hailed Willie like a Roman general who had earned a great Triumph. Although some Ulster MPs broke their normal routine by actually turning up for the occasion, Paisley's absence was conspicuous. He showed his feelings after Willie had left Northern Ireland, calling the former Secretary of State 'the man who broke his word to Ulster's loyalists'. But almost the only dissenting voice during the Commons debate came from Bernadette Devlin (now McAliskey), who thought that the deal had been cobbled together simply to allow Willie 'to depart with the flags waving and the trumpets blaring'. For her part she would be only too happy when he left.[25]

British politicians had been united with the public in wishing that the problem of Ulster, which had intruded itself so abruptly, could be swept away with equal facility. Understandably, Willie was the hero of the day when it seemed that he had pulled off the trick. The following morning, he remembered, 'The press comments were so favourable that when I look at them now I wonder if they can be describing the same person that I have sometimes read about in their columns since.' As he wrote those words he knew that in a sense he was no longer 'the same person' that he had been on 21 November 1973. On the steps of Stormont he personified a momentous, unanticipated negotiating success, which elevated him above the common run of humanity. *The Times* editorial was simply headlined 'A Great Achievement'. Even Senator Edward Kennedy, whose interventions from afar had infuriated the British, thought that only a Nobel Peace Prize would be adequate recognition for Willie's 'towering service in the cause of peace'; he had exhibited 'almost unbelievable insight, perseverence, and painstaking genius'. With hindsight, Kennedy's encomium seems fully justified. Later peacemakers enjoyed the crucial advantages – familiarity with the political terrain, and war-weariness among the people of Northern Ireland – that Willie and his officials had lacked. Even in a more helpful context, Willie's successors have still not solved the problem entirely; and no one has suggested a better general approach than the one laid down in 1972–73. Heath's decision to make Willie a Companion of Honour seemed to fall below his deserts, even though this was a most unusual award for a serving politician. But less than a fortnight later Willie had ceased to be Secretary of State for Northern Ireland, and became all too human once again.[26]

'. . . SO LOST A BUSINESS'

Even Willie would have been gratified to learn that in September 1971 his stock within Whitehall was so high that a senior civil servant considered him to be the ideal replacement in any ministry that might fall vacant. But the unsettling accompaniment for such a glittering reputation was that Willie was sure to be included in any gossip about impending government reshuffles. Edward Heath prided himself on the unity of his Cabinet, but even he could not avoid occasional changes. Incidents such as the death of Macleod and Maudling's disgrace were unwelcome enough in themselves; but while the parliamentary touts might enjoy the opportunity for speculation, the need to fill unexpected vacancies increased Heath's dismay at these losses to his team.

Whatever a Prime Minister might think, talk of a reshuffle always increases when a government loses popularity, and by the summer of 1973 the opinion polls were causing serious disquiet. In July Gallup's survey showed a 10 per cent lead for Labour; even more worrying, only one-fifth of the electorate thought the Tories would be re-elected. The gloomy prospect was confirmed by more tangible results; in July the government lost two 'safe' seats to the Liberals in by-elections, having suffered a similar reversal at Sutton and Cheam at the end of the previous year. By November the outlook had improved, and the two main parties were virtually neck-and-neck in the national polls. But still only 31 per cent approved of the government's record – 11 per cent less than the figure for Labour just before it lost the 1970 general election. Again a by-election reinforced the message; on 8 November 1973 the Liberal Alan Beith began his long tenure of Berwick-upon-Tweed at the expense of the Conservative candidate. Labour also performed badly, but Liberal revivals had always been bad news for the Tories.

In September 1973 the *Evening Standard* reported that 'Mr Heath would like Mr Whitelaw back in circulation up and down the country as soon as possible for he rates him as a charmer and the right man to spearhead a campaign to raise Tory morale'. The importance attached to Willie's presence was such that he was asked to speak during the Berwick campaign, despite his heavy commitments in Ulster. There was no constitutional requirement for a general election before the summer of 1975, but the restoration of party fortunes could not be achieved overnight. The talismanic Whitelaw would have to be in place to work his magic well in advance; the remaining difficulty was to find the right berth for him. There were no vacancies in the highest ranks of the government. It seems that an attempt was made to convince Alec Home that the Scottish Office would be an appropriate venue for him as retirement beckoned; but he loved the Foreign Office, where he had been untroubled by the domestic disasters that had befallen most of his colleagues. The Chancellor Tony Barber had already let it be known that he wished to leave politics; but Heath was determined to avoid instability in that key policy area until it became unavoidable. The Home Secretary, Robert Carr, had only been in the job for a few months.[1]

Eventually the dilemma resolved itself. Willie had been mentioned in the press as a candidate for the Department of Employment before he went to Northern Ireland. At that time the post was held by Carr, who had been subjected to constant attack by Labour during the passage of the Industrial Relations Act. In the enforced reshuffle after the imposition of Direct Rule, Carr replaced Willie as Leader of the House, where he stayed until Maudling left the government. At that time Employment was given to Maurice Macmillan, son of the former Prime Minister. Previously Macmillan had been a successful Chief Secretary to the Treasury, disproving the doubters who had referred darkly to a long-standing drink problem.

At Employment Macmillan continued to urge a tough line against inflationary wage settlements. Certainly he was no pushover for the unions. But he was not an inspiring orator, and his lacklustre performances in the Commons had long been the subject of cruel mimickry in the Press Gallery. When delivering a speech or making a statement he would grip the dispatch-box, drop his head almost onto his chest and read out the Civil Service brief in an almost inaudible monotone. By the winter of 1973 Heath felt the need for a more commanding figure in what was now the front line of government activity. A new conflict was looming with the miners, and on the day of Willie's triumph at Stormont the NUM executive rejected a generous pay offer from the National Coal Board (NCB). But the Prime Minister was anxious to avoid giving the impression that he had lost confidence in Macmillan, so in the reshuffle he retained his place in Cabinet. To accommodate him, the Wykehamist David 'Smarty Boots' Eccles was removed from his post of Paymaster-General. Ironically, in 1962 Eccles had been the most unexpected victim of the 'Night of the Long Knives' – the rather desperate Cabinet purge conducted by Macmillan's father Harold. But this symbolic sacrifice was not enough to placate those close to the Macmillan family. Improbable rumours began to circulate, to the effect that Willie had plotted Maurice's downfall. Willie thought the chief source of this fable was the former premier himself; in retirement he remained convinced that Macmillan *père* had never forgiven him for his alleged offence.[2]

The complications that arose even from the limited exercise of bringing Willie home were sufficient to show why Heath had always been determined to avoid the kind of ministerial butchery associated with the Macmillan Government. The domino effect triggered off among those concerned with domestic matters was dramatic enough; but there was also the question of finding a replacement for the man who had apparently brought Northern Ireland to the verge of peace. The *Evening Standard* proved unusually prescient in pressing the claims of Jim Prior, although the newspaper had to wait another eight years before the prediction was verified (and even then Prior's move was rightly seen as the nearest thing Mrs Thatcher could do to sending her rival to Siberia). In 1973 Prior must have been an option, but there was another man in the government who seemed almost an identikit match for Willie himself.[3]

As we have seen, Willie and Francis Pym came from similar social backgrounds, and in war and politics their careers had run in parallel. As Chief Whip Pym had obviously been guided by Willie's advice and example, but he had left his own stamp on the job. Like Willie, he had tried not to bully recalcitrant troops in the manner of Martin Redmayne; but he had also avoided Willie's emotional outbursts. By comparison with Willie he was a shy man, whose qualities were not so complementary to those of Heath. After an early Cabinet meeting Willie told Robert Carr that he thought Pym and Heath were not getting on: 'Francis hasn't yet learned to sit in silence,' he lamented. Yet Pym soon mastered his leader's idiosyncrasies. Before the next meeting Willie gleefully reported a breakthrough: 'Francis has just told me that he sat in silence for a quarter of an hour in the Cabinet room.'[4]

For some months Pym had been attending the Cabinet sub-committee on Northern Ireland, and had been kept well informed of Willie's thinking. On paper, sending Pym to Northern Ireland must have seemed almost ideal to Heath – the nearest thing to having Willie in two places at once. The obvious problem was that the negotiations which allowed Willie to return at the height of his prestige also meant that his successor would have to hit the ground sprinting. Willie's appointment as the new Secretary of State for Employment was announced on 2 December 1973. Preparations had been going on for some time behind the scenes, allowing Willie to chew over the precise nature of his new duties. On 26 November he had written a letter to Tony Barber, allaying any suspicions the latter might have nursed that he would be displaced from overall control over economic policy. But it seems that Pym was denied the luxury of advance notice. Having driven himself to Chequers for talks with Heath, he found himself flying out to Belfast at seven-thirty the following morning. On the steps of Stormont Castle he faced the usual demands for an optimistic statement, and got through the ordeal as best he could, although he could already detect that he was being unfavourably compared with Willie. That night he took to bed with him a list of internees who might be released. There was no time for quiet reflection; the tripartite talks were due to start at the Civil Service College, Sunningdale, on 6 December.[5]

For some time Pym had been urging Heath to recall Willie, and to that extent he had little scope for protest. As far as the decision affected himself, he would do his duty in Northern Ireland as best he could. But his main concern was the gap he had left in the whips' office. Possibly Pym himself, had he been succeeding to the post of Chief Whip at this climactic stage of a fraught Parliament, might have made a success of it. But the man who replaced him, Humphrey Atkins, did not. There was yet another change to the government team in January 1974, when Lord Carrington was named as the head of a new Department of Energy. It was rumoured that this appointment had been held up because Peter Walker, the Secretary of State for Trade and Industry, was reluctant to give up responsibility for this area. As a tired Cabinet faced up to its most serious crisis, it seemed to be collapsing into the kind of squabbles over personalities and political turf that had disfigured the Wilson years.

After the Stormont talks one commentator had hailed Willie as 'the only English politician since the Earl of Essex to be thrown into the Irish bog and to emerge from it not only with credit but with a shining reputation'. It was an odd comparison to choose; Elizabeth I had summoned Essex home from 'the Irish bog' in disgrace, and had her former favourite beheaded for treason shortly afterwards.[6] Even more ominous was the fate of another North Country squire, Charles I's Earl of Strafford, who in 1639 was recalled to the domestic front after a controversial spell in Ireland. As his biographer noted, 'Too long absent in Ireland, [Strafford] had but partly conceived of the deep-seated discontent at home.' Once he had realised how desperate the situation really was, he asked his cousin to 'Pity me, for never came any man to so lost a business'. For those who appreciate historical coincidences, there was an extra dash of piquancy in the prominence of a man called Pym in Strafford's situation, and some consolation in the fact that while Francis Pym was Willie's warmest admirer, John, his seventeenth-century namesake, was the chief instigator of Strafford's impeachment and judicial murder in 1641.[7]

In December 1973 Willie was better placed than Strafford had been, but he had little reason for optimism. Back in June 1970 the government had identified as its top priority the restraint of inflation, but Heath had taken radical steps to fuel economic growth in anticipation of EEC entry. To guard against the obvious danger of inflationary overheating, the Prime Minister introduced a series of measures to control prices and incomes. Initial hopes for voluntary restraint by unions and employers were dashed, and in November 1972 the government turned to legislative measures. This contradicted clear pledges given before the 1970 election, but Heath was far more interested in practical solutions than in ideological purity. Willie agreed; as he explained in his speech during the Berwick by-election campaign, the alternative was higher unemployment and (unlike Enoch Powell, the target of his remarks) he was not prepared to countenance this. At first the cumbersome machinery seemed to be working, but unfortunately for Heath his gamble coincided with a worldwide rise in commodity prices. As a result, the attempt to keep down inflation required ever more detailed intervention, so that ministers found themselves setting prices and rates of pay with an attention to detail that might have daunted even the bureaucrats in the old Soviet Union. Geoffrey Howe, the Minister for Trade and Consumer Affairs, once had to ask the vicar of Trumpington to rescind his decision to double the charge for brass-rubbing in his church.[8]

In October 1973 the government's strategy unravelled further. In response to the West's support for Israel in the war of Yom Kippur, Arab oil producers increased their prices fourfold, supplementing smaller rises earlier in the year. At the beginning of 1973 the price of oil had been $2.40 per barrel; twelve months later it was $11.65. The dangerous over-reliance on cheap fuel of the world's affluent societies was exposed; even more worrying, supplies of the more expensive oil were severely limited for a time. For the Heath Government, the problem was political as well as economic. Even before Yom Kippur, the government had decided to reverse its strategy of running down the coal industry. It was easy enough to stuff the miners' mouths with golden subsidies, but there had already been one serious clash over pay and conditions and the oil crisis greatly increased the difficulty of devising a prices and incomes formula that was flexible enough to satisfy the NUM. In July 1973 the moderate NUM leader Joe Gormley thought that he had struck a secret deal with Heath, under which the miners could be made a special case. But when Phase 3 of the government's policy was announced – two days after war broke out in the Middle East – Gormley found that the loophole he had suggested would not apply to his members alone; indeed, under its terms any group of workers could have won extra concessions. Significantly at this stage the government was being advised that it could sustain industrial action in the coalfields, provided that it did not coincide with any other crisis.

Before Willie's recall the government's plight had worsened, due to its habitual mixture of blunders and bad luck. In what was widely regarded as a disastrous tactical error, the NCB made an opening pay offer that stretched Phase 3 to the limit. Clearly this would only encourage the miners to ask for more. The Middle Eastern situation should have induced a tactical rethink, but when ministers were asked to provide some token concessions in advance of a miners' conference in late October, nothing new was offered. On 12 November the miners began an overtime ban, which cut output by almost half. The government responded by calling its fifth State of Emergency: there had been just seven over the previous fifty years. During the 1972 confrontation with the miners, energy restrictions had been applied haphazardly, causing unnecessary disruption. To avoid this the government now prepared the public for the worst by announcing a series of draconian measures based on the premise that the worst had already happened. As so often, ministers found that their attempts to implement rational plans resulted only in public-relations disasters. In addition to restrictions on heat and lighting, television broadcasting would have to close down at 10.30 p.m. – a measure which some might think a mercy today, but which in 1973 seemed to be an unnecessary breach of the British tradition of conducting 'business as usual' during a crisis. This impression was reinforced two weeks later, when Walker announced preparations to introduce petrol rationing; a 50 mph speed limit was already in force. To compound the government's difficulties, it was also in dispute with key workers in the power industry and the railways. But the most spectacular interference with the national routine – the introduction of a three-day working week – came into force on New Year's Day 1974, at the same time that the power-sharing Executive in Northern Ireland held its first meeting.

During the miners' dispute of February 1972 the government felt that it had been fighting for its life. This time the threat was made explicitly when Heath agreed to meet the full NUM executive at Downing Street on 28 November 1973. The union's communist Vice-President, Mick McGahey, is alleged to have said that his main aim was to bring down the government. After the meeting the miners' representatives retired to another room in Number 10, where they decided against allowing their members to vote on a continuation of the overtime ban. Douglas Hurd, who had been horrified by the 'surrender' of February 1972, now felt that 'the earth began to move under the Government's feet'.9

When he went to Northern Ireland Willie had inherited numerous difficulties, but Direct Rule at least offered the chance of a fresh start for the province. On 2 December 1973, by contrast, he found himself parachuted into the advanced stages of someone else's disaster. And he was aware that his recent experiences increased the more obvious handicaps in several ways. First, like Strafford he needed to readjust to politics on the mainland. He had lost touch with the mood at Westminster while he had been away, and even after his return he was distracted by the critical developments in Ulster. But his new ministerial responsibilities brought him back to a scene which he had left in 1964, when the Conservative defeat at the general election removed him from what was then the Ministry of Labour. He knew several senior trade unionists, but they tended to be moderates who were out of tune with the new harsher realities of industrial relations. Ironically, one of Willie's last decisions in Northern Ireland was to recommend the appointment of the former TUC General Secretary, Vic Feather, to head a commission on human rights. Len Murray, who replaced Feather at the TUC, was certainly no militant; but ministers doubted whether he had sufficient standing within the trade-union movement to deliver on any agreement. According to Heath's biographer, he was regarded in government circles as 'a deracinated backroom intellectual whose first loyalty was to the Labour Party'.[10]

In Northern Ireland Willie often complained that no one would allow him time to develop his strategy; but events in the province had happened in slow motion compared to the hectic rush during his days at Employment. And Willie was only too aware of a second handicap; he was exhausted, both physically and emotionally. In normal times the approach of Christmas would have offered the prospect of a much-needed rest, but in 1973 it merely increased the pressure for the Man of Stormont to conjure up a settlement that would allow the population to enjoy the festive season. Willie knew how important it was to stamp his authority on the situation as soon as possible, but his weary flesh was no match for his spirit, and observers felt that he was unimpressive when he contributed to his first debate on the crisis on 4 December.[11]

The question of authority was also central to the third handicap that Willie imported from Belfast. Later he came to realise that 'it is dangerous to be described as a born conciliator because it implies a tendency to compromise too easily. This in turn weakens one's negotiating position especially, as is true in my case, when one's instincts lead in the direction of compromise.'[12] Of course Willie could point to incidents in Ulster – notably 'Motorman' – where he had proved his ability to take tough decisions. But trade unionists could only assume that the Cabinet's 'Mr Fixit' had been brought back at this stage to cut a deal, especially since they knew that he had argued for a generous deal with the miners in 1972. For them his appointment was an open invitation to play even harder to get. To make matters worse, Willie might have been an instant success had he been asked to play the part of 'nice cop' to a more inflexible senior colleague. But although the unions liked to caricature Heath as a 'confrontational' figure, they knew that he would keep on finding scope for an agreement long after less optimistic politicians had turned from 'jaw' to 'war'. The old complementary partnership was over; in their new roles Heath and Willie were carbon copies of each other.

These difficulties were weighty enough, and in combination they made Willie wonder if he had been the right man for the job. The answer to his doubts, as at Northern Ireland, was the lack of any obvious alternative candidate with compelling credentials. Ironically, as things turned out, Pym would have been a better appointment. His knowledge of the contemporary Westminster scene was unrivalled, and no one thought he was a soft touch. He had no experience of the industrial relations field, but this would have been less of a drawback than Willie's anachronistic memories proved to be; and if Pym was unknown to the public, Willie might as well have been a newcomer, given that hardly any use was made of his communication skills. Meanwhile Pym himself was wasted at Northern Ireland, inevitably overshadowed by his Prime Minister at Sunningdale and by the ghost of his predecessor afterwards. The idea that brilliant Chief Whips make ideal Secretaries of State for Northern Ireland took a long time to die, but it should not have outlasted February 1974.

Another factor that would have made Pym a better choice was the fourth and final handicap mentioned by Willie in his memoirs. The brief allusion to this problem stands out in a book that is hardly stuffed with shock revelations. 'Although I did not realise it at the time,' he wrote, 'apparent success in politics at any moment leads inevitably to feelings of jealousy and suspicion among one's colleagues.' Presumably this sentence has escaped notice only because the remainder of the text has such an anaesthetic effect. In conversation much later, Willie confirmed what only the most perceptive insider could have guessed from the memoirs – that the colleague he had in mind was Heath himself.[13]

As we have seen, Willie's dealings with Heath during his spell in Northern Ireland were not always amicable. The Prime Minister's apparent endorsement of full integration within the UK as a possible solution to the problems of the province must have produced lasting irritation. With hindsight, it is also possible to interpret the recall on the eve of Sunningdale as an attempt by Heath to scoop up some of the praise that was due to Willie's exhausting work since March 1972. In fact, since Sunningdale was a tripartite, governmental conference it would have been difficult for Heath to avoid the limelight, whether Willie or Pym had been his junior colleague. But clearly something about the circumstances of the recall rankled with Willie, both then and later.[14]

A more serious incident occurred soon after Willie had settled into his new office, in St James' Square. Against precedent he had successfully requested that his press secretary, Keith McDowall, should come home with him. Apart from the strong personal rapport that the pair had established, McDowall had obvious qualifications for the job from his days as industrial correspondent on the *Daily Mail*. But the previous incumbent, Bernard Ingham, was understandably aggrieved and activated his contacts within Whitehall to resist. Willie prevailed. Interviewed by Ingham's unauthorised biographer, he revealed far more of his mood at the time than he had done in his own memoirs: 'I was in a fairly powerful position because I didn't want to come back anyway.'[15]

McDowall was soon reporting relevant gossip to his boss. Within a few days of Willie's appointment he learned that there had been a top-level meeting on the miners' dispute between the Prime Minister and senior civil servants. Whitelaw immediately telephoned Robert Armstrong to find out what, if anything, had been decided; understandably he also wanted to know why he had not been invited to the meeting. According to his own account, he received an ambiguous response. So he rang Heath, and found himself pleading with the Prime Minister, 'Tell me what you want me to do with this department. Do you want me to settle, or do you want war?' As he remembered years later, there was 'no reply of any clarity'.[16]

Given his fatigue, and the fact that he had never wanted this particular job, Willie would have been justified in threatening resignation in response to this bizarre state of affairs – whatever the reason for Heath's evasiveness. It seems that he did not do so, presumably because Heath would have thought he was bluffing. No one with Willie's sense of duty would have dreamed of rocking a boat that was already holed in so many places; these were precisely the arguments that he had already used in persuading Peter Walker to stay in office. Ever since March 1972 Willie had been soldiering on in the face of political setbacks and grave personal inconvenience; even before the unsatisfactory telephone exchanges he must have known that there would be no relief for him, at least until a general election.

Willie was right to feel excluded from policy-making in his own field, but his clear suggestion that jealousy was the main cause only underlines the extent to which he and his leader had moved apart over the last few months. To some extent, at least, the allegation must reflect the constant war of denigration conducted against Heath by admirers of Margaret Thatcher, up to and beyond the time when Willie wrote his memoirs. Significantly, the 'jealousy' thesis seems to have been most common in 1973 among right-wing and Euro-sceptic Tory MPs who claimed that Heath was trying to do to Willie what King David did to Uriah the Hittite – give him a job in which he was bound to fail.[17] This was a ridiculous fantasy, since failure for Willie was likely to result in the fall of Heath's government. In later years Heath might have envied Margaret Thatcher, at least in so far as she seemed to have been granted all of the political good luck that had been denied to her predecessor. But the famous feud between them owed far more to her own feelings about the man who was the clear choice of party activists at the time of their leadership battle, and whose popularity among the electorate as a whole tended to grow whenever she fell out of favour. In any case, Heath's consistent opposition to 'Thatcherite' measures was rooted in the 'One Nation' principles which had always guided his conduct. And even if Heath was jealous of Thatcher, who supplanted him as leader, there was no reason for him to nurse the same kind of grievance against Willie, who had always made clear his willingness to act as Heath's deputy. True, even before Willie's recall there were rumours that he would soon replace Heath as Conservative leader, and either become Prime Minister himself or join a coalition and offer that post to Labour's Jim Callaghan. But it seems that the original source of this speculation was John Silkin, Labour's Chief Whip; and if he ever heard of it himself, Heath must have known that Willie would not have cooperated with such a scheme.[18]

A far more plausible explanation for Willie's difficulties at Employment is that by December 1973 Heath's approach to governing had changed. Always a problem-solver rather than an ideologue, he now found it difficult to delegate in any of the key areas of government activity. His innate desire to assume complete control of any operation that deserved his attention was abetted by Sir William Armstrong, who had become Cabinet Secretary in place of Burke Trend. By December 1973 Armstrong was playing the role that formerly belonged to Willie; disastrously for a civil servant, he tried to act as a political adviser to the Prime Minister instead of restricting himself to administrative matters. In the end the pressure proved too great for Armstrong, who suffered a spectacular nervous breakdown just before Heath called the election of February 1974. The first symptom of his illness had been an apocalyptic outburst about the future of the country. When his collapse was reported, some began to wonder whether they had ever been right to listen to his advice, because the tone of his remarks had been unduly pessimistic for some time and might have led them to regard the unions more harshly than they would otherwise have done. But by then it was too late to correct any damage.[19]

Evidently Willie had expected to resume his place at Heath's right hand when he left Belfast. Instead he found there was no room for him at the top table. In the absence of clear directions from Heath, his only option was to work as a freelance. If he could negotiate a satisfactory deal with the miners, Heath would have to accept it, and the country would avoid what Willie rightly felt would be a disastrous all-out strike. To this end he arranged to meet Joe Gormley in a private room at Brown's Hotel on Dover Street in London. According to Gormley, Willie 'listened, I thought, with sympathy' as he rehearsed his members' case; in fact, Gormley was disappointed that the great peace-maker had nothing concrete to offer. Willie was behaving as if he was still in Northern Ireland; after so many months of being talked at he could be forgiven for assuming that Gormley would be satisfied with a one-sided conversation. Throughout his period at Employment he had to guard his own tongue in case he committed himself to anything that would be disowned by his colleagues. For Gormley this first impression was crucial; clearly Willie was not the organ-grinder, but he seemed no more convincing in the part of the monkey than Maurice Macmillan had been.[20]

On 20 December Gormley went to St James' Square for more formal talks, accompanied by his colleagues, McGahey and Lawrence Daly. Willie already admired the pragmatic Gormley, and found Daly 'agreeable'. But having left one type of irrational unionist in Belfast, Willie encountered another in the shape of Mick McGahey. As Willie recorded in his memoirs, 'he regarded me as a representative of the wicked coal owners and treated me as such in any formal discussions'. This was slightly disingenuous, since Willie had certainly benefited financially from the coal extracted from his Gartshore estate. But this had little to do with the situation in 1973. Presumably McGahey did not know that Willie's knowledge of local conditions had inspired him to argue against the closure of Upper Clyde Shipbuilders in the early months of the Heath Government. Even if he did, McGahey's class-based view of the world would have contorted Willie's stand into some 'bosses' conspiracy. The pair did break the ice to some extent, but Willie could guess that McGahey would prove inflexible – and he, rather than Gormley, represented the current mood of the NUM.[21]

Although Willie had only been at Employment for just over a fortnight, his reputation had been tarnished even before this first exposure to the NUM executive. He had met TUC representatives on the day that Heath announced the three-day week, without warning them of the government's intentions. Heath's decision outraged trade unionists, and threatened to drive a wedge between the miners and other workers who looked certain to find themselves out of pocket, if not out of work, because of the restrictions. Had the meeting of 20 December proceeded according to plan it might have produced nothing, but thanks to Willie's old Provo foes there was a last-minute change of venue. A Christmas bombing campaign was under way, and it was reported that a device had been planted in the building. So, as Gormley remembered, 'we all went outside and stood in the street for a bit, and then the lot of us decided to go off to a nearby Italian restaurant'. Once the beer had been served Gormley decided to play 'what I felt was my final card'. He explained to Willie that the miners could be made a special case after all. Unlike other workers, they had to have a bath after every shift because 'The dust gets right into your skin, and you get bloody filthy'. There was also some delay at the start of the shift, as miners changed and waited for a lift down to the coal face. At present, the miners were not paid for this. The case for a special allowance seemed powerful, and Gormley rightly sensed that Willie saw it as a likely solution. He left the restaurant in a confident mood.[22]

Gormley's optimism outlasted the effects of the beer, but not for long. On the following day he visited Harold Wilson and disclosed the possibility of a deal. The Opposition leader had proved reliable over Northern Ireland, but there could be no question of cross-party cooperation on industrial matters. Gormley never forgot (or forgave) Wilson's response: 'Oh! Well, of course, Joe, you do realise you're pulling the Tory Government's irons out of the fire for them?' Apparently in the Italian restaurant this thought had not even occurred to Mick McGahey, for all his desire to bring down the government. Gormley left Wilson with deep misgivings, which proved well founded that afternoon, when the latter informed the Commons of the 'waiting and bathing' idea as if it were his own. In his memoirs Willie recorded his fury at what he regarded as a cynical breach of 'the old conventions of confidentiality within parties'.[23]

The usual story is that Wilson's intervention was in itself sufficient to ensure that 'waiting and bathing' ceased to be an option. Certainly it was rejected by the Pay Board soon afterwards. Yet there is still a mystery here. Wilson had obviously caught wind of rumours that a faction within the government was pressing for a general election. Since his opinion of Willie – which had been high enough even before 1970 – had increased because of events in Northern Ireland, he had probably been expecting to hear of an early breakthrough, and prepared his tactics accordingly. When he claimed the 'waiting and bathing' idea for himself, he was not hoping to scupper the deal entirely; rather, he wanted to grab the credit for easing the fuel crisis, instead of allowing the government to go to the country bragging of its own success. In short, if the government had really wanted to end the miners' dispute it still could have done so; only narrow electoral considerations made the deal impossible. But the official propaganda was stressing that the nation faced a grave crisis. The response to Wilson's tactic revealed that some ministers were far more concerned about the future of the Conservative Party.

In this atmosphere union leaders could only regard Willie either as a typical agent of his party or as an *ingénue* who could not be trusted to deliver. But he continued to talk to the NUM and the TUC in the hope of finding a settlement. As far as the miners were concerned, he had little to offer, and on 9 January 1974 he could only suggest that if the NUM accepted the latest package there would be an inquiry into the future of the industry, with special emphasis on pay and conditions. Perhaps he hoped that the NUM would remember the last inquiry, under Lord Wilberforce, which had resulted in excessive generosity. If so he was to be disappointed; his offer was rejected. But he was encouraged by the fact that the TUC was rattled by the three-day week; indeed, Len Murray thought that Heath had the trade-union movement 'over a barrel'. At the regular meeting of the NEDC, held at Millbank on the same day, Murray made a dramatic attempt to break the deadlock, pledging that if the miners were made a special case, no other union would try to exploit the breach of the official pay guidelines.

Accounts differ over what happened next. Unfortunately for Willie he was not at the NEDC meeting, having been assured that the miners' dispute was not on the agenda. As Chancellor, Tony Barber was in the chair, and it fell to him to give the government's reaction. Some say that he left the meeting to telephone Heath; others that he spoke without the Prime Minister's authority. But all agree that his response was negative, and no one has suggested that Willie was consulted, despite the fact that before his appointment he had told Barber 'I must have charge of the industrial relations activities of the nationalised industries' and had asked to be nominated as Deputy Chairman of the NEDC. Significantly, Barber chose not to mention the incident in his memoirs. In his own autobiography Willie merely trotted out the only conceivable justification for Barber's action: that 'there was serious doubt about the TUC's ability to influence the miners in any settlement or to contain other unions'. But on the following page he resorted to his technique of coded criticism: 'perhaps mistakenly, I still obstinately held to the view that the TUC leaders at the meetings were totally genuine in their determination to make a real effort to hold the line'. In fact, the most powerful union leaders – Jack Jones of the Transport Workers and Hugh Scanlon of the Engineers – offered private reassurances, and Tom Jackson of the Communications Union was keeping the government closely informed of the mood within the TUC. Unfortunately for Willie, others who were closer to Heath at the time were equally 'determined' – to hold the unions responsible for the national crisis, and to use this as their trump card in a snap general election. For Willie it was destabilising enough that these arguments were being aired behind closed doors, but the Cabinet 'hawks' had no hesitation in dropping heavy public hints. So during the meeting between Willie and the NUM on 9 January, the atmosphere was soured from the outset because Lord Carrington had just briefed the press with comments that seemed to preclude any further negotiations.[24]

Some in the 'hawk' camp belatedly realised that Murray's suggestion had presented the government with a further tactical opportunity. If they had taken the TUC at their word, and other unions had still insisted on pressing for a deal outside the terms of Phase 3, it would have made life even more difficult for the Labour Party and brought severe discredit on the union movement as a whole. If Willie had shared this view at the time, and had pressed the argument on Heath, he might have won his battle outright. But his experience in Northern Ireland had taught him that tactical manoeuvres were justifiable only if they led to a constructive end; and once he realised that people close to Heath were agitating for an election, he could only wonder what their ultimate goal might be. Was it simply to secure another victory over Labour? If so, the Conservatives would still have to deal with the miners once they had won. It had been possible for Stanley Baldwin to show a degree of magnanimity after the defeat of the General Strike in 1926, but if the Tories were to ask the people to vote against the union movement in a general election, the situation would be far more complicated. Central Office officials had already warned the government that 'single issue' elections generally ended in tears.[25]

As election talk gripped a section of the party over the first few weeks of 1974, no one in the feverish faction ever gave a tenable answer to Willie's question. At best, the hawks could point out that the economic indicators were all poor, and that the electoral outlook would only deteriorate over time; but this in itself was a serious indictment of Conservative rule since June 1970, and implied that the party did not deserve to be re-elected. There was another justification for a tough line, but this never reached the public. The oil shortage was sure to ease before long; and at that point the miners would lose their awesome bargaining power. Once the election was won, a government endorsed by the public could settle the dispute well within the terms of Phase 3. The problem for the hawks was that their strategy for winning the election depended on the maintenance of a crisis atmosphere. If they had spelled out their real intentions, the excuse for an early poll would disappear and they would never receive their vote of confidence from the public.

At least the hawks were working to a clear timetable. They had identified 7 February as the best day for an election. Soon after this a new electoral register would be introduced, helping Labour, because the Tories had always been better at keeping track of their supporters, arranging postal votes, and so on. Since Heath would have to ask the Queen to dissolve Parliament three weeks before the poll, a decision had to be reached by Thursday 17 January. With hindsight, Willie was inclined to blame Heath for not acting to dampen down speculation in advance of this date.[26] But although the issues seemed clear-cut to the warring factions, for Heath himself the dilemma was agonising. Since Labour had adopted an anti-European stance, defeat in an election threatened to destroy his most cherished achievement. Under these circumstances the temptation to cut and run must have been considerable, with the opinion polls currently showing a narrow Conservative lead.

On 11 January it seemed that the hawks had won; the Prime Minister set the Central Office machinery rolling towards an early election. At Chequers on Saturday 12 he discussed the situation with a group of advisers who supported the hawkish line. But the following day a further meeting with party officials brought to light some practical obstacles to a 7 February poll; according to his biographer, Heath 'seized gratefully' on these points. In the evening he listened while Willie and Carr fought against Carrington, Barber and Prior. By this time he also knew that Pym was fiercely opposed to an early election, rightly fearing that the results in Ulster would be disastrous for the peace process. This factor also weighed heavily on Willie. The meeting ended in deadlock.[27]

Jim Prior thought that the 'doves' were hopelessly outnumbered, and as Deputy Chairman of the party he felt confident that he had gauged the mood both at the grass roots and at Central Office. His supporters had also been worrying away at Heath since before Christmas, when Willie was oblivious to their activities. But from the beginning of his long association with Heath Willie had known that his friend disliked being pressurised into decisions, and this insight gave him a decisive advantage.[28] At the crucial moment the hawks took their eye off the ball. One of their number should have kept Heath occupied on the evening of 16 January, when he would have to make his fateful decision. His PPS, Tim Kitson, assured Carrington that the Prime Minister planned to spend those hours at home. Probably thinking he had won the battle already, Carrington was satisfied with this news. But when his back was turned Willie whisked Heath off for a dinner tête-à-tête. This was at least the fifth occasion on which Willie had tried to persuade his leader; on previous occasions, when Willie had asked 'What happens if we lose?', Heath had retorted, 'We won't lose.' But this time the message filtered through. As Kitson recalled, 'Things seemed to change round' after that furtive meal. The deadline passed without an announcement. Despite the importance of the issues at stake, discussions had been amicable up to this point. Now the tension boiled over, albeit briefly. The frustrated Prior rushed round to Number 10 to tell Heath that Labour MPs were celebrating their reprieve; in return, the Prime Minister angrily accused him of trying to force his hand by stoking up expectations within the party.[29]

Willie might have won this round, but unlike the Labour MPs he was in no mood for celebration. If he had thought that a deal was impossible with the miners, he would probably have sided with the hawks, however reluctantly. But he did think the dispute could be solved. Inevitably, since many within his party thought the government should never repeat the 'sell-out' of 1972, his position left him open to accusations of appeasement. During one debate he took the trouble to answer this at length:

Of course, any Minister in my job has the task of seeking to resolve industrial disputes in the best interests of the nation. Certainly he must pursue the course of conciliation. But if conciliation is meant to imply plain weakness or lack of resolution, then I reject that view as decisively as did all my predecessors . . .

All Governments and all my predecessors have on occasion found it necessary to point out that conceding some claim pursued through industrial action would, in the view of the Government of the day,

(*Left*) 'A loss in one's life that can never be replaced': baby Willie with his mother and his ill-fated father, 1918.

(*Below*) A lonely boy, on the beach at Nairn, *c.* 1921.

(*Left*) Willie as a Cambridge undergraduate, *c.* 1937.

(*Above*) Willie playing in the victorious Cambridge golf team against Oxford, Westward Ho!, 1938.

(*Above left*) Willie and Celia Sprot, an engagement photograph, 1942.
(*Above right*) The celebratory cigar, May 1945.
(*Below*) The Whitelaw family outside the house at Gartshore.

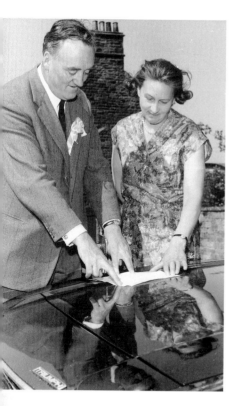

(*Left*) Willie canvassing in the 1966 general election.

(*Above*) The Secretary of State for Northern Ireland inspects the Second Battalion, the Parachute Regiment, at Girdwood Park, Belfast, 1972.

(*Below*) 'The most terrible problem…' : Edward Heath and his Secretary of State for Northern Ireland at the Conservative Party Conference, October 1972.

(*Above*) 'Feeding the Leviathan': the unstoppable Whitelaw canvassing technique, deployed in Bayswater, London, during the campaign for the October 1974 general election.

(*Below*) Willie and Margaret Thatcher express their 'full-hearted consent' to Europe, 1975.

(*Above*) Caught in the crossfire: Willie welcomes a conciliatory speech from his old leader, Brighton, October 1976.

(*Below*) The Home Secretary takes aim in East Yorkshire, 1980.

(*Above*) Willie and Metropolitan Police
Commissioner Sir David McNee (striped tie)
risk a visit to riot-torn Brixton, 12 April 1981.
(*Right*) The annual ordeal: Willie faces
demands for the return of capital punishment
at the 1981 Conservative Party Conference.

(*Above*) A rare glimpse of the Cabinet room, 1985.

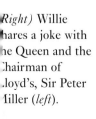

Right) Willie
hares a joke with
he Queen and the
Chairman of
Lloyd's, Sir Peter
Miller (*left*).

(*Opposite page, below*) The Prime Minister and her disunited team present the 1983
Conservative manifesto: (*front*) Margaret Thatcher, Willie (*left*) and Party Chairman
Cecil Parkinson (*right*); (*behind, left to right*) Norman Tebbit, Employment Secretary;
Geoffrey Howe, Chancellor of the Exchequer; Francis Pym, Foreign Secretary; Michael
Heseltine, Defence Secretary; and Tom King, Environment Secretary.

(*Left*) 'The sharpest loss the Prime Minister has suffered': Willie and Celia face the cameras at Ennim after Willie's resignation, January 1988.

(*Above*) Lord Tebbit poses with two Willie look-alikes on a family holiday in Portugal.

(*Below*) Three Whitelaw generations at Ennim: Celia and Willie with their daughter (*from left to right*) Mary, Carol, Susan and Pamela, and grandchildren.

damage the national interest. It always has been easy to buy industrial peace in the short term at a considerable price. If that price is so high as to cause real damage to the country in the long run, through a severe twist to the inflationary spiral, then quiet firmness and determination backed by reason must be right and should be supported by all sides of the House.[30]

It was very well put; and the official minutes of meetings with the TUC prove that Willie had no intention of repeating the 'surrender' of March 1972. But coming after his experience in Northern Ireland, his attitude during the miners' strike created the impression with some of his colleagues and the wider public that he was a natural 'appeaser'. For a 'One Nation' Conservative such a word is wholly out of place in domestic matters; the central plank of the creed is that differences within the country can never be so great as to demand that one side to a quarrel must abandon all principle in order to reach agreement. But in one regrettable respect there *was* a parallel between Willie's situation and that of Neville Chamberlain. Whenever the latter made what he thought would be a clinching concession, his opposite number raised the stakes. Intoxicated by their sudden position of power, the miners were now emulating Hitler's form of brinkmanship.

Originally Willie thought that the real problem was obstruction on the part of his colleagues. Secret canvassing for support was out of the question; as he later recalled, the Heath Cabinet did not operate like that. His hopes were now pinned on another piece of bureaucratic lumber, a Pay Board report into the relative effect of a statutory incomes policy on different groups of workers. It opened up the possibility that the government could refer the NUM case to a Relativities Board, which would be encouraged to make the helpful discovery that the miners had been adversely affected by wage controls and now deserved a bumper pay increase. Crucially, the ensuing deal could be presented as falling within Phase 3.[31]

But before the report was published Willie received a devastating blow, this time from the miners he had been hoping to conciliate. On 23 January the NUM executive called a ballot on an all-out strike. With hindsight, Willie accused himself of a serious blunder in not making more of the Relativities Report. There was, as he recognised, a problem in using this machinery during a national crisis. An objective procedure was required, rather than decisions based on 'sheer trials of strength'. At first his department's press briefings played down the report. But Willie soon realised that the difficulties might be overcome, perhaps by backdating any offer to March 1973 – the time of the last, modest pay increase for the miners. Refused permission by his colleagues, he tried to muster support from elsewhere. In the House of

Commons on 27 January Labour's Barbara Castle was startled to see Willie 'gesticulating at me frantically'. As she rightly surmised, he wanted her help in 'some game in Cabinet'; he was prompting her to make a point about Relativities which he felt unable to raise himself. The peculiar double-act had begun during a debate of 10 January on the three-day week; after Willie had anticipated that the report 'will indicate a significant way of settling these problems in the future', Castle had intervened to support him. Even if Willie did fail properly to exploit the opportunity presented by the report, Heath made up for the deficiency, referring to the idea on the *Panorama* programme and backing up the hint in the Commons. But the miners were no longer listening. On 4 February the official declaration of hostilities was delivered; 81 per cent of NUM members had voted for a strike.[32]

The doves were badly winged by the miners' ballot – Willie's officials had been convinced there would never be an all-out strike, because the mood in the coalfields seemed far less militant than it had been in 1972 – but they were determined to struggle on. Pym flew over from Belfast to repeat his warnings about the likely effect of an election in Northern Ireland. On cue, the day of the miners' ballot result also saw the murder by the Provos of twelve people, blown up in a coach on the M62. Pym also argued that the country already supported the government; the fact that production had hardly decreased despite the restrictions on working hours seemed to prove the point. Subjecting the public to a general election at such a time might dissipate existing goodwill; it was most unlikely to make voters feel better disposed towards the government. Cool reflection might have convinced the hawks that the best chance of winning the election had vanished when Willie took Heath out to dinner on 16 January, but they pressed on regardless. On 6 February Prior told journalists that 'the miners have had their ballot, perhaps we ought to have ours'. Carrington raised the temperature still further by revealing that if the miners were offered more money he would resign, along with Prior and Barber; he also thought (rightly or wrongly) that Willie would step down if he was prevented from improving the current deal.[33]

No one seemed to consider that holding an election now would give the party the worst of both worlds – it would be too late for the government's supporters, and still far too early to stifle criticism from diehard opponents like Enoch Powell. By this time, the chief dove had also switched to auto-pilot. Willie asked the NUM executive to see him yet again on the morning of 7 February, but it was clear to all concerned that he would have nothing new to offer. He and Pym had already bowed to the inevitable, accepting the case for an election on the evening of 6 February. Heath was granted permission to dissolve Parliament for an election on 28 February. Whether or not they knew of this decision – which was not made public until the following day – the

NUM executive proceeded to endorse it by declining to meet Willie, claiming with unnecessary rudeness that they were too busy. Gormley announced that his members would stop work two days later.

Thus Willie found himself 'swept into an election campaign which I dreaded', yoked in the battle with colleagues who – for all their underlying warmth and respect – had been bickering constantly for several weeks. Despite his forebodings and his fatigue, he summoned the energy for 'a massive speaking campaign all over the country'. Adrenaline carried him from Dover to Manchester, from the North-East of England to the Midlands, then into Scotland. His message was typified by his contribution to a party political broadcast of 14 February, which he opened with a familiar statement of personal commitment: 'Perhaps I'm old-fashioned but I was brought up to believe that because you were lucky enough to be born in a free country – and thank heaven, this still is a free country – if you ever found yourself in a position of any authority, then the price of that authority was a thing called responsibility.'[34]

To underline his 'One Nation' theme, he contrasted the strength of the unions with the vulnerability of 'people who don't have a powerful organisation to protect them'. Despite his own doubts, he claimed that the government was not seeking re-election just to cling onto power: unlike Harold Wilson in 1970, '*we* have a cause. *We* are most definitely fighting for something.' But the government was not fighting against the miners; instead it was trying to defend the weak from 'the sleeping sickness of inflation'. Thus Willie distanced himself from those who presented the election as a straight choice between an elected government and the 'overmighty' unions. Yet he was obviously referring to the militants in the NUM when he warned against 'allowing extremists to divide us as a nation'. The problem of combining an appeal for the whole population to 'stand by each other' with a partisan attempt to denigrate the Labour Party was emphasised by the closing images of the broadcast, which featured 'a Wilson puppet spewing forth cash for the miners, nationalisation and food subsidies'.[35]

At the beginning of the campaign Willie had referred the miners' case to the Relativities Board after all. Some have seen this as a serious mistake; the hawkish Alec Home went so far as to describe it as an 'oversight', although he knew very well that it had been entirely deliberate. In fact it was perfectly sensible; by continuing the search for a settlement with the miners, Willie was reinforcing his own message that the election should not be seen as a referendum on the conduct of the unions. On the day the election was called, both Robert Carr and Geoffrey Howe independently pressed this argument on Heath. The real problem lay in the board's preliminary findings, which were published on 21 February. These indicated that miners' wages had been calculated on the wrong basis, and that in real terms they were earning 8 per cent less than the average worker in the manufacturing sector. In fact these figures were themselves misleading, because they took no account of miners' perks such as free coal. But the news was startling enough to invigorate Harold Wilson, who had previously been fighting the campaign like a man who expects to lose and welcomes the prospect of defeat.[36]

Willie was in Birmingham when the news broke.[37] The following morning he began a journey by train up to Scotland; his assistant Robert Jackson had to disembark at every station to find out the latest news. The rest of the day was occupied with a series of meetings, ending in Selkirk, where Willie stuck to his prepared text and called for a decisive mandate from the people because 'A Government based on a weak Parliamentary situation and only formed after some weak compromise would be a complete disaster'. The speech reflected well-founded anxieties at Central Office that the contest would be close; had the result gone the other way, it would have provided Labour with some irresistible quotes. His work done for the day, Willie drove the eighty miles home to Ennim, where he arrived 'exhausted and utterly miserable'. Typically, although he knew he was not to blame for the incident, he could not suppress that feeling of responsibility which he had just identified as the inevitable price of authority. He felt the same way after a new disaster, just two days before the election, when the CBI Director-General Campbell Adamson made some unguarded remarks about the need to reform the Industrial Relations Act. As Employment Secretary, Willie was now responsible for that ill-starred legislation; and as Leader of the House he had played a key role in enacting it.

The Pay Board story is often cited as the single most important reason for the Conservative defeat. But during the campaign itself Willie soon bounced back. David Butler thought he seemed ebullient when he met him at Oxford Station on the day of the Adamson gaffe. Willie mentioned his (well-founded) worries about the Moray and Nairn constituency; clearly his mother had been taking soundings and discovering that the Scottish National Party was making progress there. But otherwise he thought the outlook was very bright. The miners' strike had continued, but there had been none of the mass picketing which had marked the 1972 dispute. He had been seriously heckled on one occasion, when during a speech in Warwickshire a group of miners shouted 'Send him back to Ireland' and shook their pay packets at him. But before he boarded his London train he told Butler that it had been a quiet campaign on the whole. He was tempting fate; that evening, in Maida Vale, he was threatened by some Irish Republican sympathisers. Since Willie had no bodyguard for the election campaign, the police had to be called.[38]

Butler's snapshot might be squared with the account in Willie's memoirs, where he wrote that throughout the campaign he had to fight against defeatism 'and maintain an outward impression of high morale and confidence in victory'. Yet it seems more compatible with the further interview he gave Butler after the election, when he admitted that he had misread the public mood. The second week of the campaign had certainly been bad, but his optimism had revived over the last few days. In contrast to 1970, this mood had been shared by most of his colleagues. Afterwards, when assessing the reasons for the result, Willie made no mention of the Relativities Report; nor did he allude to the antics of his *bête noire* Enoch Powell, who had advised his supporters to vote Labour. Instead, he was exercised by a broadcast delivered on 19 February by Barber, who had been condemned by some newspapers for his confrontational tone. This blunder seemed particularly gratuitous to Willie, since Barber had already decided to leave politics and had played an important part in thwarting Willie's efforts at conciliation.[39]

Eight months later Powell was elected as the Ulster Unionist MP for South Down. Before Direct Rule this step would have meant that he would take the Conservative whip, but the death of this arrangement was confirmed in the immediate aftermath of the February election, in the most dramatic fashion. Eleven of the twelve Ulster seats were won by unionist candidates. This was par for the course; but this time the eleven included both William Craig and Ian Paisley, who had fought in alliance with the 'Official' unionists on a platform of intransigent opposition to all that Willie had achieved. Faulkner was still Chief Executive at Stormont, but he had resigned from his party after finally losing control. According to one (admittedly jaundiced) source, Willie had declared during his time in Northern Ireland that he hoped to 'smash' the Unionist Party. If so, he had succeeded, but the shattered fragments had reassembled themselves in a most disagreeable way.[40]

When all the votes had been counted in the general election, those eleven Ulster MPs became the main focus of attention, along with the fourteen Liberals. Labour had been returned as the largest party at Westminster by just four seats (301, to 297 Conservatives). Some thought that although no one had really won the election, Heath had certainly lost it. Yet the Tories had been clear winners in terms of the popular vote, beating Labour by around a quarter of a million. Heath had no reason to leave Downing Street until he had exhausted every possibility of forming a majority government. Given their historical link with the Conservative Party, it was inevitable that he should approach the unionists; but he could only bring himself to offer the whip to the seven MPs who would not normally have allied themselves with Paisley. They replied that they would only cooperate if new Assembly elections were held, and since this would make power-sharing unworkable there could be no deal on these terms. It must have been a relief for Willie; had the unionists wrung any concessions out of Heath, he might have felt compelled to offer his resignation. Ironically, Paisley told Cecil King that he 'would welcome Whitelaw as the new PM' if the Liberals demanded Heath's head as the price of their cooperation.[41] Eventually Heath failed to secure any support from the Liberals either, and on 4 March he resigned. It was the end of his ministerial career.

Normally Willie would have been expected to take a prominent part in negotiations with other parties. But at the crucial time he was ill in bed, having collapsed after his traditional eve-of-poll dash through the constituency and woken up on the morning of the count feeling 'desperately ill' and with a high temperature. With medical help he managed to deliver 'a perfectly rational speech' after his result was declared, and went on to give an interview to Robin Day. He offered his opinion that since Labour appeared to have secured the most seats, they should be considered as having won the election. Thus Heath's negotiations were undermined by his old ally before they had started in earnest. Although Willie later considered that he would not have spoken so openly had he been feeling fit and well, it was not simply a case of the drugs talking. During the campaign he had said that a narrow victory for any party would be disastrous; it would be even worse for a party which had technically lost to try to patch together an administration. The following day he learned that his comments had caused a stir, and that Heath wanted him to fly down to London for discussions. Fortunately his doctor ordered him to stay in bed for the weekend. He only managed to struggle down to London in time to attend the two Cabinets of Monday 4 March, which were merely formal occasions to register the failure of negotiations with the Liberals. Later he revealed that he had been opposed to a last-ditch idea of asking the House of Commons for a vote of confidence in the absence of a pact with any other grouping. This, he felt, should be the prerogative of the party that had won the most seats.[42]

Even if he had been in his usual robust health throughout these days, Willie would have been forgiven for feeling dazed. Only three months earlier he had been receiving the praise of press and politicians on the steps of Stormont Castle. Now he and his colleagues had been dismissed by the electorate; and despite the hair's-breadth verdict, it soon emerged that it had been a strangely decisive election. In part this reflected the position of Heath himself. All observers agreed that he had performed even better this time than in the 1970 campaign. But it was his second defeat in three attempts as Tory leader – not an enviable record in a party that prides itself on its aptitude for government. Almost everyone regarded Willie as the natural successor, and the result in Penrith and the Border served as additional proof of his personal success. He received more than 60 per cent of the vote – 10 per cent more than he could have expected if his constituents had duplicated the national trend. Business had kept him away from Penrith and the Border for most of the preceding two years, but the population had obviously followed his deeds at a distance, with growing admiration. On the day before the poll his Labour opponent had complained, 'There seems to be a "Willie" cult in Penrith, people have forgotten that he is a Tory.' The 'cult' was not confined to Penrith. Even the angry miners who had tried to shout him down ended up shaking his hand; when he entered a pub full of strikers in Leicestershire he was visibly embarrassed as they acknowledged that he would never have called an election under such conditions, and toasted him as the Tory leader-in-waiting.[43]

Yet for Willie there could be no compensation in a feeling of quiet satisfaction at his own performance. There were too many unanswered questions. If he had come home sooner, could he have defused the miners' strike? Alternatively, if he had stayed on in Northern Ireland, might he have saved Faulkner? In the light of subsequent events, he asked himself whether he could have rescued his work in Northern Ireland from oblivion if he had persuaded Heath to hold out until the government ran through its allotted term of office. But there was another nagging doubt. In arguing so strongly against a poll on 7 February, had he condemned his party to an avoidable defeat – with all that was to entail, both for his leader and for his natural allies? For some within the party, this was the only question that mattered; and they tended to think that Willie should bear the heaviest responsibility for the events of January and February 1974. In his memoirs Willie leaves these enemies unnamed, describing them only as 'mischief-makers'. They certainly did not include Carrington, with whom friendly relations were restored. But Willie had built his career on his talent for friendship and a reputation for sound judgement. For his own part he could stick to his view that one should never look back. But it was bad enough to know that in the future he would have to work with colleagues who regarded him as a man who had given bad advice, and who could not help wondering whether he had done so for his own advancement.[44]

CHAPTER II

THE POISONED CHALICE

Thirteen months after Heath left Downing Street Labour was still in office, despite a precarious position in Parliament, and Willie's status within his own party had been officially recognised with the title of Deputy Leader. But for him the intervening period had been one of almost unrelieved misery. In his memoirs he describes the destruction of his Northern Ireland settlement by a loyalist-inspired strike in May 1974 as 'the greatest disappointment of my political career'. It was scant consolation that this was soon to be rivalled by other serious setbacks. Only Edward Heath endured more misfortune at this time, both personal and political.[1] The events between February 1974 and March 1975 determined the future political careers of both men; they also set the pattern of British politics for a generation.

For Heath and Willie the February result had been the worst imaginable. The fact that Heath had run through all his options before leaving Downing Street provided the first suggestion that he might be a 'bad loser'. Had the outcome been more conclusive – as it was in 1966 – his actions would have been very different. Presumably after a dignified acceptance of defeat he would have been persuaded (however reluctantly) to step down. As it was, he did float the idea of a leadership contest. It was reported that more than 100 MPs had told the whips there should be a change. But Wilson could call a general election at any time – as he had been able to do after the 1964 election – and once the first shock of defeat had worn off, the restive backbenchers saw the logic of keeping things as they were. When Heath met the 1922 Committee the only MP who argued for a change was shouted down. The leadership contest idea died away. Yet at best this meant that a sizeable proportion of the parliamentary party was willing to accept the status quo as the least bad option. Loyalty was alleged to be the secret weapon of the Conservative Party, but it was difficult to feel much of this emotion towards a leader whose execution has merely been deferred to a more suitable occasion.[2]

Unfortunately the same considerations that settled the leadership issue in the short term pointed to continuity in other respects. Heath was forced to act like a football manager whose team has narrowly lost the first leg of a cup tie, and who finds that his opponent is allowed to write his own rules for the rematch. Wilson could choose the moment when his own squad was at its peak; and in the 1966 contest he had used this advantage to deadly effect. But Heath had no time to change personnel or tactics before the second bout. It seemed futile to embark on a major policy review, or to conduct a far-reaching reshuffle; even if this had seemed prudent, senior members of the Shadow Cabinet were tired and depressed as the consequences of the defeat sank in. So Willie now 'shadowed' his successor at Employment, Michael Foot, and although Alec Home had signalled an imminent retirement from the front bench, he still covered Foreign Affairs. Peter Carrington was anxious to step down as Party Chairman, but he was asked to stay on in case Wilson appealed to the country before a new regime had bedded in at Central Office.

Yet the parallel with 1964–6 was inexact. This time, theoretically, the government could be brought down before it had achieved anything at all, if only the Conservatives could persuade all the opposition parties to vote against the legislative programme announced in the Queen's Speech. In the Shadow Cabinet this argument was pressed on Heath by Maurice Macmillan, who was backed by his father. The Macmillans imagined that if Wilson were defeated on this crucial vote, the Queen could send for Heath, to have another crack at forming a government. Their opponents argued that Wilson would be sure to ask for a dissolution, and pointed out that no monarch had denied this request for 150 years. In those circumstances, they reasoned, Labour would be certain to win an overwhelming majority. But given the apparent inevitability of defeat whenever the election might be called, it could have been worthwhile precipitating an immediate contest; Labour's reckless policy platform might have been subjected to more damaging scrutiny second time around, and even if the Tories had been trounced they would have been granted a lengthy period in which to refresh their team and rethink their policies.

In the immediate aftermath of the election Robert Carr had put forward this idea, adding the point that the public might blame Wilson for the inconvenience of another election and punish Labour. But once this dangerous gamble had been rejected, it seems that no one had the energy to revive it. Instead, Heath listened to the arguments of both sides and made the wrong decision. Having believed in his policy of statutory wage restraint, he was not prepared to let Labour drop it without a challenge. An amendment to the Queen's Speech was tabled, criticising the new government's decision to abandon Phase 3. For a time it looked as if this would attract decisive support; the Liberals, who evidently felt they would benefit from a new election at a time when both of their main rivals were unpopular, said that they would vote with the Tories. But this prospect merely exposed the eccentricity of Heath's decision, because some members of his own party were now ready to abandon a statutory policy which they had always disliked. Up to forty MPs indicated that they would abstain. As Heath's biographer remarks, in the circumstances it was fortunate that Foot decided to bow to the terms of the critical amendment, indicating that the government would keep Phase 3 for the time being. It fell to Willie to withdraw the amendment, which concerned his own area of responsibility. The damage could have been worse, but even so John Campbell describes it as 'a humiliating shambles'.[3]

Willie was no longer Chief Whip, of course, but even if the issue had not concerned employment policy he might have been expected to take a leading role in the tactical discussions. Yet Ian Gilmour, who fielded the best-researched arguments against the Macmillans, kept a detailed dairy for these few days – and Willie is hardly mentioned. It seems unlikely that he exerted any influence over Heath, even in private; had he done so he would surely have argued strongly against the line that was taken, since in discussions immediately after the election he had warned that the party should not try to be 'too clever'.

Probably Willie had decided to stand back from the arguments because of gossip about his own future. Having accepted that the Conservatives were almost certain to lose the next election, he knew he was regarded as Heath's natural successor. On the night of the election he had been in a bad mood, even allowing for his illness; it seemed to Robert Jackson, who spent the evening at Ennim, that Willie's 'stamper' was induced by the thought that he would be asked to clear up the mess left by the misguided decision to go to the country. Whether his advice during the miners' crisis had been right or wrong, it had inspired speculation about his motives; and the same was certain to happen again if he came down forcefully on one side or another in this new debate. So he kept his own counsel.[4]

Unfortunately for Willie, the gossip was now so prevalent that even his silence during meetings was suspect. Being Willie, he could not refrain from comment entirely, and any hint of criticism was sure to be inflated into treachery. For example, Gilmour's friend Roy Jenkins reported that Willie had made 'some fairly disloyal noises' as they walked together to hear the Queen's Speech. It had been particularly unwise of Willie to confide in the man who was being mentioned as a possible rival at the head of a coalition government. He could not stop others talking, either; Gilmour recorded that another member of the Shadow Cabinet had been overheard telling Willie that he was the obvious person to lead a coalition. This speculation was the more dangerous for Willie because it was manifestly true. In fact he disliked such talk as a matter of principle; as he put it in a private conversation with *Guardian* journalists, 'it really was very difficult if either Party insisted on the right to choose the other's leader'. At the end of March he tried to dampen things down, putting on record his support for Heath as leader, deploring the gossip and pleading for an end to recrimination after the February defeat. It had even been reported, on good authority, that Willie would only consider taking over if Heath asked him to do so. But by this time such stories were counter-productive; they made Willie seem like a man anxiously waiting to be 'drafted', as Home had been in 1963.[5]

At first the Conservatives had expected Wilson to call a new poll in June. Their tactics settled down into a pattern that had Willie's warm approval. The aim was to harry the government without provoking it into calling an election. To maintain morale on the backbenches several defeats were inflicted on the detail of legislation – for example, in May Willie forced through an amendment to the government's Bill on Industrial Relations – but not until June did Heath muster all his forces for a vote of censure. By that time he had decided it was safe to make at least one change in his team; he allowed Carrington to leave the party chairmanship. Willie was chosen as his replacement at Conservative Central Office, situated near Westminster in Smith Square.

Heath's decision produced the predictable press comment. In *The Times* the well-informed George Hutchinson claimed that 'There has been no comparable situation in recent Conservative Party history'.[6] The appointment was a serious risk for Heath, who might find himself increasingly overshadowed if Willie managed to reinvigorate the grass-roots membership. But there was a corresponding danger for Willie, who could 'probably say goodbye to any prospect of succeeding Mr Heath' if the party lost the coming election. Carrington had been widely blamed for the February defeat, and Willie was sure to be seriously damaged by a further reverse.[7]

At least there were some familiar faces at Central Office, which helped Willie to readjust quickly. But from his contacts there he knew that morale was very low, and that there was 'a mood of defeatism in the party as a whole'. A month after his appointment Willie said that he had been lucky to become Chairman just after the government had suffered its first defeat in the Commons; but this fillip was unlikely to have a lasting effect. Although the danger of a summer general election had passed there was almost certain to be a contest in the autumn, which gave him very little time to transform the situation. Even if Wilson decided to carry on into 1975 there would still be the problem of dealing with 'what promised to be an unpleasant party conference' in the autumn of 1974. All things considered, the new Chairman thought that he had been presented with 'a fairly poisoned chalice'.[8]

At least Willie would not have to immerse himself in the detailed running of Central Office. While he concentrated on relations with the constituencies, the burden of routine fell on the recently appointed Director-General, Michael Wolff. At such a sensitive time it was probably an advantage that Wolff had worked for both Heath and Willie; but he had been a strong advocate of an early election. Relations with other officials at Central Office were equally tricky. Heath's friend Sara Morrison, one of the party's Vice-Chairmen, was a 'forceful and dynamic personality'. This was the code Willie used in his memoirs to hint at friction. Mrs Morrison felt that Willie had great difficulty in dealing with a strong woman. But the relationship was not improved by her belief that Willie had 'sniffed the wind and realised that Ted could not be saved'. Feeling that he was too easily influenced by others, and thinking that the first impression of the day would always weigh heaviest on him, she made a point of seeing him as soon as he arrived at Central Office each morning. She felt that he could accept criticism if it was expressed with sufficient emphasis; at the same time, though, he always seemed disconcerted by those who could stand up to him. In the end she felt that all her efforts had been in vain, because Willie was not interested in detail or in reforming Central Office.[9]

Mrs Morrison's strictures were echoed by others at the time. After the general election of October 1974 the head of Heath's private office, William Waldegrave, confided that Willie had proved 'an appalling Chairman' who had done nothing to dissipate the air of defeatism at Central Office. 'Even if he had an agenda and was supposed to go through item by item,' Waldegrave continued, 'he often wandered off the point and rambled on.' This was a telling criticism; as Waldegrave later appreciated, Willie could be a very skilful chairman when his attention was fully engaged, and if he really was preoccupied in the summer of 1974 it would be easy to guess where his mind must have been wandering. But Willie himself would have pleaded guilty to some of the other charges. He later revealed that he had disliked working in Smith Square, which 'could make you neurotic'. As a result he had spent as much time as possible out of the building, leaving the professionals to get on with their own work.[10]

Certainly Willie was far from the top of his form while he was Chairman – and for good reasons. But the harshest reflections on his performance have come from those who apparently thought that he should forget entirely about the leadership issue. They were expecting far too much. A more balanced picture was provided by a longer-established party official, Sir Richard Webster, who believed that although Willie had indeed 'rambled on' from time to time, it would have been unfair to call Central Office a 'shambles' under his chairmanship.[11]

Actually the party organisation held up well in October 1974, despite initial doubts about Wolff, whose background was in journalism rather than management. Spending on this second election of the year was well planned compared with February, and the idea of narrowing the party's main effort to forty-five key marginal seats was held to have worked, despite initial protests from other constituencies that had been given special attention (and resources) in February. The campaign itself was always going to be difficult, but there was some creative thinking, particularly in the latter stages when at one of Geoffrey Tucker's 'breakfast meetings' at the Dorchester Hotel it was suggested that the party should set up an 'instant response unit' – more than two decades before the Labour Party stumbled on the same idea. One new initiative that did take concrete form – a 'Phrase-Making' group – was judged to be unsuccessful, spending a lot of effort in researching arcane subjects like the size of vocabulary (1,400) needed to understand the *Sun* newspaper.[12]

The latter work was undertaken because officials were aware that crisp, familiar phrases would be needed if the party's message was to reach target voters. The Conservative Manifesto, *Putting Britain First*, was attractively presented; but although the first page would not have overtaxed the average *Sun* reader (who had to cope with around 350 different words on the front cover), the whole document was necessarily long and closely argued. There was also an unpleasant shock for Willie, when a print worker stole an advance copy and it was leaked to the *Guardian* and the *Financial Times* more than a week before Wilson announced that the general election would be held on 10 October.

Since the manifesto was unusually literate – Willie described it as 'the best-written manifesto the Conservatives had ever produced' – the leak was probably less damaging than the perpetrators had hoped. Although the police were called in, and eventually there was a successful prosecution, the initial anger in Central Office soon died away. As usual Willie felt personally responsible, but at a meeting with Tory candidates he 'apologised handsomely . . . and was as handsomely forgiven' (not for the last time). Presumably after this Willie considered the incident closed. One of the journalists who published the contents of the manifesto was called in to discuss the matter with Michael Wolff, a personal friend. Instead of the dressing-down he expected, after a few token reassurances they ended up sharing a whisky.[13]

Willie's approval of the manifesto should have extended beyond the style to the substance, because it was a moderate document which pledged the Conservatives to govern in the national interest. There was no direct offer of places in a future government to members of other parties, but there was a promise that the Conservatives would 'consult and confer with the leaders of other parties and with the leaders of the great interests in the nation', whatever the result of the election. The 'national interest' theme, of course, was one that Willie had emphasised in his speeches during the February campaign. The same was true of the manifesto's concentration on the interests of groups which lacked the muscle of the major trade unions. It was, in short, a 'One Nation' programme, epitomised by an early declaration that the party was 'free from dogma and free from dependence upon any single interest'. Willie's concern that the early drafts had not focused strongly enough on the danger to society of inflation were also clearly addressed in the published version.[14]

Yet after the election it was revealed that Willie had been very unhappy with what turned out to be the main feature of the Tory campaign – national unity. An unnamed official was quoted as saying that Willie was uneasy because he felt that it would be unpopular with the party's activists. His intervention was crucial in bringing a temporary halt to momentum, which had built up while Carrington was Chairman, behind the idea of an electoral pact with the Liberals. The theme only became dominant in the last few days of the campaign, by which time, some observers felt, it was too late.[15]

In the abstract, the theme of national unity – and the idea of cooperation between politicians of goodwill, whatever their partisan loyalties – looked to be a potent one for the Conservatives. The February election had revealed deep dissatisfaction with both the Tories and Labour; hence the Liberal revival. No one had any illusions that there could be a truly 'national' coalition; Labour MPs were most unlikely to join in significant numbers. But an electoral agreement with the Liberals, leading perhaps to a deal on proportional representation (PR) and the offer of a few Cabinet posts, would be popular with the public. The clever (if not cynical) twist would be that the Tories might win an outright majority on this platform, and would therefore need to undertake only the most token 'consultations' with other leaders and interests.

There were, though, two major difficulties with the tactic. Willie had correctly identified the first, and his point tallied with his earlier argument about being 'too clever'. Privately he revealed that he was not frightened at the prospect of PR; but some of his parliamentary colleagues were strongly opposed to this concession.[16] Traditionally relations had not been warm between Tory and Liberal activists in the constituencies, and they had not been improved by the February result. To fierce anti-socialists, the vigorous campaign fought by the Liberals in those circumstances had been tantamount to treason against the national interest. The radical Young Liberals were particularly unpopular, and in one speech Willie went out of his way to stigmatise their 'disruptive activities'.[17] But it seems that his arguments omitted a more personal difficulty. The Liberals had signalled a strong preference for himself as leader if they were to join forces with the Conservatives. Heath they regarded as a divisive figure; any deal with him, they felt, would alienate their own supporters.

It was this problem that dogged Conservative attempts to devise a convincing 'national' platform before the second election of 1974. Heath himself had been a founder-member of the 'One Nation Group' and during the various crises of his government he had made regular appeals to social unity. But during the campaign the Liberal leader Jeremy Thorpe referred to Heath as 'the architect of confrontation', confident that his own supporters and many key 'floating' voters would endorse this sally.[18]

The obvious solution to the Heath difficulty was to signal that if necessary the leader would be ready to make 'the supreme sacrifice' and stand aside, should this be the necessary price of cooperation with another party. Having done so much to make Heath into a bogey-man, Labour's researchers now discovered that their propaganda might rebound on them. During the last days of the campaign Conservative strategists heard that their counterparts were worried about the 'supreme sacrifice' to the point of obsession. A dramatic announcement by Heath that he was prepared to stand aside could transform Tory prospects, their findings suggested. On 4 October the argument seemed to be clinched by a survey conducted by ORC – the Conservatives' own pollsters – which found that 10 per cent of voters would switch if Heath were no longer leader of his party. Heath was immediately bombarded with telephone calls from his closest allies, including Wolff, Mrs Morrison, Carrington, Lord Aldington and even Tony Barber. The overwhelming message was that he should make the necessary gesture. The *Guardian*'s Peter Jenkins had already quoted anonymous 'aides' who were confident that a statement on these lines was imminent. Some over-eager members of the leader's entourage were evidently trying to force his hand.[19]

The significant name missing from the list of advisers was that of Willie Whitelaw. After the election William Waldegrave reported that on one occasion the 'supreme sacrifice' was mentioned while Heath and Willie were in the same room. 'Willie lay back on the sofa and said "No, no, no" very slowly for about five minutes while Ted was looking impatiently at his watch.' To those in Central Office who remained convinced that Willie coveted the crown, this scene was sure to leave a lasting impression of a man who was afraid to strike; and MPs like Nigel Fisher, who urged Willie to talk Heath round, probably drew the same conclusion. But they were too little acquainted with Willie's history. Once before he had told a leader that it would be better to go, and that had been hard enough. Back in 1965 Heath had been the beneficiary; there had been no thought of personal advancement on Willie's part. To press the 'supreme sacrifice' on Heath at this moment was not quite the same as telling him that he had to step down immediately. One Shadow minister put it well: 'What was there to lose? If we won he was safe, but if we lost then he was out anyway.' Yet Willie would not have looked forward to broaching the subject even if he had been an outsider for the succession. For him the decisive factor was his knowledge of Heath's character. It was very likely that any hint from him would be misinterpreted, and might even reinforce Heath's resolve to fight on. As it was, one 'close friend' said later, 'When it came down to it, Ted was suspicious of the advice he was getting. He suspected that he was being got at by people who were no friends of his.' In short, at precisely the moment when the advice of a candid friend might have saved Heath's leadership and benefited the party, he had decided that anyone who spoke with candour was a secret enemy.[20]

The 'supreme sacrifice' was never promised. Heath's only concession was to become far more explicit in his references to a national coalition in the last few days before the election, even announcing a timetable for discussions with other leaders. But while the ex-Premier remained an obstacle in Thorpe's eyes, such planning could only appear hopelessly unrealistic for uncommitted voters. Behind the scenes, indeed, Willie, Gilmour and Carrington were charged with the task of 'undermining and debunking' the Liberal leader, who was clearly an asset to his own party. At the same time they would go on paying lip-service to the idea of cooperation. Willie had already taken the lead here, accusing Thorpe of combining the Liberal Party's own version of the 'national unity' appeal with bitter personal attacks on Heath and Wilson.[21]

With hindsight, this outburst does look like an attempt on Willie's part to scupper the coalition idea. Only in the last couple of days, when the momentum was impossible to resist, did he relent and tell an audience at Putney that 'We Conservatives have pledged ourselves to work with others', and that the only way forward was under 'a broad-based government that commands the support of the overwhelming weight of public opinion'. By this time Willie had probably decided that the talk of national unity had gone so far that it might as well be taken to its logical conclusion; he knew that it would never be put to the test because he was certain of defeat. According to one official, he now joined in the attempts to cajole Heath into accepting the coalition line, although the leader had reacted angrily and 'torn the whole idea to bits' when it was suggested at an earlier stage.[22]

From the outset Willie had regarded the election campaign as a damage-limitation exercise for his party. When it was over he said that he had hoped people would like the notion of national unity and vote accordingly, without asking too many questions about the detail. But he still thought the sudden focus on the coalition idea was an unwelcome intrusion – bringing the prospect that the Tories might form part of a government after all, but only at the price of enraging many of their own activists. Whatever others were thinking, Willie drew a clear distinction between national unity and a coalition government. He genuinely believed that the Conservative Party alone represented the best interests of the nation; hence a new Conservative government would be a 'government of national unity' without the need for any deal with other parties. It was his own characteristic answer to the enthusiast who complained that during the campaign national unity 'became a slogan instead of an intellectually respectable answer to the crisis'. Willie would have agreed instead with another anonymous 'insider', who said that the line 'was most strongly recommended by those with no sense or knowledge of history and a boy-scoutish idea of political life. These people did not understand what a slow-moving animal a political party is: you can't steer it or expect quick responses or understanding.' From the fringes of the 'boy scout' camp it was even proposed that the Conservatives should withdraw their candidates in forty-nine constituencies, to give the Liberals a better chance of unseating the sitting Labour MP.[23] Lurking behind this was Churchill's old idea of a lasting anti-socialist union between the Conservatives and the Liberals.

Although to the participants everything seemed straightforward, in reality the situation was extremely complex, and highly depressing for Willie. Heath's reluctance to embrace the coalition idea showed that he was closer in his thinking to Willie than he was to those whose loyalty even he could not doubt. Unfortunately the days of the intimate partnership between the two men had ended when Willie went to Belfast, and since that time they had been driven further apart. The crucial difference between the two sides to the argument over 'national unity' was not that the advocates of coalition had a limited grasp of history. Rather, like Churchill himself, they lacked sympathy for the wider Conservative Party. According to one source, even Carrington had ended his term as Chairman 'loathing' the average activist. In private Willie and Heath might have expressed similar opinions; in his memoirs the former was quite ready to admit that when he was Chairman he had used his wartime tactic of shouting 'Splendid! Keep up the good work!' to deflect awkward questions as he toured the constituencies. Even so, they remained instictively loyal to the party as an institution.[24]

Some thought that Sir Keith Joseph had different ideas. Since February 1974 the former Secretary of State for Social Services had been conducting a crusade on behalf of free-market policies, having initially refused any specific brief within the Shadow Cabinet. Monetarism, his proposed remedy for inflation, was held by the overwhelming majority of his colleagues to be unworkable and dangerously divisive; certainly a policy that was sure to cause mass unemployment was most inconvenient for a party which was trying to present itself as the custodian of the national interest. It seems that Willie made no attempt to restrain Joseph; this job was left to others, including Joseph's friend Margaret Thatcher, whose admiration for the dissident made her an impotent intermediary. During the campaign it was a recurrent nightmare for the Central Office team that Joseph might don the mantle of the departed

Enoch Powell and say something disastrous. Yet in this respect the October campaign was a great improvement on February; there were no self-inflicted wounds.

Willie was unlikely to forgive Joseph's open (if ingenuous) attacks on his own party's record. But in one important respect he agreed with Joseph. Disdaining the highbrow debate about economic theory, Willie focused instead on the practical import of Joseph's message that inflation was the main threat to British society. Even so, it was probably an accident that he chose to make his most stridently anti-socialist speech at Upminster, where Joseph had given one of his most celebrated performances. On 7 October Willie claimed that Labour's plans 'would turn Britain into the largest state-owned, state-controlled economy outside the Communist bloc'. Even the infatuated Joseph would have been warmed by Willie's encomium of free enterprise, of:

> the companies that have been built up from humble origins all over the country, in every part of the British Isles, by energy, initiative and skill . . . They have given our people security, the chance to earn a good livelihood and hope for the future – and they have given us choice in our custom and the resources with which to improve our social services, to help those who need help and to make Britain a more civilised country in which to live.[25]

The only way to preserve free enterprise, Willie thought, was to throw out the socialist government by voting Conservative.

In private conversation after the election Willie emphasised his Upminster speech as a last-minute attempt to 'save the thing slipping away': in other words, to galvanise the bedrock of Conservative support. But the theme had been fairly consistent in all of his public oratory. If he had been hell-bent on the leadership, Willie would have jumped at the coalition idea, but for him the choice in October 1974 was only different from that of any other post-war election because it was more urgent this time. It lay between socialism and what he regarded as the free society. Willie recognised that Wilson had been skilful in watering down the radical commitments embraced by his party in opposition, and in distancing himself from his controversial Industry Secretary, Tony Benn. Yet he saw the 'Social Contract' – the government's plan for voluntary cooperation with the unions – as a sham. The nation's underlying problems, he thought, were being kept out of sight for the duration of the campaign; but there would have to be a reckoning once the votes had been counted. He was particularly angered by the evasiveness of the Chancellor, Denis Healey, about the real inflation figures. At one meeting he suggested that Labour's strategy should be attacked as 'Operation Cover-up'.[26]

Ironically, just at the time when Heath seemed to have warmed to the coalition idea he joined Willie in stepping up his attacks on Labour, saying that the party had been taken over by 'the neo-Marxist Left'. Meanwhile the Tory whips were telephoning candidates to make sure that they were emphasising the party line on a coalition. The response of one MP, Alan Clark, was to point out that the party would never make progress with any policy while Heath remained as leader. Afterwards Clark telephoned Willie at Ennim to urge that even at this late stage he should move against Heath. Understandably Willie ignored his hints, merely bellowing his wishes for 'a very great success, a very good success, a good result'.[27]

In the orthodox campaign that Willie wanted to fight, the Opposition should have balanced its attacks on the government with constructive proposals. So he warmly approved the idea, first suggested by Heath, that the Conservatives should offer extra incentives for home-owners. He helped to overcome the reluctance of Mrs Thatcher, the Shadow Environment Minister, to pledge that mortgage interest rates would be cut to below 10 per cent by Christmas, and would be pegged at that level. There would also be help for first-time buyers. It was a popular idea, which rattled Labour (and greatly enhanced Mrs Thatcher's profile). But even this ran into trouble during the talk about coalition. Mrs Thatcher's initial misgivings were transformed into a violent attachment to a policy that might have to be sacrificed in any talks with prospective coalition partners. Miles Hudson, who had been drafted into Central Office to help with the campaign, noted in his diary for 4 October that Mrs Thatcher had asked to see the Party Chairman 'in a high state of excitement'. She told Willie that 'she was damned if she was going to give up her housing policy'; Willie 'had a hell of a time with her'.[28]

Despite this setback Hudson recorded on that day that 'for the first time during the campaign one did begin to see a little bit of light'. On 5 October the experienced Deputy Chairman, Sir Michael Fraser, thought the contest was 'wide open' and that there was still everything to play for. Like almost everyone else, he thought that 'national unity' could still bring the long-awaited breakthrough. But the tide of anticipation soon receded. On the eve of the election Tucker's breakfast group heard that Labour's people were confident of victory.[29]

At the beginning of the campaign Willie had made another of his rallying speeches, telling Central Office staff that he 'would not tolerate pessimistic comments from anyone'. More effective than his words was his manner, which galvanised his colleagues even on the most dismal days. Hudson felt that Heath had been lacklustre at the press conference of 24 September, the first day of the official campaign; but when Willie presided the next day with Jim Prior 'the contrast was enormous. Willie Whitelaw dominated the conference with his personality.' This was true throughout the campaign; out of fifteen press conferences he was absent for only three, and on each of these occasions the atmosphere was subdued. After the election, though, Willie confessed that he thought the conferences had been a waste of time. At least they provided scope for two marvellous 'Willie-isms'. The first, like so many good political anecdotes, has been distorted. Folklore suggests that he accused Labour of 'going around the country stirring up apathy'. Actually the key word was 'complacency', which the admiring Simon Hoggart thought was 'a slightly different thing, and, in an intriguing metaphysical way, almost meaningful'. At another conference Willie denied that morale within the party was low. When asked to back this up with evidence, he said 'Well, I have the thermometer in my mouth and I am listening to it all the time.'[30]

Later Willie reported that he had felt depressed in the last few days of the campaign, and that there had been a sense of panic in Central Office. Partly this mood was generated by Mrs Thatcher; she had not secured a guarantee that the housing pledge would survive, and Miles Hudson felt that 'at the end of the campaign she was in a fair old state'. But two days before the vote Willie himself made a remark that punctured any remaining optimism. At a tactical meeting he announced that 'he would go to ground after the election and would not be interviewed by anybody'. Obviously he was thinking of his post-election gaffe in February; but, as Hudson immediately grasped, his statement took another defeat for granted.[31]

In February Willie had been kept away from his constituency for most of the campaign by his governmental duties. In Penrith and the Border, at least, he had been like Churchill in 1945 – a national figure who was readily forgiven for the fact that he also belonged to a political party. He knew that the post of Conservative Chairman would have diminished him in the eyes of uncommitted Cumbrians, so it was no surprise that the swing against him in October was higher than the national average (2.8 per cent compared to 2.2 per cent). Of course this still left him with a massive majority.

Of far more concern to Willie was the national picture. On the evening of 10 October he left his own count and took the train down to London, to be at Smith Square for the results. He was greeted at Euston with the news that a BBC exit poll predicted a Labour majority of 150. It seemed that his worst nightmare – a repeat of 1966 – was going to happen after all. It was easier to swallow the story because a late survey by NOP had produced a Labour lead of 14.5 per cent. But even after years of refinement, exit polls can still produce wildly inaccurate predictions, and in October 1974 the technique was in its infancy. The first 'real' result – from the Guildford constituency of Willie's old colleague David Howell – showed a swing to Labour of 3.5 per cent. While this suggested a very different scenario from a Labour landslide, it was worse than the national average proved to be. So the mood improved at Central Office as the night wore on. The next day was even better; Labour failed to make a single gain in any of the late-declaring seats.[32]

The final outcome showed that Labour had gained eighteen seats from the Conservatives, leaving a margin of forty-three between the two main parties. But the overall majority was only four. As a damage-limitation exercise it could not have been bettered. But who would get the credit? Willie knew that the result 'could only increase the pressure inside the Conservative Party against Ted Heath's leadership'. The speculation intensified further when Lord Carrington visited Heath's Bexley Sidcup constituency, as he had done in 1970. According to one account, Carrington merely discussed what would happen if the Tories won, but his biographer believes that he told Heath he would have to stand down. The only safe conclusion to draw from the conflicting stories is that some people found it difficult to tell Heath what they really thought; and that this proved particularly awkward for those who had known him longest. Whatever he had said in Sidcup, the following day Carrington accepted an invitation to a dinner at which all the other guests were people who had urged Heath to stay on. Willie was not among them. Faithful to his strategy, he was keeping a low profile in Cumbria where Alec Home joined him to discuss the situation.[33]

Miles Hudson, who had been close to Willie throughout the campaign, thought on the morning of polling day that 'on balance' he was likely to take over. More than a week later he committed his views to paper:

> Willie Whitelaw is a born politician with all the instincts and expertise that are endemic to the politician. Ebullient, noisy, dominating, shrewd and amusing – he is a leader. He is caustic in private about many of his colleagues. He also makes a virtue of being a non-intellectual – 'I don't understand all that stuff', he will say. He is a pragmatist without any clearly defined philosophy, except an instinctive reaction against extremes. He gives an impression of firmness which is in fact not always justified, and he is rather apt to be convinced by the most cogently argued case without subjecting it to his own judgement. On the other hand he would be a good leader of a team as long as there were no fundamental disagreement among the members of it. He would encourage his colleagues and understand their human feelings. But he would be very apt to have a small circle of friends within which the real decisions would be taken. This is, of course, the reality with almost all political leaders – but it would be enhanced if Willie Whitelaw were to become leader.[34]

It is an invaluable snapshot, not just because of the insights and the absence of sycophancy, but also because it takes up so much of Hudson's three-page post-mortem on the election. Heath was hardly mentioned. The message was clear: although he had hated every minute of the campaign, Willie Whitelaw had ended it as the dominant character in the Conservative Party.

CHAPTER 12

'ALEC'S REVENGE'

It all seemed perfectly simple. The February 1974 defeat had been a terrible shock to the Conservatives, but October was far less traumatic. Given the situation in the country, it had been, as some party workers were already saying, 'a good election to lose'; even better that it had been close. As in June 1970 the pollsters had been confounded, and although the party had registered its lowest ever share of the vote, the Commons' arithmetic offered plenty of encouragement. But Heath had now lost three elections out of four, and a humane boxing referee would have ushered him back to his corner. He could retire with his honour repaired. There could be no recompense for the 'Who Governs?' election, but Heath had shown himself to be a dogged fighter who would be respected as an elder statesman when he accepted the inevitable post of Shadow Foreign Secretary from the new Conservative leader – Willie Whitelaw.

Heath's decision to banish this benign vision by hanging on as leader is usually identified as the point at which his resilience hardened into stubbornness. In fact his predominant trait at the time seems more like masochism, given the unenviable prospect ahead of him. Bad advice from his closest supporters is also blamed, although as so often individuals are cited in various places as having argued in different ways.[1] Along with Ian Gilmour, Sara Morrison and others, Jim Prior told Heath that his only chance of survival was to resign from the leadership and offer himself for re-election – and he thought that even this course would end in tears. Afterwards Prior reflected that Heath was now 'only hearing the advice he wished to hear'. This is almost invariably true of embattled leaders. But at least Heath was receiving encouragement from outside his immediate circle. One of these welcome counsellors committed his thoughts to paper, so whatever other people said there can be no doubt that Willie's cousin Lord Thorneycroft told Heath that 'the Conservative Party will be very much weaker unless you are still at its head'. Apparently another veteran of leadership battles, Lord Hailsham, said much the same.[2]

Apart from Heath's personal sense of mission, two reasons could be offered in justification of his stand. The first, to which Thorneycroft alluded, was the state of the country. It was widely felt that Britain was becoming 'ungovernable', and rampant inflation conjured visions of Weimar Germany, with workers heaving their worthless wages home in wheelbarrows. Prices rose by 19 per cent over 1974 as a whole; wages leaped by 29 per cent, while industrial production fell by 3 per cent. The *Financial Times* share index had stood at over 300 when Heath left office; by 9 January 1975 it had fallen to 146. This was even worse than the stock-market collapse of 1929–31. Shadowy figures were rumoured to be planning a *coup d'état* – a story that Willie scouted before the October election, though he might have taken it more seriously had he maintained close relations with Cecil King. The situation was far worse than it had been in 1966, when Heath had issued gloomy prophecies, which proved well founded after Wilson had been re-elected. But that was no reason to keep Heath as leader this time round; rather, it could have been regarded as an additional motive for replacing him with Willie. Even if things really fell apart, Wilson would be unlikely to call a general election; his response would have been to call in other party leaders to form a 'grand coalition'. And in these circumstances Heath might still be seen as an obstacle – while Willie would certainly be welcomed as an important asset.[3]

The second reason was equally tenuous. Heath told Prior that he was determined to stay on and 'fight the right wing' of his own party. Prior replied that 'if he refused to go he would probably end up giving them exactly what they wanted'. It was brutal, but true. If there really was to be a trial of strength within the party, the moderates would be seriously handicapped if they went into battle behind a lame leader. There were other problems beside the three defeats and the successful myth that Heath had conducted an ideological 'U-turn', abandoning correct (i.e. right-wing) ideas in favour of the soft, 'consensual' option. As Heath remarks in his memoirs, with some backbenchers the objection was more personal; he had not given them the promotions or the knighthoods that they felt they deserved. It was not in his nature to perform a real 'U-turn' now, and rekindle his popularity by showering honours on those he had previously overlooked. He could not even bring himself to patronise his troops with flattering personal attentions in the Commons tea-rooms – those costless gestures that Willie had quickly mastered. One MP, Julian Critchley, was dining with Prior one day when Heath came up. He spoke warmly to Prior, but ignored Critchley and two other Tory MPs. Critchley admitted that he was sufficiently 'piqued' to let the incident affect his choice when the leadership was finally contested.[4]

When Parliament reassembled, Critchley heard that Willie had told his friends '("in total confidence") that Ted was not behaving like a gentleman. He should have resigned'. As Miles Hudson had noted, Willie was quite capable of making cutting comments about his colleagues; and had he drawn any parallel with the conduct of Alec Home in 1965, he might have spoken irritably. It was a pity that these rumours were circulating, since in public Willie had begun to declare his support for Heath even before the last votes were counted. On election night he told reporters, 'We are in a party that has fought the campaign together under Ted Heath . . . Loyalty is something that really matters – loyalty to a friend, loyalty to a leader, a party and overall loyalty to the country. There will be a large number of Conservatives who will be returned to the House of Commons, and we will be a loyal and united team.' A week later he went further, issuing a statement that affirmed his 'admiration and support for Ted Heath as our Leader', a feeling which 'does not waver, least of all in times of difficulties. Naturally, I accept all members of the Conservative Party are entitled to their own views about the leadership of their Party. Yet surely, at this time of crisis, as Conservatives our priority is clear. It is our nation first.'

This, of course, was the Thorneycroft line. And before the end of October Willie had made a speech at Didcot which the *Sunday Express* interpreted as an explicit disclaimer of interest in the leadership. It was announced that he would stay on as Chairman, though he would also lead for the party in the Commons on the subject of devolution for Scotland and Wales. This was likely to be a key strategic post in any Conservative recovery, reflecting Willie's personal concern for Scotland, where the nationalists had won nearly one-third of the votes and the Tories had been reduced to just sixteen seats.[5]

None of this made the slightest impression on the more cynical Fleet Street commentators. 'Crossbencher' in the *Sunday Express* was particularly biting during these months. Just a couple of days after Willie took the trouble to issue his personal statement, the anonymous columnist asked his readers to 'Picture him before the glass brushing up that expression of reluctant acquiescence, of humble surprise that the services of a North Country squire could be valued so highly'. The author even issued a warning: if the leadership election was held immediately Willie would win; but a delay would give the Tories time for reflection. 'The old hands who valued Willie as Chief Whip will be tackled, he knows, by the sharp young new recruits who question his intellectual grasp and who reckon his particular brand of Greyfriars School camaraderie an electoral liability in the Britain of 1974.'[6]

Unfortunately Willie's memoirs lend inadvertent support to the cynical explanation of his behaviour. He wrote that only after the October election did he realise there was 'bitterness, dissension and general bad feeling' directed against Heath; and that even then he was unaware of its extent. One might say that if this was true he had obviously stopped listening to his thermometer, and had lost all of the sensitivity to party opinion which he had demonstrated as Chief Whip. Against this should be set the fact that as Chairman he talked most often with ordinary members of the party, whose loyalty to Heath proved exceptionally tenacious. But his reaction to Alan Clark's telephone call just before the October election suggests a habit of evasion on this issue. And long before he published the sanitised account in his memoirs, he had tacitly confirmed that he had written off Heath's chances after the second election of 1974. The MP Nigel Fisher consulted him while preparing the 1977 book that remains the best account of the leadership crisis. The published version includes the statement 'Whitelaw himself realised that Heath could not survive'.[7]

Certainly Willie was acting in accordance with a plan. But his main aim was to avoid the mistakes he had made in February 1974. Although he might mutter from time to time, he would do nothing with the deliberate aim of destabilising the leadership. When approached by some of his parliamentary supporters who had already compiled a list of MPs who had pledged their votes to him, Willie told them to desist.[8] If by some miracle Heath had managed to save his position, Willie would have been content. At the same time, experience in Northern Ireland had convinced him that he had the ability to lead his party if the circumstances were right, and he could not see any obvious alternative among his colleagues, if Heath had to go. So after October he was ready to accept the top job, and even to campaign for it under certain conditions. But the first two of those conditions were that Heath should no longer be leader – and that he, Willie, would not try to persuade him to resign. Probably this would have been the case even if Willie had not been made Party Chairman by Heath, but that did make life much more difficult. It left him with no alternative but to issue supportive statements after the election defeat, and subsequently there was no way that Willie could have stood against Heath without betraying all the rules of conduct that had governed his life. So in early November when Airey Neave, Heath's most determined personal enemy on the backbenches, offered to run a leadership campaign for Willie, he was rebuffed. Neave was reluctant to give up so easily, though, and after a brief flirtation with Joseph, he asked Heath directly if he would stand down.[9]

With well-timed cruelty, two months later 'Crossbencher' jeered that Willie had 'manoeuvred himself into immobility'. This was a cheap way of saying that, since he did not navigate by Fleet Street's moral compass, he now found himself in a blind alley thanks to Heath's decisions – and some unfortunate coincidences. Following the election, events had hardened the leader's resolve to plug on. The executive of the 1922 Committee met by prior arrangement at Edward du Cann's house on 14 October. The name of du Cann – who had been dubbed 'Oily Edward' by some Westminster wags – always provoked

Heath's wrath, and Willie shared his feelings. But this meeting merely reflected a widespread disillusionment within the party, and afterwards du Cann asked to see Heath, Willie and Atkins, the Chief Whip. In 1965 du Cann's predecessor as Chairman of the 1922, Anstruther-Grey, had gone to see Alec Home longing to be told that a resignation would be inappropriate. But times had changed. Given the personal edge introduced by his presence, du Cann would have been wise to delegate the mission to a less provocative colleague. Over dinner with du Cann, Willie tried to prevent an unpleasant confrontation. Suppressing his own feelings, he conceded that du Cann had been badly treated by the party and even hinted that he should be given a place in the Shadow Cabinet. Du Cann ignored this flannel, and declared that he would still deliver his message to Heath in person. Having done his best and failed, Willie admitted that he was 'unsurprised' by du Cann's decision. The meeting with Heath went ahead, and was predictably frosty. When the 1922 executive reconvened the following morning, at du Cann's City office, the press had been alerted. Some members were photographed as they left the building; others delayed their departure, or made dramatic escapes.[10]

Willie's response to this fiasco – and to a *Times* leading article which pushed his own claims to the leadership – was to reaffirm his support for Heath in the press statement of 17 October, quoted above. Anything less would have seemed like a tacit endorsement of du Cann and his colleagues, who were dubbed 'the Milk Street Mafia' to commemorate the venue of their second meeting. The 1922 executive deserved the bad publicity; in acting like camera-shy celebrities they were betraying a collective guilty conscience. But Willie had been wounded by the crossfire between Heath and the 'Mafia'. If Heath was now regarded as stubborn, his Heir Presumptive was beginning to look spineless. The stakes were raised further after Parliament reassembled on 22 October. Some of Heath's supporters told members of the 1922 executive that their positions would come under threat if they continued to seek a change of leadership. Probably this tactic would have rebounded even if the executive was out of touch with Tory backbenchers. Since it actually provided a reasonable reflection of their views, the gamble proved disastrous. The next full meeting of the 1922, on 31 October, was conducted in a feverish atmosphere. Someone briefed the press that du Cann had primed the speakers beforehand. If so, he would have been following Willie's own maxim that one should never call a meeting unless the outcome is known in advance. As it was, Nigel Fisher dismissed the press reports as another example of 'dirty tricks' from the Heath camp; Critchley, a more impartial observer, thought that the meeting merely verified the predictive law laid down by his friend David Walder – 'that the first three people to speak on any subject at the 1922 are mad'. Certainly if du Cann really had fixed the proceedings he could have done better, since the anti-Heath message of the speakers was not unanimous. But du Cann was re-elected as Chairman unopposed, to loud acclamation.[11]

Now Heath had no alternative but to offer himself for re-election. On 14 November he agreed that a committee should be set up, with Alec Home in the chair, to re-examine the rules for such a contest. As Party Chairman, Willie was made a member, along with Carrington, Atkins – and du Cann. The task was probably miserable enough for Willie; everyone must have been watching him closely to see how he reacted to provisions that might shortly affect himself. By this time du Cann's own (short-lived) ambitions were obvious, but his candidature would be unaffected whether or not Heath chose to run. The 1922 meeting had been another blow for Willie in this respect; demonstrating their own lack of spine, its members had been cowed by Heath's presence into giving him the kind of reception that encouraged him to fight on.[12]

The new rules were eventually dubbed 'Alec's Revenge' – as if, during a decade of close partnership with Heath, Home had simply been waiting for a chance to strike back against him for the whispering campaign which had led to his own resignation in 1965. But the rule changes compared to the last contest did make life harder for Heath, and James Douglas of the CRD, who had been a key participant in the meetings that formulated the rules in both 1964 and 1974, later confirmed that the new arrangements were deliberately framed to unseat the leader.[13] It was now almost ludicrously easy to launch a leadership challenge; only two MPs were necessary to support a nomination, and whether in government or opposition the leader could face this threat every year. Previously the successful candidate had to win 15 per cent more votes than the runner-up; this was changed, so that the winner would now have to be in front by a margin equivalent to 15 per cent of those *eligible to vote*. This made the first ballot even more tempting for tactical calculators; if they wanted to eject Heath, but had no liking for any of his rivals at the initial stage, an abstention would be almost as effective. Since there were 277 Tory MPs in the House, to win outright on the first ballot in 1975 would require a tally of 160. Although Atkins consistently misinformed Heath as to the state of opinion among MPs, no one on the committee can have been unaware that even after the February general election more than a hundred MPs had wanted a change; that figure was unlikely to have diminished in the meantime. The other change was that some provision was allowed for consultations with the wider party membership. In the end this had no effect on the result; but on paper it seemed to improve the chances of a popular Party Chairman.[14]

So a more accurate tag than 'Alec's Revenge' would have been 'Willie's Last Chance'. But this was diminished immediately after the announcement of the new rules, just before the House rose for the Christmas break. In fact Heath had extinguished any possibility of a bloodless departure when he accepted the need for revised rules; if he backed down after that it would have looked like cowardice. It was also very likely that there would be a challenger from outside Heath's circle, although in November 1974 Keith Joseph had made one gaffe too many and decided not to stand. Meanwhile Neave was busy, sounding out du Cann and finally Margaret Thatcher after his failures with Willie and Joseph. Although Neave was far from the only MP to champion du Cann, the latter pulled out because of adverse rumours concerning his City dealings. Symptomatic of the concern among Tory MPs at this time was the typical response whenever a journalist mentioned du Cann's name: 'Ha ha, you chaps have got files on him as thick as a phone book, haven't you?' When the nominations closed on 30 January 1975 'Oily Edward' was not among them, although in his official capacity he could look forward to overseeing the count. Heath and Thatcher had both declared to run, along with the right-wing backbencher Hugh Fraser.

Willie declared his support for Heath before the ballot. Although he knew that a decisive win was most unlikely, that was the only way to save Heath in the long term under the new rules, so he urged the party to give the incumbent leader an overwhelming majority. Even this was interpreted in the press as a devious way of saying that Heath should retire from the contest if he received anything short of a landslide majority. But on 4 February Heath was beaten, with 119 votes to Thatcher's 130. The peculiar state of the party was reflected by the tally of sixteen for the improbable Fraser; there were eleven abstentions. The behaviour of Heath's campaign team was also strangely contradictory; they over-estimated his support while using heavy-handed tactics to squeeze out every last vote. More seriously, it has been estimated that around forty MPs were conned by Neave and his team into supporting Thatcher with the argument that only in that way could they secure a second ballot in which Willie would be a candidate. Certainly Neave chose the perfect form of words when asked how his candidate was faring: 'Very well, but not well enough'. Michael Heseltine, who supported Willie on the second ballot, has denied that he was talked into voting for Thatcher first time round; but other prominent Whitelaw men, including Sir Paul Bryan, did make the fateful switch.[15]

After the result the Conservative Party lurched even further from reality. It might have been facing a long period of opposition, but it was monopolising the media spotlight and MPs were loving every minute. Alan Clark set the tone. Jim Prior's train had been delayed, and he arrived in London too late to cast his vote for Heath. When he finally reached Westminster his first indication of what had happened was the spectacle of Clark dashing out of Westminster Hall, yelling, 'She's won, she's won.' Regrettably, Clark's excitement during the campaign had been so intense that he failed to keep his diary.[16]

But the only surprising thing about the result was that a woman had won. Even that unprecedented facet of Thatcher's victory could be explained; chauvinism and courtly love are two sides of the same coin. Any other senior figure – even Joseph, whose judgement was almost universally distrusted – could have beaten Heath on that first ballot. Yet Clark's exultation was mirrored by loud lamentation from moderate MPs, including even the placid Reggie Maudling.

Sometimes hailed as the world's most sophisticated electorate, the Parliamentary Conservative Party behaved like children who have just elected the naughtiest pupil as Head of School. The hysteria spread to parts of Fleet Street – especially to those newspapers with a strong female readership. In the Heath Government Mrs Thatcher had been an obscure minister; and where she was known she was generally disliked as 'the Milk Snatcher'. The result on 4 February 1975 transformed her into an heroic figure from the Boadicea stable. A truly sophisticated electorate would have paused to ponder what it had done; for example, if anyone really thought Mrs Thatcher deserved support in the next ballot because of her undoubted courage in standing against the leader, they should have clamoured for Fraser, who had been brave enough to stand in the sure expectation of a crushing defeat. The real argument was that Mrs Thatcher had won, and MPs thought that the party might look silly if it embarked on a mass defection to other candidates. In short, Thatcher now benefited from a real 'bandwagon effect' – her position strengthened because some opportunist Tory MPs wanted to be seen backing a winner. Some who had lost their sense of proportion never recovered it. Nigel Fisher was greatly impressed when Mrs Thatcher kissed him and exclaimed, 'Isn't it exciting, Nigel.' Yet the campaign had exposed deep divisions in the party and ended in the humiliating defeat of a long-standing leader. Someone who could find that 'exciting' was only likely to increase the rifts in the ranks. That evening a party was held to celebrate the defeat of the man who had been Prime Minister for more than three years, during which time Margaret Thatcher had kept her worries to herself.[17]

Willie was with Heath and some other close friends when Timothy Kitson brought the news. Very soon Hugh Fraser turned up in tears, quite unable to explain why he had stood in the first place. Lord Hailsham also wept. It would not have been out of character if Willie had followed suit. But after a decent interval he slipped away to meet some of his own supporters. One MP remembered that he 'bounced into the room' and declared, 'Ted's out of the running. I'm going to have a go.' Although some members of the launch party had also helped to set the Thatcher 'bandwagon' rolling, at this time there was no feeling that the first ballot result had scuppered

Willie's chances. After all, Home's new rules had been consciously designed to ensure (as far as possible) that the result of the first ballot was not decisive. Willie's announcement was greeted with loud cheers, and the decision was immediately made public. Probably this was the right thing to do, but it still left an unfortunate impression after so many months of waiting for Heath to step aside. At a subsequent meeting of the party's National Executive there were dark mutterings in Willie's presence about candidates who had 'hidden behind the lady's skirts'.[18]

Before the night was over there came a further blow. Prior and the newly promoted John Peyton, who had both commiserated with Heath after the result was known, insisted on fighting the second ballot. Willie failed to talk them out of it, and other emissaries were equally unsuccessful. Prior's emergence was particularly serious for Willie; and, as it turned out, for himself. The idea of 'putting down a marker' for the future had occurred to Enoch Powell in 1965, but his mark turned out to be a black one, and Prior met a similar fate. Peyton's decision was equally mysterious, giving the impression that Heath's supporters were hopelessly divided as well as demoralised. Mrs Thatcher's team was rattled by Geoffrey Howe's decision to enter the contest; but although Howe was a monetarist, he was not widely known as a right-winger (or indeed as anything else); he had voted for Heath in the first ballot and in the second round he might have chosen Willie. Since his supporters included moderates such as Norman Fowler, Kenneth Clarke and Leon Brittan, probably the real effect of Howe's candidacy was further to damage Willie rather than Mrs Thatcher.[19]

At least there was no shortage of volunteers for Willie's campaign team. He was particularly touched that so many of those who had worked with him in government and the whips' office offered their support. Several people were heavily involved, including Colonel Michael Mates, a newcomer to Parliament who had served in Northern Ireland. Mates later described his role as that of 'driver, batman and orderly'; on one occasion he and Celia had to try to change Willie's trousers while the candidate spoke to a journalist on the telephone, lifting one leg after the other like a patient horse waiting to be shod.[20]

Willie's team also included David Howell, Sir Dennis Walters, Christopher Tugendhat, Sir Paul Bryan and Mark Carlisle. But there was a problem of accommodation, since Willie refused to take the slightest advantage of his base in Central Office. He even wrote to Mrs Thatcher asking for permission to use his party-funded secretary, since Joy Pemberton-Pigott, who helped with his constituency work, was on holiday. Mates started planning the campaign on the bed of the spare room of Willie's London home in Clabon Mews; the operation later moved to Interview Room J in the basement of the Commons. A new member of the Shadow Cabinet, Nick Scott, allowed Willie to use his room for meetings with some of the recent intake of MPs.[21]

Immediately after the first ballot Willie was the odds-on favourite, with Mrs Thatcher at even money. But by the following evening it was clear there were no wheels on Willie's wagon. A canvass by Thatcher's team revealed that their candidate was ahead of Willie by 106 to forty-six. Peyton and Prior stood on eight and six respectively, Geoffrey Howe on eleven. Mates somehow assembled an audience of 300 in his own Hampshire constituency for Willie to deliver the first speech of his campaign, but although the meeting went well it was not enough to reverse the momentum. Even at the grass roots there was a dramatic swing of opinion behind Thatcher. To activists who had assumed that the Conservatives were the natural party of government, and were bewildered by the setbacks of 1974, she had provided the perfect pressure-valve. Willie was being blown away.[22]

Willie's leadership bid was based on the idea that he alone could unite the party. This position demanded some genuflections towards the right-wing, and when he promised that no one should be excluded from the Shadow Cabinet because of 'his or *her* ideas' he obviously meant that Mrs Thatcher would be offered a senior position. There were limits, though; one over-heated commentator suggested that he might bring back Enoch Powell, which was more than even Mrs Thatcher managed. Although he could not match his rival, who boldly declared that she and her colleagues had 'failed the people', in the *Daily Telegraph* Willie came as close as he could to disowning some of the 'modernising' policies of the Heath Government, notably the local government reorganisation which had outraged many grass-roots Tories. 'For some years,' he wrote, 'change for the sake of change has been the order of the day . . . But as some of the changes have not turned out for the best, that mood is altering.' Willie would return to the party's traditional approach, mixing 'the ability to improve' with 'a disposition to preserve'. At the same time he indicated his continuing dislike of monetarism, saying that it was a mistake to be 'overawed by voluble expertise'. And he struck what must have seemed a shrewd blow against Mrs Thatcher's image, saying that a truly national party should be able to attract support from all regions, not just London and the Home Counties.[23]

The difficulty for Willie was to establish exactly what he stood for apart from unity and a dislike for unpalatable changes. His admirers compared him with Stanley Baldwin, claiming that he would unite the country as well as the party; but since Baldwin was regarded in some quarters as the father of appeasement, this was not a happy parallel. At Wimbledon two days before the ballot Willie appealed to the reforming Tory spirit of 1945–51, which had inspired him to join the party. But this merely invoked the period when the Conservatives had endorsed the post-war 'consensus'. Although the 'New Right' was numerically weak in the parliamentary party, it was now making the ideological running, tapping into a feeling that Heath's failure discredited the pragmatic approach that Willie had always followed.[24]

'Woolly, bumbling and platitudinous,' John Campbell has written, 'Whitelaw was in fact a very unconvincing candidate to put up against Mrs Thatcher in the full confidence of her first round victory.'[25] This verdict says more about the excitable state of the party at the time than about Willie himself. His platform was anything but 'woolly' and 'platitudinous' compared with the rhetoric of Tony Blair, for example, and in 1975 no one could guess that the 'One Nation' tradition within the Conservative Party was on its last legs. In fact, it was Mrs Thatcher who had been 'put up', against Heath. Once she had won the first round, any conceivable candidate from what now had to be seen as the moderate 'wing' of a divided party was bound to seem 'unconvincing'. More important than the profound philosophical differences between them was the fact that she and Willie represented contrasting political styles. John Biffen, who agreed with Thatcher on economic issues, nevertheless voted for Willie in the second ballot because he recognised the limited shelf-life of a leader who, even at this stage, saw political life as a constant crusade.[26] By contrast Willie spoke for those who understood the inevitable ebb and flow of popularity and knew that, unless the Conservatives frightened the voters, their time was sure to come again. So, in himself, Willie remained the best option among the moderates after Mrs Thatcher's first-round victory.

After the second ballot Willie showed the value of his philosophy of never looking back. He seems to have convinced himself that he had not expected to win – indeed, that he had never really wanted to stand in the first place. At a lunch only two months later he talked very freely to a group of journalists. Alastair Hetherington made a note of his remarks, feeling that this was useful 'as a footnote to history because what he said about the Conservative leadership race and his own part in it rang very true':

> He said that he was not a man of any particular ambition or particular capacity. He knew that he did some things well. On the other hand he knew that he was a lousy orator and could never become any better. Everything he had done in politics – apart from the original decision to stand for Parliament in the first place – had been handed to him on a platter. He had merely done the jobs that had come about . . . He was not surprised, frankly, that Maggie had won . . . especially he was not surprised by his own defeat in the second round. He had not privately expected to win. He wasn't sorry that he had not won. On the whole he

thought he probably didn't have the capacity to be a good Conservative leader.[27]

Probably Hetherington found Willie's confession more credible because it had been inspired by some excellent claret. But while some of his remarks do have a 'ring of truth' – he was certainly not ambitious in any orthodox sense, and his shortcomings as an orator would have been a severe handicap, particularly in Opposition[28] – the overall impression is that of a man trying to rationalise a serious personal misfortune. His showing in the second ballot turned out to be more of a slap in the face even than Heath's defeat; he was beaten more easily, yet he was still far more popular than the ex-leader had ever been. Rather than cursing his bad luck, it was natural for him to overcome his disappointment by adopting as his own views the questions that had been raised about his suitability for the post during the campaign, by some of his closest non-political friends, among others.[29] Even if the realisation of impending defeat had come early on, he could not have expected 'Maggie' to beat him when he first declared his candidature. As for his lack of capacity, the feeling that he could do the job had come upon him very suddenly, in Ireland, and there had been plenty of time for doubts to set in as he awaited his chance. But he was not the man to apply for a job which he felt to be beyond his abilities, and although his spell at Employment might have knocked his confidence, he must have known that this had been an unfair test of domestic departmental aptitude. Unfortunately, the pose of 'reluctant candidate' worked too well, and he stuck to it for the rest of his life whenever the subject was mentioned. This could only undermine his own power base within the party, by implying that those who had wanted him as leader – backing their opinion with hard work, and earning enemies for themselves in the rival camps – had overrated their man.

Of course Willie could never refer publicly to the role in his defeat of its real architect – Edward Heath. Almost everything Heath did in 1974 worked to Willie's disadvantage. Even trivial decisions worked their way through and afflicted him. In the summer, for example, Heath had asked Keith Joseph to shadow Home Affairs. The only excuse for this unlikely appointment was the hope that it might shut Joseph up on economic matters; but even that didn't work. Almost the only notable speech which Joseph made with direct relevance to Home Affairs came just before the Christmas recess, when he had abandoned his own fleeting leadership ambitions. In a debate on capital punishment, Joseph argued that terrorist murderers deserved the death penalty, but that this should not apply in Northern Ireland where juries had been abolished. By previous arrangement with the Home Secretary, Roy Jenkins, Willie intervened to say that although he knew public opinion was against him, he still felt that the execution of terrorists would be counter-productive. Coming so soon after November's Birmingham pub bombs, which killed twenty-one and injured more than a hundred, this was a courageous statement, as Jenkins fully recognised. But it was also a clear sign that Willie shared none of the visceral instincts of so many grass-roots Tories, not to mention the MPs who would soon be voting for a new leader.[30]

Another of Heath's appointments caused more spectacular damage. As deputy to the Shadow Chancellor, Margaret Thatcher had made a strong impact with her speech of 21 January 1975, attacking Denis Healey's Finance Bill. Ironically, at a Shadow Cabinet meeting held in advance of Healey's budget, it was Willie who had suggested that the time had come for the Opposition to speak out more strongly against Labour's economic policy.[31] By contrast, important though it was in itself, Willie's brief of devolution was unlikely to present him with many openings at this time – 'lousy orator' or not. On the Saturday before the second ballot, Thatcher and Willie travelled to Eastbourne to address the Young Conservatives' Conference. Both candidates had agreed that they would stick to their Shadow subjects. Willie's worthy speech was greeted with lukewarm applause, and he had to field awkward questions concerning some YCs who had not been selected as candidates in the general election. But Mrs Thatcher's speech brought the house down. There was some ill-feeling afterwards, since Thatcher had addressed a wide range of policy areas instead of sticking to her brief; but had she followed the rules, she would still have had much greater scope to make an impact.

At least Willie had not perpetrated one of his celebrated verbal slips, as he had done in December 1974, when at a business lunch he congratulated the City of London on its contribution to 'our national economic problems'. But it was a pity that, as Party Chairman, he had no alternative but to fulfil an engagement in front of a group that had harboured some of Heath's most vigorous opponents.[32] By contrast, when Mrs Thatcher was advised not to take part in a *Panorama* debate with the other four candidates, a decision dictated by fear of a slip-up created the impression that the new front-runner was too dignified to court public favour. In one of the less successful quips in her memoirs, Lady Thatcher has compared the programme to '*Hamlet* without a princess'. Supporters of the other candidates would have been reminded instead of the leading female part in another of Shakspeare's tragedies.[33]

The Eastbourne conference took another adverse turn when the warring couple posed for photographs outside. Willie agreed to kiss Mrs Thatcher, who claimed (improbably) that this was not the first of their embraces. Clearly embarrassed, Willie resorted to bluster, saying that he had kissed her often: 'But we have not done it on a pavement outside a hotel in Eastbourne before'. Probably no two politicians in Britain were less attuned to the double entendre, and neither can have realised that they were sounding like a risqué music-hall double act. But Mrs Thatcher's team could not have conjured up a more effective way of presenting their candidate as an attractive woman, while Willie just looked bashful. The worst incident of this kind, though, was a fearful own goal. Willie agreed to be filmed doing the washing-up at home, wearing an apron. It was all too clear from the picture that he was unfamiliar with the procedure, but in case anyone doubted this Celia provided confirmation in the accompanying interview. It all looked hopelessly contrived; and all to no purpose, since very few housewives had a vote in the election (besides Mrs Thatcher herself). By contrast the new front-runner made the most of every photo-opportunity lined up by her professional advisers. A half-admiring Barbara Castle understood the sudden transformation, writing, 'She is in love: in love with power, success – and with herself.'[34]

But Willie's greatest handicap besides Heath was Northern Ireland. The collapse of the Executive in May 1974 had been particularly difficult for him to take. There was no way that he could break the informal cross-party consensus which had been faithfully observed by his opposite number, Merlyn Rees, during his own time in Belfast. But Willie remained convinced that the breakdown could have been averted, feeling that the army would have been allowed to keep the power stations going, provided they had secured cooperation from middle management and technicians. This chance, he thought, had been wilfully tossed away by Wilson, who discussed the crisis in a television broadcast of 25 May. The Prime Minister was quite right to describe the strike as 'a deliberate and calculated attempt to use every undemocratic and unparliamentary means for the purpose of bringing down the whole constitution of Northern Ireland so as to set up there a sectarian and undemocratic state, from which one-third of the people of Northern Ireland will be excluded'. But this was not a million miles from what the miners had so recently tried to do on the mainland. And Wilson was ill-advised to refer to the subsidies that the British taxpayer poured into the province, talking of 'people who spend their lives sponging on Westminster and British democracy'. The contrast with Willie's conciliatory methods could not have been greater, and the result was the complete destruction of his work.[35]

In private, Willie described Wilson's broadcast as 'a total disaster', and although he approved of new proposals advanced by Rees, he remained concerned that the Labour Government was doing nothing to dissuade people who wanted the troops to be withdrawn. Strangely, it seems that he had neither offered advice to Rees nor asked for a confidential briefing. If he had, he would have known that Faulkner had been despairing of the Executive long before the strike delivered the *coup de grâce*, and concluded (as a recent historian has done) that 'the strike was sufficiently popular that to try and break it by using the army and police would have simply made it more effective'. In fact, despite the IRA bombing campaign on the mainland, Northern Ireland was almost a non-issue by the time of the October general election; even in February 1974 less than 10 per cent of Tory candidates had mentioned it in their election addresses. Had the Executive survived, at least Willie would have had a constructive achievement to his name, even if few people cared about it. At best, by February 1975 it seemed that he had wasted his time. Those who thought about his service in Ulster at all tended to remember only his talks with the Provos. Conflating this with his abortive spell at Employment, they concluded that for all his good nature Willie was nothing more than an unsuccessful appeaser. Against this background a hard-hitting article on Northern Ireland reminding the party of Willie's achievements might have been helpful. Instead, on the day before the election *The Times* published a piece by David Howell that was too thoughtful and balanced to punch home the positive message.[36]

At four o'clock on 11 February, Michael Mates sprinted over to the Norman Shaw Building to break the news that Willie had lost. Perhaps the worst of it was that his elderly but indomitable mother was furious that he had allowed himself to be beaten by a woman.[37] At least he had done better than the Thatcher team had initially expected, winning seventy-nine votes to Mrs Thatcher's 146. Prior and Howe trailed with nineteen votes each; John Peyton received eleven.

Willie was braced for bad news. His own campaign team had been slow to adapt to the new atmosphere within the parliamentary party, in which MPs were quite prepared to lie to each other about their intentions. After the poll, Mates discovered that at least six of his colleagues had written to both Thatcher and Willie, claiming that they had voted for them. But in the end the forecast was almost right – Bryan had estimated support at eighty-two. In his memoirs Willie wrote that he found 'the internal divisions and bad feeling among one's parliamentary colleagues most disagreeable'. Attention has focused largely on the clumsy and counter-productive attempts to denigrate Mrs Thatcher before the first ballot. But while Willie's team fought fairly, it seems that Neave and his associates did all they could to undermine the man who had failed to make a clear distinction between himself and the hated Heath. In an editorial of 6 February *The Times* complained that Willie 'is now being liberally daubed with the mud of politics'. In one ridiculous slur, it was claimed that he had telephoned Lord Carrington before the first ballot to plead for his support. In fact, Carrington had rung Willie to say that if Heath lost 'he would be wholly for Mr Whitelaw from then on'. No wonder Nigel Fisher felt wretched when he found himself casting his vote in Committee Room 14 at the same time as Willie. Although he regarded him as an 'old and valued friend' Fisher was unable to wish Willie good luck since he had just voted for a candidate who was worlds apart from his own liberal brand of Conservatism.[38]

There should have been some consolation in defeat for Willie. Since speculation began about Heath's position, he had been under constant pressure from others – the gossips who were pushing him towards the top job, and the leader who prevented him from taking it. Now it seemed that he was free. Some of his supporters advised that he should take a little time to reflect. Even if he decided to offer his services to Margaret Thatcher, he should do so only after playing hard to get for a while.[39]

But Willie had already finished his reflecting. Mates remembers that when he brought him the bad news, Willie said, 'Well, the party's made the right decision. The party needs Margaret and it needs change.' That night he held a small party in Clabon Mews, to thank his supporters. True to form, he was very emotional and wept openly. Shaking hands with each member of his team, he promised never to forget what they had done for him. Some harsh words were spoken, particularly of Humphrey Atkins, the Chief Whip, who had tarnished his office by encouraging both Prior and Howe to stand. But before Mates helped Willie to bed, the vanquished candidate announced that for the sake of party unity he had already promised his loyalty to Mrs Thatcher. After all, he was still a prisoner – of his own upbringing, and of the recent past in which he had constantly banged on about party unity. Mrs Thatcher knew him well enough to have seen straight through any delaying tactics. And he really had been trounced in the election. Thinking all this through, Willie realised that an instant pledge of loyalty would be the best way of preserving – maybe even increasing – his existing influence. It proved to be a highly controversial decision among his political allies.[40]

Later Willie said that Mrs Thatcher 'had to make the initial approach'; if so, she only saved him the trouble of asking for a meeting that would have happened quickly anyway. It also emerged that one condition had been attached to Willie's promise – that Mrs Thatcher should never appoint Sir Keith Joseph as Shadow Chancellor. To this extent, at least, he could settle old scores. He also tried to persuade the moderates that they should join him in the Shadow Cabinet. In at least one case he succeeded too well. Robert Carr had been anxious to give more time to his business interest, but after talking to Willie he decided that he would stay on, provided that he was offered the post of Shadow Foreign Secretary. This was no more than his seniority demanded, but Mrs Thatcher had other plans. In fact the post went to Reginald Maudling, who had been heard after the first ballot to declare, 'The Party's taken leave of its senses. This is a black day.' Mrs Thatcher obviously resented Carr, who had threatened to resign as Shadow Chancellor because his understrapper insisted on making speeches without clearing them with him. As a distinguished name from the 1960s, Maudling added (temporary) weight to the team; and Mrs Thatcher probably calculated that, unlike Carr, he would be more dangerous on the backbenches. Lord Thorneycroft was another renowned elder statesman to be brought back. Whether Thorneycroft had really changed his mind in the two months since he had assured Heath that he was indispensable remained to be seen.[41]

So from the outset Willie had some influence over his leader, but there were clear limits. Peter Walker, who had been the most outspoken front-bench critic of monetarism, was dumped, as was the Housing spokesman Nicholas Scott, who had helped both Heath and Willie. Naturally Willie wanted a senior post for Heath, but this proved impossible to arrange; Heath signalled his intention to return to the backbenches. Like all ideological purges, this one extended to the party's officials. Michael Wolff was abruptly removed from Central Office. Mrs Thatcher attributed this unpopular decision to Thorneycroft, but his only knowledge of Wolff must have come from Willie. Mrs Thatcher would not have been anxious to work with Wolff; but Willie might not have fought very hard to save someone who was heavily implicated in the 'Who Governs?' election.[42]

Despite these portents of a bumpy ride ahead, the Shadow Cabinet had a similar balance to the one that Heath had appointed after the October election. Willie himself was named as Deputy Leader, and kept his responsibility for devolution. In numbers and ability, those who opposed Mrs Thatcher's economic views – and her hostility to Europe, which was difficult to conceal even at that time – held a clear majority. Some felt that the new leader could be tamed; and in this task they looked to the new Deputy Leader for guidance and action.

CHAPTER 13

'THAT AWFUL WOMAN'

'She'll be out by Christmas!' Lord Carrington is supposed to have crowed after Mrs Thatcher's victory. He was not alone in thinking that his party had done something inexplicable, although the Labour MPs who toasted the 1975 result in the belief that it doomed the Tories to defeat at the next general election obviously felt that the aberration would last beyond the festive season. They would have been as astonished as Carrington if someone had told them that Mrs Thatcher would celebrate fifteen Christmases as the leader of her party.[1]

It was assumed by many of Mrs Thatcher's allies that, at heart, Willie really agreed with Carrington. They might have found backing for that view in the letter he wrote in sympathy with the discarded Robert Carr: 'I am only so sad that having taken on the task of running for us all I failed you. Of course it is now becoming clear that her cohorts a) have little talent, b) have no idea at all about running a party.'

Like Sara Morrison and Ian Gilmour, who wrote similar letters to Carr, Willie had felt unable to refer to Mrs Thatcher by name. But he continued, 'I suppose rather ironically I am there to save them!!' His words might be unflattering, but there was no direct contradiction of his loyalty pledge. As so often, he was prepared to do his duty, even if this time he would have to brace himself more than usual.[2]

Even so, Willie's instant offer could be seen as a clever move in a long game; once the party realised its mistake he would be ready to step forward amid the apologies of his chastened colleagues. These suspicions came naturally to a group which felt that Mrs Thatcher owed her position almost entirely to good luck. For his own part, Willie certainly doubted his chances of forging a fruitful relationship with Mrs Thatcher. Apart from his doubts about her abilities and those of her team, he wondered about her physical capacity for the draining job of Opposition leader. But in retirement he rightly admitted that his concern had been based on 'male chauvinism of the worst order' – after all, he had once predicted that Mrs Thatcher would prove impossible to get rid of if she were ever promoted to the front bench, and his closest relatives had given him ample evidence of female durability. Yet when Willie's fears on the score of stamina were allayed, traces of his 'chauvinism' remained. In deference to his leader's sex, for example, he resolved never to argue with her in front of others. Willie probably knew that his critics took this as a sign that he was frightened to contradict her, but a man of his generation and upbringing could do no other.[3]

Social status was even more important, though not decisive; after all, the difference in background had not prevented Willie from working well with Heath. Mrs Thatcher, though, presented almost a caricature of the attitudes associated with the middle class; she would have verified all the fears of Willie's Victorian ancestors. She also typified a new breed of MP, whose advent Willie regretted. Long before her arrival at Westminster she had been obsessed with politics; yet Willie believed that without a range of outside interests, her view of the world would always be distorted. In short, she lacked the crucial knowledge that politics was 'the art of the possible'. That insight would have to be supplied by someone close to her: Willie would have to 'save her', although he put this more politely in public when he told his colleagues, 'Just as we need her she needs us.' If he could establish a working partnership with the new leader, the result might be a winning blend of impetuosity and pragmatism. The only question was whether or not he would be rebuffed. This possibility had obviously occurred to him when he prepared his speech for the party meeting of 20 February 1975, where he seconded the formal motion to endorse Mrs Thatcher's victory. When he repeated his pledge of loyalty he thought it necessary to add, 'When I say that, I mean it.'[4]

At the same time, Willie saw no reason to compromise on his own views. In a speech to his constituents on 3 March he warned that Conservatives would not 'carry conviction if we appear either selfish or narrow-based in our approach to politics'. The individual should be released from some of the restrictions imposed by Labour; but 'a true and successful Conservative Party will always seek to look after those who are not in a position to care for themselves'. Willie pointedly referred to Keith Joseph's generosity as Secretary of State for Social Services under Heath. Undoubtedly the speech was a reminder to Mrs Thatcher that any attempt to break with 'One Nation' policies would be resisted. But in the context of Willie's recent declaration of loyalty it could also be interpreted as an offer to complement a leader who had already established an 'uncaring' image.[5]

The situation was not helped by wider political developments. The Labour Government was deeply divided on the subject of EEC membership – far more so than the Conservatives, although a vocal minority on the Opposition side had always been worried about the perceived erosion of British 'sovereignty'. To paper over the cracks in his own party Harold Wilson had conducted a superficial 're-negotiation' of the terms of entry and had introduced the necessary legislation for Britain's first ever referendum. A month after her election Mrs Thatcher delivered her maiden speech as Conservative leader in the debate on the White Paper. She managed to score partisan points while sounding statesmanlike, denouncing Labour's use of the referendum in this instance without ruling out the use of the device in other circumstances. In obedience to this line, she and Willie both announced that the Conservatives would not be bound by the referendum result – a position that would have triggered a constitutional crisis if the people had voted 'No'. Years later, though, she began to think that in 1975 the constitutional conditions had been right for a referendum after all. By that time she was itching to give the British public a chance to reverse a decision which apparently cemented for all time the place of the UK in an institution she had come to loathe.[6]

In 1975 Mrs Thatcher's feelings were relatively temperate, and she denied that membership of the Community had made the Germans feel less German or had wrenched the French from their sense of nationhood. But she had no affinity with European culture – and none of the memories of war that inspired Willie's strong commitment to the EEC. The cross-party 'Britain in Europe' (BIE) campaign was organised with impressive speed, and it was suggested to Mrs Thatcher that Willie should be nominated as a vice-president. According to Philip Goodhart, 'the idea was accepted with alacrity', and although Mrs Thatcher did urge the public to vote 'Yes', she was relieved to be something less than a backseat driver throughout the campaign. Reggie Maudling, the Shadow Foreign Secretary, was also made a vice-president, although unlike Willie he was not on the executive committee. It was Willie, rather than Maudling, who opened for the Opposition in the debate on the second reading of the Referendum Bill on 7 April 1975, and of all the senior Conservatives Willie paid the closest attention to the day-to-day running of the campaign – a role that reunited him with the dynamic Geoffrey Tucker. He was also pencilled in to deliver seven major speeches from Portsmouth to Glasgow; for Labour only Roy Jenkins was scheduled for so many. The venues varied from the Free Trade Hall in Manchester to the Odeon in London's Leicester Square.[7]

But there was another senior Conservative on the vice-presidential roster – Edward Heath, who understandably chose this issue to break his silence in the Commons since the leadership election. Heath remained opposed to referenda: although the remark was endlessly quoted against him, when he had spoken of EEC membership depending on 'the full-hearted consent' of the people he had been referring to consent expressed by their elected representatives. But once Wilson had decided on the expedient, Heath threw himself into battle. *The Times* hailed him as 'The Achilles of the European cause', and it seemed that at last he had overcome his own Achilles heel – his inability to project his warm personality in public. Ironically, the opinion polls in which he had so often trailed Harold Wilson now showed him to be marginally the more popular of the two. At the same time Mrs Thatcher's 'honeymoon' with the electors was abruptly terminated; her approval rating, almost two-thirds in February 1975, had been halved by June. For her it was equally unwelcome that the 'national unity' idea was given belated (if not posthumous) endorsement, as Heath willingly shared platforms with Labour and Liberal leaders (though not with Wilson himself, who followed Mrs Thatcher's low-profile example). Roy Jenkins, the leader of Labour's pro-marketeers and President of BIE, still found Heath 'a difficult morsel to digest', but his admiration of the ex-premier increased during the campaign.[8]

Willie was far less troublesome to Jenkins' digestion. The pair had already combined, during the capital-punishment debate of December 1974, and the referendum campaign confirmed to Jenkins that Willie was 'a fine ally' and 'a pleasure to be with'; he was 'my most important collaborator'. Their rapport was essential to prevent friction within a broad umbrella organisation; Willie would defend Labour's people against complaints from his own side, and Jenkins returned the compliment. Jenkins was impressed by the organisational expertise which the Tories brought to the campaign, and was amused when party officials treated Willie 'with an almost military obedience'. But he recognised that Willie had also played a key role in reassuring voters with his homely style – his contribution was epitomised by a television broadcast in which he spoke about the beauties of Cumbria 'while he drove a Land-Rover with more speed than attention'. His journey ended safely 'just as, with a splendid logical leap, he announced that the quality of the English countryside proved that we would be safe in Europe'. To confirmed opponents of the EEC this was contemptible blather, and it was unlikely to impress the more committed on Willie's side – such as the businessman and later Europhobe James Goldsmith, who was anxious that a positive decision should be reached by a public that felt fully informed. But the polls suggested that most voters needed emotional reassurance – not facts – since the statistics produced by both sides could be endlessly contested. Until the first few months of 1975 a substantial majority wanted to withdraw from the Community, but detailed findings suggested that most people were just waiting to be convinced that membership on the right terms would be a good thing for Britain.[9]

If Willie had not been such an artful conciliator his message during the campaign might have unsettled some of his new allies. Before the White Paper was published he had argued that the real question would be 'Are we in Britain, by staying in Europe, prepared to look outwards to the world both politically and economically, or are we going to withdraw inwards on ourselves, fearful, introspective and small minded?' But during the campaign he sounded 'introspective' himself. For some time he had been warning about the rise of the left within the Labour Party, and now he stepped up his rhetoric, suggesting that a 'No' vote would pave the way for a socialist state. But this would hardly explain why idolators of the capitalist system such as Enoch Powell were pleading with their countrymen to turn their backs on Europe. Mrs Thatcher's supporters were unlikely to be comforted, either; the party rank-and-file would be enthused by these assaults on the socialist enemy, but Willie's speeches could also be read as an appeal for moderates of all parties to stay in some kind of combination once the referendum was over. Now that it had seized the leadership, the Conservative right wing was less anxious than ever to join a coalition government that was sure to embody the values of the post-war 'consensus'. But the cooperative mood was enhanced by new press attention on other European governments – many of which were, of course, themselves coalitions. Fortunately for the 'Thatcherites' and tribal politicians of all parties, normality re-established itself very quickly; in one area, at least, drunken arguments broke out among rival party activists within minutes of the referendum result. The Labour minister Reg Prentice, who had made a public appeal for national unity, was demoted by Harold Wilson at the first opportunity. But the foot-soldiers had enjoyed their flirtation; and if a similar issue were to arouse them again, they might find it easier to reach a true consummation.[10]

What Willie feared most was a low turn-out in the referendum, and in the days leading up to the vote (held on 5 June 1975) he was tempted to patrol his constituency with his loudspeaker.[11] He need not have feared. The result was very satisfactory to the 'Yes' camp. More than seventeen million votes were cast for continued membership – more than twice as many as those who wanted Britain to pull out. In Cumbria, despite his own doubts concerning the farming community, almost three-quarters of the electorate supported Willie's case. In fact, every area of the country voted 'Yes'. The lowest percentage (52 per cent) was registered in Northern Ireland, where Ian Paisley had campaigned on the platform that a vote for Europe was an endorsement of the Pope. Willie was consoled by an opinion poll which found that although both men were recognised by 83 per cent of the electorate, only 3 per cent 'respected and liked' Paisley (for Willie himself the figure was 33 per cent – the same as for Enoch Powell).[12]

When Edward du Cann declared for a 'No' vote during the campaign, he ensured that almost everyone in Willie's personal rogues' gallery was lined up against the Community. Willie may have felt it to be no accident that so many people he regarded as untrustworthy (or worse) were numbered among the

'No' ranks. But as Tony Benn rightly complained, the media obsession with personalities rather than issues detracted from the campaign and devalued the result. Also, the press was virtually unanimous in supporting the EEC. Even the cartoons in the *Daily Mail* (which would later deploy any flimsy evidence to discredit 'Europe') presented a uniform 'Yes' message. Only the *Morning Star* bucked the trend. All of the pro-EEC editorials in papers like *The Times* and the *Daily Telegraph* represented free advertising; but if this were not enough, BIE heavily outspent its opponents on more conventional forms of publicity. The 'Yes' camp could argue that this was only natural, since the overwhelming majority of businessmen supported membership, and their interests would be affected more than most by the result. But this argument cut little ice with anti-market Tories, who now discovered the attractions of pure democratic theory. As for Willie, he probably felt much as he had done after the border poll in Northern Ireland – regretting that it had been necessary to use the referendum as a tactical device, but relieved that it had produced a result he could live with.

Within two decades of the referendum all the underlying divisions of the Thatcher years had crystallised in the issue of 'Europe', and the Tory Party decided that arguments about 'sovereignty' were far more enjoyable than the business of governing. Back in 1975 internal debate focused on the economic legacy of the Heath Government, with particular reference to the statutory incomes policy, which had produced the confrontation with the miners. Mrs Thatcher and Sir Keith Joseph regarded this as an almost blasphemous contravention of sound economic theory, and were determined to ditch the policy. The majority of the Shadow Cabinet saw it for what it really was – a fairly desperate expedient, which had proved unworkable in too rigid a form. They acknowledged that the alternative remedy for inflation – a monetarist 'squeeze' leading to a sharp rise in unemployment – was likely to work in time. But for 'One Nation' politicians the prospect was unappealing for many reasons, not least of which was the increased likelihood of further electoral defeat.

Shadow ministers were given an early chance to air their views. At a meeting of 11 April 1975 they discussed a paper, jointly written by Joseph and Angus Maude, the party's new Deputy Chairman. The document invited the Shadow Cabinet to join Joseph in denouncing almost everything the Heath Government had done. Maudling, Gilmour and Pym reacted angrily. Fortunately Lord Hailsham realised the importance of the discussion, and knew that the official minutes would provide only a neutered summary; so he jotted down a verbatim report of some exchanges. Joseph and Thatcher asserted that the post-war 'consensus' had been forged by socialists, and that Conservatives (themselves included) had failed to offer an alternative to the public. When Gilmour denied this, he was challenged by Mrs Thatcher to attest his belief in capitalism. Geoffrey Howe suggested a compromise, arguing that the 1970 Conservative Manifesto had been a departure from the consensus and that Joseph was only asking his colleagues to return to the 'Selsdon Park' principles. This was to become a familiar position, but as we have seen it was historically dubious and in any case Howe's colleagues were too angry to listen.[13]

Willie was alarmed. Pym had rightly described the paper as 'a recipe for disaster'; it had polarised the Shadow Cabinet at a time when party unity was more important than ever. The moderates were ready to admit that mistakes had been made between 1970 and 1974; but they could not allow that the whole of their political careers had been based on semi-socialism. Like so many recent converts, Thatcher and Joseph were desperate to prove their new-found virtue, and forgot that others had yet to be fired with the same inspiration. There was no room for compromise, but the atmosphere could still be lightened. According to Hailsham's record, Willie cut across the debate on economic theory and recent history to say, 'The most fatal thing in politics is to try and look different from what we are. People always complain that I look very large on TV. What w[ould] they say if I appeared in a bathing dress?'[14]

In the context of that fierce argument it is more difficult than usual to work out what Willie might have meant. But his remark conveyed a general truth that was deeply uncomfortable for anyone who wanted a united Shadow Cabinet. It was illustrated on 21 July 1975, when Mrs Thatcher gave a dismal performance in the Commons because she had been forced to 'try to look different from what she was'. The government had imposed a £6 limit on pay increases. According to monetarist theory, this was just as bad as Heath's Phase 3; and in her memoirs Lady Thatcher describes it as 'nonsense'. But at the time she was persuaded that the urge to theorise should be mastered by tactical considerations. In August Wilson backed his policy with a patriotic appeal, and even the monetarists had to recognise that all-out opposition would cost votes. Willie certainly thought so, and since his leader was on holiday at the time he made positive noises on behalf of the Opposition without clearing the text in advance. In hindsight Lady Thatcher described his televised response as 'a rather warmer welcome than I could have been persuaded to [give]'. Actually she had allowed herself to be 'persuaded' into even greater warmth; in the Commons she had merely protested that the government had acted too slowly. And although some commentators thought that Willie was sailing close to the wind in offering support for the policy, he had pointed out that limits on pay could not cure inflation unless they were accompanied by cuts in government expenditure. This could only be regarded as a symptom of disloyalty by a deeply insecure leader – or, perhaps, one who was still fuming from the Commons debate, in which Heath had 'made Margaret look like a tinny amateur'. Barbara Castle, who made that observation, also recorded that

Thatcher's poor effort had rekindled speculation about her leadership.[15]

Significantly, on the day of Mrs Thatcher's ill-starred speech – but before Heath made his own contribution – Lord Hailsham suggested a reconciliation between the warring couple. He asked Mrs Thatcher to offer an olive branch, arguing that there was no ideological difference between them. Yet he combined his appeal with an admission that the breach might be too great, and he cannot have been surprised by Mrs Thatcher's response: 'I do try, but it takes two'.[16]

Mrs Thatcher's reply showed how far her fears of a National Government had been increased by the referendum campaign. If Heath, Peter Walker and other Conservative moderates could be enticed into a coalition with Labour and the Liberals, then the short-term prospects for the Tories – and their new leader – would be grim. At the time this idea was being canvassed by Harold Macmillan, who thought that Wilson could reverse the situation faced by Ramsay MacDonald when he headed a coalition dominated by Tories. While Macmillan seemed to relish such speculation, Hailsham and his closest colleagues were terrified by it. If Heath were asked to associate himself with the Labour government, his old allies would come under tremendous pressure to follow him, which would split the Conservative Party. The only solution was to keep a channel of communication open with the fallen leader. Hailsham wrote to him at the end of July, repeating his implausible denial of ideological disagreements ('Most of them are differences of emphasis') and expressing the hope that Heath would not blame him for serving under Mrs Thatcher.[17]

If Hailsham felt torn between two leaders, the situation was even worse for Willie. He knew that a prolonged quarrel could be disastrous for the party – even, perhaps, resulting in a rerun of the Corn Law controversy, with Heath playing Peel to Thatcher's Disraeli. He was the obvious go-between if things got out of hand; but he knew Heath too well to expect him to forgive the colleague who had accused him of betraying Conservatism. Whatever Hailsham might say, Willie also knew that the real quarrel was about ideology rather than personalities, and that given Heath's determination to resist the right wing at all costs, he would be certain to attack at the first sign of a policy shift.

Even before the referendum Willie had unburdened himself on this subject to the *Guardian*'s Peter Preston:

frankly he wished Heath would now get out of politics altogether because the position he was playing by choice on the back benches put a tremendous strain on the Conservative Party. If Heath got up and agreed with the front bench, that would be taken as no more than a routine endorsement of what Thatcher and Joseph were planning. If he showed even a modest differing of line, it would immediately be taken as rebellious and petty . . . as soon as Heath began to seem critical of Thatcher on a consistent basis he would be ostracised by the majority of Conservative members and would find his position untenable.[18]

Willie had taken a serious risk in spelling this out to a group of journalists, and he hastily added that he would be grateful if it was kept confidential. According to Preston's notes, Willie claimed 'that at some stage he might indeed be asked to give that advice [to Heath], and he did not wish it to have a secondhand flavour'.

By the time Hailsham made his own appeal, the situation had deteriorated. In June Mrs Thatcher had released a questionable account of her dealings with Heath after the leadership election, suggesting that he had been discourteous when she visited his home and claiming that she had made a direct offer of a Shadow Cabinet post. In fact Heath had already made it clear that he wished to return to the backbenches. The infuriated Heath issued a correction. With hindsight, Mrs Thatcher's tactical purpose in this exchange seem fairly clear, and her timing suggests that Heath's performance in the referendum campaign had left her seriously rattled.[19]

At the Party Conference of October 1975, held at Blackpool, Heath received a standing ovation when he entered the hall. Mrs Thatcher wisely led the applause, and at her initiative they shook hands before leaving the platform. Willie decided to press for a rapprochement. According to Lady Thatcher, the following evening he asked if she would be prepared to visit Heath in his hotel suite. When she agreed, 'Willie said that that was "absolutely splendid" and that he would ring me back to confirm'. Nearly two hours passed, and the telephone was silent. So Mrs Thatcher contacted Willie again, to be told that the meeting was off. According to Alistair McAlpine, 'Tears filled her eyes, not at Heath's rejection of her attempts at peace, but at Whitelaw's casual attitude to the whole affair.'[20]

Whatever the precise course of events – the accounts differ – apparently the exercise was never repeated. In an interview for this book, Willie asserted that the rift was 'none of his business'. Long before the 1979 general election it was understood that Heath neither wished for, nor expected to be offered, a place in a Thatcher Cabinet. By that time Willie's sympathy for Heath had been eroded and privately he expressed his frustration at the ex-leader's failure to give any credit to his successor. In retirement he used a newspaper interview to claim that, although he had kept up good relations with Heath, 'The fact that he's so bitter has been very distressing to his friends and it's tragic for him. He's too great a man not to have played a bigger role in recent years.' Willie could have been more tactful had he wanted a return of the old intimacy now that he was freed from government responsibilities; when he was shown the offending passage, Heath asked for it to be kept on file. But it seems there was never anything like a row over the years, although Willie occasionally delivered mild public rebukes whenever he judged that his old boss had clearly overstepped the boundary of constructive opposition to Mrs Thatcher's policies. Helped by their mutual friends, such as Lord Aldington, the two men found a way to tolerate their divergent political paths.[21]

Willie's half-hearted attempt to bring Heath back into the fold at the 1975 conference rounded off a difficult few days for him. The audience seemed to reserve all of its understandable frustration for the debate in which he made his own contribution. As an indication of the depth of feeling, party managers had been forced to allow discussion of a hostile motion, deploring the ineffectiveness of the parliamentary Opposition. At least two of the previous speakers (including Michael Ancram, who had lost his seat in October 1974) were directly critical of Willie himself. The party wanted to feel that its MPs were striving night and day to bring down the Labour Government; yet Willie repeated his conciliatory line towards the incomes policy: 'I cannot believe it makes any sense at all to oppose something which you believe is vitally necessary at this time in the country's interests.' Those who took 'a dogmatic line' (Joseph? Mrs Thatcher herself?) should 'remember that no single one of us can have it all our own way'. At the next general election there would be 'no question of holding back'; and by that time Labour's internal divisions should have damaged the government far more than any Tory sniping. In the meantime Conservatives should themselves remain united; Willie lashed out at 'those members who sometimes seem to indulge themselves in critical and malicious gossip for its own sake'.[22]

Despite the tension, Willie kept control of his temper and observers considered it a good-humoured speech, which had transformed the debate. The *Daily Mail*'s headline the next day was 'Whitelaw holds party together'. But the more resolute critics – mainly Young Conservatives – had ignored his plea for a show of unity by pressing (in vain) for a vote on the motion. There was more trouble later, as Willie addressed a meeting of the newly formed Tory Reform Group (TRG). When he argued that some kind of incomes policy was necessary, some right-wingers yelled 'rubbish' – to which he replied, characteristically, 'It's perfectly reasonable to shout "rubbish".' Although he defied the line being trumpeted by Sir Keith Joseph, declaring that he was 'not in the least apologetic for what the Conservative Government did between 1970 and 1973', Willie was forced to say that if he had thought the TRG had been designed as an anti-Thatcher faction within the party he would not have addressed the meeting. To prove his open-mindedness, he even agreed that it was worth looking into the feasibility of denationalising the Post Office.[23]

Ironically, the events at the conference improved Willie's relationship with

Mrs Thatcher, at least to the extent of clarifying a few things. Roy Jenkins thought that 1975 was 'a great lost opportunity for Heath and Whitelaw and a whole regiment of discarded Conservative "wets"'. But if such an opportunity really existed, it passed with Mrs Thatcher's own speech to the Blackpool conference. Very nervous beforehand, she was exultant when it was over. 'Now I *am* leader,' she told her closest supporters. Almost certainly a flop would have been fatal. But after the speech it was impossible to think of a challenge to her leadership; even if an overwhelming national crisis had produced a coalition government, the enraptured party membership would have withheld their support unless she was a senior member.[24]

An enhanced feeling of security meant that Mrs Thatcher could relax in her attitude to Willie, despite the botched rendezvous with Heath. At the same time, Willie had shown a similar mastery of the conference mood; and although his speeches were 'unsound' from the leader's point of view, he was a model of orthodoxy compared to others who were delivering thinly coded attacks. By this time he had sworn allegiance in public so often that it only made sense to take him at his word. Apparently it still took an intervention from Norman Tebbit before Mrs Thatcher felt she could trust Willie, but in the Shadow Cabinet reshuffle of January 1976 she gave a clear sign of her faith in him by adding the Home Affairs portfolio to his existing responsibility, devolution. Probably the fact that at this time Sir Keith Joseph asked Willie to chair important policy committees – on parliamentary reform and public spending – should be taken as another indication of a thaw in relations, given the symbiosis between Mrs Thatcher and her eccentric policy supremo.[25]

Willie was in charge of devolution until November 1976, when his reliable substitute, Francis Pym, was brought in to replace him. Pym later marvelled at Willie's dexterity in discarding a subject that had never greatly appealed to him, at exactly the time when instead of 'gently simmering beneath the surface . . . it boiled over'. In that month Labour's legislation to set up devolved assemblies in Scotland and Wales was given its second reading. Mrs Thatcher authorised the imposition of a three-line whip against the bill, but more than thirty of her troops disobeyed. Two of these – the Shadow spokesman for Scotland, Alick Buchanan-Smith, and his deputy, Malcolm Rifkind – resigned. Three other Scottish front-benchers offered their resignations, but Thatcher refused to accept them. Only recently has it come to light that Lord Hailsham would have followed suit without an intervention from Peter Carrington. Hailsham exercised his feelings by telling Angus Maude that he was increasingly unhappy with the party's direction; instead of broadening its appeal, it was falling back on its ever-shrinking band of 'core' supporters, he felt.[26]

Willie seems to have supported Mrs Thatcher over devolution. This is slightly mysterious, since he was particularly sensitive to opinion north of the border, while (as her biographer wryly notes) 'Mrs Thatcher never understood Scotland, though she liked to think she did'.[27] Willie might have felt that his influence should be reserved for other topics, but if so he blundered badly; at the time of writing the party holds only one Scottish seat, and this situation can be traced directly to 1976.

It could all have been so different. The Conservatives had been the first major party to embrace devolution for Scotland to deflect the growing demand for full independence. In 1968 Heath had accepted the argument for an assembly, and set up a committee under Alec Home to flesh out the details. But Mrs Thatcher preferred to appease grass-roots activists in England, who cherished the abstract idea of the United Kingdom, whatever they might think of the Scottish population. To make matters worse, the Conservatives had no constructive alternative to offer – a fact that was made abundantly clear when the leader spoke during the December debate. Although she thought that her effort had been adequate, others felt differently, perhaps because once again she had tried to conceal her true feelings. Unable to force an immediate policy U-turn, she attacked the proposals in Labour's bill while claiming that she still believed in the principle of devolution. As Heath and the resigning spokesmen had guessed, her purpose was more radical, and she prevailed; while the 1970 Conservative Manifesto had offered 'a new chance for the Scottish people to have a greater say in their own affairs', the 1979 version contained only a half-hearted promise of 'discussions about the future government of Scotland'.[28]

The only explanation for Willie's behaviour at this time is that he saw devolution as an unsatisfactory compromise, which would only inspire demands for full independence. In April 1975 he had presented proposals to the Shadow Cabinet, and his colleagues had agreed that 'the Party should not be motivated simply by electoral considerations . . . mistakes would involve drastic consequences for the whole United Kingdom'. Ironically, Lord Hailsham might have helped to start the panic that led to the policy change; at the April meeting he agreed that nationalists in Scotland would not be satisfied with a fairly toothless assembly, but unlike his colleagues he thought that the party should exploit this mood and go for a constitutional 'big bang', with similar bodies for all the regions of the UK, a Bill of Rights and even a Supreme Court. This kind of meat was far too strong for Willie. With his memories of Selsdon Park, he doubted whether Opposition parties should engage in anything more than minimal policy-making; pettifogging detail was bad enough, but majestic radical blueprints were anathema to him. In keeping with this approach, he kept aloof from Joseph's anarchic policy exercise, concentrating on the Machinery of Government committee and coolly ignoring Joseph's suggestions even in that area.[29]

In his own memoirs Norman Tebbit hails Willie's handling of devolution as a masterpiece of political tactics: 'At the time he took on responsibility as our spokesman the Party had favoured devolution. By 1978 we opposed it but no one could quite remember how or when the U-turn had been made. It was the stuff of genius'. This was going too far; the credit (if such a word is appropriate) should really have gone to Pym, who in this job proved yet again that in parliamentary tactics he was at least Willie's equal. But in winning the admiration of Tebbit, Willie showed that he was indeed a 'genius' in man-management. Despite their marked differences in background and outlook, they became warm friends and close political allies. By the time of his death in March 1979 at the hands of the Irish National Liberation Army (INLA), Willie had also established a good working relationship with Airey Neave. When Winnie Whitelaw died in January 1978, Neave sent his heartfelt commiserations. It would have been interesting to see how they would have collaborated if Neave had lived to be Secretary of State for Northern Ireland. Willie was not aggrieved that the party dropped its commitment to power sharing in Opposition, since he recognised that the unionist strike had driven this off the agenda, at least in the short term. Neave's successor was Humphrey Atkins, who was not among Willie's favourites.[30]

For Willie, shadowing the Home Office promised to be a congenial Opposition posting. There would have to be some preliminary thinking, in sensitive subjects like immigration and law and order. But a Home Secretary's attention is often engrossed by unexpected events, reflecting the ad-hoc nature of the department. As Peter Hennessy has aptly remarked, from its inception 'the Home Office was Whitehall's charlady mopping up the pools of activity that did not fit tidily into any other institutional container'. Roy Jenkins, who was twice Home Secretary, has reflected that although mistakes made within the Home Office might be relatively trivial compared to the blunders of a Chancellor of the Exchequer, they are at least as likely to be publicised, since the impact on individuals is immediate. Most of these events will be short-lived sensations, but for an Opposition spokesman the potential to score political points and to boost morale among MPs is obvious.[31]

In September 1976 Jenkins left the Home Office to become President of the European Commission, and for the next two and a half years Willie faced Merlyn Rees across the dispatch-box. The pair had personified the cross-party consensus when they covered Northern Ireland. Now they appreciated that the rules of engagement had changed, but they would never take personal offence. So when in February 1978 Rees accused the Tories of racism Willie lashed back at a 'baseless lie' in a speech at Loughborough University. But they remained the best of friends.[32]

On the race issue Rees sympathised with Willie more than usual. Willie had been out of London for the second week of January 1978, attending to the arrangements following his mother's death on the 10th. While his back was turned right-wing newspapers reported that the Conservatives were planning to stop immigration from the 'New' Commonwealth. Perhaps he was too preoccupied up in Scotland to notice the stories, but they clearly emanated from 'sources close to the leader'. On 20 January Mrs Thatcher tried to overturn Willie's earlier decision to nomimate a young Tory MP, John Moore, to a Joint Committee Against Racialism. Apparently there had been a heated conversation on the subject, and while Willie was still away representatives of the party's National Union insisted that the leader's decision should be reversed. Not to be outdone, in a televised interview at the end of the month Mrs Thatcher referred to public fears of being 'swamped by people of a different culture', and did her best to deepen any anxieties by comparing the current immigration rate to the addition of 'two new towns' arriving every year.[33] In fact in 1978, 30,000 immigrants from the 'New Commonwealth' were accepted for settlement. Mrs Thatcher's 'New Towns' would have been pitifully small, and the figure represented a drop of 15,000 on the previous year.

Like Enoch Powell in 1968, Mrs Thatcher had not cleared her remarks with the Shadow Cabinet, and Willie was taken by surprise. In his rage, he offered his resignation. This was at least their third clash within two months. In November 1977 Mrs Thatcher had given a radio interview in which she endorsed the pay claims of striking firemen. Willie had already agreed that the police should be made a special case and deserved an award outside the government's pay policy; but if the firemen were also exempted, there might be no end to such concessions. After a sharp exchange of words their feelings died down on that occasion. But the provocation of the race interview was far more serious for Willie. The previous year he had warned that 'Anti-immigrant extremists have a marvellous time exploiting fears about the number of coloured people coming into the country'; now he had to accept that his own leader was one of those 'extremists'. Three days after the programme he told Roy Jenkins 'how absolutely ghastly life was with that awful woman, how he was thinking of resigning'. Asked to advise, Jenkins said that Willie should not resign but should carefully distance himself from his leader. '"Quite right, quite right," he said, "quite right. It's better not to resign, but distance myself. That's right."' Jenkins thought that the resignation threat was just typical bluster from Willie. But he was probably in earnest at the time. While Labour MPs, like Neil Kinnock, responded to the controversy by urging Willie to topple Mrs Thatcher before she destroyed Britain's tolerant society, Willie knew that there were many Conservatives who only disagreed with the leader because she was not outspoken enough. As it was, her remarks coincided with a surge in support for the Tories – and inspired a Powell-like deluge of laudatory letters.[34]

Mrs Thatcher's worst offence was to claim that her party should assuage public fears by offering 'the prospect of a clear end to immigration'. As the subsequent leap in Conservative support demonstrated, appearing tough on immigration could bring dividends. But far from hoping to put a stop to all immigration, Willie was content to work towards a reduction in what he considered to be an unsustainable level of entry. *The Right Approach*, a policy document presented to the 1976 Tory Conference, suggested that this could be achieved through a more rigorous application of the existing rules, which permitted married and engaged couples to settle in Britain provided that one of them had British nationality. In conversations with party colleagues Willie had pointed out the difficulties, in terms of discrimination on grounds of sex or ethnicity, which would arise if he tried to amend the rules. But he had authorised Keith Speed (who had joined the Conservative Home Affairs team in November 1977 along with David Howell) to explore possible changes.[35]

After Mrs Thatcher's broadcast Willie went on television himself, saying that the language of 'swamping' was too lurid, disputing the statistics that his leader had quoted and admitting that the immigration figures were already coming down. The *Sunday Times* felt that he had indeed 'distanced himself', but without seeming disloyal; his strategy had been 'to disown Mrs Thatcher's emotive phraseology while defending her judgement in giving expression to public fears'. It was noted that he was the only front-bencher even to offer his leader this double-edged support, which he repeated in his Loughborough speech while reintroducing the key qualification deliberately omitted by Mrs Thatcher – that the party wanted to hold out 'the prospect of an end to immigration *on the scale we have seen it in post-war years*'. In the circumstances, Rees had helped Willie by accusing the Tories of racism; this offered a welcome opening to restate the true position of his party in the context of a counter-thrust at his opposite number. He showed his real feelings on race after the Loughborough meeting, when in pouring rain he shook hands with a group of Asian protestors and spoke of his three-year-old granddaughter who had many black playmates: 'She does not know the difference between them. That gives me hope for the future.'[36]

This personal touch proved how different Willie was from his leader; he genuinely thought that good race relations would be fostered if the rate of settlement was checked, while she gave the impression of wanting fewer (black ot Asian) immigrants, whether this helped race relations or not. But after the 'swamped' speech an all-party committee came out in favour of new restrictions, making it impossible for Willie to shirk the issue. In a speech to the Conservative Central Council in April 1978 he unveiled his proposals, claiming that they were 'tough but fair'. For all its harshness of tone, the *Guardian*'s Hugo Young thought that the speech was not really a departure from Willie's habitual 'woolly acuteness, ruthless niceness, vacuous solidity, acute woolliness'. The real goal of the extreme right-wing – a policy of forcible repatriation – was dismissed as 'totally unacceptable to many people in this country', and Willie had described the voluntary alternative (already provided for in the 1971 Immigration Act) as 'a delusion'. *The Times* editorial, cheekily headlined 'So that is what Mrs Thatcher meant', welcomed Willie's proposals and closed with the thought that ending all immigration had been a chimera in the first place.[37]

If Mrs Thatcher read that article she cannot have been surprised by Willie's subsequent moves. After meeting a delegation from the Asian community, he followed his leader's example by speaking without prior authorisation. The difference was that this announcement really did foreshadow a policy departure. His proposed register of dependants hoping to enter Britain would not be limited to the Indian subcontinent, as Mrs Thatcher had hoped. Willie knew that such a register would be unworkable anyway, but his move went beyond symbolism. In fact, along with Keith Speed and his former colleague in the whips' office Jack Weatherill, Willie had been taking a close interest in the formation of Conservative Anglo-Asian groups in several constituencies, and unlike his more hot-headed colleagues he had recognised that the wilful alienation of immigrant voters would damage his party. The advertising company Saatchi & Saatchi had been asked to run a campaign in Asian newspapers, reassuring recent immigrants about Conservative intentions. James Callaghan had won the trust of the Asian community, partly because he had visited India. Willie had gone there himself as part of a parliamentary delegation in 1975, meeting Mrs Gandhi and opposition politicians before joining Kenneth Clarke for a ride on an elephant. Now he sent Speed on a further fact-finding mission.[38]

Willie's problems on the emotive race issue continued until the end of the Parliament. In March 1979 he addressed the Conservative Home Affairs Committee in an attempt to head off what seemed likely to be a major rebellion against a government bill, which would allow central funding to local authorities that wished to promote the interests of ethnic minorities. Willie's appeal to MPs to abstain was backed by the committee's secretary, Roger Sims, who subsequently became his PPS. Some right-wing members of the committee refused to back down, regarding the legislation as an example of 'reverse discrimination'; one of them, Alan Clark, branded it 'corrupt'. But in the end only six Tory MPs opposed the bill, including Clark and the inheritor of Enoch Powell's Woverhampton seat, Nicholas Budgen. Roughly the same 'awkward squad' had voted against the second reading of Roy Jenkins' Race Relations Bill in March 1976 – minus Ivor Stanbrook, the MP for Orpington, with whom Willie had some of his most unpleasant conversations, both before and after the election. If there was anyone Willie disliked more than Stanbrook, it was the right-wing *Daily Mail* journalist Andrew Alexander. At one function in 1977 Willie 'bore down' on Alexander and boomed, 'Fair criticism I can take. But why do you persistently write about me as if I were stupid? Let me tell you, I-am-not-stupid.'[39]

At least law and order was more straightforward for Willie to deal with. Recorded crime had been rising since the 1950s in most developed countries, but for Britain 1977 produced an unwanted record for offences. The greatest public concern focused on vandals and football hooligans. To meet the demand for action against young offenders, Willie deployed the perfect slogan for hardline Conservative audiences: the 'Short, Sharp Shock'. At the 1977 Party Conference he used the phrase as the basis for what was perhaps the definitive Whitelaw performance. Later he advised one of his successors, Douglas Hurd, that every conference speech should include at least one proposal that would be unpopular with the audience; the secret was to smuggle this in under a smokescreen of harsh rhetoric. On this occasion he warmed them up from the start, invoking imaginary left-wingers who claimed that law and order had no place in party politics. 'What a load of sanctimonious rubbish!' he spluttered. After thrilling the audience with his new slogan, he used the same straw-doll technique: 'Of course, when I have advocated this, I have been accused in some circles [of being] a wicked old ogre determined to send every young offender to a form of borstal.' Even grass-roots Tories might find an ogre unsuitable for the job of Home Affairs spokesman, so they were probably relieved to hear that Willie had some compassion in his heart. He managed to slip in praise for the probation service and even for social workers, going on to hint that in office he would try to alleviate overcrowding in prisons. He praised his own policy as 'a calm, reasoned and commonsense approach . . . No one can suggest that it is some emotional, vengeful response to a serious and worrying situation.'[40]

When Willie made that speech he probably expected it to be his last conference appearance before a general election. The Labour Government (headed by Callaghan since Wilson had stepped down in March 1976) was limping on, sustained by a pact with the Liberals. At the time of the 1977 conference Labour was level with the Tories in the polls, but most people thought that an election would bring Mrs Thatcher to power, even though Callaghan had established a higher approval rating. By October 1978 Labour had actually pulled ahead, but the Prime Minister doubted that this could be translated into an election victory. He backed away from an autumn contest. This meant that Willie had to face the conference one more time in his present capacity, and his 1978 speech lacked the ebullience of his previous effort. If anything, the mood in the hall was even uglier. Speakers advocated a return to public floggings and incarceration in the stocks, while members of the audience signalled their desire to adminster these punishments in person. In a debate which featured an early outing for Ann Widdecombe, some speakers hoped that the party would commit itself to a referendum on capital punishment, although Willie had opposed this in Shadow Cabinet and Mrs Thatcher accepted his objections. Maintaining a prudent silence about his own position, Willie could only try to mollify the conference by repeating the promise that there would be an early free vote in the Commons. In March 1979, after the assassination of Airey Neave, it was reported that he was thinking again, but probably this was just another attempt to disarm his right-wing critics. It was bad enough for him that the pro-hanging Humphrey Atkins was appointed as Neave's successor at Northern Ireland.[41]

When Willie's critics on the left of the party doubted his commitment to the fight against 'Thatcherism', they were overlooking the fact that he had his hands full defending his own patch, where he was faced by the united and vociferous voice of 'reactionary' sentiment. Perhaps when the first Shadow Cabinet was selected he could have made a greater effort to ensure a more eclectic mix of spokesmen covering economic subjects; but he did blackball Joseph, and at that time he probably did not suspect that Geoffrey Howe would prove to be such an inflexible follower of the monetarist doctrine. He threw his weight behind *The Right Approach*, in which Mrs Thatcher's followers compromised on incomes policy, and his ally David Howell drafted the follow-up document, *The Right Approach to the Economy*, which was a great disappointment to the monetarist faction. Thorneycroft, who talked with Willie in advance of every Shadow Cabinet meeting, worked closely with his cousin in ensuring that Mrs Thatcher stuck to the terms of the truce on this issue.[42]

Nevertheless, in retirement Willie thought he could have done more to restrain Mrs Thatcher, both in Opposition and in government. Whatever Willie might have said to his leader in private, to Ian Gilmour he appeared terribly indecisive; under pressure before meetings he would agree to speak up against the right, but when the chance came he would rarely advance even muffled objections. But on general economic management, 'wets' like Gilmour were familiar with abstract economic arguments and rightly deplored the misleading simplicity of monetarism. Willie had never been at home in these debates, and given that he shared with the monetarists an overriding concern with inflation, he could not be expected to recoil instinctively from the doctrine, as some of the 'wets' had done. In turn, he was blind to the possible consequences of monetarism – and incapable of predicting that the ideologues in his party would stick to it long after it had proved unworkable. Inadvertently he revealed his ignorance in a private conversation of June 1978, when he expressed approval of Keith Joseph's phrase 'monetarism is not enough'. He seemed to think that Joseph had spoken in support of a mixture of policies – similar to his own preferred pragmatism – which was far from Joseph's intention. He went on to praise the series of speeches that Joseph had made in Britain's universities, but apparently contradicted himself by complaining that 'the Right Wing of the party believe they are in the driving seat', and blaming Joseph's Centre for Policy Studies (CPS) for this development. In October 1977 he had agreed with Hailsham and Carrington that Joseph was an 'Albatross' for the party.[43]

Carrington has observed that the moderate faction in the Shadow Cabinet was itself divided. Willie, Hailsham and Carrington were older than the real 'wets'; they had also served as chairmen of the party. They had seen so many battles, and had been exposed so often to the views of the activists, that instead of fighting against the right-wing takeover they preferred to act as if it had never happened. Meanwhile, although they despised dogmatic politics of all kinds, unlike the 'wets' they disliked the style of 'Thatcherism' more than the content. They were themselves inclined to move to the right in the months before the 1979 general election. The changed mood can be traced in the foreword written by Lord Home to a pessmistic volume of essays published in 1978. Home presented stark alternatives for the British electorate; unless it could be brought to its senses, democracy itself could be destroyed. Home had never been a 'wet', but he had no taste for Joseph's doctrinaire brand of politics. His foreword represented a new blend in his thinking, with echoes of the 'New Right' drowning out the voice of the old 'consensus'. Hailsham contributed a more sophisticated essay to the volume, but he seemed to have accepted the Joseph line that post-war politicians as a whole had failed the people, before conjuring visions of the Weimar Republic and accusing Labour of having 'more or less declared open war on the middle class'.[44]

In the early days of Mrs Thatcher's leadership Willie had risked a row by arguing that Conservatives should back the Labour Government if it pursued policies in the national interest. By October 1978 his thinking was very different. At the Party Conference Heath had urged that Conservatives should not 'gloat' at the nation's difficulties. When asked about this, Willie confided to a journalist, 'I'm not gloating. Oh no. Wrong to gloat. Mustn't do it, no, no, no. But I can tell *you*, I'm gloating like hell.' Not only was Britain's decline more evident than ever under Labour – symbolised by the government's humiliating request for funds from the International Monetary Fund (IMF) to shore up the pound – but the social democrats who had generally dominated the party's thinking since the war were in retreat. Willie genuinely believed that their internal opponents, like Tony Benn, were a serious threat to Britain's remaining prosperity and social harmony. He rarely indulged in personality politics, but he was as responsible as anyone on his side for making Benn into a public bogey-man. Similarly, in 1974 Willie had wanted to conciliate the unions; but he could hardly be blamed if the 'Who

Governs?' election had changed his mind about a movement that had used its power irresponsibly. To the surprise of Mrs Thatcher's adviser John Hoskyns, Willie quickly accepted his proposal that the party should tackle the issue of union reform head-on.[45]

At times Willie might think of his leader as 'that awful woman', and to symbolise the change since his close relationship with Heath he stuck to his rule of never telephoning Mrs Thatcher at weekends. But he did appreciate her good qualities. In a 1978 interview he praised her personal kindness, her stamina and her instincts.[46] But for Willie the final consideration was that although Mrs Thatcher did not owe her position to her views, she had been elected leader and he wanted his party to replace an incompetent Labour Government. Once again Willie's position arose from his general approach to politics; he knew that if Mrs Thatcher became Prime Minister she would be much harder to restrain. By now he was widely known as 'Woolly Willie' – a tag that was reinforced when Jim Callaghan (plagiarising Denis Healey on Sir Geoffrey Howe) said in the Commons that being attacked by Willie was like 'being nuzzled by an old sheep-dog'. But he knew his own mind, and followed his own preferences, no less than the ideologues in the Shadow Cabinet. The only 'woolly' thing about him was an outward manner that convinced almost everyone that he agreed with them. This could infuriate colleagues or journalists with more rigid views – and a corresponding belief that political opponents could never be friends. But Willie's outlook had been shaped in a more tranquil environment, and he could not have changed, even had he wanted to.

Callaghan's decision to delay the election may not have made the difference between re-election and what turned out to be eighteen years of Opposition for his party. But the winter of 1978–9, which featured a series of strikes by public-sector workers against the government's pay policy, ensured that the voters were more impressed by Labour's frailties than by any doubts about the Opposition and its headstrong leader. As a final indignity, the government had to call the election as a result of a Commons' vote of 'no confidence' – the first time this had happened since 1924. The pact with the Liberals had ended, and the Scottish National Party (SNP) was angered on 1 March 1979 when a referendum on devolution produced a favourable majority, but on too small a turn-out to legitimise constitutional change.

Mrs Thatcher tabled the confidence motion for 28 March. Labour still outnumbered the Conservatives by twenty-four MPs, so the issue would be decided by the forty-three representatives of minor parties. In some frantic horse-trading, the Ulster Unionists tried to sell their support to the government in return for a gas pipeline from the mainland to Ulster, but this was a deal too far for a government that had already lost credibility with the nationalist community in Northern Ireland. In the end even Powell voted with the Conservatives; Gerry Fitt of the SDLP, who thought that the current Northern Ireland Secretary Roy Mason was a dismal substitute for Willie, abstained along with Frank Maguire, an 'Independent Republican'.

In the days before the vote Willie played down expectations, rating his party's chances at no better than 'even money'. Winding up for the Opposition, he gave what he proudly described as the dullest speech of his career. He could never have competed with Michael Foot, who delivered a sparkling riposte for the government; but in any case Willie was anxious to fill up the required thirty minutes without saying anything to alienate potential waverers. After Foot's closing speech, as members filed through the lobbies, there was gloom on the Conservative side. Humphrey Atkins reported that a couple of MPs had not returned from dinner, and on his calculations this looked likely to decide the day. Mrs Thatcher, sitting beside Willie on the front bench, kept repeating 'I'm so sorry'. She had forced two confidence votes in January, both of which the government had comfortably survived. Misjudging the arithmetic for a third time would be a serious blow to Tory morale; Callaghan was being urged to call an election whatever the result, and his own image would be burnished if he went to the country as the man who had beaten off everything the Opposition could throw at him. But even if Mrs Thatcher felt responsible for the decision to force a vote, she must have taken advice from Willie, Pym and Atkins. They all looked glum as a government whip gave a 'thumbs up' signal to his colleagues.[47]

But everyone had miscalculated. In a macabre echo of Willie's experience as Chief Whip, one Labour MP was too ill even to attend the Palace of Westminster in an ambulance. Consequently, a tie that would have been decided in favour of the government by the Speaker's casting vote had become an Opposition victory, by 311 to 310. Callaghan immediately announced that he would ask the country for a new mandate. More than four years after he had kissed her for the cameras in Eastbourne, Willie put his arm around Mrs Thatcher. This time the gesture looked spontaneous, but with Willie one could never be quite sure. It could easily have been a gentle reminder that although she could take great credit for the outcome, whatever happened in the election campaign she would still have to rely on his support.[48]

CHAPTER 14

'OF COURSE IT WON'T WORK!'

When Callaghan fixed 3 May 1979 as the date of the election, Willie plunged into his tenth national campaign. His canvassing technique was celebrated by the political sketch-writers, who could always rely on him to provide good copy. At one by-election in the late 1970s he had said that a report on legal reform 'deserved careful consideration', only to be told by a journalist that the Conservative candidate had already remarked that it should be thrown into the waste-paper basket. 'Quite right, quite right,' Willie shot back, 'it should be thrown into the waste-paper basket, then taken out, smoothed down, and given very careful consideration.'[1]

In April 1979 the *Guardian*'s Simon Hoggart, who had covered Willie's period in Ulster, marvelled at a typical performance in Barrow:

> Mr Whitelaw meets the electorate in the way a combine harvester meets a field of wheat, with impressive, even ruthless efficiency. 'Hello, how nice to meet you, how very nice to meet you, thank you so much, so very good to meet you, thank you so very much,' he will say to a single voter.
>
> Show him a group of shoppers and he is among them, scattering greetings and handshakes like grapeshot. 'Very nice to meet you, very kind of you, so nice to see you!' While greeting one group he might spot another moving out of range a few yards away. But there is no escape. 'How are you? Oh good! Very nice to meet you!'
>
> A team of Tory campaigners is sent on ahead to line up people to be introduced. Feeding the Leviathan is a full-time job and sometimes they accidentally catch journalists, Mr Whitelaw's detectives, and each other – anyone to gorge the endless appetite.

Hoggart attributed to Willie a canvassing-rate of thirteen voters per minute

– 'more than 700 an hour, quite enough to swing a marginal seat'. The secret was to drive ahead with a fixed grin, whatever anyone might say. As another sketch-writer put it, 'the tone in which he says "Pleased to meet you" signals a simultaneous goodbye'. Everyone recognised Willie, and most people seemed delighted to confront the whirlwind: 'some were so smitten that they hung round and were introduced two or three times'. His bonhomie was so infectious that even when he expressed disagreement with the views of those he met, they still went away feeling better for the encounter. He was only stopped in his headlong course by a question about Northern Ireland: 'I had such hopes when I was there, and I can never get quite away from my feelings about it,' he confided mournfully.[2]

From Willie's point of view, his party fought an eminently sensible campaign. Although the need for unity ensured that the manifesto lacked detail, Willie and his cousin Thorneycroft regarded even this vague document as nothing more than an abstract starting-point. The young Tristan Garel-Jones, who was advising the latter at the time of the election, was concerned about one of the very few policy commitments, and asked Willie and Thorneycroft whether they thought it could really work in practice. The Party Chairman was aghast. 'Work, my dear boy? Of course it won't work. Nothing works. The thing to do is the best we can in the circumstances.' There was no sign of dissent from Willie. To the sceptical cousins the teetotal Garel-Jones was an unfathomable creature. Their puzzlement was such that when Thorneycroft tried to explain his misgivings to the Conservative Party Treasurer, Alistair McAlpine, he could only say the opposite of what he really meant: 'Garel-Jones hasn't got a political idea in his head.'[3]

The Thorneycroft-Whitelaw approach to politics was anathema to Mrs Thatcher, who believed that she had been chosen by her party to restore Britain's past glories. But generally she heeded her cautious counsellors; for example, she rejected Callaghan's challenge to a televised debate, after Willie had joined Thorneycroft and her speech-writer Gordon Reece in warning that she had nothing to gain from this unprecedented exercise. Apparently the only time that she kicked against Thorneycroft's advice was halfway through the campaign, when she angrily rejected the idea that Heath should feature in a Conservative broadcast. In public, at least, she reined in her radicalism, thwarting the Prime Minister's attempts to portray her as a dangerous extremist. But even at her meekest she could not hope to compete with Callaghan's emollient image. Among senior Conservatives Willie was the closest approximation to the Labour leader, and although this time he did not feature in any party broadcasts he worked hard to spread reassurance, visiting numerous marginal constituencies throughout the country. He left

Penrith and the Border in the capable hands of Celia and his election agent, Norman Dent.[4]

During each of the previous elections that Willie had fought as a front-bencher he had tried to suppress a feeling of impending defeat for his party. In 1979 the Conservatives were heavy odds-on favourites throughout. But although the campaign ran without a serious hitch, Willie suffered his habitual attack of pessimism two days before the election, when a *Daily Mail* poll forecast a narrow Labour victory. It proved to be a false alarm. On 3 May the Conservatives were returned to office with an overall majority of forty-three. Willie won his own seat by just over 17,000 votes.

Looking back, Willie remembered 4 May 1979 as 'one of the most exciting days of my life'. This ranked it below 19 June 1970 in his estimation, partly reflecting his greater awareness of the pitfalls that lie ahead of any government on its first day in office. More important, though, was his knowledge that Mrs Thatcher's first Cabinet would be far more divided than Heath's had been – and that in advising his leader on appointments he would have to consider the balancing of factions, not simply the aptitude of the various candidates for the available posts. As in 1970, Willie's count in Penrith delayed his arrival in London until the afternoon. He was joined for the discussions at Number 10 by his protégé, the new Chief Whip Michael Jopling. Having scored a decisive victory Mrs Thatcher was in a strong position, but there was still no chance of Sir Keith Joseph becoming Chancellor. Instead, Geoffrey Howe took over the post he had shadowed, while Joseph went to Industry, which was always likely to be a severe test for him. The biggest surprises in the new line-up were a recall for Peter Walker, who became Agriculture Secretary, and Lord Carrington's appointment as Foreign Secretary.[5]

Even if these decisions were not suggested by Willie, he was happy with them. Although Walker had been regarded as the most cutting of Mrs Thatcher's internal critics, he had remained in close touch with Willie. Over lunch just before the election Walker had politely demurred at Willie's suggestion that a few supportive speeches might be helpful. Willie departed 'looking lugubrious'; but he must have helped to convince Mrs Thatcher that Walker 'was safer in than out'. Although Carrington's translation from the Shadow Leadership of the House of Lords displaced Francis Pym, the latter was compensated by a posting to Defence. In turn, the fact that Carrington could not be held accountable in the House of Commons opened a space for a deputy, and Ian Gilmour moved from Defence to fill this role, with a place in the Cabinet and the title of Lord Privy Seal.[6]

The Thatcherite Nicholas Ridley was going too far when he claimed that 'In many respects, it was Willie Whitelaw's Cabinet which [Mrs Thatcher] first appointed'. But, as Gilmour has written, the first Thatcher Cabinet 'was palpably not a happy or united body', and Willie's part in its construction left him vulnerable to criticism when things began to go wrong. While some of his colleagues thought from the outset that inevitable failure would widen the existing divisions, Willie hoped that modest success would bind them together. The Treasury team consisted entirely of monetarist 'believers', and this might have been a price he consciously paid to secure his own influence elsewhere; but for him that was a price well worth paying if it meant that the majority of Cabinet posts went to people of sufficient stature.[7]

But there could be no place for one well-qualified figure. As John Campbell has pointed out, 'There was no precedent for a former Conservative Prime Minister still in the Commons being excluded from a subsequent Conservative Government.' Although Mrs Thatcher had vetoed his participation in the election broadcast, Edward Heath had campaigned vigorously for his party. The Foreign Secretaryship was an obvious placement for this least insular of British politicians. The fact that he had signalled his intention of remaining on the backbenches need not have been an insuperable obstacle. But instead of testing out the ground, Mrs Thatcher sent Heath a note to advise him of Carrington's appointment. In his memoirs Heath writes that he 'was not in the least surprised', although he would have been even less human than the cold creature depicted by his enemies had he not been disappointed. And no one could have retained their equanimity faced with the provocation that confronted him ten days later. Mrs Thatcher wrote to ask if he was interested in becoming Ambassador to the United States. Not only was this an open hint that the new Prime Minister would be gratified to see the back of her predecessor; a positive response by Heath would have implied an unconditional surrender, since there was no concrete offer even of a post that would have been grossly unsuitable for a man who had devoted most of his career to the task of turning Britain's attention away from the States and towards Europe. Even though Willie thought his old colleague would be well advised to leave the Commons, it is barely conceivable that he could have given his sanction to this hare-brained initiative. The only possible tactical justification was that it clarified the situation; after this gratuitous insult there could be no more hypocritical pretence of friendly feelings on either side.[8]

By this time Willie had met his new departmental colleagues at 50 Queen Anne's Gate – the location of the Home Office since a recent move from Whitehall. The building (designed by Basil Spence) was a typical award-winning modernist effort, with an Orwellian aspect all too evocative of the department's chief responsibilities. At least Willie's office on the seventh floor afforded a view of the Guards' Chapel. But the room was equipped with garish yellow furniture selected by Roy Jenkins – Home Office humourists suggested that Jenkins had made this choice in the expectation of a rapid removal to the presidency of the European Commission. Morale was quite low when Willie arrived; the department had worked hard (and without tangible reward) to keep the country moving during the 'Winter of Discontent'. As usual Willie's arrival was a tonic, coinciding with the brighter May weather. During his four-year stint at the Home Office he was appreciated for his ebullient spirits – although, as he conceded in his memoirs, some of his officials took time to realise that when his booming voice echoed around the building it was usually a sign that the minister was enjoying himself. But he also won loyalty through his steady application to business and his consideration for junior colleagues. In a typical incident, he showed his PPS the text of a speech prepared by the department and spluttered, 'Look at this – have you ever read such a load of balls in your life!' But when the offending officials trooped into his room he thanked them all for their work, and after offering gentle suggestions for improvements he invited their own views. His working methods gave rise to many affectionate anecdotes. It was remembered that after reading another speech drawn up on his instructions, Willie scribbled beside one section, 'Weak point. Shout.'[9]

In his own memoir one of Willie's greatest post-war predecessors, Lord Butler, had described the Home Office as 'the residual legatee of every problem of internal government not specifically assigned to some other department'. The main responsibility was for law and order, covering the courts, the prisons and the Metropolitan Police. But (among other things) the department also dealt with the fire service, equal opportunities, licensing and gambling laws, measures for civil defence, broadcasting, domestic espionage – and immigration, which had caused great unrest on the Conservative benches even before Enoch Powell's fateful speech in 1968. Some of the decisions within Willie's remit seemed more appropriate for a Minister of the Interior in some totalitarian state; for example, he was charged with setting the fees for taxi journeys in London. Thankfully Willie was an enthusiastic delegator, and he was supported by competent junior ministers throughout his time at the Home Office. Initially his team consisted of Timothy Raison (who was with him until moving to Overseas Development in January 1983), Leon Brittan and Lord (John) Belstead.[10]

The higher ranks of the Home Office also furnished some distinguished civil servants. At first Willie's permanent secretary was Heath's great friend Robert Armstrong, soon to win promotion as Cabinet Secretary. Armstrong was succeeded by Brian Cubbon, who had worked with Willie during the passage of the European Communities Bill. Admiring public servants as he did, Willie disagreed with Mrs Thatcher's own attitude, which was based on a theoretical distrust of the bureaucratic approach rather than an assessment of the real qualities available in Whitehall departments. In Opposition Thatcher and Keith Joseph had envisaged swingeing cuts in Civil Service numbers, but although the ranks were pruned rather than decimated, after a year there had been no thaw in relations. So Willie helped to arrange a dinner at Number 10, to allow the Prime Minister to acquaint herself with senior officials in more relaxed circumstances. Reasonable enough on the drawing-board, the plan failed lamentably in execution. Ian Bancroft, the Head of the Home Civil Service, made a speech that seemed insufficiently penitent to Mrs Thatcher. It may have dawned on her that it was easy enough to win the loyalty of Conservative MPs, who had good reason to adapt to a new regime even after a *coup d'état*; but civil servants owed their loyalty to the Crown, and officials who had already reached senior positions had no incentive to prostrate their professional judgement. Not even Willie could liven things up. The meal dragged itself out until Mrs Thatcher announced, 'Gentlemen! Your cars are waiting', and the cream of Britain's bureaucrats rushed to the exit.[11]

Willie might have farmed out some of the most demanding work in his department – he kept only his favourite areas of broadcasting and horse-racing entirely to himself – but overall responsibility for such a heterogeneous empire remained a crushing burden, leaving aside his other duties as Deputy Leader of his party (and de facto Deputy Prime Minister, although that title had no constitutional basis). Having secured the loyalty of his officials, he took immediate steps to ensure that his ministerial team was happy and united. Every morning they gathered (along with senior officials) to discuss developments within their areas of responsibility, and for a general gossip about political events. To stay in touch with backbench party opinion, Willie relied on his PPS Roger Sims, who was ideally qualified, as a good listener, an MP from the South of England and the outgoing Secretary of the Conservative Home Affairs Committee. Securing Sims was a typical piece of poaching on Willie's part. Sims had been asked by the new Environment Secretary, Patrick Jenkin, to be his PPS. He had not expected even this lowly government post and was ready to accept, once Downing Street had given its approval. Probably Willie got wind of the plan at this stage, because the following day he walked up to Sims and said, 'Roger, you're going to be my PPS.' A polite refusal, referring to his previous engagement, was not an option. Alan Clark's diaries for this period testify to Sims' success; that scheming backbencher knew he would always have to deal with the PPS as if he were addressing the Secretary of State himself.[12]

Another MP who gained his first insights into the working of government inside Willie's Home Office was John Major. First elected in 1979, Major was unhappy that he had been overlooked for two years; even then he was only offered the post of PPS to Raison and Patrick Mayhew (who succeeded Brittan in January 1981). The credit for spotting Major's talents should go to Michael Jopling rather than to Willie; the latter thought that Major 'blossomed' only after he left to become a junior whip in January 1983. At one stage the frustrated Major confided to Sims that he was considering giving up this humble post to devote more time to banking. But from his first day he had been made to feel welcome by Willie, who singled him out for a typical greeting at his first morning meeting: 'Come in. Come and sit down. So pleased you've joined us. Very good news. Yes, very good news indeed. Yes, very!' Major's loyalty to Willie, and his efficiency in reporting any stirrings on the backbenches, ensured that Alan Clark was soon referring to him as 'that toad John Major'.[13]

Major and Clark provide conflicting testimony concerning Willie's relationship with another important constituency, the Conservative Home Affairs Committee. Major remembered that before meetings with this restive group Willie would groan, and make sure that plenty of drink was available before he let them in. Once his guests were refreshed he would flatter them by listening carefully, but he would never act on their wishes unless he saw no means of escape. From the other side of the fence, Clark has left a different account of one such meeting. He recorded that Willie 'thundered and blundered about his Ministry being loaded with so many responsibilities [that] he would find himself "at breaking point", etc'. Clark had been watching with special care during the meeting, having decided a few months earlier that Willie was determined to block his own promotion. Probably this was true – and there are times when the biographer regrets the lack of more objective published testimony from other first-hand witnesses. But more than any other source the Clark *Diaries* reveal how, with minimal effort, Willie could disarm his critics – even one who imagined that he had fathomed his methods and thought that he could match his cunning. The last glimpse of Willie in the *Diaries* is at a dinner held at Number 10 in February 1988 – a month after he had finally left the Cabinet. In the past Clark had plotted for Willie's removal from office, but now he recorded that 'with him any conversation, however brief, is always a pleasure'.[14]

These skills had been sorely tested before, but in the circumstances of 1979 Willie was not surprised to find 'the Home Secretary's job easily the greatest strain of my political life, as far as workload was concerned'. Apart from everything else, he later claimed that he had to sign 10,000 letters every year.[15] Departing from his prepared text at the 1980 Party Conference, Willie offered his own perspective on the department, explaining that:

> The Home Office deals inevitably with human cases, with individuals and, therefore, with their lives. We have to give decisions on many sensitive and emotional problems. We try to balance hard and ruthless decisions where they are obviously in the best interests of the community with sensible compassion in particular personal cases where that seems to be justified.[16]

'We will get the balance wrong and we shall be criticised for it,' Willie added, 'but that is the task to which we dedicate ourselves.' Knowing this in advance, he 'went to the Home Office in a mood of keen anticipation tempered by considerable anxiety'. At least he knew that his first significant decision would be widely welcomed. The Conservative Manifesto had identified law and order as one area that would be immune from the cheese-paring tendencies of the Treasury. Having promised a generous pay deal for the police, in his first week in office Willie announced an immediate 20 per cent increase, in line with the findings of the Edmund Davies Committee set up by Labour. With typical cunning, Willie maximised the psychological impact by putting out his announcement before the Ministry of Defence awarded an even bigger increase to the armed forces. Apart from reviving the spirits of the existing force, the decision reversed a recent decline in numbers. When Willie left the department he was able to boast that 9,000 additional officers had been recruited. While the effects of this munificence were sure to wear off, in the short term, at least, he had bought some valuable goodwill from the police. Delegates at the Police Federation's annual conference in May 1980 gave him standing ovations when he entered and left the hall, even though he alluded in his speech to allegations of police corruption.[17]

Bolstering the ranks of Britain's policemen was a logical response to a problem that had dominated Willie's speeches in the run-up to the general election. Recorded crime had risen by around 50 per cent since 1973, and as so often public fears had more than kept pace with this increase. Extra 'bobbies on the beat' could act as a deterrent to would-be criminals, and were even more likely to restore confidence among potential victims. The problem for Willie was that although an increased likelihood of detection would indeed prevent some crime, most Conservative supporters demanded that this should be backed up by a strict sentencing policy. When he had spoken of a 'short, sharp shock' for young offenders, Willie had raised expectations that he would be an inflexible Home Secretary. It was easy for party activists to overlook the significant 'short' element in the catch-phrase, but Willie was well aware that Britain's jails were already hideously overcrowded. New prisons were being built, and the law-and-order lobby within his own party might have been satisfied if Willie had seen greater capacity as the solution to the problem. But it was less than half an answer. New prisons could not appear overnight; one of the projects that Willie approved, London's Belmarsh, had yet to open at the beginning of 1990. And modern buildings were needed to replace the existing accommodation, not to create more space; one-third of Britain's prisons had been built before 1900, and they were showing their age. Even if one believed that criminals should serve their time in dismal conditions, it was hardly fair that prison officers shared the discomfort. Besides, it cost £500 per week to keep an offender locked up – ten times more than non-custodial alternatives. Since the party members who called for stiffer sentences tended to be the same people who demanded lower taxation, wide publicity for these figures should have provoked some hasty rethinking. But the hardliners had even more dramatic savings in mind. At the 1979 Party Conference Willie referred to 1,800 people who had been jailed for ten years or more after committing serious crimes. This news was greeted with cries of 'Hang them!' So perhaps Willie was prudent not to make too much of the economic argument. Instead, in March 1980 he announced his aspiration to reduce the prison population by 4,000. At that time almost 45,000 people were in jail – 3,000 more than the number that Roy Jenkins had described as 'intolerable' when he was at the Home Office. Even 41,000 inmates would have been 5,000 more than the existing prisons had been designed to hold.[18]

Prison policy provided compelling support for Thorneycroft's dictum about the inevitability of failure. Anticipating trouble ahead from his own backbenchers, Willie had ensured that the relevant section of the 1979 manifesto foreshadowed a reduction in custodial sentences, but in a form of words that was a masterpiece of imprecision. A clear statement that 'long prison sentences are not always the best deterrent', and a promise that 'a wider variety of sentences' would be made available, were followed by some tough talking on young offenders. Only in the next paragraph did Willie return to the subject of alternatives to prison; presumably he calculated that the intervening rehearsal of the 'short, sharp shock' treatment would distract hardline Conservatives from his central message.[19]

On taking office Willie was presented with a report, based on an inquiry commissioned from Mr Justice May by the Callaghan Government. The suggestions, which included alternatives to prison for minor offenders, chimed with Willie's own thinking. But this sweet reason ran up against the brute reality of a rising crime rate, and a public demand for retribution that no Conservative Home Secretary could ignore. Ironically, the problem was only compounded by other elements of Willie's strategy. A larger, better-motivated police force was likely to improve the clear-up rate for crimes, resulting in more convictions. Until the new prisons came on-stream anyone receiving a custodial sentence would face conditions which, Willie accepted, were likely to 'brutalise human beings still further'. This would balance any deterrent effect created by the increased likelihood of detection once the prisoners were released. The result would be more crime, renewed public demands for longer sentences and more policemen, setting off a new tour around an increasingly vicious circle.[20]

Whenever possible, Willie praised prison officers in public, and on visits he was always ready to listen. Accustomed to hearing complaints from the staff, he was determined to offer friendly encouragement to everyone he met. The method worked well on election tours, but in the prisons it could have been applied with more discrimination. On one visit he accosted a prisoner who was diligently mopping the floor. Asked about his crime, the prisoner began a detailed and grisly narrative of the murder of his wife. Willie's hosts, and the officials who accompanied him, were horrified by the account. But Willie had activated his morale-boosting auto-pilot, and once this was engaged it was relentless. 'Splendid! Splendid! Carry on!' he boomed, as he resumed his quest for new targets for exhortation.

Whether or not this encouragement worked on the wife-killer, the application of soft soap to the prison officers was unavailing. Even Merlyn Rees freely acknowledged that recent governments had given in too readily to the officers' demands, and some governors were finding their staff more difficult to control than the prisoners themselves. A significant proportion of officers' pay came from overtime, and the Prison Officers' Association (POA) claimed that 'our members are working themselves to death just to keep the system on an even keel'. Yet in some prisons it was said that televisions were having to be brought in to keep surplus staff occupied. In this context some of the findings of the May report were deeply unwelcome to the officers. Proposals accepted by Willie included the appointment of a Chief Inspector of Prisons, who would work independently of a new Director-General of the prison service and publish an annual report. It seemed like a deliberate act of provocation when Willie appointed as the first Chief Inspector William Pierce, who had previously worked in the probation service. This profession was almost as unpopular with prison officers as the network of prison visitors; and Willie was keen to encourage the latter, in his drive to win wider publicity for the conditions within Britain's jails.[21]

The prison officers felt that they had many reasons for discontent, but the tension came to a head over pay. The May report had also dealt with this issue, and it seemed that the POA had accepted what Willie considered to be a generous offer. But the association was internally divided, and many members felt that their leaders could have prised out more concessions. It was claimed that the May report had exposed an anomaly, whereby officers working on one shift system were paid for certain meals, while others following a different routine were not. To a veteran of the 1973–4 miners' dispute, replete with wrangling over rituals such as 'waiting and bathing', the complex causes of contention must have induced an unpleasant sense of *déjà vu*. Willie was determined to resist the demands, arguing that the best solution was a new duty system for all. He refused to entrust the dispute to arbitration, pointing out that even if this decided in favour of the officers, there would be no money to pay them; the claim was backdated, and a capitulation would cost the Treasury

£5 million. Further negotiations failed, and at the beginning of October 1980 21,000 officers began to take disruptive action.

The overcrowded prisons now became a weighty bargaining counter for the POA. They could argue that admitting new inmates into buildings that were already bursting at the seams lay outside their prescribed duties. By 23 October most jails were refusing to take new prisoners; more than 3,000 convicted people, including violent offenders, were being held in police cells. It was reported that some prisoners were having to sleep on the floor in poorly ventilated rooms. Willie told the Cabinet that he regarded the dispute as a direct challenge to his authority. Emergency legislation was drawn up, to allow prisoners to be held in temporary camps. At the same time Willie arranged for Frankland Prison, near Durham, to be opened eighteen months ahead of schedule and staffed by soldiers. Frantic preparations were necessary; when Willie took his decision the walls of the building were rocket-proof, as designed, but there were no locks on the cell doors.[22]

Although Willie was infuriated by the POA action, it gave him an unexpected opportunity to advertise the problems in the prisons, and to impress on judges and magistrates the attraction of non-custodial sentences. The same agenda was pursued in the Imprisonment (Temporary Provisions) Bill, which gave the Home Secretary the right to order the release of prisoners in certain categories. Generally the judiciary exercised common sense in the face of the emergency, but others were less cooperative. This was the heyday of the celebrity law-enforcer, with senior policemen such as James Anderton from Greater Manchester regularly winning headlines with uncompromising statements. Now Judge James Pickles joined the game, announcing in court that he might bend his strict sentencing policy a little, but that his duty was to the public and not to the government, who would just have to find room for the people he convicted. Pickles was only giving forthright expression to a view which would continue to hamper Willie's reforming efforts. Judicial independence from politicians was fiercely guarded, even if it was difficult to define with any clarity since judges enforced the laws laid down by parliament.[23]

Eventually Willie's stubborn stand paid off, and the POA suspended its action at the beginning of 1981, although there was still no agreement on the revised duty system by the time Willie retired from the Cabinet seven years later. Before the Christmas of 1980 a firemen's dispute was also settled. Willie told his colleagues that the blame lay with the local authorities, which had not fully honoured a national pay settlement; but he recognised that the public would see the government as the culprit. Certainly the dispute added to Willie's workload, since it demanded detailed planning on the part of the Cabinet Civil Contingencies Unit, which he chaired. In this capacity he was also asked, in April 1981, to draw up a plan to combat another miners' strike. This was two months after the Cabinet had backed down when the NUM started industrial action to resist planned pit closures. Ministers fully expected another clash over the issue – and next time they would be ready to avenge 1973–4.[24]

Apart from law and order, the only Home Office issue covered at length in the 1979 manifesto was immigration. Willie described this section as 'a balanced compromise', but it was undoubtedly a compromise dictated by the right wing of his party. True, there was the usual incantation of support for improved race relations, but this was held to be dependent on 'the effective control of immigration', based on the full range of restrictions suggested in Opposition – a register of Commonwealth dependants, a quota system for all outside the European Community, and an end to the automatic right of husbands and male fiancés to join their partners in Britain. The centrepiece of the policy would be a new British Nationality Act, 'to define entitlement to British citizenship and to the right of abode in this country'. None of this was likely to reassure the existing immigrant population, and during the 1979 general election campaign Willie had tried to compensate. At Preston on 23 April, for example, he explained 'that all dependants will be allowed in as soon as possible, and that the controversial quota system will largely restrict new white immigration, since Asian entry is now as restricted as it can be'. This message was reserved for Asian community leaders, and the contrast with the general tone of the Conservative campaign left Willie's audience 'baffled and suspicious'.[25]

By the summer of 1980 suspicions had spread to right-wing backbenchers, and in July a delegation met the Prime Minister to restate their demands for tough new controls. That month, in a speech at Dorking, Enoch Powell waded back into the controversy, claiming that even if the present rate of immigration slowed down, the New Commonwealth population would soon be 'sufficient to constitute a dominant political force in the United Kingdom able to extract from government and the main parties terms calculated to render its influence still more impregnable'. He connected the immigrants with 'urban terrorism'. The White Paper on British Nationality was due for release at the end of July, and Willie felt compelled to strike back once again at his old enemy. 'The best defence against false fears is plain truth,' he asserted; public apprehension was 'fed not by facts but by myths: by misinformation and misunderstanding'.[26]

When the White Paper was published Willie came under fire from his left flank. The Runnymede Trust – representatives of what Powell had sneeringly called 'the race relations industry' – described it as 'an abysmal and mean document'. But criticism from the Labour Party was relatively muted, mainly because the proposals were broadly similar to a Green Paper produced by the Callaghan Government in 1977. The bill itself, published in January 1981, gave full citizenship only to those with an intimate connection to the UK. A second category related to citizens of existing British Dependent Territories, and was designed to guard against a mass influx in 1997 when one of these territories, Hong Kong, was scheduled to be handed back to China. Finally, there would be a British overseas citizenship, which affected Asians still in East Africa, unlike those who had been evicted in recent times from Kenya and Uganda. As one academic commentator has written, this category 'was hardly a citizenship at all – rather, [it signalled] the phasing-out of British subject status'.[27]

The provisions of the bill were extremely complicated, and before its publication there had been thorough consultations. This gave plenty of advance warning to people abroad who were concerned about their status, leading to a significant surge in the number of those applying for naturalisation, even though the government more than doubled the fees. In 1982 nearly 100,000 applications were received. Later the Home Office was criticised for 'incompetence and inexcusable delays' in processing the applications; it was also censured by a Commons Select Committee for turning a rush that it must have anticipated into a profit of £6 million. Certainly the rise in fees laid the department open to accusations of class-discrimination, in addition to the earlier charges of sexism and racism; charging £200 for naturalisation was an inventive way of restricting the right of entry to those who could be expected to assist the UK economy, rather than living on benefits.

Immigration policy had been delegated to Tim Raison, and Willie was very grateful for his hard work on such an important and controversial piece of legislation. But as the Secretary of State he took the brunt of the inevitable criticism. The most serious clash with his right-wing foes came after the crucial second reading on 28 January 1981. Having secured a majority of fifty, Willie felt it safe to announce a major concession, accepting that children of naturalised British citizens would inherit that status, even if they were born abroad. After the third reading in June the government agreed to a sheaf of further softening amendments from the Lords. From the right, Ivor Stanbrook accused Willie of 'betraying' manifesto promises, and of treating backbenchers with 'a contempt' that 'he would regret'. There would be an obvious opportunity for Stanbrook and company to strike back before the Nationality Act came into force in January 1983; the right hoped that before then Willie would have been replaced by a more abrasive Home Secretary, but if he was still in place he would have to present new immigration rules for the House's approval.[28]

Powell had timed his latest outburst to influence the debate on British nationality, and he calculated that his inflammatory remarks about 'urban terrorism' would reactivate his admirers because of an event which even the accident-alert Home Office had not expected. In fact, the Bristol riots took most people by surprise; when the leader of the council was telephoned with the news, he thought he was having his leg pulled. On 2 April 1980 more than a thousand youths – mainly black – confronted police for several hours in the (relatively) deprived St Paul's area of Bristol, leading to thirty-one injuries and more than twenty arrests. As Willie recorded in his memoirs, there were numerous incidents of 'looting, arson and criminal destruction', and he regretted the fact that police resources in the area were so thin that for a time the rioters were unchallenged. The disturbances had begun after a raid on a café favoured by the black community. Although St Paul's 'was known to be a difficult area from the policing point of view', the authorities had consulted local community leaders beforehand. But these sensible precautions were nullified by the nature of the operation. Whatever had been going on in the café – and even in the eyes of the police illegal drinking and the consumption of soft drugs were hardly serious offences – it was unnecessary to assign thirty-nine officers to the raid. The regular customers already had good reason to fear that one of the few congenial meeting-places in the area had been targeted for closure. Although the great majority of the rioters were black, sympathy for them was widespread in St Paul's. One white witness told reporters that his only regret was 'that more of the white residents did not join in to drive the police back'.[29]

With hindsight, Willie felt that his response to the Bristol riots had been 'inadequate'. In a written reply to a parliamentary question from Alan Clark, he denied that there was any need for a fundamental review of police tactics. Willie was most reluctant to introduce the kind of riot-control methods deployed by the security forces in Northern Ireland. Probably he hoped that the outbreak would turn out to be an isolated incident, which (unlike so many US riots) had at least ended without loss of life. He was generally averse to calling public inquiries, but his refusal to do so in this instance must have been informed by a suspicion that it would dwell on matters that he preferred to leave unexamined – particularly the extent of racial discrimination in the job market. Between 1977 and 1980 unemployment among blacks in Bristol doubled, while the rate among whites actually declined. Willie had only just decided to leave unpublished the findings of an inquiry into another violent episode – the clash on 23 April 1979 between the police Special Patrol Group (SPG) and Anti-Nazi League demonstrators in Southall, leading to the death of one protestor. But *The Times* reporters, at least, were prepared to speculate on the cause of the Bristol troubles, clearly identifying the lack of jobs and racial tension as the main contributory factors. By an unfortunate coincidence the St Paul's riot was followed by the news that four black members of the Commission for Racial Equality (CRE) had been removed after calling for an investigation of the immigration service within the Home Office. One activist said, 'Mr Whitelaw is seriously mistaken if he believes that he can have any credibility left within the immigrant community by removing those from the CRE who have fought his racialist immigration policies.'[30]

Before the end of April 1980 the Home Office had been plunged into a more protracted – and dramatic – crisis. On the morning of Wednesday 30 April six armed Iranian dissidents seized control of their country's embassy at 16 Prince's Gate, Kensington. Twenty-six hostages were taken, four of them British (including a BBC reporter and the solitary police guard, Trevor Lock, who became an instant celebrity). There was a well-practised routine in the event of such emergencies, and a team of ministers, officials and advisers, with Willie at its head, quickly assembled in a basement room of the Cabinet Office. He asserted his authority, carefully ensuring that his colleagues all agreed that the terrorists' demands were unacceptable.[31]

In January 1980 Willie had told Lord Hailsham that the West German Interior Minister was staying with him for a week. They were getting on very well: as Willie explained, 'He is very keen on terrorism. So am I.'[32] Since the early 1970s terrorism had been a key area of any Home Secretary's responsibility. Willie had good reason to know that the Northern Ireland problem was as far as ever from a solution; he was the obvious man to chair the relevant Cabinet committee, and in that capacity had warned Mrs Thatcher against a knee-jerk response to the murders of Lord Mountbatten and a total of twenty-one others in two separate bomb outrages on 27 August 1979. The troubles in the Middle East had impinged on the Heath Government, but the Iranian Embassy siege was entirely unexpected. If anything, difficulties from that part of the world were more likely to be triggered off by the new Iranian regime, which for more than a year had held forty-nine US hostages and continued to be regarded as a source of instability. But the Iraqi-trained gunmen were opponents of the new government, acting in support of the Arab inhabitants of an Iranian province. They threatened to kill their hostages and blow up the embassy if the Iranian government refused their demands, which included the release of ninety-one fellow Arabs.

Compared with some of the crises Willie had faced in Northern Ireland, the siege was uncomplicated. Britain was on the verge of imposing economic sanctions on Iran, under pressure from the Americans. Even if relations between London and Tehran had been warmer, the Iranian Government would still have declined to negotiate with the terrorists; it merely let it be known that if any hostages were killed, reprisals would be taken against the Arab minority in Iran. Douglas Hurd, then a junior minister at the Foreign Office, tried to persuade the Jordanians to intercede, but this approach came to nothing. In his memoirs Willie mentions that Kuwaiti and Syrian diplomats were also contacted on the Sunday, four days into the siege. But his own position had been signalled on the Friday, when he told Mrs Thatcher that 'there was to be no accession to the gunmen's demands for mediation by Arab ambassadors'. According to Hurd's biographer, negotiations with the Jordanians failed because the British Government would not promise safe conduct for the gunmen even if the siege ended peacefully. Again, it seems that Willie persuaded Mrs Thatcher to take this decision. In effect, Willie had ensured that the incident would be treated as if it were an instance of domestic criminal activity, while Hurd willingly provided 'cover'.[33]

At first it seemed that the inflexible line would pay off without bloodshed. By the Sunday four hostages had been released. But Willie ensured that he was either in or near London throughout the episode. On the Monday 5 May he hosted a lunch party at his official residence, Dorneywood, near Slough in Berkshire. The situation at Prince's Gate seemed to be calm, but preparations had been made in case the lunch was interrupted by bad news. In fact, Willie had not started on the first course when he was told that two shots had been heard in the embassy. He rushed out to his ministerial Jaguar, where his driver (and great friend) Jack Liddiard[34] was waiting. The twenty-mile journey to Whitehall took just under nineteen minutes – a remarkable feat, even if the traffic was lighter than usual on that Bank Holiday Monday. Willie and his private secretary John Chilcot were too busy with phone calls to judge the average speed, but at Hammersmith Willie noticed that they were travelling at 120 mph. On the way, a police escort of six vehicles joined them and somehow kept up the pace. Thanks to rapid traffic diversions, Liddiard was also able to take some shortcuts, whizzing up the wrong side of Constitution Hill. Trafalgar Square was completely cordoned off for their benefit.[35]

According to the SAS Commander Peter de la Billière, Willie had already decided that there should be an assault on the embassy if two or more hostages were killed. For his part, de la Billière knew at once that it should be an SAS operation; there was no possibility that the police could handle it. In any case, according to Willie (and much to his frustration), the Metropolitan Police Commissioner Sir David McNee was keen to persist with negotiations. The SAS had been alerted immediately, and a team was ready near London while others carried out reconnaissance on the spot. In the meantime, listening equipment was brought in; the gunmen would not even have the chance to plot in private. To cover up the installation of devices, some workmen from the Gas Board were instructed to dig unnecessary holes nearby.[36]

When Willie arrived at Whitehall he discussed the situation with de la Billière. They had no confirmation that a hostage had been killed, but this seemed the most likely reason for the gunfire, and since the government was determined to stand firm against blackmail it could only be a matter of time before there was a second shooting. When de la Billière stressed that the decision to go in would have to be made by the politicians, Willie replied without hesitation, 'If and when the operation is launched, I will not interfere in any way . . . if it goes wrong, I will take the responsibility afterwards.' De la Billière was greatly heartened, and impressed by Willie's resolve; as he wrote later, 'here was that rare being, a politician who was not trying to protect his own career, but was prepared to shoulder responsibility.'[37]

As tension grew inside the embassy, at about six o'clock the gunmen threatened that they would kill everyone inside at regular intervals. Soon afterwards three more shots were heard, then the body of a hostage was flung into the street. It turned out that the new firing was a bluff; the dead hostage had been killed in the earlier burst of gunfire, and no one else was murdered at this stage. But Willie had no means of knowing this, and in any case it would have been perverse to stick to his arbitrary threshold of two dead hostages. While Mrs Thatcher relates in her memoirs that she gave permission for the action to proceed, in an interview for the present book Willie stressed that she had already given him full authority to act on his own initiative. The SAS went in soon after seven o'clock. Five terrorists were killed – one of them picked off by a sniper who had been stationed in Hyde Park – and the survivor was arrested. Only one of the remaining hostages was killed before the SAS team carried out their deadly work. As de la Billière revealed in his own vivid account, there were moments when the assault seemed to have gone badly wrong. No doubt this made the celebratory whisky even more refreshing to those who had been waiting for news. Partly captured by television – Willie himself watched the execution of his orders – the end of the siege remains one of the best-remembered images of the 1980s, and sealed the reputation of the SAS at home and abroad. The only humorous moment at the dinner given by Mrs Thatcher to senior civil servants a few months later came when Frank Cooper (now at Defence) went to the lavatory; one Whitehall wag remarked, 'Thank God! Frank's gone to get the SAS to get us out of here!'[38]

For Willie it was not quite a rerun of Motorman, where a failure might have plunged Northern Ireland into civil war. But his career could still have ended in a few minutes, and he could be forgiven for sharing the excitement as he thanked everyone he could find at Prince's Gate. He was worried that at the subsequent press conference he might have appeared too pleased with himself, as he had done after the Stormont talks in 1973. The parallel with Northern Ireland did not end there. As he might have guessed, although he was a hero to the press on 6 May 1980, his crucial contribution to the successful outcome was no guarantee of favourable coverage on other matters, when all the fuss was over.[39]

The prison officers' strike was not the only headache for Willie in the last few months of 1980. In February he had presented a bill on broadcasting, drawing partly on proposals first advanced by Lord Annan in a 1977 report. Willie had always been very interested in broadcasting, and had many friends in the industry, including George Howard, his nominee as Chairman of the Board of BBC Governors. Although he had signalled broad agreement with Annan's suggestions, Willie felt that this was an area where he could forge a lasting personal legacy and he paid the bill close personal attention.

Willie's main objection to the Annan Report was that the proposals would have tied broadcasters in excessive red tape. The most important issue facing the industry was the structure and status of a new fourth television channel. Willie proposed that this should be supervised by a subsidiary of the Independent Broadcasting Authority (IBA), as Labour had intended, but at his insistence it was specifically designed to encourage independent programme makers, who should be 'experimental and innovative'. He also saw off a group within his own party that wanted to use this opportunity to break ITV's monopoly of television advertising; it was said that he called the key sub-committee meeting at a time when he knew that his chief opponent, the junior Trade Minister Sally Oppenheim, had a hair appointment. Not long after its first broadcasts in November 1982, Channel 4 was damned by social conservatives (and some ministers) as far *too* 'experimental and innovative', and normally Willie would have shared their misgivings. But he regarded the channel with the benevolent eye of a parent, and to the end of his life insiders could rely on him to defend it against the threat of privatisation.[40]

Willie's attitude to Channel 4 was unlikely to endear him to the average Conservative voter. It was an even worse offence that he habitually defended the BBC, doing his best to preserve the real value of the licence fee and offering advice when he thought it had gone too far, as in the case of a *Panorama* interview with IRA leaders conducted in October 1979. Before he became Home Secretary he had put on record his view that 'the first principle of broadcasting must be to defend the independence of the authorities from Government and Parliament', but he was well aware that the existing institutions could be swept away if they forfeited the goodwill of the lawmakers. Soon after the Iranian Embassy siege he gave striking evidence of his commitment to incisive film-making, speaking out strongly in favour of the ITV documentary *Death of a Princess*, which caused a temporary severance of diplomatic relations with Saudi Arabia. Less predictable was the outcry in Wales against Willie's Broadcasting Bill. Despite a manifesto commitment, he decided that up to twenty hours a week of programmes in the Welsh language should be transmitted on BBC and ITV, rather than the new Channel 4. He should have known that Welsh nationalism is more of a cultural than a political movement, and that the same people who had been lukewarm at the prospect of a Welsh assembly would not be satisfied with a halfway house where television was concerned. On 15 September 1980 Willie's constituency offices in Carlisle were ransacked; the former nationalist leader Gwynfor Evans had already started a hunger-strike. The Welsh Secretary Nicholas Edwards asked Evans whether it was really worth risking his life so that his co-linguists could watch their programmes without changing channel now and again. But more moderate community leaders lobbied Edwards, and he convinced Willie to establish Sianel Pedwar Cymru (SC4) as originally promised.[41]

Although Willie was nervous about the prospect of major upheavals in broadcasting, he also gave tentative encouragement to the development of cable and satellite television. Elsewhere, though, he proved less than a steadfast friend of freedom. At the urging of the Commons' Committee on Home Affairs he abolished the old 'sus' law, under which people could be stopped by the police if they suspected criminal intent; but this indiscriminate power was merely rationalised in new legislation. Willie did introduce a bill in the House of Lords to reform the notorious Section 2 of the Official Secrets Act, but this was withdrawn before the opposing cannons had even been loaded with grapeshot. As Willie admits in his memoirs, the proposed reform was hardly a libertarian move; the existing, all-embracing law was a blunt instrument which juries were increasingly reluctant to use, and there was never any question of offering a free licence to whistle-blowers. Willie's attitude to official eavesdropping was even more provocative to the civil-liberty lobby. The number of warrants issued in England and Wales had risen by 260 per cent between 1958 and 1977, but Willie seemed unconcerned at the possibility that even he was being kept in the dark about the true extent of intrusion by the security services. Possibly he was working on the assumption that technological advance would enable government spooks to listen into private conversations with or without old-fashioned 'bugging' devices.[42]

While Merlyn Rees remained as the Labour spokesman on Home Affairs Willie could rely on the sympathetic understanding of his opposite number. At the end of 1980, though, Rees was replaced by Roy Hattersley, who made libertarian issues a top priority. Hattersley was an idealistic intellectual; Willie merely claimed to be less stupid than he looked. Although there were times when Willie was grateful for Hattersley's refusal to exploit crises for political advantage, the differences between them were too great to allow mutual respect to deepen into true comradeship. In September 1982 Hattersley launched an intemperate (and inaccurate) personal attack, describing Willie as hopelessly incompetent and claiming that his 'enthusiasm for shooting small birds' was matched by his 'antipathy to reading books'. Unfortunately Willie was guilty on the first charge, but he had a well-stocked library at Ennim and read political biographies for relaxation. His public comments on Hattersley were more restrained, but the last thing he said in the House of Commons was a characteristic rebuke to his shadow, who had seemed amused during a debate on police interrogations: 'If the right hon. Gentleman thinks that that is funny, he is entitled to his opinion.' He also made fun of Hattersley in private. During one discussion of forthcoming parliamentary business he told Michael Jopling that if he wanted Hattersley to be more cooperative, 'you will have to hit him on his large head'. 'You can't miss,' Mrs Thatcher chipped in.[43]

Whatever their differences, Willie was particularly grateful to Hattersley for his support during the next drama to affect the Home Office. On the evening of Saturday 11 April 1981, serious rioting broke out in Brixton, South London. Although this was another unwelcome surprise for Willie, Brixton had been identified as a much more likely trouble-spot at the time of the Bristol outbreak. Here, too, insensitive policing was the spark; a crackdown on petty crime, involving more than a hundred plain-clothes officers, had been launched five days before the riot with the code-name 'Swamp 81'. Probably the echo of Mrs Thatcher's pronouncements before the election was unconscious; but for the police to have come up with a more unfortunate name they would have had to have trawled through the speeches of Enoch Powell. Nearly a thousand people were stopped on suspicion during the operation. Although the ethnic mix of the suspects was fairly equal, the black residents of Brixton felt they had been victimised for some time; and to top up discriminatory treatment from the authorities, it was estimated that over half of the blacks in Brixton under the age of nineteen were unemployed. The April riot broke out after a misunderstanding, when two policemen trying to help an injured black youth were wrongly suspected of having caused his wound. But after 'Swamp 81' there was no need for a major incident to make feelings boil over. There was a short-lived fracas on Friday 10 April – the day when the black youth had been injured. But the real trouble occurred the following evening, after a black taxi driver had been searched for drugs. The violence continued on the Sunday, after Willie and McNee had risked a ten-minute visit to the area. Some youths shouted 'Sieg Heil' at Willie – a bizarre insult to level at someone who had risked his life in the struggle against Hitler.[44]

The tally of injuries and damage was far worse than it had been in St Paul's. Petrol bombs had been used and several properties gutted by arsonists. Looters – many of them white – helped themselves to consumer goods while the police were pinned down. Well over a hundred policemen were injured. Visiting some of them in hospital, Willie was shocked at the number of head injuries and resolved to improve the protection available to officers. Riot shields, as well as special helmets, were ordered and tactics were reviewed. This time he knew that there would have to be an inquiry to seek the underlying causes of the trouble. With Mrs Thatcher's permission, Willie approached Lord Scarman to head the investigation. This, he subsequently felt, was 'one of my best decisions', notwithstanding the private complaints of Tory backbenchers who confused an objective approach with appeasement. Enoch Powell was on hand inadvertently to rally support after the Home Secretary had reported to the Commons; he chilled even right-wing Conservatives by warning the government that 'they have seen nothing yet'. Powell must have been worried that his admirers had forgotten his notorious forecasts just at the moment when they were being verified. By comparison, Mrs Thatcher's statement that such violence could not be justified in any circumstances was a model of dignified restraint.[45]

Unlike Powell, who had a theory to prove, Willie knew that the riot was the product of complex causes. But although he paid proper attention to the presence of many whites in the ranks of the rioters, he knew that race had been an important factor. He had already shown that on this subject he was more enlightened than most of his colleagues; yet a man of his age can be forgiven for failing to keep up with changes in British society that left his own constituency almost untouched. In the wake of the (belated) outcry after the murder of Stephen Lawrence and the supposed imposition of 'political correctness' on the police, reading accounts of British racism during Willie's time at the Home Office is a surreal experience. In October 1982 a senior police officer told the Conservative Monday Club (the natural home for the party's Powellites), 'There is in our inner cities a very large minority of people who are not fit to salvage . . . The only way in which the police can protect society is quite simply by harassing these people and frightening them.'[46]

Although such attitudes were clearly fostered within an institution like the police, they would have had less purchase if they had not reflected more general social attitudes. A more pertinent search for the source of the poison would have started with certain sections of the media; but the newspaper editors thought they were merely echoing the prejudice of their readers. So – to take just one example – when a Pakistani was murdered in Wandsworth in May 1981, the incident was dismissed in five lines on an inside page of the *Daily Mail*. But after the killing of a white youth, also in South London, the *Mail* headline screamed 'Race Murder in Suburbia'. For once the tabloid was surpassed by its ideological stablemate, the *Daily Telegraph*: 'Rampaging Blacks Kill Youth After Wrecking Pub'. Politicians who drew much of their support from the same audience were equally culpable. The Deptford fire, which claimed the lives of thirteen young blacks in January 1981, passed with barely a comment from the government, even though the tragedy occurred in suspicious circumstances. In the month before Brixton 10,000 people marched through London to demand a full investigation. If the police had been inactive after the fire they compensated with their firm handling of the demonstration; there were 23 arrests. By contrast, when some young Dubliners were killed in a discothèque blaze soon afterwards, Margaret Thatcher immediately sent her condolences. We have already seen what many Tory MPs really thought of the Irish, and during the passage of the Nationality Act they gave further evidence of their true feelings, attacking Willie for failing to eradicate the anomaly that allowed Irish citizens the right to vote in British general elections.[47]

After Brixton Willie could only hold his breath while he waited for Scarman's report. Unfortunately the judge's deliberations were interrupted by further trouble – a sustained outbreak of lawlessness which, at times, seemed to have built up an unstoppable momentum. Almost every area of England was affected in July 1981, and not just the inner cities. The chaos provided a thought-provoking backdrop to the national celebrations following the wedding of Prince Charles and Lady Diana Spencer; when Ian Botham inspired the English cricket team to an improbable victory over Australia soon afterwards, he rounded off a month that would provide ample material for a doctoral dissertation on the English mentality.

The first in the new series of riots took place in Southall, where a 300-strong group of skinheads specially bused in for the purpose provoked a clash with local Asians on Friday 3 July. The police were attacked when it seemed that they were protecting the racist intruders. More than a hundred people were injured, nearly half of them policemen. Since Southall was not economically disadvantaged to the same extent as other affected areas, the outbreak introduced another alarming factor for the Home Office. The nightmare evoked by Powell could be conjured into reality by white thugs, touring the country and inciting violence in any town or city with a sizeable ethnic community.

On the same evening trouble broke out in the Toxteth area of Liverpool. In a reversion to the previous pattern, the immediate cause this time was an operation that was taken by the local black population as further proof of police prejudice. On the Friday fighting was short-lived, but the following night saw another worrying development, when police were lured into an ambush. Petrol bombs and other weapons had been prepared for the confrontation. On the Sunday the disorder was even worse. Around 800 policemen were overwhelmed by the hostile crowd, and as reinforcements poured in from surrounding areas the Chief Constable of Merseyside, Kenneth Oxford, woke Willie at home to ask permission to deploy CS gas for the first time on the mainland of the UK. Willie agreed, trusting Oxford's judgement as the man on the spot. Five rioters were injured by the gas cartridges; later it emerged that these were not designed for riot control. When the trouble was rekindled on the Monday, Liverpool city council asked for troops to be put on standby, though they proved unnecessary. The cost had been appalling; the police recorded 781 injuries sustained during the battles. Willie later described the mayhem in Toxteth as 'concerted violence of a wholly new ferocity and intensity'; in the face of criticism he continued to support Oxford, and never apologised for the use of CS gas, which he saw as a necessary evil.[48]

Toxteth was the worst individual episode, but it was far from the last. On 7–11 July the violence spread to Moss Side in Manchester. Here the police tactics were far more aggressive; many officers had already seen action in Toxteth, and it was alleged that some of them actively stirred up trouble in an attempt to avenge what they regarded as a defeat. But if the police were consciously fighting back they had chosen to do so when it seemed that the whole of Britain's youth was taking to the streets. On Friday 10 July there were more incidents in London, where Brixton and Southall rejoined the lists; but the epidemic also embraced such widely dispersed towns as Reading, Nottingham, Sheffield, Slough, the Handsworth district of Birmingham – and Preston, where Willie had made a conciliatory speech to community leaders before the election. Even Cirencester in Gloucester got a taste of trouble on the Saturday night, along with Southampton, Leicester and Leeds.[49]

It was the worst peacetime nightmare faced by any Home Secretary in the twentieth century. On the Friday Willie had visited Manchester – this time, prudently, he stayed in his car as he toured the affected areas – before delivering a speech to community leaders in Liverpool. This gave him the opportunity to lash out at racism as 'brutish and irrational hatred'. On the drive down to London he heard a long stream of dismal reports from around the country. Back at the Home Office there was 'a suppressed atmosphere of impending doom', which reminded him of the mood at Stormont during Belfast's Bloody Friday. He tried to throw off his own depression, and offered encouragement to his officials. Then he was driven to Dorneywood for the weekend.[50]

Willie rarely indulged in philosophical reflection, but a period of soul-searching was in order over that weekend. The country seemed to have suffered a nervous breakdown. Some of the riots had obviously been inspired by events elsewhere, but these 'copycat' incidents were even more worrying than those that had been triggered off by misunderstandings or deliberate provocation. If even Cirencester could fall under the contagion, then the potential for trouble seemed infinite. Beyond this, Willie could not forget the other objects of his personal loyalty. The Queen, understandably, was deeply concerned, and her views added to Willie's sense of responsibility. The Conservative Party had been unpopular enough even before the anarchy, and in the coming week it faced a key electoral test, with Roy Jenkins standing as the candidate for the newly founded SDP in the Warrington by-election. And the Prime Minister was on a war-footing. She had concluded that much of the trouble had been inspired by 'left-wing extremists'. Later she toured Toxteth, and convinced herself that the problems were nothing to do with a lack of amenities. The root cause was a breakdown in authority, fostered by a media which gave the impression that 'rioters could enjoy a fiesta of crime, looting and rioting in the guise of social protest'. Since authority and self-respect had been undermined by the welfare state and the bloated bands of professional do-gooders, the problem could not be killed by kindness. For Mrs Thatcher it was all a question of restoring respect for the law, by supporting the police and giving them extra powers. A revival of the Riot Act, under which rioters could be shot if they refused to disperse, was under contemplation. Willie was under great pressure to make some legislative move against the rioters. Sir David McNee, whose differences with Willie were encapsulated by his nickname 'The Hammer', was reported to favour an amended Riot Act.[51]

Willie and Celia loved Dorneywood, although the fastidious Alan Clark dismissed it as 'a dreary red brick house in flat country'. They spent more time there than at Ennim, and regularly entertained either ministerial colleagues or Home Office staff, who particularly appreciated the fact that they could bring their partners along.[52] Reflecting in his tranquillity that weekend, Willie felt he could trust his own instincts instead of listening to the alarmists. Mrs Thatcher regularly boasted of her intuitive understanding of the British people, but her reaction to the riots exposed an important qualification to her claim. No doubt her outlook accurately reflected the feelings of a section of the community, but her political stance had always been one of confrontation against 'the enemy within'. Possibly she did envisage an ideal situation in which every Briton shared her attitudes and could accumulate property in peace with each other. But in the present, imperfect world, her political faith could only burn at high intensity in the presence of a potent antagonist; if left-wing agitators did not exist, they had to be invented. A mass conversion to the path of righteousness would put crusaders out of business. After visiting Brixton, the Prime Minister was satisfied that her just cause had to be prosecuted with greater vigour.

Willie's approach was also the product of his instincts, but they were far more optimistic. As he later wrote:

> I remember sitting out after supper on a beautiful hot summer evening, looking at the fields and trees of Burnham Beeches. It was a perfect, peaceful English scene. Was it really the same country as the riot towns and cities which I had visited during the week?

Whether or not his reasoning was any more realistic than that of the Prime Minister, he reached a more consoling conclusion: 'Surely, I thought, this peaceful countryside represents more accurately the character and mood of the vast majority of British people.' They would demand calm resolution from those in authority, knowing that this actually required more courage than the reactionary remedies being suggested elsewhere. Hinting at his differences with Mrs Thatcher and McNee without naming them, Willie admitted that his own view might be biased: 'Perhaps because it reflects my own instinct, I do not believe that [the British] respect those who talk more toughly than they are prepared to act.'[53]

Perhaps Willie remembered a speech he had delivered in Cambridge the previous October. Given the right-wing canard that he was an appeaser himself, Willie might have thought twice before accepting an invitation to give the inaugural Stanley Baldwin lecture. But the occasion offered an opportunity to expound his own conservative philosophy, which in the domestic sphere had much in common with that of a Prime Minister who had been in office when he was a student at Cambridge. Paying tribute to Baldwin's skill, Willie remembered that:

> His responses sometimes surprised his contemporaries. But he always tried, before acting, to feel the grain of the public will. Better than anyone he understood how to gauge the importance of various currents of popular opinion and how to balance them and to apply them against the traditional attitudes and established practices of his Party and his country.

Baldwin's greatest achievement, Willie thought, was that:

> at times when the unity of the nation was threatened by divisive forces, he held both Party and nation together. He relied on his understanding of the people of this country. He pursued policies which were rooted in their everyday concerns and attitudes.

Although Willie went on dutifully to yoke Mrs Thatcher's very different outlook to the Baldwinian world-view, as he addressed himself to the disturbances of July 1981 he knew which Prime Minister provided the best example to follow.[54]

The Cabinet had already discussed the riots, on 9 July, and Willie had provided his own assessment of the causes. He referred to a general sense of alienation among the young; since some of the rioters – and looters – had been well under employment age, the issue of jobs was obviously not the sole cause. Racism had played a central part in some incidents, and the Home Office would press ahead with existing studies of this problem. On the question of how to deal with the political fall-out, Willie's influence is clear from the Cabinet minutes. The Opposition would recommend a change in economic policy, while some government supporters were sure to demand draconian laws. The best policy would be to steer a middle course, while offering full support to the police. For her part, Mrs Thatcher denied that a lack of resources had contributed, but agreed that there could be better coordination of expenditure. Concentrating on the law-and-order issues, she felt that the rioting might prove to be a watershed in British political life.

The subject was discussed again on 16 July. It was too soon to say with confidence that the crisis was over, but the remaining outbreaks seemed to be the product of sheer criminality. Three days earlier, at a meeting of the Conservative Home Affairs Committee, Willie had announced that army camps were to be made available for the housing of rioters. He had been criticised for not reporting this decision to the House of Commons, but previous governments had used similar tactics and in this case Willie could tell the Cabinet that his action had been fully justified by the results. What could have been an awkward meeting with angry backbenchers had gone smoothly, and he had been well received in the House afterwards. It had been a typical Willie manoeuvre; he had exploited the crisis to win agreement for a decision that he had wanted to take anyway, since the army camps could now be used to ease the pressure on the normal prison population (still scandalously high at 44,600). In the meantime, the feeling that the media had done nothing to reduce social tension had led him to contact both the BBC and the IBA, which had promised not to show violent films and to encourage more 'responsible' reporting.

The triumph for the 'middle course' was not quite complete. After the Cabinet meeting Willie had to lead off a Commons debate on the disturbances. His audience was in the kind of responsible mood that Willie considered to be the hallmark of the British, but he was still under extreme pressure when he began his speech. He succeeded magnificently. A later speaker, the Tory backbencher John Wheeler, described his effort as 'one of the finest speeches that I have heard him make. He struck the truth and spoke common sense.' More dramatically, Roy Hattersley had to reassure his own side that he still wanted the government to fall, before congratulating Willie, 'Long may he continue in his present office.' By contrast, Powell's contribution to the debate was mean-spirited, even by his own standards. Although the complex origins of the rioting were clear to everyone else in the House, he insisted on repeating the all too-familiar 'Rivers of Blood' themes. For his pains he was heckled throughout by incensed Labour backbenchers, who included 'bloody rubbish!', 'cattle trucks!' and 'gas chambers!' among their sedentary interjections.[55]

Willie won through this new ordeal because his heartfelt speech offered something for everyone (except Powell). He showed his dismay at what he later described as 'a shameful episode in our nation's life', but did not labour the point. He gave his full support to the police, and outlined the new equipment that would protect them. But his vague remarks on a new Riot Act reassured those who had feared an unthinking reaction; and (as he had promised in Cabinet) he acknowledged that although nothing could excuse the violence, social deprivation had undoubtedly been a factor.

It was a message he would soon repeat in less formal surroundings, when after a government strategy meeting he beckoned Mrs Thatcher's adviser John Hoskyns into the lavatory and said that something had to be done about unemployment, 'especially after the riots'. In the debate he had foreshadowed the most dramatic gesture in this field ever made by any of the Thatcher Governments; the Secretary of State for the Environment, Michael Heseltine, would undertake a fact-finding visit to Liverpool. Willie was slightly suspicious of this initiative, even after his junior minister Tim Raison had gone to Liverpool with Heseltine to protect the Home Office beat. The problem for Willie was not the measure but the man; he had distrusted Heseltine since 1976, when he seized and brandished the Mace in the House of Commons in protest against underhand tactics by the Labour whips. For someone like Willie, accustomed to making his objections quietly through 'the usual channels', this was unforgivable behaviour. Willie's closest allies shared his suspicions of Heseltine. During a Cabinet meeting the previous summer Hailsham had scribbled a note to Carrington: 'Old Goldilocks is always vociferous. And always wrong.' The more conciliatory Carrington had inserted 'nearly' in the final sentence. Now, with the government in deep political trouble, and the Prime Minister breaking records for unpopularity, Willie thought that Heseltine was trying to exploit a crisis to improve his public image.[56]

Within a week of his departure from the Home Office, Willie told Tony Benn, 'The thing I am proudest of is that I managed to handle the riots in 1981 without having to take more repressive measures.' He did have every reason for pride, to balance his regret for having failed to gauge the real importance of the St Paul's outbreak. Now the police were equipped for future trouble, but the nightmare conjured up by Willie in Cabinet – of armoured cars patrolling the streets, as they did in Belfast – was banished, at least in the medium term. Willie was thwarted in his attempts to interest chief constables in water-cannon as a method of crowd control, but the alternatives of CS gas and rubber bullets remained in storage. He had always known that the police would be most reluctant to use them except in the last resort.[57]

Lord Scarman's acute and beautifully written report was the most significant constructive legacy of the riots, but he would not have been appointed without Willie's championship. Mrs Thatcher's biographer Hugo Young has written that Willie implemented 'almost all that Scarman had to say about strengthening the police, and almost nothing he had to say about social reform'. In so far as 'social reform' lay within the province of his department Willie did water down Scarman's proposals. But the pursuit of the 'middle course' prevented him from ruffling too many feathers among a profession that was sure to resist undue political interference, whether it came from Westminster or from left-wing police committees. So the police complaints procedure was beefed up, but it was not made independent, as Scarman had wished; and although Willie encouraged the development of liaison groups between the police and deprived communities, under pressure from the Association of Chief Police Officers he dropped plans to put these on a statutory basis. Even so, the very fact that liberals eventually felt short-changed was a testament to Willie's skill, given the hysterical atmosphere in the immediate aftermath of the riots.[58]

Willie's comments to Benn ring true because he accompanied them with what was a regular refrain from him at this time. The right wing of his party, he complained, 'had made his life absolute hell for not being tougher, particularly in the *Daily Mail*, the *Express*, and the *Sun*'. These journalists were, of course, prime examples of 'those who talk more toughly than they are prepared to act'. He felt that he had done a good job in withstanding such saloon-bar critics. As the trouble on the streets died away, Willie and Celia could travel to Sandwich to watch the Open Golf as they had planned before the storm broke. But they knew that Willie would soon have to face another right-wing audience, more fearsome than anything Fleet Street (in its final days) could offer. Hugo Young found that in retirement Willie 'retained a strangely exact memory of each onslaught the [Conservative Party] conference had made against him'. As the 1981 reunion approached he had every reason to expect another skirmish. Willie might have blocked the reactionaries as Brixton burned, but at Blackpool he would make an ideal scapegoat for all the government's troubles.[59]

CHAPTER 15

HOLDING THE LINE

Few Conservatives can have relished the prospect of the 1981 Party Conference. That October only a quarter of the electorate approved of the government's record. The party was marginally ahead of Labour in the polls, but more than 10 per cent behind the Liberal-SDP Alliance, which had been picking up support ever since its formation in March. The most worrying figure, though, concerned the future. Only 14 per cent of voters thought that the Conservatives could win the next election.

Mrs Thatcher's economic experiment seemed to have failed. Britain was now a net exporter of oil, which had once again risen sharply in price. But in obedience to monetarist theory the Chancellor Geoffrey Howe had raised interest rates, and together these factors had subjected the pound to irresistible upward pressure. High domestic inflation made life difficult enough for exporters; now even efficient companies were unable to compete, and borrowing for future expansion was ruled out by the penal interest rates. For an administration that was supposed to cherish entrepreneurial energies it was an ignominious situation. Manufacturing industry entered a prolonged recession, and unemployment soared under the party which had recently jeered that 'Labour isn't working'. The 'official' figure stayed below three million until September 1982, but it exceeded two million throughout 1981. At the time of the Party Conference it stood at more than 2,700,000.

While the government was taken aback by the increase in unemployment, there was nothing accidental about other measures which widened the gap between rich and poor. Geoffrey Howe's first budget, in 1979, gave a trial run to a trick that worked far better than anyone in the Treasury can have hoped. Howe almost doubled the rate of VAT in June 1979, to compensate for a reduction in the basic rate of income tax, from 33 to 30 per cent. In a nation fixated with rates of direct taxation, many people still believe that the Thatcher Governments were aggressive tax-cutters. In reality, they relied increasingly on indirect taxation to collect a fairly constant proportion of the national revenue; and since indirect taxes like VAT had an equal effect on rich and poor, the strategy was a deliberate attempt to reverse the post-war trend of income distribution. At the same time, welfare benefits were now linked to inflation rather than average wages, ensuring that the long-term unemployed fell further behind those lucky enough to keep their jobs. Those who prospered, and those who were hustled into the economic scrapyard, were chosen by a 'market' mechanism that made the spin of a roulette wheel look like a moral arbiter of life-chances. At least the arrangement described by Disraeli as a Britain of 'two nations' was held together by social attitudes that were almost universally shared. In the Britain of 1981 this adhesive had run out.

Many Conservatives of Willie's generation had been appalled by the experience of the last terrible economic slump, in the 1930s. When Willie was first elected in 1955 three-quarters of Conservative MPs had been educated in public schools. By 1979 the proportion was almost the same, but the ethos of the party had been transformed along with the society that spawned it. Social deference was dying, dragging down with it the feeling that Conservative MPs ought to consider the interests of all their constituents, regardless of how they had voted. The fact that the slump tended to hit hardest those areas that traditionally returned Labour MPs reduced the electoral risk of prioritising the demands of middle-class voters. So the unpopularity of the government outside its heartlands was unprecedented both in its extent and its intensity; and yet under the British electoral system the Conservatives knew that they could stay in office provided they satisfied a minority of voters, mainly concentrated in the Home Counties of England.

Unemployment on this scale had never been envisaged by Conservative moderates, even those who had agreed that tough action was required against inflation. With his paternalistic outlook – and a northern constituency which included several industrial towns – Willie was a most unlikely ally for the new school of Conservatism. The majority of his Cabinet colleagues were equally miscast. But for him the 'conflict of loyalties' was especially acute. His offer of support to Mrs Thatcher in February 1975 had been as near to unconditional as any such statement can be in the fluctuating world of politics. On economic policy his room for manoeuvre was particularly limited. It was the major theme of the Thatcher premiership, so action against the government's policy in concert with the Cabinet 'wets' would be an obvious threat to the Prime Minister's position. The fact that Mrs Thatcher was outnumbered in the Cabinet might have consoled sceptics at the outset, but her refusal to revise her economic course had transformed the arithmetic into a serious handicap for anyone who wanted even a minimal detour from the monetarist itinerary. The 'wets' were like an army that lacked any conventional forces; they had only a nuclear device, which could not be deployed without serious risk to themselves, to the party and (so they had reason to think) to the country. So when Ian Gilmour, Peter Walker and Jim Prior discussed the 1981 budget, which defied Keynesian logic by raising taxes in a slump, they agreed that although the measures were 'astonishingly perverse', they should not resign. Gilmour later expressed his regret that they had decided to stay on, but he also felt that the gesture would not have altered government policy. Indeed, the departing ministers would only have been replaced by people who shared Mrs Thatcher's outlook.[1]

Howe always discussed his budgets with Willie on the day before delivery, by which time it was too late to contest any details. Lord Prior has recorded that although Willie was uneasy about the 1981 package, he felt that the Cabinet should trust the Chancellor's judgement. This was a line that he pursued in other crucial ministerial meetings, notably the so-called 'Star Chamber', which adjudicated on disputes between the Treasury and individual spending ministers. As Chairman of these meetings Willie was naturally anxious to seek a compromise, but in order to deter supplicant ministers from dragging out the (often tiresome) process he made it a general rule that they would get more if they settled in bilateral meetings with Treasury ministers. Had the Home Office budget ever been in dispute Willie would have suffered from a conflict of interests; but his department enjoyed favoured status even before his junior minister, Leon Brittan, was promoted to the Cabinet as Chief Secretary to the Treasury. One of Brittan's performances at the Home Office had pleased his boss so much that he marked the occasion with a new 'Willie-ism': Brittan, he boomed, had 'made a lot of straw without any bricks'. Before the spending round of 1982 senior officials in the department were worried that their full expenditure wish-list might not be approved, but Willie seemed very confident of winning the argument. When asked why he was so relaxed, he chuckled that for Brittan the forthcoming discussion would be more like a promotion board than a bargaining session. After the meeting had passed off to everyone's satisfaction Willie's officials knew that Brittan could expect further advancement at the next major reshuffle.[2]

For all the rhetoric of the Thatcher camp, public spending continued to increase. The original plan was to cut the total by 4 per cent between 1979 and 1983; instead, it rose by 6 per cent. Since this reflected the inevitable costs of higher unemployment, rather than spending for constructive purposes, it was still not enough to satisfy the 'wets'. But it was intolerable to Mrs Thatcher. The 1981 riots coincided with a series of unpleasant arguments in Cabinet. In mid-June, after a long and vigorous discussion, ministers were reminded of the need to appear united in public. But that argument was only a warm-up. Gilmour has written that during the meeting of 23 July, 'The Prime Minister found herself virtually isolated, alone in a laager with the two Treasury ministers, Geoffrey Howe and Leon Brittan.' Mrs Thatcher later described that meeting as 'one of the bitterest arguments on the economy, or any subject, that I can ever recall taking place at Cabinet during my premiership'. The overwhelming majority of the Cabinet had balked at a planned cut of £5 billion in public expenditure. For the first time John Biffen and the Defence Secretary John Nott joined the dissenting chorus. Hoskyns recorded in his diary, 'It sounds like the beginning of the end – or at least a step in that direction.' He also noted that Thorneycroft had warned Mrs Thatcher 'that unless she learned to work with her colleagues her own position would be in jeopardy'. Her desperate search for soulmates had just led her to invite Enoch Powell for lunch at Chequers. As this was less than a fortnight since Powell had shocked the House with his analysis of the July riots, it was an astonishing lapse of judgement and members of her coterie were frantic at the prospect of the news leaking out.[3]

Lady Thatcher has written that during the July crisis Willie was 'as loyal as ever'. Since he is not named among those who actively defended the economic policy at that time, she must have really meant 'Willie was far more loyal than I had any reason to expect'. He did have serious misgivings about Howe's general handling of the economy; and there was a more specific grievance. Civil servants had been taking industrial action since March. After six weeks Christopher Soames, the responsible minister, thought that the union would settle for 7.5 per cent. But Mrs Thatcher refused to authorise the settlement, saying that 7 per cent was her absolute limit. At the end of that fateful July the civil servants did settle – on the terms that Soames had suggested three months earlier. Jim Prior calculated that £250 million was lost because of the Prime Minister's intransigence. Probably she agreed that this was a regrettable episode; in her memoirs she relegated it to a footnote, and mentioned the cost to the taxpayer without indicating that she herself was to blame. Instead, Downing Street claimed that the culprit was Soames, when his sacking was announced two months later.[4]

Willie's own feelings at the dismissal of Soames are indicated by his tactful decision to avoid the subject completely in his memoirs; Lords Carrington and Hailsham are equally reticent. It was true that Soames had often made tactless jokes about the Prime Minister, and had irritated her by his behaviour in Cabinet. He frequently flicked notes across the Cabinet table; before one meeting some of his colleagues ran a sweepstake on the number of such messages, which turned out to be eight. It was said that on one occasion Mrs Thatcher, who was in the habit of kicking off her shoes during meetings, found that one shoe had gone missing when she was about to stand up; under the table, Soames had manoeuvred it out of her reach. Whether or not this even happened – and the usual seating arrangements at Cabinet meetings make the story very doubtful – Soames did seem to bring out the childish side of several ministers.[5] These, though, were hardly hanging offences. And Willie and Soames were close friends, who often went shooting together. On the day of the sacking, Monday 14 September 1981, Mrs Thatcher discovered that Willie and Soames had something else in common. When she broke the news to Soames, the incensed minister:

> assailed her for twenty minutes for her various shortcomings . . . He had never been spoken to by a woman, he told her, in the abusive way she had spoken to him [during the Civil Service strike]. His thunderous curtain-lines, it was said, could be heard out of the open window halfway across Horseguards Parade.[6]

It is not known whether Soames conducted a high-volume duet with Willie on the same subject – certainly they remained on good terms after the incident – but if he did he would have been well within his rights. In the past other politicians may have been shunted aside for being proved correct, but this seemed like a stupendous act of pettiness. And Willie bore much of the responsibility. It was he who had originally persuaded the Cabinet to back Mrs Thatcher's line on the Civil Service. Jim Prior has written that after the strike Willie divulged that 'she had told him she would resign if she didn't get her way'. He adds that no one should have believed such a threat on such an issue – but it seems that Willie, at least, took her seriously, canvassing hard to rally his colleagues behind the Prime Minister. After his retirement he gave an additional reason for acquiescence, claiming that Mrs Thatcher was supported by most of the parliamentary party on this issue.[7]

The reshuffle was agreed in Willie's presence, at Chequers on the Saturday before the announcement. Mrs Thatcher had imported several key advisers with limited experience of the workings of British politics; they tended to reinforce her own feeling that half-hearted friends were (if anything) even worse than open enemies. On 26 August she had revealed her thoughts to her entourage. John Hoskyns, who was present at the discussion, noted that a week later they were still working on a strategy for dealing with the likely objections of Willie and Jopling. Willie needed very careful handling, because his own cousin was lined up for the sack, along with his friend Soames. But at sixty-two, Lord Thorneycroft had enjoyed a reasonable innings. His successor as Chairman, Cecil Parkinson, felt that Mrs Thatcher had already forgotten the contribution Thorneycroft had made to the 1979 victory; but if the premier's memory was short, Thorneycroft himself may well have considered that it would be better to bow out on a winning note, rather than presiding over what looked sure to be a dismal defeat in a couple of years.[8]

More straightforward were the departures of the moderate Mark Carlisle from Education and of the thoroughly disenchanted Gilmour. But the real key to the reshuffle was the Employment Secretary Jim Prior, who was to be sent to Northern Ireland. The Thatcherites wanted a symbolic confrontation with a major trade union, but only when they had devised a framework of law that would strip workers of the weapons they had used to such deadly effect in the disputes of the 1970s. Although it was designed to avoid a repetition of the Industrial Relations Act fiasco under the Heath Government, Prior's cautious approach to reform infuriated the Prime Minister and her friends.[9]

After the reshuffle it was said that Willie was initially prepared to speak up on Prior's behalf. The latter's mistake – possibly in an over-reaction to the passive 'wet' response to the budget – was to tip off media friends that his position was in jeopardy, and to let it be known that he would fight hard to keep it. While Gilmour had remarked that the government was heading for the rocks, Willie thought that the Prime Minister ought to be in charge of the steering; his own self-appointed task was to avoid a mutiny, even if the vessel was miles off-course. Prior's defiance had made the reshuffle into a question of Prime Ministerial authority; and in February 1975 Willie had sworn to support his leader, however much he might prefer to be serving someone else. Mrs Thatcher hesitated before calling Prior's bluff; she might easily have backed down, had Willie not swung behind her at the last moment. The new Employment Secretary was Norman Tebbit, whose determination to shackle the unions was reflected in new legislation. But although he moved faster than Prior would have done, Tebbit still recognised the importance of keeping in line with public opinion.

In his memoirs Prior reflects that 'any individual Minister, unless he is very strongly backed by his colleagues, is in a weak position to challenge an established Prime Minister's appointments'. He acknowledges that he had over-played his hand, but adds that 'when it came to the crunch those who had advised me to dig in were the first to say "Well, you'll have to take it, won't you? There isn't much we can do."' After Mrs Thatcher had offered Prior the Northern Ireland job he decided that it was still worth consulting Willie and Jopling. But if Willie had previously told him to stand firm, the advice was now very different:

> they gave me the old guff, as you would expect: how important it was that I should do it, how she really wanted me to do it, what a blow it would be to the party if I didn't.

I said to Willie, 'But surely it's become almost impossible for me to take it on, because I've said quite openly that I don't wish to go to Northern Ireland.' He blithely replied, 'Oh, they don't mind that sort of controversy over there. In fact, they rather like that sort of thing. That will make no difference. And you can take it from us that you will have our full support.'

It was indeed 'guff' – if not worse. Given Willie's feelings about Northern Ireland, his reported remarks on the subject are particularly suspicious. If Prior had been sent there under happier circumstances he might have made important progress. But far from relishing the arrival of a demoted minister, the contending parties in the province were likely to regard his appointment as a slight; and more than anyone else Willie knew that first impressions are crucial in Ulster. Quite possibly, during the interview with Prior – which in itself was something of a departure from the normal procedure on these unhappy occasions – he was going through the motions of repeating the positive argument for a move, while secretly hoping that Prior would leave the Cabinet entirely. With hindsight, that would probably have been better for all concerned, although Prior served honourably for three years.[10] At his insistence he remained a member of the key Cabinet Economic Strategy Committee, but this proved to be a token concession because he was hopelessly outnumbered by Mrs Thatcher's allies.

Politically, Willie was strong enough at the time to have revised the hit-list which Thatcher had discussed with her friends. After the riots one Conservative backbencher, Richard Shepherd, had called for his resignation; but thanks to his speech of 16 July, Willie had shored up his position. A forceful word from him in these circumstances might have made a lot of difference; he could not have gone into bat for all of his endangered colleagues, but Soames could have been spared and Prior kept at Employment. What the latter seems to have overlooked is the possibility that in entrusting an ultimatum to the press, he was putting other allies at risk. Once Willie had accepted that the Prime Minister must be allowed to have her way over Prior, it was hardly necessary for her to use the same argument against Soames. Mrs Thatcher hailed the reshuffle as a devastating defeat for the 'wets', but dangerous dissidents were still in place; Francis Pym, who had been making restive noises, was secure as Leader of the Commons and Walker survived at Agriculture. Sir Keith Joseph was removed from the economic scene, taking Education at his own request. Even so, as he contemplated the messy fall-out from the Cabinet rows of July, Willie could agree with the verdict of the The Times: if Mrs Thatcher failed, at least after the reshuffle she would have no one to blame but herself.[11]

Unversed in economics as he was, Willie had been forced to take sides by the reshuffle of September 1981, and he isolated himself from the 'wets' who had supported him in 1975. Once he met a deputation of moderate backbenchers including some old friends, but he kept them standing in his office after guessing that they had come to sound him out on the subject of the leadership. When a group of young MPs lunched with him it was delicately suggested that he might do more to uphold 'One Nation' principles. The result was one of Willie's 'stampers'. 'I've no idea what you're talking about,' he stormed. 'You don't know what it's like. I'm sitting around the Cabinet table with the most ghastly people.' The most prominent of the younger dissidents, such as Chris Patten, Garel-Jones and Waldegrave, were intellectuals rather than instinctive conservatives in the Whitelaw mould; he tended to keep them at arm's length. Garel-Jones remembers that for at least his first year in the Commons the slightest provocation would trigger Willie's stock conversation-stopper: 'I know what you young people think. You think that I'm a bloody fool. I'm telling you, I am not a bloody fool.'[12]

In Opposition Willie had complained privately that Mrs Thatcher's leadership victory had encouraged right-wing Conservative activists to think they were the dominant force within the party. The September reshuffle did nothing to diminish that view, and at the Party Conference Willie knew that they would feel no inhibitions in demanding the reintroduction of the death penalty. As promised in the manifesto, there had been an early (and free) Commons vote on the subject. On 19 July 1979 Willie explained once again his reasons for opposing the measure, now reinforced by Home Office advice. He knew that although many of his new parliamentary colleagues disagreed violently with his position, the fact that the Conservatives now enjoyed a majority in the Commons would make no difference to the outcome. The motion was rejected by 119 votes.

No one imagined that the parliamentary battle was over. Willie had to rehearse the same arguments again before a further vote in May 1982. But the rank and file felt that they were faced by a phalanx of alleged 'do-gooders' within their own party who were ignoring the clearly stated wish of the people; and their impotence gave an extra edge to their wrath. Willie had worked out a technique for handling his critics. He would 'make a serious, dull speech on the main issues [of law and order], making understanding noises about support for capital punishment at the same time as giving no ground'. It sounded workable on paper. But in May 1981, when he restated his position at a Conservative women's conference, Willie was booed by the assembled *tricoteuses*. The admixture of male retributivists at the October gathering was unlikely to temper the mood, and the fact that those proceedings would be televised made no difference to the frustrated lynch-mob. Willie's speech would have to be a masterpiece of tedium if he hoped to emerge unscathed. So the final text was burdened with statistics and platitudes in sufficient quantity to produce an outbreak of somnolence at an accountants' annual dinner. To satisfy anyone who stayed awake he included one or two hardline comments, including a positive reference to the 'short, sharp shock' policy, which he already knew to be failing. In retirement he hinted that officials in the Home Office had sabotaged his pet project, but it was said that some of the young inmates actually enjoyed what was supposed to be an effective remedial experience. The Prison Officers' Association remarked that the system merely produced 'fit young burglars able to run faster than the police'. The cost per inmate, at £1,000 a month, was double the fees at Eton. Magistrates stopped sending young offenders to detention centres. But officially the policy outlasted Willie; politically, at any rate, it had served its purpose.[13]

Willie's strategy for repelling his critics had one serious flaw. It might have worked if he was to open the debate; but instead he had to reply at the end of it. Speakers could be carefully screened to ensure that both sides of the argument at least received an airing, but party managers knew that someone was bound to put the case for hanging in the emotive form so familiar to saloon-bar visitors. When this duly occurred Willie noticed that Mrs Thatcher applauded the 'fiery and brilliant' speaker, who advocated a three-line whip on hanging and urged the de-selection of Conservative MPs who disobeyed. Having tasted blood, the pack found an appetising quarry in a Young Conservative who argued that there should be no room for racists in the party. Presumably in calmer moods the audience would have argued that racists have a right to free speech, but in that overheated moment they forgot to extend the same courtesy to their liberal-minded colleague, who tried to expose an organisation called 'Tory Action', which later denounced Willie as 'unspeakable' and described the heroine of the conference as 'basically a weak prime minister surrounded by a bunch of toadies'. But the same people who deplored the influence of Labour's Militant Tendency had no problem with extreme Conservative 'entryists', and they howled down the speaker. 'I was witnessing scenes of intolerance which I had never expected to see in the Conservative Party,' Willie later reflected. In combination with Mrs Thatcher's applause – and, perhaps, the sight of the young Edwina Currie brandishing a pair of handcuffs – this unsavoury mood ensured that when his turn came to speak Willie was geared up for a full-scale 'stamper'. Had he been able to give the usual expressions to his fury, the emotion might have faded quickly. But he was stuck on the platform with no immediate outlet. When his turn finally came to read out his text – so lovingly crafted to sidestep the very subject that now dominated the debate – his temperature was still rising.[14]

In his memoirs Willie said that he regretted the ensuing outburst, feeling that it had only made matters worse. In fact, although he did rebuke those who wanted a whipped vote on hanging, his unscripted remarks were peppered with qualifications and apologetic noises. Afterwards the conference defeated a resolution backing the government's policies on law and order. Willie had not asked for support at the end of his speech; under the circumstances that would only have added to the humiliation. Short of announcing his resignation on the spot there was nothing he could have done to change the outcome.[15]

After the debate Willie did offer to resign, during a protracted and sulphurous argument behind the scenes with Mrs Thatcher. It might have seemed bathetic to end a long ministerial career because of a tactless burst of applause, and Willie had always known that his leader was a devotee of the rope. But having supported the Prime Minister over the budget and the reshuffle, he had every reason to deplore what amounted to a very public endorsement of a constructive vote of no confidence. Finally, though, the storm blew itself out and Willie realised that resignation at that point would have precipitated all the bad consequences he had wanted to avoid during the reshuffle. Bill Pitt was about to win the Croydon by-election for the Liberals, showing that the new Alliance could pose a threat even without a celebrity candidate in the field. And Heath, who delivered a heartfelt plea for a change of economic policy at the conference, had re-emerged as a focus for discontent within the party. Less than 40 per cent of Tory voters endorsed the present leader; opinion polls found that around one-fifth of them wanted a Heath restoration. Willie retained his high regard for Heath, but his return in the circumstances of October 1981 was unthinkable.[16]

As so often, in his memoirs Willie skirted round an unfortunate episode, claiming, 'The mutual understanding between Margaret Thatcher and myself had even by then grown so strong over the years that it was capable of withstanding such strains . . . In the end we carried on happily as if nothing had happened.' He was unruffled when the Prime Minister failed to endorse his work at the Home Office in her own speech to the conference. He chose not to reveal whether or not she apologised at the time; she did, at least, keep her hands out of sight at future conferences when anyone supported the death penalty.[17]

Two months after the conference one journalist wrote that Mrs Thatcher's relationship with Willie had developed into a 'habit of total reliance'. But at lower levels there was no doubt that Willie's stock had fallen; and even Lord Burghley might have been handed his cards by Elizabeth I if the whole court had turned against him. As one right-wing MP put it in early December, 'the magic is wearing thin and too many people know how the tricks are done. Willie is still a reassuring cuddly bear – but this Christmas he looks just a bit shopsoiled.' On the left the comments were ever more disrespectful. The previous year one of his Cabinet colleagues privately informed Hugo

Young of the *Sunday Times* that Willie was '"a burned-out case": a pathetic
Thatcherite bootlicker, blind to the economic crisis, the once acceptable face
of Conservatism who was now reduced to providing the cover behind which
every kind of depredation was being attempted. Some of the language,' Young
concluded, 'was very strong.'[18]

Willie's anger at the conference must have been compounded by his
knowledge that it would scupper a key element of his strategy at the Home
Office, resulting in a further loss of face. He had hoped to marshal support for
his plan to include in a Criminal Justice Bill the Home Secretary's right to order
the release, under supervision, of offenders who were serving sentences of less
than eighteen months. After the conference he knew that he had no chance of
persuading his parliamentary colleagues; in any case the judges and magistrates
were implacably opposed. Their cooperation was essential, because they could
always escape the constraints of the legislation by imposing longer prison terms.
In order to build confidence between his department and the judiciary, Willie
had invited them to an unprecedented supper-party with his ministers and
officials. Thanks to his political setback, he had to fall back on the idea of
allowing judges to impose partially suspended sentences. Politically it was a
reasonable compromise, since the principle was already enshrined in an act of
1977. The judges would have less room for complaint about undue ministerial
interference. Even so, Willie was disappointed with the results of his act, which
was passed in 1982. If anything the prison problem was worse when he left the
Home Office than it had been in 1979. This was a regrettable reflection of
the political and social conditions of the time. Certainly Willie could not have
acted more energetically than he did, and none of his successors have fared any
better. In 2002 the prison population exceeded 70,000.[19]

In another of his numerous attempts to interpret Willie's motives, in
February 1982 Alan Clark guessed that he was only supporting Mrs Thatcher
while biding his time before taking a leading role in a coalition government
after the next election. In his ministerial role, though, Willie was acting as if
a government of the soggy centre was already in place. He had 'made himself
indispensible on the broad canvas, and [wa]s allowed a free hand to implement
by stealth or otherwise the progressive policies of the Home Office', Clark
thought. When it emerged that Willie had admitted defeat on sentencing,
Clark was exultant. On 22 February he dined at the Garrick Club with Willie
and other officers of the Home Affairs Committee. On this occasion Willie
temporarily forgot his distaste for this kind of company (although the egregious
Ivor Stanbrook insisted on haranguing him). Perhaps wisely, though, Willie
directed his inevitable 'stamper' not at his chief parliamentary tormentor, but
at the *Daily Mail*. His 'great bellowing rampage' included the unlikely allegation
that the newspaper's editor was hell-bent on toppling the whole government; as

Clark reflected, Willie was nearer the truth when he narrowed the indictment, roaring that David English wanted his resignation:

At intervals Willie yelled that he would 'resign his seat' (the wrong phrase, he cannot really have meant this, surely?) or lapsed into melancholia, chin slumped on his waistcoat . . . Promptly, however, at two minutes to eleven, he snapped out of it, rose to his feet, literally in the middle of somebody else's sentence, delivered a short farewell homily and made his way out to his armoured black XJ6.[20]

These were black days for Willie. Recently released crime figures set a new record. Did they reflect better reporting, the effects of high unemployment, or an incipient breakdown of respect for the law? Willie thought such statistics were always misleading, but he had used them freely to attack Labour before 1979. In March 1982 the *Daily Mail* added to its list of offences by publishing an opinion poll which showed that 80 per cent of the public wanted tougher sentences. While other papers introduced new alliterative insults, such as 'Waffling Willie' and 'Whitelaw the Weak', the *Mail* plumped for 'Mr Wetlaw'. Its unrelenting parliamentary sketch-writer, Andrew Alexander, jeered that 'Mr Willie Whitelaw at bay is a curious sight. It is as if someone had cornered a bad-tempered blancmange. Loud too. And repetitive'. At the time the press was particularly exercised about rape – which was a likely candidate for better reporting rather than a massive real increase, as women at last began to assert their right to equal treatment under the law. But concerns were also growing over burglaries, and Willie had a personal insight into this problem. In 1982–3 his daughter Carol, who was living in Brixton, suffered five minor break-ins. Although the story conflicted with its distorted 'Powellite' view of Brixton – how could it be that the daughter of a prosperous white politician was happy living in such an area with her family? – the *Daily Mail* inevitably caught up with Carol. She loyally supported her father's line, saying that the problem had been reduced by the introduction of 'community policing'.[21]

By now the Home Secretary was at the centre of every Westminster rumour. At the time of the Garrick Club dinner even Tristan Garel-Jones – who had quickly become a reliable barometer of party opinion – thought that Willie ought to make way for a more robust Home Secretary. There was talk of a 'Save Willie' campaign, instigated by the Prime Minister; others said that she was only waiting for a revival in Willie's fortunes because she preferred not to sack him when he was already prostrated by bad news. The latter rumour seemed to be verified when Mrs Thatcher let it be known that, since the worst of the economic slump was over, she was now free to focus on law-and-order issues. In fact, in an interview for this book, Willie disclosed that he was sure

Mrs Thatcher would have been happy to see him leave the Home Office in the first few months of 1982. This explains the champagne-fuelled threat at the Garrick Club. Unless he was under terrific pressure, no amount of refreshment would have been enough to make him hint at an imminent departure in the presence of someone like Clark.[22]

Apart from Willie's current unpopularity, Mrs Thatcher had to consider the future in deciding his fate. Westminster was hardly in the grip of election fever at the time – with so little good news to report, the government was likely to hang on for as long as possible in the hope of something better, and it could put off an encounter with the electorate until the early summer of 1984. But in December 1981, after Shirley Williams had secured an astonishing victory at a by-election in the Conservative seat of Crosby, only 23 per cent of the voters said they would support the government when an election came. As the historians of the SDP note, this was the lowest figure for any ruling party since polling began in the 1930s – yet another feat for a government which had set many of these doleful records. The economic outlook remained grim. Law and order was one of the few issues on which the Conservatives might have any reason for hope. Even if the figures failed to improve, a Home Secretary with a blood-curdling line in rhetoric might turn public fears to political advantage. Although Willie was willing to play politics with law and order up to a point, there was no chance that he would capitulate to his critics, and he was damned if he was going to hang on as a lame-duck deputy. In his memoirs he recalls a time when he considered 'resigning from the House of Commons or staying there while sitting on the backbenches'. Although its position in the text suggests that he considered these options at the beginning of 1983, the idea had clearly been in his mind much earlier than that.[23]

It was down to Willie to fight for his political life, with the assistance of any friends he could muster. On 22 March 1982 Bill Deedes, editor of the *Daily Telegraph*, came up trumps with a strongly supportive editorial. Later that day Willie confronted the Home Affairs Committee once again. More than a hundred MPs were crammed in to hear his twenty-minute speech. The substance was nothing special. He repeated his opposition to capital punishment, and his promises of tougher policing can hardly have convinced the critics who wanted action, not words. But he later wrote, 'I felt, as I spoke, that the audience were just waiting to stand up and that, provided I did not actually fall down during the speech, they would do so.' While they waited to deliver their standing ovation, the MPs banged their desks in the approved Tory fashion. The committee's Chairman, Sir Edward Gardner, emerged from the meeting to claim that he had just witnessed 'one of the most remarkable demonstrations of support for the Home Secretary that one can remember'. This accolade loses some of its force when one reflects that Gardner was a long-standing friend of Willie's – and that since May 1979 there had been very few demonstrations of support for him that would have allowed a meaningful comparison. But whether or not the meeting had been 'packed' and the officers primed to load the speaker with compliments, Willie could not have survived if he had not enjoyed genuine support in the parliamentary party. He would soon discover that although he could save himself by his own exertions, others were lacking in the unique skills that had thwarted his enemies.[24]

Stanbrook and Clark were both present at the meeting, and it would have been interesting to read the latter's views in his published diary. But that evening Clark's attention was diverted by news of an incident thousands of miles away. In the House of Commons Library he scribbled, 'A bunch of Argentinians are horsing around in South Georgia.' Actually the horseplay had begun three days earlier, although Argentinian troops did not land on the Falkland Islands themselves until 2 April. For a frustrated military strategist like Clark it was time to turn away from the pseudo-conflict in the Commons and consider the implications of a real war.[25]

The Argentinian invasion of the Falklands Islands transformed the fortunes of the first Thatcher Government, and it could hardly have happened at a more crucial juncture in the relationship between the Prime Minister and her Deputy. If Mrs Thatcher still doubted Willie's qualities in March 1982, for his own part he had seen nothing yet to banish his original misgivings. Whatever the precise reasons for the Argentinian attack, he shared the general admiration for the Prime Minister's conduct after the crisis broke. In fact, his presence from the outset in the War Cabinet proved that, whatever his departmental difficulties, Willie was someone to whom she instinctively turned when tough decisions were required. But before this inner grouping was formed Willie lost another of his Cabinet friends, this time to a genuine resignation rather than a sacking. Within a fortnight of his own success at a backbench committee meeting, Willie failed utterly in his attempt to 'rally vocal support' behind the Foreign Secretary, Carrington, who saw himself as the responsible minister. He appeared at a special gathering of the 1922 Committee on Saturday 4 April.[26]

With characteristic understatement, Carrington has described the meeting held in Committee Room 10 as 'fairly disagreeable'. As far as unequal contests go, it can only be compared to the Christians against the lions. When Willie had encouraged him to meet the backbenchers, he had warned Carrington that he should not gauge the political mood from the response of his colleagues in the Lords, whose own debate had been civilised. But even if he appreciated this point, Carrington was not prepared to butter up an unmannerly audience with insincere apologies. According to one witness, he mistakenly treated the MPs 'like normal people', courteously asking for questions when he had finished his speech. But the mob needed no invitation. Clark recorded that he was one of thirty critical speakers, and that when he made his point 'Carrington sat staring at me in haughty silence'. He had never been a member of the Commons, and had disliked the experience of being Chairman of the Conservatives; perhaps, as he glared at Clark, he realised that standards within the party had gone steeply downhill even since then. He also seems to have doubted Mrs Thatcher's decision to resist the Falklands invasion, and he was attacked in a *Times* leading article that particularly dismayed Willie. Over the weekend Carrington travelled to Dorneywood, where Willie and Jopling tried hard to persuade him to stay on. But he stuck to his resolution and left the Foreign Office on Monday 5 April. Francis Pym replaced him, and was appointed to the War Cabinet along with Nott and the Party Chairman Cecil Parkinson.[27]

At the emergency Cabinet called after news of the invasion first reached London, it was Willie who had expressed the situation in the starkest terms. The government, he thought, could not survive unless it took immediate steps to recapture the Falklands. In fact, initially he shared Carrington's misgivings about the practicality of the operation; but having delivered his political assessment he was prepared to back it wholeheartedly. He was involved in most of the key decisions over the next ten weeks; he thought, for instance, that the sinking of the Argentine cruiser, *General Belgrano*, on Sunday 2 May was fully justified because although the vessel's movements were difficult to predict, it did represent a threat to the British task-force. His most significant intervention had come a week earlier, when Pym returned from negotiations in the US with a package of peace proposals that Mrs Thatcher regarded as tantamount to 'conditional surrender'. The situation was far more complicated than that. For many years the Foreign Office had hoped to find a way either to share sovereignty or to negotiate a handover of the islands; Willie had reflected this view during the early debates on his British Nationality Act, when he resisted backbench pressure to make the Falklands a special case like Gibraltar, and thus denied full citizenship to about 800 of the islanders. Remembering Suez, Willie was also concerned that ultimately the Americans could force the British to accept peace proposals.[28]

While Pym was discussing the ideas with officials and other ministers, the Prime Minister invited Willie up to her study to explain her opposition. Downstairs, Cecil Parkinson noticed that the pair had left for a private chat and nervously awaited the outcome. When he saw them descending the staircase together, evidently on cordial terms, he knew that Mrs Thatcher's arguments had prevailed and that the peace plan would be rejected. Even so, the Prime Minister felt constrained to tell the Commons that the ideas would be carefully considered; with hindsight, Willie was glad that the Argentinians themselves refused to negotiate.[29]

Ironically, it has been suggested that Parkinson was only in the War Cabinet to counter what was assumed to be an automatic alliance on every subject between Willie and Pym. This was nonsense: as Foreign Secretary, Pym was obliged to seek a negotiated settlement for as long as any chance for diplomacy remained, while Willie had shown during the embassy siege that he preferred not to drag out the talking. Within the Thatcher camp the misreading of the characters of both men was still so great that someone started a rumour of a pact between Willie and Pym: if everything went wrong and the Prime Minister had to resign, only one of them would stand after they had decided between them who was best placed to succeed. Needless to say, this story was entirely groundless. Once the real action had started, the Cabinet was united, and Willie and Pym gave it the benefit of their similar wartime experiences. They acted as an indispensable channel between the politicians and the armed services, advising both sides of the real military risks and the political calculations.[30]

There were, of course, times when the hazardous operation to eject the Argentinians seemed on the verge of disaster. By 25 May the task-force had lost five ships, and the whole fleet seemed defenceless against the Exocet missile. At this time, Willie confided, he was 'lying awake at night with visions of Suez'. At least the British had secured US support. But he was terrified that mounting casualties, and the loss of essential equipment in the sinking of the *Atlantic Conveyor*, would force a retreat and bring down the government. 'We must not leave our chaps with the job half done,' he warned on several occasions. Tory MPs also thought that the 'chaps' deserved the unreflective support of the broadcasters, and an edition of BBC's *Newsnight* which tried to be impartial between the two sides gave them a chance to turn their own fire against a hated enemy well within reach. Willie advised his friend George Howard, chairman of the BBC, to walk the plank as Carrington had done, and he duly appeared before the backbench media committee. This time there was no resignation, and although one MP prodded Howard and called him a 'traitor' Willie thought that this meeting had been a harmless way for his parliamentary colleagues to let off steam.[31]

Thames TV also caused offence, by screening an interview with the Argentinian leader General Galtieri. In both of these cases Willie tried to mediate, in his departmental capacity; he was assisted by opinion polls which showed that the public shared none of the outrage of the bellicose MPs. Even after the war was over, he was called upon to protect another friend, Robert Runcie, when the Archbishop of Canterbury fell below approved standards of Tory jingoism during the Service of Thanksgiving on 26 June. This must have been particularly distasteful for Willie, who was well aware of Runcie's personal courage and thought that he had struck exactly the right tone. Tristan Garel-Jones remembers watching in admiration as Willie fended off questions about Runcie in one television interview. Having checked how long the interview would last, he blustered about nothing in particular for half a minute before looking straight into the camera as if he were about to say something profound. But the expectant audience learned only that in his opinion 'Robert Runcie [pause] is a deeply religious man'.[32]

Runcie's crime had been to remind the British public that war was at best a highly regrettable necessity. But like Willie, the Archbishop had reason to feel some of the reflected glory from one of the decisive actions of the war – the capture of the heavily defended Mount Tumbledown on 13–14 June, by a battalion of Scots Guards who fought through the night in appalling conditions. Willie heard of this decisive success at the same time that news came through of British troops entering the Falklands capital, Port Stanley. But if Willie 'rejoiced', in line with Mrs Thatcher's advice after the earlier recapture of South Georgia, he was keenly aware of the price of victory. Nine Guardsmen had been killed and forty-three wounded.[33]

According to one witness, Mrs Thatcher was 'spitting blood' after Runcie's sermon. Her reaction was a further reminder to Willie of the gulf of personality that divided them. But he genuinely felt that the Prime Minister had proved herself during the Falklands campaign; and if her exploitation of the war for political advantage was in dubious taste, he had always differed from her on standards of propriety. As ever, though, his opponents were ready to place the most cynical constructions on his conduct. When Alan Clark rushed to prostrate himself at Mrs Thatcher's feet on the day after the Argentinian surrender, he noticed Willie 'shuffling benignly three paces behind'. He could not help adding, 'What must he have been thinking?' Presumably Willie was thinking, 'We'll be in for a lot of trouble if this lot insist on treating her like a goddess.' As it was, he merely looked 'grumpy' when he overheard Clark's slobbering tributes.[34]

There was nothing Willie could do about the right, for whom the Falklands had been a one-woman show. If they thought about Willie's part in the victory at all, they tended to assume he would be brooding over an episode that ended for ever his hopes of a Whitelaw-led coalition government. On the left, the feeling that he had betrayed the 'One Nation' cause was now accentuated by frustration. With poll ratings approaching 60 per cent, Mrs Thatcher had switched from unelectable to unassailable, and at the next election the mismanagement of the economy would be a subsidiary issue. So while the war helped the government (which had slowly been recovering in the polls anyway), and burst the SDP bubble, it left Willie more exposed than ever to fresh troubles.

Willie always dreaded the month of July, which among other things had brought him the Home leadership crisis, 'Bloody Friday' and the worst of the 1981 rioting. His experience in 1982, though, capped anything that had gone before. The first disaster was a break-in at Buckingham Palace. The intruder, Michael Fagan, had found his way into the Queen's bedroom on Friday 9 July, after several previous attempts that had not been so successful. Apparently he had told his mother that he had 'a girlfriend called Elizabeth living in SW1'. The Queen had reacted with remarkable sang froid, agreeing to Fagan's request for a cigarette before help arrived; he had already sampled some of the royal wine. Willie expected the story to leak out over the weekend, but nothing happened until the Monday when most of the newspapers ran it. The *Daily Express*, in particular, made it the focus of a general story about inadequate palace security. At this point Willie realised his mistake; to make the best of a bad job he should have publicised the incident himself, either on the Friday or over the weekend. But he had heard the news on his way to give a speech at Glenalmond School, and had decided not to change his schedule given that the Queen had escaped unmolested. When the storm broke Willie felt ashamed that his department was being blamed for putting her at risk, particularly since she had visited the Home Office only four months previously, on the occasion of its 200th anniversary. In his mortification he drove to Downing Street and offered his resignation. With the Falklands behind them, Mrs Thatcher would not hear of him breaking their partnership over an incident for which no one could reasonably blame him, even if he held overall departmental responsibility. Sir David McNee was not directly responsible either, but if people wanted a high-profile scapegoat he was the obvious candidate. With Willie's approval Brian Cubbon put this view to 'The Hammer', who refused to fall on his sword; he was due to depart in the autumn anyway.[35]

But this was far from being the end of the matter. Willie gave a statement to the House, outlining new measures to ensure there would be no repeat visit from an uninvited subject. A hasty inquiry was already under way; eventually this led to disciplinary action and at least one resignation. There was also an investigation into the law of trespass, which began after Willie discovered that Fagan could not be prosecuted under existing statutes. When Patrick Mayhew informed him of this he was incredulous: 'Do you mean to say,' he spluttered, 'that if I went home and found *Ivor Stanbrook* in my bed, there would be nothing I could do?' The elements of absurdity, combined with a feeling of misery that grew as he spoke, meant that Willie was not at the top of his form when he addressed the House. Later he defended himself (yet again) in front of the Home Affairs Committee. Lord Cranborne, then an MP, remembers 'a palpable feeling of antipathy' towards Willie; the meeting had been moved to a bigger room to accommodate the gloating crowd. The victim had donned a striped suit and his Guards' tie; this was a sure sign that things were bad. But almost as soon as Willie started to speak the atmosphere changed. He began with a disarming comparison, saying that he was like a cricketer who arrives at the crease without a bat (whether consciously or not, Sir Geoffrey Howe later borrowed this image to even greater effect). 'I know what you're thinking,' Willie continued, '"Whitelaw, you're a bloody fool." I want to say that I don't believe there's anyone in this room who hasn't been a bloody fool.' It was the perfect tactical performance – a wild exaggeration of his own part in the fiasco, delivered with apparent humility, was the best way to make everyone realise that he was not to blame in the slightest. At the end of the speech, amid much applause and murmurs of 'Good old Willie!', he was thanked for having explained everything with such clarity. Only later did the majority of his listeners realise that he had hardly explained anything at all.[36]

However, not everyone was taken in. For once even some of his personal friends thought the Home Secretary had not treated the break-in sufficiently seriously. One of them, Jack Page, was described as being 'apoplectic' after the committee meeting. Years later Page considered the incident to be one of the most shocking of his many years in Parliament. He, at least, would not call for Willie's head, and he might not have been so enraged if he had known at the time that Willie had submitted his resignation. But others had private reasons to foment further trouble. When Downing Street discovered that Alan Clark planned to draw an unflattering parallel between Carrington's resignation and Willie's refusal to stand down, Ian Gow rang to dissuade him. His 'awkward squad' colleague Richard Shepherd broke ranks, describing Willie's performance over Fagan as 'abysmal'. But even he ended his renewed call for Willie's resignation by rehearsing all of the qualities that Mrs Thatcher would badly miss.[37]

On the day after his statement Willie lunched with his old friend Bill Deedes, gladly accepting a 'consolatory glass of champagne'. The first glass 'went down virtually without touching the sides'; over the second, he revealed the extent of the security blunders and coincidences that had helped the intruder, who apparently was as surprised as anyone that he had got so far. Willie had been handicapped in making his statement by the fact that a thorough explanation would have been extremely long, and even then people unaware of security arrangements might not have been very enlightened without the revelation of sensitive information. Among other things, a window had been left open, and although the Queen had telephoned for help, at first no one had responded.

Only a week later Willie would require additional sustenance. Commander Michael Trestrail, who was in charge of security outside the palace, had resigned after admitting to a long-term relationship with a male prostitute. Over Fagan, Willie had weakened his position by leaving it to the newspapers to break the news. This time he was at the British Open on Saturday 17 July when the Home Office learned of the resignation. For some reason they decided not to alert him, and he first learned of the new disaster on arriving back at work on the Monday. He decided to make an immediate announcement, and this worked in his favour. When MPs heard that he was about to make a statement they assumed it would refer to the Fagan incident; when they gathered that something else had happened, they were more incredulous than angry.[38]

Once again, Willie could not escape with a single bound. When he was questioned about the vetting procedure in Trestrail's case, he confirmed that the usual inquiries had been made. It was a purely factual reply, and there was no reason for him to add that Trestrail, who had worked at the palace for sixteen years, had only been vetted for the first time four months previously. Ironically, this had happened at all only because it was felt that palace security had been too lax; but obviously the inquiries could have been more exacting. Apparently Trestrail had enjoyed the Queen's special trust; perhaps Willie had kept his account as short as possible to avoid embarrassment.

Early in the morning after his statement Willie was telephoned by a reporter who had learned the truth. Tired and depressed, Willie shouted that he had not given the House all of the details because no one had asked him. In an editorial comment *The Times* claimed that he had actually misled the House. At worst, though, he had fallen very slightly below his self-imposed standard, when on 19 July he had promised to 'report everything . . . at the earliest possible opportunity that I can find'. But after reviewing all the relevant facts concerning Fagan and Trestrail, a constitutional expert has rightly concluded that 'Even using an absolute version of ministerial responsibility, there would not be a requirement for Whitelaw's resignation'. This seemed relatively straightforward for an academic commentator, but for the minister at a miscellaneous department like the Home Office the situation was much more complex and Willie had found it difficult to provide a clear definition of his responsibility. After the escape of an IRA man from the maximum-security Brixton Prison in January 1981, he had told the Commons that although he took overall responsibility for everything done by his department, he could not be expected to resign whenever something went wrong. When the Fagan incident had been forgotten by the public he could argue that he could not have been blamed unless he had been patrolling the palace himself; he could even chortle that 'At the end they felt so sorry for me, I got away with murder'. The trouble was that even if he could be exculpated in each individual instance, by the summer of 1982 the chapter of accidents was getting long enough to verge on the 'carelessness' category.[39]

Looking back on these desperate days, Willie thought that 'if anyone had written a novel based on the whole story, it would have been ridiculed as too absurd and impossible'. But the story was not quite over, and the denouement put into perspective the fact that although the palace troubles had been potentially very serious indeed, they had not led to any fatal consequences.

On 20 July, when Willie and his officials were preparing a statement about the inquiry, they heard a loud bang. For a moment they all thought of the palace, because the explosion came from that general direction. In fact the IRA had attacked a squadron of the Queen's Household Cavalry in Hyde Park, killing several soldiers and leaving many horses dead or maimed.

In his memoirs Willie admitted that for a few moments he found it difficult to cope, and members of his staff noticed this. What he failed to mention was that the chaos of the previous fortnight had come after two years of almost continuous crisis management; it was only a month since the recapture of Port Stanley, and as far back as March he had wiped away a tear while confessing at the Conservative Central Council in Harrogate that he had been suffering from stress. The only surprise is that Willie recovered his composure so quickly after hearing of this new calamity. With his officials he continued to work on a revised statement, only to be interrupted by news of a further IRA bomb, planted in Regent's Park with a view to killing military bandsmen. The final death toll for the day was eleven. As a result, while some of the outrage about the palace had been synthetic, the House was in a sombre mood when Willie read out the finished statement and sat down to 'a muted cheer'. It had been an 'absurd and impossible' period, and the best he could hope for was a lull before the next attack. The Queen, at least, was understanding; it was made known that Willie enjoyed her full support, and her private secretary sent a note congratulating him on his handling of the security issue.[40]

At least there were no serious riots in the summer of 1982, and – if such a remark can ever apply to a Home Secretary – Willie's life was relatively free from fresh troubles as the conference season approached. The predictable speculation began well in advance, and Willie was very nervous; but this time he had girded himself up. The arrival of a new Metropolitan Police Commissioner, the ex-RUC officer Kenneth Newman, provided an excellent excuse for some tough talking on law and order (Willie saw Newman as an improvement on McNee, not least because his experience in Northern Ireland made him more attuned to the requirements of community policing). In an article for the conference newspaper, Willie set out his record in the way best calculated to appease hardline delegates. Creative graphics showed a very steep rise in police manpower, and a precipitate slide in immigrants from 'the New Commonwealth and Pakistan'.[41]

At Brighton on 6 October it was noted that Willie seemed to be coordinating his applause with that of Mrs Thatcher, regardless of whether or not he agreed with the speaker. His own debate featured none of the ugly scenes that had marred the previous year. In fact, everything was suspiciously quiet. There would be no repeat of the crossed wires of 1981. This time Willie could stick to his text, which opened with a ritual swipe against the monsters of

Tory imagination – 'those who condone crime, those who justify it, and those who neglect their responsibility to prevent it'. He listed irresponsible parents, teachers and 'those in public life who are more interested in undermining the police than they are in supporting them'. There were one or two interruptions; towards the end of the speech someone yelled, 'What about the death penalty? When are you going to bring that back?' It was like asking Mrs Thatcher when she planned to introduce collective farming. Willie sat down to polite applause; Mrs Thatcher did not rise, and the audience followed her example. Later there was a question-and-answer session on Home Office matters, but as Andrew Alexander noted, the questions had been carefully vetted. Even so, he thought that Willie 'scowled at the conference and the conference scowled back'. But it was enough; he had survived again, and he had reason to believe that it would be his last ordeal of that kind.[42]

Yet Willie could not relax and look forward to his annual shooting holiday over Christmas and the New Year. No sooner had he escaped from the baying band at Brighton than he stumbled against an unexpected foe. He was still very popular with individual police officers, who appreciated his courteous informality whenever he met them on duty. But their representative bodies had become disillusioned with the Thatcher government. At a Metropolitan Police conference he was 'heckled, slow-handclapped and barracked with cries of "rubbish" and "guilty"'. The grievances were wide-ranging: police pension contributions were being increased, and cut-backs were expected in the special rent allowance. But while Willie could sympathise with these financial difficulties he was enraged by other, politically motivated attacks. He had already defended the police against the full force of the Scarman Report, but there were still many who objected to the idea of community policing. Willie had also refused to call a public inquiry into the 'Operation Countryman' operation, which had looked into more than 600 allegations of corruption against the Metropolitan Police, leading to just two convictions. But even this was not enough. It was rumoured yet again that he was thinking of resignation. On the Home Affairs Committee even old friends like Sir Angus Maude and Sir Paul Bryan were beginning to question his policy. The prospect of addressing a by-election meeting with only twenty-eight people at Peckham must have seemed almost enticing. But instead of quietly expressing his approval of the candidate – John Redwood, about as far removed from Willie's style of Conservatism as could be found – he was caught in the verbal crossfire between right-wing members of his own party and a CND activist. And while all this was going on, Willie had to give evidence against the National Front leader Martin Webster, who was accused of having orchestrated a demonstration at London's Caxton Hall earlier in the year; a smoke bomb had been thrown towards Willie as he was speaking. During his testimony at Webster's trial Willie seemed very angry, red in the face and gripping the rail, against which he 'rocked himself to and fro'.[43]

This time Willie might well have thrown in the sponge without an unequivocal declaration of support from Number 10. Although his most vehement critics were still the kind of people he had spurned at the time of the riots – 'those who talk more toughly than they are prepared to act' – his position in the Cabinet had cost him several friends, and ill-informed attacks were always a sore trial for him. His demeanour during the court case had betrayed the toll that unrelenting pressure had taken on his health; and the political cost was equally high, as he looked back on a year that had featured so many attacks on his performance (if not his integrity). Thankfully at the crucial moment Mrs Thatcher proved that, whatever their differences, she could recognise the value of loyalty. Asked in the Commons about the Metropolitan Police, she seemed 'pale with indignation' as she branded their antics 'disgraceful' and hinted that they had done themselves a great deal of harm. Her intervention conveyed a direct threat: the police could not rely for ever on their political patrons.[44]

The Prime Minister had given an unambiguous public signal: Willie was untouchable. Had she paid a lyrical tribute to her right honourable friend, MPs would have suspected that she was protesting too much. Before the Falklands she might have chosen this approach; ever sensitive to nuances, Willie himself had noticed that after one debate she had congratulated him in a way which implied that it had been a good day for him, rather than for the government as a whole. Despite the media prominence of the Prime Minister's devoted spokesman, Bernard Ingham, this government was not wholly given over to 'spin'. But the rumour that Willie was thinking of resigning seems on this occasion to have been a challenge to would-be rebels to 'put up or shut up', rather than a serious suggestion by Willie himself. There was good reason for this tactic; at least two more parliamentary battles lay ahead for him before the next general election, and any excuse to show that the Prime Minister had total trust in her Home Secretary would help to concentrate rebellious minds.[45]

Willie had tried to keep on good terms with the Opposition. In November 1981, after rebuking a Labour MP who had suggested that high unemployment among blacks excused the Brixton riots, he met his antagonist in the Members' Lobby and put an arm around his shoulder. '"Sorry about that," he confided. "Hope you understand. Knives at my back, knives at my back."' But by the winter of 1982 Labour strategists knew that the next election would not be about toppling a hated government; instead, their party would be hoping to retain the status of official Opposition. The slightest chance of a morale boost had to be considered carefully – regardless of the principles involved. Willie had to win parliamentary approval for his new immigration rules before the beginning of 1983, and on 12 November 1982 fifty-two Tories ostentatiously abstained after a preliminary debate on the relevant White Paper. On this occasion only three Labour MPs actually voted against the proposals – finding themselves alone in the lobby with Enoch Powell. But the Tory whips were worried that Labour would exploit right-wing discontent when the House voted on the new rules in December. A full turn-out by the Opposition, backed by a significant number of Conservative dissidents, would pose a serious threat to the government's majority. At the end of the debate on the White Paper Willie betrayed his anxiety by rounding on Hattersley, who had asked if the rebellion would force a change in his proposals. After saying that he would consider the points made in the debate, Willie snapped, 'If you don't understand that you are even more stupid than I thought you were.'[46]

The key point for the right was Willie's decision to allow male spouses and fiancés to settle in Britain after all. It was anticipated that the original plan would have fallen foul of the European Convention on Human Rights. During his regular talks with minority groups, Tim Raison had also found an unusual level of opposition to the proposals. But the proposal had featured in the Conservative Manifesto, giving the rebels a fig-leaf to disguise their prejudices. For a former Chief Whip it was a familiar dilemma, but none the easier to resolve for all that. The most tempting escape-route was to offer the right a few token concessions, while refusing to back down on the main point. But the slightest movement in the direction of the Stanbrooks and the Powells would give Labour an excuse to vote against the rules. In particular, the Home Office would be treading on treacherous ground if it tried to introduce special checks to ensure that marriages between Asian couples were 'genuine' rather than arrangements of convenience; but since this was the chief argument of the hardliners, there had to be at least a token effort to appease them. The fact that the left thought the rules too restrictive, while the right denounced them for their leniency, meant that Willie had probably already struck the best compromise. But this would be no comfort if the unholy alliance could muster enough votes to beat him.

By 6 December the Home Office had come up with a new formula. Anyone who came to Britain in order to marry would be deported if the marriage broke down within two years. Presumably the officials who drew up this scheme knew that it would be ineffective; anyone who really did get married with the sole intention of beating the system would suffer the trivial inconvenience of living a lie for twenty-four months rather than twelve. No doubt there would have been a stampede to the divorce courts by couples fresh from the celebration of their second wedding anniversaries. Still, it provided a basis for negotiation with the dissidents. Willie met a group of around eighty prospective rebels, and afterwards declared himself optimistic. Loyalists thwarted an attempt by the right to pack a meeting of the Home Affairs Committee in the days before the debate; Jonathan Aitken seemed to be reflecting the general mood when he said that he was content to have made his point by abstaining on the White Paper.[47]

At the committee meeting Michael Mates identified the real issue, saying that if the rebels thought they could undermine Willie without enraging Mrs Thatcher they were quite mistaken; despite her own views, the Prime Minister had promised her support at an earlier meeting with Willie. But this could work both ways. Willie's tormentors were an assemblage of those right-wingers who had hoped for preferment from a Prime Minister who agreed with them on almost everything. Their rewards had been a long time in coming, and some of them rightly suspected that the call from Number 10 would never be made. Many, like Clark, believed that Willie lay behind this unjust treatment. If they could humiliate him enough to force his resignation, Mrs Thatcher would be very angry; but her rage would be temporary (especially on this issue), while Willie's departure would be permanent. At the very least, if he lost the vote he would be far less likely to contest the next election.

In this context it was probably a mistake for Willie to let it be known before the debate that he would stay in his post even if the vote went against him. Perhaps he thought that this would smoke out those among his critics whose interests in changing the immigration rules had been eclipsed by a personal vendetta. But in a debate which was characterised by emotion rather than cool reason, Willie's right-wing opponents would draw on an inexhaustible supply of superficial arguments. Ivor Stanbrook, for example, had suggested that immigration was largely responsible for the high level of unemployment. This hardly explained why unemployment had shot up while immigration had been declining – in fact, contrary to tabloid mythology, between 1972 and 1984 the British population suffered a net loss of 400,000 people through migration – but it was bound to play well with the Tory grass roots.[48]

Furious arguments broke out within the Conservative Party after the vote, in the early hours of 16 December. As the rebels walked into the Labour lobby, Norman Tebbit shouted, 'You fools! You fools!' Later there were angry scenes in the tea-room. Twenty-three Tories had voted with the Opposition, and twenty-eight had abstained. The result was a government defeat by eighteen votes – the only such reversal suffered by the first Thatcher Government. It was easy to blame the whips, but they had worked hard, even on some of the worst previous offenders like Alan Clark (he had been told to expect promotion at the next reshuffle, and Michael Jopling had pulled off a master-stroke by including the military historian in a fact-finding mission to the Falklands). But on this issue, at this point in the Parliament, the buttering-up and the arm-twisting were never going to succeed. Ian Gow, and Mrs Thatcher herself, talked to some dissidents; but to no effect.[49]

The defeat would have upset any minister, but for Willie it was particularly hard to take. Watching him leave the Chamber, Mrs Thatcher told Tim Raison hat they should all make an effort to comfort him; at Question Time on the following day she rebuffed Stanbrook when he hinted that the quarrel was not with her. At a surreal Home Office questions session no one referred to the accursed rules; a strange taciturnity also descended at the 1922 Committee meeting. But at last Willie's position had become fragile enough for Mrs Thatcher to decide that a direct public expression of confidence in her Home Secretary was needed. The master of parliamentary tactics had come unstuck, in spectacular style. With hindsight, the concessions to the right had been a fatal misjudgement. Predictably Willie had been forced to admit during the debate (under pressure from Hattersley) that husbands would not automatically be deported if their marriages ended within two years; there would be exceptions if the wife died or abandoned a young family. The cynical concession had rebounded – and deservedly so. As Hugo Young commented, it had always been clear that there was an overwhelming majority in the House for the original rules. Now, he continued, the issue had become an acid test for the Conservative Party: 'The decent men will have to stand up and declare that in no circumstances will they permit Britain's immigration policy to be decided by Mr Tony Marlow and Mr Harvey Proctor.'⁵⁰

The final act of this shoddy drama was played out in February 1983, when Willie reintroduced his rules as they had been before his concessions. But the Opposition parties still insisted on voting against, forcing Willie to go out of his way to conciliate the right. He announced that the rules would be kept under constant review, and some of his replies to the wilder Conservative spirits brought cries of 'Nazi' from the Labour benches. Hattersley landed several effective blows at an opponent who was cowering on the ropes. But at least this time the vote was won. Only five Tory diehards opposed the rules; a further ten abstained.⁵¹

Willie had one last chance of leaving a constructive legacy – his Police and Criminal Evidence Bill, published just before the right-wing ambush on immigration. The highly complex legislation (which at first included seventy-five sections) followed a Royal Commission which had reported early in 1981. The delay since then reflected the need for widespread consultation, and to absorb lessons from the riots; but it allowed cynics to say that the Home Office had been working overtime to extract all of the liberal suggestions from the commission's report. The object was to define the limits of police power in such areas as searches of person and property, interview procedures and detention; a new body was also proposed, to deal with complaints from the public.

By early May 1983 the bill had almost negotiated the parliamentary obstacle course. There had been forty-one debates, and Willie, who took a very active part at every stage, had already accepted 134 amendments. Despite all the preparatory work almost every relevant pressure group had some objection – the list included the Law Society, the Criminal Bar Association, the National Association of Probation Officers, the National Council for Civil Liberties and, the most dangerous of the lot, the Police Federation. As this roll-call suggests, once again Willie was being assailed from both flanks because, as he put it, he was trying to strike a 'balance between law enforcement and personal liberty'. Undoubtedly the left had more reason to complain about the original proposals, under which the police would have been allowed access to confidential documents, including medical records; it was also pointed out that although in theory everyone would have access to a lawyer after arrest, there was no reference to a suspect's right to silence. But in other cases the new law was designed to clarify existing powers, and some of the liberal outcry was based on a misunderstanding of how the rules would work in practice. To keep things (relatively) simple, detailed safeguards, such as the tape-recording of police interviews, would be included in a Code of Conduct once the bill was passed. Yet the liberal response was far more considered than the backlash from the Police Federation, whose anger inadvertently proved the case for greater regulation. In the wake of 'Operation Countryman', and well-publicised incidents such as the wounding of an innocent man, Stephen Waldorf (who was shot several times by police who mistook him for a fugitive), it was clear to everyone except the police themselves that an independent complaints procedure was overdue. In fact, public complaints would still have to be made to the police; and once the independent panel set to work it could always be stymied by a lack of police cooperation.[52]

The police did have one good reason for misgivings. The act produced a significant increase in paperwork. According to one authoritative account, the new measures reflected a fundamental flaw in the British approach to policing: 'we do not trust the police so we build safeguards into the way they exercise their power. However, we have enough faith to allow them to police those very safeguards which our mistrust has impelled them to impose.' But this 'average' view of the police disguised conflicting attitudes in a nation increasingly split between those who despised or feared the police and those who thought they deserved unquestioning support. Real attitudes to policing, in short, reflected the fact that Britain was becoming more polarised than ever. In these circumstances, Willie's unflinching and instinctive support for a 'middle position' – shunning the extremes and upholding the viewpoint of the 'reasonable' citizen – could make him look more isolated than ever. During the debate when he accepted the 134 amendments to his bill, the *Daily Telegraph* sketch-writer thought that Willie was 'quivering with passionate fair-mindedness'. No doubt the impression was reinforced by the fact that much of his work on that day involved inserting 'reasonable' and 'reasonably' throughout the legislation, at a time when opinions differed so widely about the 'reasonable' exercise of police powers.[53]

As it entered its Report Stage, the most serious threat to the Police and Criminal Evidence Bill was the possibility of an early election. Since the beginning of the year June had been the clear favourite. Willie would have preferred October, and the fate of his bill must have been a significant factor for him. But he was also unsure about his own future. If he was going to the Lords, as Mrs Thatcher wanted, he would have to warn his constituents in good time to allow the choice of a new candidate. By March, though, no decision had been taken; and since he was pretty sure by then of a summer election he formally announced that he would stand again. His hunch proved to be sound. So decisive in other respects, Mrs Thatcher was strangely hesitant about elections. But after Cecil Parkinson had presented a detailed analysis of local elections held on 5 May, she was convinced. According to Parkinson, all the ministers who gathered at Chequers the following weekend agreed to a June poll 'with varying degrees of enthusiasm'. Willie, who was also present, must have been resigned rather than enthusiastic; he knew that his bill would now have to be reintroduced in the next session of Parliament, almost certainly by a new Home Secretary.[54]

On Saturday 4 June Willie was visited on the campaign trail by Simon Hoggart. Four eventful years had passed since their last encounter on the stump, but some things never change. The air reverberated with Willie's benedictions: 'Marvellous to see you. So pleased to meet you. Very nice to meet you. Thank you very much!' When Willie started to use the public-address system his voice seemed quieter: 'Peasants try to flee, but it is too late. Willie is upon them, padding down their garden paths like a hungry grizzly.' Later Willie was asked into a pub for a drink by someone who had already imbibed too freely, but he quickly re-emerged. '"I escaped my drunk," he confides, "by my well-practised technique of *having a pee*. You go in, and when they offer you a drink, you say, "No, I must have a pee."'[55]

After Willie's death it was often said that people had underestimated his cunning, falling instead for his carefully crafted image of a well-meaning buffoon. In fact, by 1983 he had begun to play a double game. His Billy Bunter routine could still be deployed at will, but the man who delighted in explaining his preferred method for eluding over-friendly constituents obviously wanted to be seen as the wise old bird he really was. Yet for some within the Conservative Party there was no place for either persona. Just before the election was called, *Crossbow*, the journal of the Bow Group, published a typically humourless attack. In an editorial Willie was accused of 'failing to get on top of his department'. Once again, the call went up for a more 'abrasive' replacement. The editorial did more damage to the Bow Group than to its intended victim; two prominent members, including the subsequent MP Nirj Deva (who felt that he would never have entered politics without Willie's encouragement) wrote to *The Times* to dissociate themselves. But while the *Guardian* noted that the *Crossbow* article had been 'marked by a surprising degree of ignorance', it understood the underlying reason for the charges:

> Mr Whitelaw has become disposable. Isolated by the party conference, humiliated by the Prime Minister, under constant and simultaneous attack from left and right for being too liberal and too illiberal, he is no longer seen as indispensable, the healer of splits, the arch-fixer. He has become a charming anachronism, an embarrassment even, a reminder of a tradition that has been well and truly junked – the avuncular, land-owning, upper-class Tory gentleman with a conscience.[56]

Perhaps Willie's style was becoming 'anachronistic', and he admitted himself that he was 'somewhat battle-scarred and probably more tired than I knew'. But although Willie had suffered more than the usual quota of unexpected mishaps in his department, most of the criticism merely reflected the fact that no British Home Secretary can please anyone all the time; indeed the most balanced decisions in that department tend to leave everyone dissatisfied. Perhaps Willie's achievements at the Home Office had been negative in character – holding the line against his critics of all political persuasions rather than leaving the constructive legacy he would much have preferred – but even this was a great public service. The journalist John Cole thought that without Willie's rearguard action 'Britain would have been a less civilised place'.[57] And he was still loved and respected on his home turf. There had been boundary revisions, and parts of Westmorland were now included in Penrith and the Border. Once again Willie was faced with the consequences of holding official responsibility without having any real input; boundary revisions were a Home Office matter, but it would have been improper for him to interfere in any way. Knowing that he would be saddled with much of the blame for an upheaval that offended irrational local feelings, he spent more time than usual in the area. But he had no reason to worry. At 15,421 his majority was down on 1979, and his percentage of the vote in what was now a larger constituency had been cut. Even so, Penrith and the Border remained one of the safer Tory seats, as the man who had represented it for twenty-eight years headed south once again.[58]

CHAPTER 16

'THE EMPIRE STRIKES BACK'

On 16 June 1983 the House of Lords was introduced to its new Leader – Viscount Whitelaw of Penrith. Eleven years after leaving the office to tackle Northern Ireland, he also became Lord President of the Council once again. Willie's predecessor as Leader of the Lords, Janet Young, had spent less than two years in the post. She was compensated with a junior position in the Foreign Office, and (although she could not know it at the time of her demotion) a place in history as the only other female to have earned a seat in a Cabinet led by Mrs Thatcher.

Willie had prepared himself for Mrs Thatcher's decision, but he was sad to leave the Home Office. His popularity with his staff was attested by an unusually large number of letters regretting his departure; senior policemen, and even leaders of the Prison Officers' Association, also sent warm messages. Willie claimed that his last service to his department was to prevent Norman Tebbit from taking his place. His growing regard for Tebbit did not extend as far as a belief that a supporter of capital punishment would make an ideal Home Secretary, but for Mrs Thatcher the hard man from Chingford (who in 1981 had thrilled the same conference that heckled Willie) was the perfect law-enforcer. Willie may have talked the Prime Minister out of offering the job; but in any case Tebbit would have refused it. Instead, Mrs Thatcher appointed another of her current favourites – Leon Brittan. At first this seemed an excellent choice; Brittan impressed the department with his mastery of detail. But he lacked Willie's ability to delegate wisely and before long ran into a succession of misfortunes. He was moved to Trade and Industry in September 1985.[1]

Despite his own problems at the Home Office, Willie had enjoyed the human side of his job. He particularly relished the banquets held at the Chief Officers' Autumn Conference, where he would clamber onto his table and drown out the regimental band with renditions of songs such as 'Do You Ken

John Peel?' and 'Lassie from Lancashire'. On one occasion he managed to put his back out while singing 'Land of Hope and Glory'. As usual he won special admiration from the protection officers who had guarded him constantly since 1972, providing some amusement for his neighbours every time he returned to Cumbria. Willie's refusal to take himself too seriously kept the officers entertained. Despite the security that surrounded him he tried to keep up a social life, and the policemen would eat separately. After one visit they were slightly miffed to have been given fish fingers. One of them observed that the Secretary of State probably didn't know what fish fingers were. 'Of course I know what they are,' Willie boomed from the back of the car, 'I've seen them on the television.'[2]

Another fond memory for those who worked with Willie was his attitude to Prime Minister's Question Time. During the Opposition years Willie had deputised for Mrs Thatcher several times. But taking questions as the representative of the party in government was a much easier job. Partly this was because up to half the session would be taken up by friendly comments from Conservative backbenchers, who would either disguise a fawning statement as a question or, on rare occasions, ask something really interesting, but only after giving the Prime Minister ample notice. Political advisers could normally provide telling ripostes for the Prime Minister when the Opposition had their turn, and civil servants could provide background briefings for the more detailed inquiries. But Willie chose a different way of exploiting the incumbent's advantages whenever he was asked to stand in during Mrs Thatcher's overseas forays. In his memoirs he claims that he found the task 'daunting', and 'was always extremely nervous beforehand'. If so, he had a strange way of showing it. He would wrap up the regular Downing Street meeting quickly, suggest lunch and declare that he would play the rest by ear. He could expect that the 'awkward' questions awaiting him would fall into two categories. If anyone attempted to divide him from the Prime Minister he would be deliberately evasive; and if he was asked something he knew little about, he would confess his ignorance, rather than trying to paper over the cracks by reading a pre-prepared answer. In extreme cases, he would stand up with a knowing grin, say 'I'm far too old a hand to be caught out by a question like that', then sit down again.[3]

Willie's strategy was based on the assumption that he would not have to deputise very often; as he wryly recorded in his memoirs, 'the Prime Minister's immense sense of parliamentary duty ensured that she only missed Question Time when her attendance abroad was absolutely essential'. So he was free to perform an act that would have worn very thin had he tried to repeat it twice every week. It was also consistent with his more general pose as a politician whose ambition was dead; no aspirant to higher honours could have pulled it off, and he would surely have chosen a different technique had he been leader himself. As it was, his routine produced several vintage 'Willie-isms'. In June 1980, for example, David Steel tried to draw him out by following up an earlier question with a barbed inquiry: 'When will the sensible people in the Cabinet, such as the Right hon. Gentleman, assert themselves in order to ensure that we have a sustained and agreed incomes policy with which to defeat inflation?' Since Willie had annoyed Mrs Thatcher by speaking out in favour of incomes policy when it was being conducted by the Wilson Government, this was a shrewd attempt to expose crucial differences within the government. Willie replied, 'I am glad to know that the Right hon. Gentleman believes that I am sensible. The answer to both of his questions is "Yes, sir".' Even by Willie's standards this was a baffling non sequitur; but Steel had been given his reply, and it was time for someone else to have a go. During the Falklands War even a friendly full-toss from the Tory MP Geoffrey Dickens was subjected to the same blocking tactics. Dickens asked if Willie knew that some of the territory claimed by Argentina was further away from that country than Heathrow Airport was from Moscow. Willie replied, 'If I knew the correct answer to that question I would say "Yes, sir", but as I do not I'm not sure.' Reviewing one of Willie's performances, the *Guardian*'s Michael White wrote admiringly, 'It is a triumph of tone and volume over content and consistency, but he gets away with it.'[4]

Home Office questions were usually trickier and Willie was glad to leave behind that part of his life in the Commons. But moving to the Lords troubled him for two reasons. The first was the need for a by-election at Penrith and the Border. Several attempts had been made to persuade him to relinquish his seat at the general election, but he was reluctant to commit himself to this step. In fact Willie had wanted to keep his options open; if the opinion polls had been wrong, and the Conservatives lost, he hoped to be on hand to oversee the succession to Mrs Thatcher. In an unguarded moment at a press conference during the by-election campaign he actually admitted as much; for once, the press missed a real opportunity for speculation when he let slip that he would have stayed in the Commons even if his party had narrowly won. Originally it was planned that Willie's elevation would be delayed until the autumn, but Cecil Parkinson knew that such 'unforced' contests usually caused local resentment, and thought that the party should get this one over with as soon as possible. Willie had to agree, despite the embarrassing fact that his Liberal opponent had predicted an inconvenient second poll during the general election campaign. The constituency chairman was mollified when he was assured that the local party would not have to bear the expense.[5]

To compound Willie's unhappiness, although his replacement as Tory candidate, David Maclean, was another shrewd Scot (who later became

Conservative Chief Whip), he was a determined right-winger. Willie put on a brave face, saying, 'It would be impossible to imagine anyone better.' But the vote itself, on 28 July 1983, was a personal blow. After a recount, the Conservative majority fell by nearly 15,000, to a precarious 552. It was no comfort to Willie that during the post-mortem at Conservative Central Office Leon Brittan was implicated; the new Home Secretary had just given an unconvincing speech at the end of yet another debate on capital punishment.[6]

The second worry for Willie was that their Lordships might not take kindly to an old Commons hand being parachuted into the leadership without first serving as an apprentice. Peers were jealous of their independence; and any suggestion that their new Leader had been given the job simply to find space for him at the Cabinet table was sure to be resented. Knowing the importance of first impressions, Willie stressed his 'humility' on taking up this fresh challenge, 'as the House of Lords is a very considerable place'. With a sure instinct, he turned the source of possible misgivings to his own advantage, suggesting that because he still enjoyed 'considerable influence' within the Cabinet he might raise the standing of the second chamber. He was also careful to be introduced to the House by Viscounts Rochdale and Eccles, rather than any of the 'A-list' hereditary peers whose services he could have requested.[7]

In another sense Willie's elevation hinted at a revival for the Lords. Back in the early 1970s he had urged on Heath the case for hereditary peerages. After the 1983 election his own viscountcy was quickly followed by a similar award to the retiring Speaker of the Commons, George Thomas. Neither title would survive into the second generation; Thomas was a bachelor, and there was no stipulation that Willie's viscountcy could be inherited through female descendants. But in Willie's case this was probably a fortunate coincidence; he was able to enter the Lords with a dash of prestige without arousing any of the controversy that might have been stirred by a meaningful breach of recent precedent. Some of the old friends who greeted him in the Upper House, such as Lords Carrington and Home, could point to a much longer pedigree. But Willie's new ermine-lined robes suited him admirably. In this new environment, where excessive partisanship was a breach of good form, he also discovered that he had been unconsciously smoothing his own path to acceptance through years of affability in the Commons. The Lords was a refuge for many Labour and Liberal life peers who in past years had cut a deal with Willie in 'the Other Place', or shared a drink with him after a debate. Thus it could hardly be a source of 'amazement' (as he claimed in his memoirs) to find that 'most peers, including those on the Opposition benches, wished me well and wanted me to succeed as Leader'.[8]

Finally, to fill the gaps in his knowledge of procedure, Willie could rely on his Chief Whip, Lord 'Bertie' Denham, with whom he quickly forged a remarkable partnership. Denham, an enthusiastic thriller-writer in his spare time, had already been a government whip for more than twenty years, rising to the top job in 1979. He was acute, good-humoured and far more discreet than his new Leader. A partnership that 'seemed to come out of the pages of P.G. Wodehouse' worked so well because Willie knew when to defer to his Chief Whip. It was said that 'If Willie is making a mess of things, Bertie moves out to the middle of the Chamber and glares at him until he shuts up and sits down'. Although the Lords was not the place for the kind of high-jinks that Willie had enjoyed as Conservative Chief Whip, he always chuckled as he remembered the time when a vote had been called on the controversial Sunday Trading Bill as the bishops, his most determined opponents, were still scrambling into their robes.[9]

Government business managers in the Commons regard a lost vote as a personal affront. Without Denham's advice, Willie might have fallen back instinctively on that attitude, at least during his first few weeks in the Lords. There was the occasional 'stamper' after a defeat; once he even swore that he would leave politics in the face of such repeated acts of 'disloyalty' by his own troops. But he had appreciated that things should be handled differently in his new workplace, even before Lord Thorneycroft tactfully advised him 'that the Lords will I think expect the boss to pay a trifle more attention to what they say!' In March 1984, after less than a year in the job, Willie laid down the Denham-Whitelaw doctrine in a speech to the Press Gallery. Since the Conservatives had been re-elected with an overall majority of 144, he explained, it was inevitable that the Lords would come under greater scrutiny from those hoping for a government defeat. He claimed that 'the introduction of life peers, and so more cross-bench peers, has destroyed the myth of the automatic Tory majority' in the Lords.[10]

In fact, the government would only have to work a bit harder to ensure victory. The hereditary peers (or 'backwoodsmen' as Fleet Street dubbed them) could usually be relied upon to heed the call of their whips before crucial votes; although on paper they were outnumbered by the Opposition parties and the independent peers, their descent en masse would usually be enough. But, as in his dealings with Margaret Thatcher, Willie was aware of the law of diminishing returns. To be effective, his influence over the Prime Minister had to be used as sparingly as possible. Similarly, the more often he summoned elderly Tory peers from their rustic retreats, the less likely they were to obey. At the same time, a number of government defeats in the Lords would keep up morale among the peers. So, making a virtue of an unavoidable situation, Willie promised that whenever the government lost a vote under his leadership – which it was sure to do – he would present the House's objections to Cabinet. But the licence to dissent was limited. He saw the Lords as 'a revising chamber'. If it passed amendments to government bills, its opinion should be carefully considered by ministers, 'for after all it is their purposes [*sic*] to get both the policy and the detail of their legislation right'. But if ministers refused to accept amendments, he would support them; and 'while it may prove sensible and right to give in on details, I will do my best to ensure the Government will not be defeated on major issues of principle'. The final category was left undefined, but it clearly included any manifesto commitments.[11]

It was Willie's way of explaining how he had resolved a new conflict of loyalties. By delivering his message he was 'representing the true value of the House of Lords and acting as its Leader on a broad basis'. There was an important role for their Lordships, so long as they restricted themselves to occasional hints that ministers should think again. If they overstepped this mark they would lose their influence; direct confrontations with the Tory-dominated Commons would produce a stalemate at best, and even if their case was good, persistent rebellion would only draw attention to their lack of democratic legitimacy. In short, Willie was inviting the Lords to imitate his own example during the first Thatcher Government. If they wanted to achieve anything constructive they would have to come to terms with the regime, and satisfy themselves with a series of minor concessions.

The timing of Willie's dissertation was significant. It was true that the Lords gave the government's opponents their only realistic chance of winning any parliamentary votes. But they were unlikely to rebel just for the sake of flexing their muscles. In reasserting the value of the Lords as a revising chamber, Willie was predicting that it would soon be presented with legislation that badly needed revision. In one policy area the government's proposals were particularly vulnerable. Having failed to restrain public spending, Mrs Thatcher and her allies were keen to find scapegoats; and Britain's local authorities provided a tempting target. The six Metropolitan Councils, and the Greater London Council (GLC) were identified as the worst offenders. When Mrs Thatcher took office four of the Metropolitan Councils had been controlled by the Conservatives, who also ran the GLC with a comfortable majority. But in the local elections of May 1981 Labour swept the board. The result in London had been very close, but the Labour Party in the capital was as doctrinaire as Mrs Thatcher herself. After a coup Ken Livingstone emerged as a charismatic, publicity-hungry GLC leader. The next elections were not due until 1985, and ministers were too realistic to expect a comeback; after all, the Conservatives themselves had only done so well in the 1977 contests because they gave the voters a chance to register a protest against an unpopular government. There was one way to erase Livingstone's irritating grin. The 1983 Conservative Manifesto included a promise to abolish the GLC and the Metropolitan authorities. At the same time, powers would be taken to curb the power of local authorities to increase the rates to compensate for the fact that central government was no longer so generous with its subsidies. This move was nakedly political, since local government spending had actually decreased slightly in real terms since 1977.

More than its economic policy, which began with dogma and ended in something like pragmatism, the attack on local government was the defining theme of Thatcherism. Nothing illustrates better an attitude to opposition which managed to be at the same time both arrogant and suicidal. The 1983 election result disguised the fact that the Conservative vote had fallen by nearly 700,000 since 1979 – in spite of the 'Falklands Factor'. Yet ministers behaved as if they were living embodiments of the popular will, with a mandate to emasculate those institutions that they could not hope to persuade. Even so, they seemed to be haunted by the memory of the time before the Falklands, when a sustained run of terrible opinion polls signalled a decisive rejection of their domestic programme. With unemployment running at over three million and still rising, they had developed the habit of thinking that they should make the most of their power before it was brought to an inevitable end. Like Macbeth, they assumed they would meet a violent fate, whether they ploughed on regardless or switched to a more conciliatory course. In the long run the divisions between the Opposition parties that prevented a change of government proved most damaging to the Conservatives themselves. Sir Ian Gilmour had been right in September 1981, when he compared the government to the *Titanic*; it was just that it failed to encounter an iceberg until 1997, by which time most of the passengers were praying for a collision to put an end to a miserable journey (and quite a few Conservative MPs had jumped ship).

Local government also demonstrates the limits on Willie's own influence. The principle of abolition was not difficult for him to accept; after all, the doomed Metropolitan Councils had only existed for a decade, having been devised by the Heath Government in a fatal hour. The GLC was also a Conservative creation, dating back to 1964. But there were ample practical grounds for concern. For example, who would be responsible for the fire service, or for liaison with the police? As a general rule Willie agreed with Macbeth's wife; if anything unpleasant was really unavoidable, it were best done quickly. But these problems implied careful deliberation before the legislation was introduced. As chairman of the government committees that dealt with local government, he had tried to block radical measures. But this was an area of particular interest to Mrs Thatcher herself, and he had to admit defeat. Asked to come up with proposals on local government finance, a committee headed by Willie had reached the disagreeable conclusion that there was no satisfactory alternative to the rates. The Prime Minister took charge of the operation herself, and the rate-capping proposal was 'hurriedly cobbled together' just before Parliament was dissolved for the 1983 general election.[12]

To compound the irony, at the end of 1983 Willie had replaced John Biffen as the minister in charge of the presentation of government policy – or, as the press immediately put it, for detecting potential 'banana skins'. Bernard Ingham, the Prime Minister's press secretary, had wanted this change for some time. He would later describe Biffen as 'semi-detached', and he already found him difficult to motivate. But it always seemed an improbable task, for Willie or anyone else. An example of the kind of 'banana skin' lying in wait for the government was the US invasion of the Commonwealth island of Grenada in October 1983. It was President Reagan who pushed Mrs Thatcher onto this discarded fruit. The dominant partner in the so-called 'special relationship' was difficult enough to restrain, but the government's approach to decision-making could cause plenty of trouble on its own. When Geoffrey Howe announced the abolition of union rights at the secretive Government Communications Headquarters (GCHQ) only a month after Willie accepted his new responsibility, he was amazed by the outcry. But although Willie had been consulted along with a handful of other ministers, Howe had been so obsessive in guarding his plans that he did not even take his PPS or his political adviser into his confidence. More seriously, in Willie's view of politics there could be no room for what we now call 'spin'. If government is a process of muddling through, then massaging the news to present the appearance of smooth progress is bound to be counter-productive in the end, when a public lulled by a constant stream of reassurance finds itself in a serious crisis and turns on the politicians who have disguised the truth. By contrast, Willie thought that to govern was to err. He crystallised this idea in a delightful new 'Willie-ism': 'As long as there are bananas, there will be banana skins'.[13]

Perhaps Willie accepted the job in the hope that it would strengthen his hand when he warned Mrs Thatcher against unpopular initiatives. In practice, though, it only added to the pressure on himself. If the Lords dug in their heels against poorly drafted or contentious bills sent up from the Commons, Willie would be blamed for any delay; and if the controversy was followed by adverse media comment it would look as if he had failed to anticipate a rash of bad publicity. Even before Willie was put in charge of policy presentation, Adam Raphael of the *Observer* had predicted that local government would be the next 'banana skin'; he reported that Willie had been 'heard muttering discreetly that the Government's proposals to reform the rating system will end in tears'. Raphael also pointed out another good reason for Willie to think twice before taking on this extra responsibility. His 'elevation to the Lords has robbed his noble proboscis of none of its sensitivity'; but although Willie could pass on his worries to friendly MPs, he was no longer in day-to-day attendance at the Commons. In order to sense the mood in both Houses of Parliament he would have to grow a second nose.[14]

When he gave his speech to the Press Gallery Willie had already been given notice of the kind of trouble he could expect in the Lords when the local government proposals were debated. In the Commons in January 1984 he had watched as Ted Heath lashed the government. Those who saw Willie 'twisting himself into a series of agonised attitudes' that night were left in no doubt that he expected serious trouble from his own flock in due course. The government might have won the vote, but Heath and his dissident allies had won the debate. To many peers this placed them under an obligation to 'speak for England'. The first serious skirmish came on 11 June, when the Conservative whips had to pull out all the stops to vote down an Opposition amendment which described the 'Paving' Bill to prepare the way for GLC abolition as 'a dangerous precedent'. The majority was only twenty-one; more than 200 peers had turned up to register their discontent. Mrs Thatcher telephoned Willie while he and the whips were celebrating the narrow victory in his room. While Denham was denying that any 'arm-twisting' had been involved, another whip conceded that he alone had telephoned twenty-five peers.[15]

Willie was celebrating prematurely. The vote of 11 June was only a warning shot, while the peers found a more subtle amendment that could detach some of the government's supporters. This was tabled on 27 June, when Lord Elwyn-Jones proposed that legislation to scrap the forthcoming GLC elections should not be passed until the government had come forward with detailed plans for the institutions that would replace the GLC and the Metropolitan Councils. Elwyn-Jones took pains to argue that his amendment fell within Willie's own guidelines. He claimed that he was not asking the Lords to oppose a manifesto commitment; peers could object to what he called the 'Crazy Paving Bill' while still approving the abolition of the councils. But for his own part he thought that the government was riding roughshod over the parliamentary system. It was a remarkably prescient speech; years later the technique of destroying an institution without having any idea of what would replace it would be used by the Blair Government against the Lords themselves.[16]

Willie was present during the debate, but did not speak himself. He left this unsavoury task to the junior Environment Minister, Lord Bellwin. After the vote, which the government lost by 191 to 143, he hurried away, possibly to mollify Bellwin (who left the government soon afterwards). The Minister for Banana Skins had to pick himself up quickly. He began hurried negotiations, while the press speculated on the future of Patrick Jenkin, the Cabinet minister with departmental responsibility. The government capitulated to the rebels on the point at issue. Existing councillors would remain in place until the councils were abolished in 1986; previously it had been proposed that they should be replaced by nominated 'interim authorities'. Despite this climbdown Denham had to work hard to secure a government majority of ninety-three when the peers voted on the revised Paving Bill.[17]

Livingstone and the London left, who detested the House of Lords as a haven for undeserved privilege, hung a banner from County Hall thanking the peers 'for saving London democracy'. This was over-egging the irony; the GLC still looked doomed. But in April 1985 opponents of abolition in the Upper House tried another tactic. While the government wanted London to be governed piecemeal by the old borough councils, the Alliance proposed that after the disappearance of the GLC there should still be a single Londonwide authority. Again, although this would have thwarted the government's true intentions, it was debatable whether it contradicted the letter of the Conservative Manifesto. A further defeat would have been a serious embarrassment to Willie, who was aware that Mrs Thatcher was 'getting very fed up with the Lords'. He and Denham 'read the riot act' to wavering Tory peers, while the Opposition pointed to opinion polls revealing that 70 per cent of Londoners wanted to retain the GLC. Somehow Denham and his whips scraped the necessary votes together, as the opponents of abolition advanced a series of amendments varying their main theme of a Londonwide authority, even if only to oversee waste disposal in the capital. On 20 June Tory peers had to organise a filibuster while some of their colleagues (including Willie himself) rushed back from Royal Ascot to clinch another narrow victory.[18]

The summer of 1985 was a season of rebellion in the Lords. In all, the Opposition managed to win four votes on GLC abolition, but none of these was fatal to the principle of the bill. Willie and Denham may have beaten off the friends of the GLC, but they had to admit defeat in other votes, on corporal punishment and salary increases for senior public servants. By the time Willie retired he was happy to admit that he had presided over more defeats than any post-war predecessor. But underneath his good humour there were clear signs of profound concern. It was one thing for ministers to push an ever-increasing flow of legislation through the compliant Commons, as they sought to win favour with the Prime Minister by imitating her own revolutionary zeal. But often these bills amended previous government proposals which had proved flawed in practice; and since the Upper House refused to lapse into an automatic rubber stamp, it demanded time to give the legislation the scrutiny it ought to have received from the Cabinet and the Commons. To make matters worse, the introduction of life peerages was beginning to produce its inevitable result, as eloquent and able politicians dominated proceedings in 'the Other Place'. After the 1987 general election Jim Callaghan, Roy Jenkins, Francis Pym, Jim Prior and Keith Joseph were among the new boys forming a distinguished queue for admittance. It was difficult to deny them a hearing; and, freed from the wearying discipline of the Commons, elevated MPs were likely to vote on the quality of the arguments rather than bow to the limited sanctions wielded by Denham and his team of whips.

The inevitable defeats clogged up the hectic timetable in the Lords. Even more serious was the tendency of the government to delay its second thoughts until the legislation was presented to the Lords. For example, after the fiendishly complicated Financial Services Bill had been passed by the Commons in July 1987, peers were invited to consider 230 amendments tabled by the government itself. It was a perfect example of 'more haste, less speed'; but Willie had never been able to persuade Mrs Thatcher to honour the spirit of this piece of homespun wisdom.

By the time of the 1987 Party Conference Willie had decided to go public with his concerns. Speaking to the Bow Group – which had long ceased to call for his resignation – he hinted that the situation was running out of control. 'As long as I am Leader,' he said, 'there will not be reforms. But there will come a day when there will be so many extra life peers who want to take part in debates that the time factor will be more difficult. Then it might be right for hereditary peers to elect a number [from] their ranks to participate in the chamber.' To one commentator it seemed as though Willie was speaking as Leader of the Opposition as well as Deputy Prime Minister. At one point he resorted to something rarely heard from his lips – sarcasm. 'There is the possibility that even the hardest-line people would accept that just occasionally the government might be wrong,' he said. 'I would resist it if the Commons tried to ride roughshod over the Lords, a group of people who want to see legislation as good as possible. It would be dangerous arrogance.'[19]

This kind of language was unprecedented for Willie. But the following month he went even further, predicting that the government would be defeated in the Lords on its proposals to allow schools the right to 'opt out' of local authority control. It had been another involuntary remark, following an agreeable and relaxed radio interview with Peter Hennessy. But Willie was suggesting that Kenneth Baker's massive Education Reform Bill would be too much for the Lords to swallow; and his comments had been broadcast. Whether knowingly or not, he had singled out a proposal that enjoyed special support from Number 10 – the 'opt out' clause, after all, would strike another blow against the detested local authorities. Mrs Thatcher was furious, and education ministers were said to have gone 'into orbit'; the bill had not even been published. Willie made a half-apology, denying that his comment had been calculated to dish Baker's ultimate leadership chances. Bertie Denham claimed that he envisaged no difficulties over the government's programme, and predicted that the whips would get the bills through – 'we always do'.

He was right, though the government did suffer six defeats in the process. But Willie's original remark had stiffened the resolve of Baker's critics (as the minister recognised) and no one else would have been forgiven for this act of sabotage.[20]

If Willie had remained as Leader of the House throughout 1988 it would have been interesting to see how he handled the most slippery 'banana skin' of the lot – the Poll Tax. In the days after Willie's retirement the whip Richard Ryder remembered the time early in the 1987–92 Parliament when he had innocently asked Viscount Whitelaw what he thought of the tax:

> The great man stopped in his tracks, and glared . . . his face became empurpled and sweat poured down his forehead, cheeks and the end of his nose. He wrestled with some deep impediment of speech; finally burst, spluttering out the single word – 'TROUBLE'. Then he turned on his heel.[21]

Yet, ironically, the ill-fated 'community charge' has been identified as an example of the 'noble proboscis' failing to twitch. Even worse: while Willie's direct influence on legislation is usually impossible to trace, in this instance his role is well documented. It might even be argued that he was the vital catalyst whose intervention produced the Poll Tax.

The rating system of local government finance was a long-standing grievance for Conservative voters. In 1974 Mrs Thatcher had been ordered by Ted Heath to hunt for alternatives to the rating system for raising local government finance. Although she disliked being bullied in this way, and the search proved unavailing, a shift from this tax on property was an idea that appealed to her even then. When it suited her, she was quite prepared to deviate from her theoretical attachment to 'market forces'; and her mood tended to soften when housing was at issue. A rigid dogmatist would say that a poor widow living alone in a valuable house should sell up if she could no longer afford to pay the rates; it also seemed anomalous that home-owners should be subsidised through mortgage interest tax relief. But Mrs Thatcher was wedded to her own version of the old 'One Nation' ideal of a 'property owning democracy', feeling that the act of buying a house reinforced a sense of personal responsibility. At best the rates seemed to be a means of taking back with one hand what the government was providing with the other, through tax relief. For a while the Prime Minister restrained her radical impulses, feeling that a cap on the rates would at least ensure that home-owners were not unduly penalised for living under profligate councils. Whatever else one thought of a tax on houses, at least it was easy to collect. A scheme to divert the burden onto individuals had been considered (only to be rejected) back in 1981. 'Try collecting that in Brixton,' one official had joked as the Department of the Environment included the idea in a Green Paper 'for the sake of completeness'.[22]

By March 1985 that improbable idea had become a definite runner. The Thatcherites had developed a plausible rationale in its favour. A tax levied on individuals would re-energise local elections, since every resident would be affected by the level of expenditure. This would concentrate minds, and the electorate could be trusted to vote for the party that offered services at the lowest cost. Naturally, in most cases this would mean that local elections would be won by Conservatives, instead of local Labour politicians like Ken Livingstone, who (as the right-wing press alleged) frittered away rate-payers' money on hare-brained causes like gay rights, and spent the rest of his time silencing 'racist' songs like 'Baa Baa Black Sheep'.

A meeting to discuss possible reforms was to be held at Chequers on 31 March 1985. But before ministers gathered to hear the results of recent studies conducted by the Department of the Environment, Willie had met a group of Scottish Conservatives, who told him that the party would be in serious trouble north of the border unless something was done to mitigate the effects of a new rating revaluation. Willie said that his visit to Scotland had been 'one of the most uncomfortable experiences of my life', and his colleagues were 'shocked' by his report. Regrettably, the Chancellor Nigel Lawson was absent from the Chequers meeting. But given the determination of Mrs Thatcher, reinforced by Willie's feeling that something – anything – should be done to shore up the party's position in Scotland, Lawson's chances of checking the momentum in favour of the uncollectable tax would have been slim. Even the moderate William Waldegrave presented the case for a gradual move towards a Poll Tax, which at that stage was euphemistically termed a 'residents' charge'. When Lawson finally heard of the proposal he presented a devastating Cabinet paper, and Leon Brittan (in his last months as Home Secretary) also had serious doubts. But despite his own earlier view that the existing rating system was the least unacceptable of the various options, Willie failed to support the formidable Chancellor in the Cabinet sub-committee on local authority finance. The Poll Tax had become an unstoppable 'steamroller', and in January 1986 the then Environment Secretary Kenneth Baker published a Green Paper which foreshadowed its inclusion in the next Party Manifesto. Lawson did win the concession of a five-year transition period, but this was swept away in the face of opposition at the conference of October 1987.[23]

Kenneth Baker remembered that Willie had made several well-founded objections to the details of the tax; for example, he argued (in vain) that there should be no concessions for people (like himself) who owned more than one house. But if he had developed serious misgivings on the principle itself during the gestation period, he could have joined forces with Lawson, who had taken over from Howe at the Treasury after the 1983 election. In 1981 Lawson had hoped to be made Chief Secretary to the Treasury and felt that Willie had blocked his promotion. More likely, Willie had put in a decisive word in favour of Leon Brittan; certainly Mrs Thatcher had no hesitation in promising Lawson that he would be in the Cabinet after the next reshuffle, which she probably would not have done if Willie had really given him the feared 'black spot'. Once Lawson had risen to the Treasury he established an excellent working relationship with Willie, accepting like so many others that he had underestimated the Deputy Leader.[24]

For his part, Willie quickly grasped the possibility of yet another complementary mix; the aloof, intellectual Lawson was the perfect 'straight-man' for him. He was so pleased with the partnership that in advance of one meeting he revealed his game-plan to Tristan Garel-Jones while they were sharing a taxi. He began with his familiar routine – 'You youngsters think I'm stupid', and so on. Then he brightened. 'I'm just off to a Cabinet economic sub-committee. I'm the only one there who supports the Chancellor on an important issue. Before Nigel comes in I'll say "This is a very serious matter. I think Nigel is wrong on this one, and it could be a resigning issue. Dear, dear." That will put them all off guard. Then Nigel will come in and say his piece. I'll pretend to listen, then at the end I'll sum up. "Well, you all know what I think. This is a very serious matter. But I'm bound to say that after listening to the Chancellor we'll have to support him." Then they'll all agree.'[25]

But while Lawson guessed that the Poll Tax would be a nightmare for the Treasury, strictly speaking it was a matter for the Department of the Environment. If Lawson had taken his objections to the brink of resignation, things might have been different; but although all his fears were realised when the Treasury was asked to subsidise the tax, he never went that far. It seems that the Poll Tax was an example of Willie inadvertently setting a ball rolling, and then shrinking away as he watched it gather momentum. After his resignation he spoke in the Lords against any 'wrecking' amendments, stressing the need to avoid a clash with the Commons rather than saying very much in favour of the tax, which was forced through the House by a massive influx of 'backwoodsmen'.

The full consequences of the Poll Tax were unknown when Willie stood down from the Cabinet in January 1988. But despite her election victory Mrs Thatcher's position was rarely secure. After the American invasion of Grenada some of her staunchest supporters in the press, including even Rupert Murdoch, turned against her. In March 1985 the miners returned to work after their year-long strike, reinforcing the claim of Mrs Thatcher's admirers that her resolution had succeeded where the Heath Government had failed. But by the summer of 1985 there were rumours of a leadership contest, and Willie was fielded to deny that the Prime Minister's position was under threat. Even so, 'some senior backbenchers' were saying that Willie and the Chief Whip, John Wakeham, 'should tell Mrs Thatcher that she had become a liability and should make way for a successor'. It was an early outing for Willie in a new guise – at the head of the 'men in grey suits' who would gently advise their leader that she was working too hard and was due for a well-deserved rest.[26]

In October 1984 Mrs Thatcher survived a more deadly attack, when the IRA blew up Brighton's Grand Hotel during the Conservative Party Conference. Fortunately for Willie and Celia, they had been invited to stay in a flat owned by a golfing friend. When Willie arrived at the scene he advised that the unscathed Prime Minister should deliver her speech as planned. His own earlier speech, on the subject of the government's public relations, had been a typical attempt to overwhelm potential critics with winsome apologies. Accepting that the party should 'smarten up' its presentation, he promised in his own blunter phrase that he and his colleagues would 'get a bloody move on'.

After the bomb the Attorney General Michael Havers revealed what would have happened if all the ministers in the Grand had been killed. He assumed that the Queen would have appointed Willie as a temporary caretaker leader, and while the government machinery came to grips with the crisis, 'All the time we would have been pumping out the message: don't worry, we've got Whitelaw.' But no one imagined that Willie would have renounced his peerage and made a run for the permanent leadership. More than ever, journalists were now crawling over every supportive statement, looking for coded hints of an imminent visit to 10 Downing Street by the grey-suited deputation. But at least Willie was no longer suspected of seeking a change for his own purposes. There were some, though, who credited him with superhuman powers. When a self-styled 'Satanist' launched a successful drive to persuade some gullible evangelical Christians into giving him hundreds of thousands of pounds, he claimed that he was fighting a rival church led by Viscount Whitelaw. It must have been a very 'broad' church; Enoch Powell was named as one of Willie's alleged assistants.[27]

Even the government's fiercest opponents would not have accused Willie of placing his services at Satan's disposal; but they regarded Mrs Thatcher as the Devil's earthly incarnation, and there was an element of wizardry in Willie's work. In the autumn of 1984 his reputation in Whitehall was higher than ever before. Almost invariably his name was the first on the team-sheet for every government committee. The mastery of one-off meetings, which he had revealed to Garel-Jones, was surpassed by the tactics he deployed during more protracted discussions. When one committee was set up he told Norman Tebbit that during the first meeting he would pretend not to understand the issue, asking a series of dumb questions. At the second he would give the impression that he was gradually getting the point. This elaborate ritual would soften up his colleagues; at the appropriate time they would be more willing to accept his authoritative summing up because he had made such a show of wrestling with the problem. Tebbit felt that he was a privileged observer, as the process unravelled exactly as Willie had predicted.[28]

But Willie was not omnipotent, and even he floundered during the Westland Affair – a departmental demarcation dispute, and a clash of ministerial egos, which almost brought the government down. When Michael Heseltine walked out of a Cabinet meeting on 9 January 1986 the Minister for Banana Skins was 'surprised and amazed'. According to his memoirs, he had never been in a position to mediate between Heseltine and his direct antagonist, Leon Brittan, because he was a strong partisan of the latter. Given that the Chairman of Westland helicopters, Sir John Cuckney, had decided to merge the ailing company with its American rival, Sikorsky, apparently there was no reason for ministers to get involved. When Heseltine continued to argue for an alternative deal, with a European consortium, Willie 'became increasingly bored with the argument and irritated by what I regarded as an unnecessary and potentially damaging controversy'. In retrospect he wished that he had tried to assert 'the vital doctrine of Cabinet collective responsibility'. But given the characters involved, this was just another of Willie's expressions of regret that he made no attempt to achieve the impossible.[29]

Willie distrusted the flashy, headstrong Heseltine – 'the sort of man who combs his hair in public,' he is said to have snorted – and his (pre-arranged) replacement at Defence was Willie's friend George Younger. But Willie was not entirely blinded by personal prejudice. In a television interview after his retirement he conceded that Heseltine might have been given more opportunity to put his case. Writing his own memoirs years later, Heseltine seized on this comment, putting into Willie's head the further reflection that 'it is impossible to think of any other country on earth where a defence contractor would be sold to a foreign purchaser with the government refusing even to allow a discussion about the merits of an alternative solution'.[30]

By 1993, when Willie gave his television interview, he had softened his attitude to Heseltine. But his remark only supplemented a typically Willie-ish comment in his memoirs, where he claims that not until the dramatic resignation did it dawn on him that Heseltine was 'labouring under what he regarded as a genuine grievance'. Actually Willie had known for some time that Downing Street had bent the rules in its anxiety to thwart the wayward Defence Secretary. On Monday 9 December 1985 a dispute about Westland at the Economic Affairs Committee had ended in stalemate, and Mrs Thatcher had angrily brought proceedings to a close by calling another meeting for Friday 13 December. This meeting was subsequently cancelled –

indeed, Downing Street tried to deny that it had ever been arranged – in order to block Heseltine and the European consortium.[31]

At the Cabinet of 12 December Heseltine protested at the cancellation. Willie and the Chief Whip John Wakeham asked Mrs Thatcher to 'let Michael have his meeting', but she rejected their advice. Willie's preference for fair play, rather than any belated recognition that Heseltine deserved to win the argument, accounts for his later televised comment. At the time he was dismayed as the Cabinet teetered on the brink of anarchy. 'It's bloody, absolutely bloody' he admitted at the height of the crisis.[32]

The most serious breach of the Queensberry rules occurred after Heseltine's resignation. A letter to Heseltine from the Solicitor-General, Willie's friend Sir Patrick Mayhew, had been partially leaked to the press, to create the impression that the ex-minister had included 'material inaccuracies' in a published letter of his own to Sir John Cuckney. By now Westminster was seething with rumours of 'dirty tricks' against Heseltine, and the Prime Minister knew that her own position was in jeopardy. At the Cabinet meeting on 22 January 1986 Willie advised her that 'The truth must be told. And it must be told in full.' Later, among friends, he qualified this; the Prime Minister must at least 'be seen to be telling the truth' and have satisfactory answers to the most damaging questions. Otherwise 'God knows what happens'. Unfortunately his leader had already drawn up a statement for the House, which obviously told something less than the whole truth. When she read the proposed statement to her colleagues 'more than one shook his head in disbelief'. This made life deeply unpleasant for Willie, who had to recite the same statement in the House of Lords. But whatever his own reaction, Willie felt that this round of constitutional improvisation had been initiated by Heseltine's decision to publish the Cuckney letter. He told his colleagues that it was 'outrageous . . . I've never heard anything like it in my life'. After his statement in the Lords he said that he felt 'deeply and bitterly' about Heseltine's activities throughout the crisis: 'I have never in my time in the Cabinet seen more extraordinary behaviour to his Prime Minister and to all his colleagues, than was exhibited through this period of time by the Member for Henley.'[33]

Mrs Thatcher scraped through the Westland Affair, after a speech on 27 January which only satisfied her backbenchers because the Opposition leader, Neil Kinnock, fell below his usual standards in reply. Leon Brittan was not so lucky – he became another of Willie's friends to be defenestrated by a kangaroo court of Tory backbenchers, but he was also undermined by a conspicuous lack of support at the decisive moment from Number 10. For Willie it was a dismal end to an ignominious business; he had told Brittan not to carry the can, even if his own conduct had been open to question. After Brittan had resigned, though, Willie conceded privately that the departure had been inevitable, because his former protégé had 'made a dreadful muddle of everything'. No doubt Willie was referring to Brittan's spell at the Home Office, where he had wavered in his opposition to hanging. In fact, Brittan had put forward the best idea for putting an end to the Westland problem before it spun out of control, when he urged Mrs Thatcher to sack Heseltine as early as 18 December. The same day Willie and Wakeham had argued that the Prime Minister should at least send Heseltine an ultimatum. But Bernard Ingham demurred, pointing out that Mrs Thatcher was already seen as too authoritarian. The Prime Minister took his advice, rather than that of her Chief Whip and her Deputy.[34]

It was, as the historians of the scandal have written, 'a grave error', and although Willie omitted it from his memoirs he was unlikely to forget it. Looking at his own conduct from the time of Westland to his resignation two years later, it is difficult to resist the impression that the incident changed Willie's assessment of the Prime Minister. On 7 February 1986, amid new allegations that the honours system had been used in an attempt to detach one of Heseltine's key allies, Willie appeared on both radio and television to defend Mrs Thatcher. He claimed that 'it would be a total disaster' if those who sniped at the Prime Minister had any effect on her position. As usual, his remarks were deconstructed by Whitelaw-watchers; and when they failed to find a coded message they decided there was something sinister in the fact that he had felt it necessary to speak out at all. In fact Willie only wanted to sweep away this dangerous banana-skin. Even so, from time to time he must have wondered if his grey suit was going to get an airing. That might be the kindest way, given the forces now ranged against the Prime Minister. Under the party's rules Heseltine would be free to launch a leadership challenge if he received the nomination of just two MPs (who could remain anonymous); and there were plenty of disgruntled backbenchers to enlist in his cause along with remaining 'wets' who opposed Mrs Thatcher as a matter of principle.[35]

Willie himself had no intention of plotting against his leader. He would find it difficult enough to offer unprompted advice even if her situation became impossible. As one Tory told the *Daily Mail* after Westland, 'Sending Willie along to have a word is just not on. Half of us wouldn't believe he had actually told her anyway.' But Willie was bolder than his 'wet' critics imagined, even if his methods were oblique. On specific issues he was now quite prepared to use the press against a weakened premier on specific issues; and in doing so he must have known that he was fuelling the general mood of instability.[36]

At the House of Lords Willie enjoyed his weekly briefings to the press. The feeling was reciprocated by his visitors. At first, only a few would attend at noon on Fridays. But word quickly spread that Willie was excellent value for hacks hunting a tasty morsel of gossip; and he and Denham were very generous hosts, dishing out liberal quantities of drink. When reports of these gatherings reached Mrs Thatcher she was alarmed, and Number 10 sent observers to monitor the situation. But when any informants were snooping around Willie could always retreat into a dreary recital of the coming week's business in the Lords. If he still wanted to convey a message to the media, other channels were available to him.[37]

On 6 February 1986 the Cabinet split over the sale of British Leyland's truck division, plus the profitable Land-Rover. There were two bidders, both American – Ford and General Motors. Mrs Thatcher saw this as a purely commercial proposition, just like Westland. Tough negotiations with General Motors were entrusted to a ministerial sub-group, which included Tebbit, Brittan's replacement as Secretary of State for Trade and Industry, and Willie. But when news of the talks leaked out, Tory backbenchers, including Heath and Heseltine, protested against an overseas company taking control.[38]

On 22 February, with an official statement expected any day, 'a senior member of the Cabinet committee' was quoted as musing that 'No deal is a perfectly possible proposition as far as the Government is concerned'. The unnamed source was Willie. At the same time Tebbit subtly differed from the Prime Minister, stressing that any decision would be based on 'a mixture of politics and commerce and good sense'. When Wakeham reported the extent of backbench unease, Mrs Thatcher was forced to accept that the deal was impossible unless General Motors was denied a majority vote on the board. As she wrote in her memoirs, 'GM in the end were not prepared to wear this and I do not blame them . . . Britain just could not afford to indulge in Anti-Americanism of this sort.' It was a bitter defeat. For his part, although Willie was certainly not anti-American, his appreciation of British political realities was more profound than that of his leader. For the same reason, although he gave his backing to Ronald Reagan's bombing of Libya in April, privately he agreed with Lord Hailsham's view that Mrs Thatcher's ideological soulmate was 'a madman'.[39]

All this was serious enough in the aftermath of Westland, but what followed was a remarkable act of insubordination. In June 1986 Mrs Thatcher was reported to be facing pressure from senior ministers, including Howe and Willie, to follow up the report of an Eminent Persons Group which had been dispatched to investigate conditions in South Africa. Whatever they might find, Mrs Thatcher was determined not to impose meaningful sanctions against the apartheid regime. At the 1985 Commonwealth Conference she had been enraged by fellow leaders who snubbed her after she decided to ban only the import of krugerrands. As she herself boasted at the ensuing press conference, this measure would make not the slightest impression on the racist government. She continued to voice her opposition to sanctions in principle, and the ministerial pressure of June 1986 came to nothing. The following month it seemed likely that African countries would boycott the Commonwealth Games in protest. A Commonwealth heads-of-government meeting was due to be held in London in August; if Mrs Thatcher refused to back down there was a possibility that the impasse might lead to the dissolution of the Commonwealth itself.[40]

For Willie, the crisis meant yet another conflict of loyalty. With his close connections to Buckingham Palace, he knew that the Queen was deeply troubled. On Wednesday, 16 July – just before Willie went to Turnberry to watch the British Open – both *The Times* and the *Daily Telegraph* carried stories about a looming constitutional crisis. 'Senior Cabinet ministers' were said to have confided their worries about the position of the Queen if she was dragged into the row over sanctions. As Adam Raphael put it, 'When two rival papers carry nearly identical stories of political intrigue, it is invariably the fruit of a large liquid lunch somewhere in the West End with an eminent person.' In this case Willie was identified as the culprit. A government statement describing stories of his involvement as 'ludicrous and unfounded' was generally disbelieved on Fleet Street.[41]

Fortunately, perhaps, the *Sunday Times* now waded in with explosive revelations, leaked from the palace itself, about the Queen's alleged view of Mrs Thatcher. But this did not entirely deflect attention from Willie. Andrew Neil, editor of the *Sunday Times*, was told by another of those mysterious 'senior cabinet ministers' that unnamed 'Tory grandees who hated the Prime Minister' were actively stirring up trouble between Downing Street and the palace. Apart from Willie himself – and some of his close friends – it would be hard to name any other plausible suspects among the 'Tory grandees'. Ironically, according to Neil, Willie was instructed to tell the palace that it should 'ignore the dissident Toffs and behave itself'. Whether he discharged this errand or not is another matter; it would have been a difficult task, since his own indiscretion had triggered off the public row in the first place.[42]

Soon after this diplomatic squall Willie himself was sent abroad on behalf of his country. Mikhail Gorbachev had visited Britain in December 1984, just before he became General Secretary of the Soviet Communist Party. To maintain the improvement in Anglo-Soviet relations that followed his rise to power, a suitably senior British politician was needed to head a parliamentary delegation. After a few other names had been suggested and turned down, it was clear that only someone of Willie's rank would fit the bill – although some of the deference he commanded during the visit might have arisen because his title was mistranslated as 'Deputy President of the Secret Police'. Willie's delegation included his old friends Robert Jackson (now an MP) and Roger Sims. Denis Healey was the main representative from the Labour Party. Willie was glad to have such a knowledgeable (and talkative) foil; when Gorbachev invited him to state the British view on nuclear weapons, he neatly avoided any commitment by claiming that Healey knew far more about it than he id and that in any case he had already monopolised the conversation. One drawback for the delegation was that Gorbachev was conducting an anti-alcohol drive. But when they got to Georgia Willie made a speech thanking the local dignitaries for their welcome, and hinted that his friends had heard all about the fine wines for which the region was justly famous, and so on. Alcohol was prohibited at this official function, but it turned out that Tbilisi was more relaxed about these matters than Moscow had been; if anything, their hosts over-compensated, including in the itinerary one meal that enforced 'three or four toasts in brandy during every course'. Although Willie disliked travelling – as soon as he arrived anywhere he always looked forward to going home – this visit was a great success, and he returned with a letter from Gorbachev to Mrs Thatcher which led to further fruitful contacts.[43]

In the midst of all this Willie was maintaining his close interest in Cabinet appointments. Together with Wakeham, he was said to have persuaded Mrs Thatcher in September 1985 that it was too early to bring back Cecil Parkinson, who had left the Cabinet in 1983 over his affair with Sara Keays. On that occasion Willie had been supportive of Parkinson, whose abilities he rated highly. But by December 1983 Parkinson was reporting to Alan Clark that he suspected Willie of being his enemy, along with Wakeham, whom he accused of being 'the greatest leaker known to man'.[44]

The reshuffle of September 1985 seemed to happen in a rush, after a protracted delay. Obviously Parkinson's position lay behind Mrs Thatcher's indecision. Press speculation suggested that Willie and Wakeham may have had 'ulterior motives' in preventing Parkinson's re-appointment. Given his previous warm words to the fallen minister this was too much for Willie to take, and he met Parkinson to reassure him that he was 'not impeding his return' after all. Such was the atmosphere of intrigue which surrounded Willie that the seasoned parliamentary observer Alan Watkins commented 'we may make of that what we will'. Yet Willie's gesture was probably sincere; in the days before the reshuffle it was reported that 'the whips' were doubtful that the party would accept so swift a return, which suggests that Wakeham was the prime mover, with Willie merely deferring to his judgement. But afterwards Parkinson could never be sure what Willie really thought of him. At the 1987 Party Conference, shortly after his return to the Cabinet as Energy Secretary, he was given a standing ovation. He later told the journalist John Junor that Willie 'lumbered up to me and embraced me in full view of the TV cameras at the Conference. He did it all just to impress the Conference, whereas I discovered later that he had been going around delegates and friends saying, "He didn't deserve a standing ovation. There was nothing in his speech. I can't understand why he got one." '[45]

At least Parkinson was the sole beneficiary in the press coverage. 'He is back to stay,' the *Daily Telegraph* asserted. 'One knew as much when Lord Whitelaw, upstanding, clapped him for three minutes. All must be forgiven.' Willie was capable of orchestrating applause; in 1985 when he was worried about the likely reception for Nigel Lawson he 'made a great fuss of bounding to his feet and whacking his great palms together as if he had just been listening to Cicero'. In Parkinson's case, though, the ovation had begun before the bear-hug. The real problem for Willie was that his words and actions were scrutinised far more closely than those of any other minister. In August 1986 it was even rumoured that Willie was plotting against Tebbit, of all people; this time 'friends' issued a blunt denial. The attitude of the press resembled that of the nineteenth-century diplomat, who when told that one of his more cunning colleagues had died, quipped, 'Now, what could he have meant by that?' And if members of the press were always trying to second-guess Willie, their informants were playing the same game. At a time when all of the possible contenders for the succession to Mrs Thatcher were alert to every nuance from the key figures in the party hierarchy, the everyday hypocrisies of social interaction were inflated into deliberate snubs, pregnant with consequences. Junor had already convinced himself that 'Willie would not be two-faced if there were a third one available' – because, in an incident tellingly similar to the one related by Parkinson, Willie had offered polite congratulations after a Junor speech which he had described to others as 'disgraceful'. It would be reasonable to conclude that the almost incessant stories of Willie's skulduggery were the price he paid for retaining his prominence in the court of Queen Margaret. He had not changed; he still hated the idea of making personal enemies, and his ability to get on with almost everyone, whether they were rising or falling in favour, was very useful to the government. Yet his party was now divided as never before, on grounds of personality and principle. It was impossible for anyone as outspoken as Willie to avoid alienating some of the faction-fighters (although even his enemies found it prudent to keep up the appearance of friendship).[46]

Among those who did win promotion in September 1985 were Douglas Hurd, who moved from Northern Ireland to the Home Office, and Kenneth Clarke, who gained his first Cabinet post. Another decision was far less congenial to Willie. Mrs Thatcher had suggested that Jeffrey Archer should go to the Lords as Minister for Sport. Willie could veto this idea, but he was unable to block Archer entirely. Even as an unpaid Deputy Chairman, Archer soon proved as embarrassing as Willie had warned. The animosity – undoubted, in this case at least – dated back to the time when Willie was Chief Whip, and Archer, then a candidate for the Louth by-election, had been accused of financial malpractice by Humphry Berkeley. Although Archer was highly popular in the constituencies, Willie's feelings were unchanged by 1985: 'over my dead body' he is said to have growled in response to the idea that the novelist could be a useful cheerleader. Even if Willie had to relent over the Deputy Chairmanship, he was immovable on the question of a peerage for Archer. Lord Parkinson recalls that during one meeting on the subject of honours before the 1983 election Willie had enthusiastically advanced the claims of one of his own friends, then settled back in his chair with a contented expression. The Prime Minister decided to tease him. After winking at Parkinson, she innocently reported that she was hearing a lot of requests that something similar could be done for Jeffrey. Willie obligingly produced one of his 'stampers'.[47]

John Wakeham joined the Cabinet in 1987, as Leader of the House of Commons. He was following Willie's career path. In an interview for this book Willie expressed his doubts about Wakeham's subsequent performances. But for a while they were seen as an effective double-act – the Cabinet's 'fixers'. When Brittan fell on his sword after Westland they joined forces to persuade Mrs Thatcher that it would be better to replace him with a compromise candidate, Paul Channon, rather than the fire (and smoke)-breathing Transport Secretary, Nicholas Ridley – a particular *bête noire* of Willie's. The duo had to come between the dragon and her wrath again in May 1986, when Mrs Thatcher wanted to sack John Biffen for suggesting that the party would be best served if it fought the next election with a 'balanced' team. Willie persuaded the Prime Minister that a severe dressing-down would be punishment enough. Against expectations Biffen survived until the 1987 general election.[48]

The greatest coup attributed to 'the Wakeham-Whitelaw axis' was dissuading Mrs Thatcher from making Lord (David) Young Chairman of the Party. During the 1987 general election campaign her suspicions of Tebbit, the existing Chairman, had created a poisonous atmosphere in which senior Conservatives and advertising agencies fought each other more vigorously than the Opposition. There was never any chance that the in-fighting would cost them the election, but on 'Wobbly Thursday', a week before polling day, the inhabitants of the Central Office hothouse sensed impending disaster. Lord Young enjoyed Mrs Thatcher's complete trust, and had worked efficiently as Secretary of State for Employment. But he had never fought an election, which should have disqualified him as a key member of the campaign team; by contrast, Tebbit was a seasoned veteran. Mrs Thatcher had other ideas, and in the run-up to the election Young and Tebbit were uncomfortably yoked together, with no clear guidance from the top about their respective areas of responsibility.

Willie deliberately took a back seat during this campaign, which was probably a good thing because he could never have sorted out the problems at Central

Office. The only direct initiative he took seems to have been an insistence that the Party Manifesto should have a special section on unemployment. As far as Young was concerned, Willie had invited him to Dorneywood before the campaign began and treated him with all the respect due to a rising minister. But when the feuding began Willie admitted to fears of a re-run of Westland, with squabbling between two colleagues plunging the whole team into turmoil. And, as with Westland, he could not be an impartial mediator, given his much longer association with Tebbit. At the same time, his dismay at the suspicions of Tebbit evoked pessimistic thoughts for the future. On 'Wobbly Thursday' Willie merely 'rolled his oyster eyes' to show his sympathy for Michael Dobbs, then the party's Chief of Staff, as Mrs Thatcher took out her frustrations on him. Later he muttered to Dobbs, 'That is a woman who will never fight another election'. Recalling this comment a few weeks later, Dobbs was inspired to begin work on *House of Cards*, his bestselling novel of murderous intrigue in political circles.[49]

The petty infighting of the 1983–87 parliament was a far cry from the atmosphere within the Conservative Party when Willie had embarked on his first election campaign. But some traditions could be upheld as he went out on the stump once more. In Batley he inspected the premises of a sweet manufacturer, who told Willie that he would soon be going to Hemel Hempstead to see a machine that once made hamburgers, but now produced truffles. 'Gracious me!' Willie exclaimed. The staff were lined up to meet him. 'I was originally from Manchester,' one of them explained. 'Manchester! My goodness me!' Willie marvelled. He did not comment on the fact that all of the workforce seemed to be female – or ask whether their jobs, like so many in the new British economy, were only part-time. A photographer who wanted him to pose with handfuls of sweets poured out too many and several spilled over. '"Oh, Lord" he said as they tinkled on to the ground. "Deary me. O, well. Jolly good."'[50]

Sustained by a booming economy the Tories won again, with a majority this time of 102; the voters of Penrith and the Border had forgiven the party, and Maclean almost restored Willie's old majority. The dreaded Poll Tax had hardly been mentioned during the campaign. After an historic win – secured on an almost unchanged proportion of the vote, despite all the troubles since 1983 – Mrs Thatcher really did seem set to 'go on and on', as she had predicted during the campaign. But her authority was not beyond challenge. Although in his memoirs Willie rather pointedly gave all the credit to Tebbit and Mrs Thatcher, Young duly received his reward for his own efforts during the campaign, moving to the Department of Trade and Industry (DTI) immediately afterwards. By the middle of October he was widely tipped to take on the party chairmanship (which Tebbit had resigned) without giving up the DTI; it was even said that Young's elevation would mean the end of Willie's reign as the government's 'Lord of the Strings'.

But then there was a sudden change. Young heard rumours that Willie and Wakeham were determined to stop him. At his own request, he saw Willie and was told that although he, Willie, had no objection to Young becoming Chairman, if asked he would advise the Prime Minister against her plan to give two important jobs to the same person. The real argument concerned the nature of those jobs; a party that depended so heavily on financial contributions from industrialists could not appoint as its Chairman a minister with so much potential influence over the fortunes of their businesses. No decision, though, had been taken, and it was suggested in the media that Young was ready to compromise by relinquishing some of his responsibilities at the DTI. But during the Party Conference Young heard that some unpleasant stories – 'against my origins rather than my policies' – were circulating. He decided to announce that he would not be available to take the chairmanship after all. Mrs Thatcher was 'furious'; it was seen as 'a humiliating defeat' for her. Reflecting on another triumph for the 'Wakeham-Whitelaw axis' one Tory commented, 'The Empire strikes back, I think'.[51]

This incident followed closely on yet another ministerial departure. After years of waiting for Hailsham to retire, the Attorney General Sir Michael Havers had finally become Lord Chancellor in June. But his health was poor. He had undergone heart surgery, and in September 1987 he suffered an acute reaction after eating a lobster. Very soon the newspapers were reporting that Havers had 'been made the butt of private remarks in the Lords'. Hailsham was accused of saying that Havers could not hold his post for long. Despite his own marathon service, which had ended at the age of seventy-nine, Hailsham had not wanted to step down even though some colleagues, including Willie, had become impatient at his rambling contributions in Cabinet. Yet he hotly denied making any derogatory remarks about Havers.[52]

On Monday 26 October Havers was summoned to Downing Street, to be greeted by Willie and the Prime Minister. The latter told him that 'I really must have your resignation'. Havers had just returned from a trip to the United States, where he caused embarrassment by complaining of being ignored by members of Reagan's administration. But his real offence was his absence from the Lords during the passage of a new Criminal Justice Bill. This legislation had been 'mauled' by lawyers in the Upper House; Willie cannot have been impressed. It was agreed that Havers should pretend to have stood down because of a sudden conviction that the job was too onerous for his health, but his letter of resignation was wholly unconvincing because the ex-Lord Chancellor actually felt better than he had done for years. In this case, at least, Willie had acted ruthlessly to prevent further trouble in his own patch. After the 'Empire' had also triumphed over Young, it seemed that Willie was modelling himself on a character from another Hollywood film, *The Terminator*. Duly impressed, one of the present authors noted that:

> Suddenly, harmless peers who encounter the lumbering figure of the Lord President in the corridors of power flatten themselves against the wall in genuine alarm. For there is real blood on those vast, ham-like hands, and two illustrious political scalps now dangle from his belt.[53]

In fact, if the lumbering Lord President had been responsible for all the bloody deeds confidently attributed to him, every minister beside Mrs Thatcher herself must have quailed at his approach. It was even said that he had been responsible for Leon Brittan's demotion from the Home Office to the DTI in 1985, because Willie felt that the Cabinet could not afford to have two senior ministers who looked unappealing on television (Lawson was the other aesthetic offender). At that time Brittan had answered the call from Number 10 thinking that he was about to be consulted on the reshuffle, only to find himself being ordered to clear out his desk. Reports were soon circulating that once he had received secret assurances that Young would no longer be a candidate for the chairmanship, Willie arranged a meeting with him and promised his full support; when Young confided that he had already thrown in the sponge, Willie feigned surprise and offered his sympathy. A student of Machiavelli would say that even if the majority of these stories were distorted, and some of them pure fabrication, the important thing was to have won such a remarkable reputation for the unflinching exercise of power. Most chilling for hopeful courtiers was the suspicious tendency of contenders for the succession to come to a sticky end almost as soon as their chances were being openly touted. So much for 'Woolly Willie', and 'Mr Wetlaw'. Three months later, when Willie had retired, he explained why he would never have been a good Prime Minister: 'It isn't that I wouldn't have been ruthless enough about people. If I'd thought people weren't sufficiently up to the job I'd have been ruthless about sacking them. It's events where I wouldn't have been ruthless enough.' Several recently retired colleagues would have said 'Amen', at least to the first bit.[54]

The blood-letting of October 1987 happened just after the Party Conference where Willie had supposedly double-crossed Parkinson. Since the latter once again seemed a good bet for the succession, it would have been easy for gossip-mongers to convince him that Willie was sharpening his butchery tools. What is certain, though, is that this conference saw a new turn in Willie's rhetoric. His reference to the 'dangerous arrogance' of those who failed to take proper account of the Lords seems to have passed without notice in Downing Street; but his subsequent warning about the likely fate of the 'Great' Education Bill earned him a Prime Ministerial reprimand. Who can say what might have followed?

While Willie was Leader of the Lords he had more chance of engaging in exercise to keep up his own health. His favourite activities, shooting and golf, brought very contrasting results. During one shoot as Home Secretary he ventured onto a swampy patch and became stuck fast. He had to be winched out by a Land-Rover, leaving his boots behind. While he could laugh off incidents like that, he was badly shaken when on another shoot near Barnard Castle in August 1984 he stumbled and accidentally peppered his friend, 'Partridge Joe' Nickerson, and a grouse-beater. In his shooting-book, instead of the usual tallies of pulverised wildlife, he simply wrote 'The Tragic Day'. It was a sign that, after what had been a charmed life for nearly seventy years, Willie's luck was beginning to run out. But there was a far happier moment in August 1986, when he was playing in a competition at Penrith Golf Club. Taking a four-iron for his tee-shot at the 174-yard fourth hole, he was overjoyed to see the ball run into the cup. It was his first ever 'ace', and was no mean stroke for a sixty-eight-year-old whose handicap had crept up to sixteen through lack of practice (and whose backswing was noticeably shorter than it had been). Unfortunately it was also costly, since the President of the club could hardly avoid buying the drinks afterwards.[55]

In the first two weeks of December 1987 Willie had already been shooting, and had spent a weekend with Bertie Denham. Over the New Year he was planning to do more of the same, as usual. Looking back on this period, he could only remember one ominous portent. Discussing the cluttered legislative programme with Denham and the whips, he had suddenly exploded: 'I simply can't stand these late sittings any longer. I am getting too old for it.' Afterwards he felt that he had acted 'quite unreasonably'; but he also guessed correctly that none of his colleagues would have found this unusual. In fact, the master of the coded message probably only mentioned the outburst in his memoirs to send a warning to the government he had left by that time; why else would he go on to say that 'I cursed myself inwardly for giving vent to such trivial feelings', when his speech at the 1987 conference showed that he considered the crushing burden on the Lords to be anything but 'trivial'? It was also true that he was getting rather old for such late nights. When he was made Chairman of a government committee on AIDS in November 1986, questions were raised about his suitability for the job, and some of the more explicit evidence 'set his eyebrows quivering and his jowls shaking'. In one session he made a typical joke about his fustiness. When someone suggested that there should be special advice for older people, who 'had the same desires as the youngsters', Willie piped up, 'I can assure you that they haven't.' In fact he was the epitome of common sense compared to those (including Mrs Thatcher) who flirted with the idea that the disease was a form of divine retribution; and at least he had given his troops advice on venereal disease when he was in Palestine. The responsible minister at the time, Norman Fowler, later recalled that the committee had made little progress before Willie joined, and that his chairmanship 'was absolutely essential in saving many lives in this country'. The problem was not Willie's age, but the fact that he was a willing victim of his own success, and continued to accept new duties after so many years in a high-stress, sedentary occupation. He had already asked his doctor, John Gayner, to warn him at the first sign that he should cut back on his commitments. [56]

On 14 December Willie enjoyed what he described as 'a quiet and frugal' lunch with Trevor Kavanagh of the *Sun*, then walked over to St Margaret's Church, opposite the House, for a carol service organised by the Wives of Westminster Committee. The organisation raised funds for the nearby Westminster Hospital; Celia was a founder-member and the current Chairman. After reading one of the lessons Willie returned to his seat, next to Lord Home. Trying to cough, he made a strange noise instead; then he began to yawn. When the congregation stood for the next carol Willie was unable to rise with them. Fortunately, Dr Richard Staughton from Westminster Hospital was close at hand, having just read a lesson himself. His presence, and that of two sisters from Westminster's Intensive Care Unit, was another sign that Willie's lucky star was still twinkling. Celia was there too. As Willie put it, 'On the whole no one could have collapsed in more fortunate circumstances.' But his condition would have been alarming enough wherever he was, for it was obvious that he had suffered a cerebral attack of some kind; and the Deputy Prime Minister was rushed to the very hospital that Celia had supported for more than two decades. [57]

CHAPTER 17

TOO LATE TO MOURN

It turned out that Willie had suffered a Transient Ischaemic Attack (TIA) – in layman's language a 'mini-stroke', whose effects last for less than twenty-four hours. Although those who attended him in St Margaret's had every reason to think that his condition was more serious, by the time Willie reached the hospital there were encouraging signs. But his ability to speak was restored more rapidly than full control over his limbs. 'I must be able to play golf again,' he kept repeating in the ambulance as he tried to flex his right hand.[1]

If the scene of Willie's attack had been ideal in ensuring the best emergency treatment, it also meant that the news travelled fast. Mrs Thatcher sent a note to Celia 'hoping for a full and speedy recovery'. The Queen added her own sympathy and good wishes; she asked for regular bulletins on Willie's condition. As it became clear that his life was not in danger, the relieved messages reflected the full range of friends and well-wishers that Willie had acquired. Golfers and Guardsmen; political allies and opponents; staff from the Home Office and the Lords – all were represented in his mailbag. Even a complete stranger from Belfast, who had never written to a politician before, sent her prayers for Willie's future health. As he recorded in his memoirs, the most moving message came from the golfer Henry Cotton, who sent a humorous card and the instruction that Willie should accept his infirmities on the course, at least to the extent of driving from the 'forward tees' in future. The card offered no clue that Cotton was himself in hospital; he died a week later.[2]

Willie himself was home for Christmas 1987. Later he heaped praise on the National Health Service, but he could hardly be treated like a normal patient. Security considerations meant that he was consigned to a bed that would normally be occupied by a private patient paying £175 per day. Ironically the same concerns condemned Willie to the kind of indignities that regularly inspire outraged newspaper headlines. The financial plight of Westminster

Hospital meant that it lacked the equipment for a thorough brain-scan. The nearest facility was at Charing Cross Hospital; but to get Willie there without attracting disagreeable publicity it was deemed necessary to wheel him into an ambulance via the service lift.

Willie took the decision to resign from the Cabinet while he was in hospital, after consultations with his own doctor. When Dr Gayner approached his bed, Willie said, 'I know what you're going to tell me.' The two had become good friends. When Willie was at the Home Office, Gayner had issued strict dietary instructions. No doctor can impose round-the-clock surveillance on an active patient, but Willie did his best to conform. Now the doctor felt that Willie had been issued with a salutary warning, and only a drastic reduction of his workload could prevent a much more serious episode. His advice was reinforced by Celia and the family. But Willie himself felt that it would be an unfortunate time to step down. The government front-bench team in the Lords could have been stronger, and the legislative programme which had provoked public complaints from Willie would have to be entrusted to far less experienced hands.[3]

Into the New Year there were persistent reports that Willie would be back in harness as soon as he felt strong enough. It was suggested that some of his tasks within government could be allocated to others, while he remained Leader of the Lords. If not directly inspired by Downing Street, these stories would certainly have been welcome to the Prime Minister and her aides. Mrs Thatcher was most anxious that Willie should stay on, encouraging this decision when she visited him in hospital – 'But Willie, you've never been ill!' she protested – and even contacting Gayner in the hope that he could be persuaded to reconsider his professional advice. A few days after Willie's attack Mrs Thatcher told Woodrow Wyatt that a successor would have to combine 'bonhomie and steel'. It was precisely because these qualities were so rare in public life that Willie had become so important to her. Finding an adequate replacement in the Lords would be difficult enough; but no one could be expected to match Willie's performance as multi-purpose 'trouble-shooter' within government. In this role the 'bonhomie and steel' had been reinforced by Willie's lack of personal ambition. Sir Geoffrey Howe, who could offer the nearest approximation to his experience, had been increasingly estranged from the Prime Minister since becoming Foreign Secretary. Willie's departure would remove a firebreak between the two.[4]

As he considered his decision Willie was well aware that his departure would create new difficulties for the government. But he had finally reached the point where his own interests, and those of his family, would have to drown out the call of duty. Superficially, reducing his commitments while remaining in the Cabinet seemed a plausible compromise; but this would deprive him of his general overview of government activity, and he would no longer be on call for emergencies. A part-time anchor-man can only be of much use on a tranquil sea; the Thatcher Governments had never known calm waters for long, and things looked very choppy ahead.

On Sunday 10 January 1988 it was announced that Viscount Whitelaw would be leaving the government after all. The press were invited up to Ennim, and Willie rounded off his dignified departure by expressing his regrets as he strolled around the grounds with Celia and their cocker spaniel, Judy. It seemed like a throwback to the Roman ideal of a leader retiring to his estates, full of honours, when his public tasks were over. Certainly few departures from the Thatcher Government were anything like this.

In his own memoirs Nigel Lawson wrote that after Willie's resignation 'the Thatcher Government, which for more than eight years had been such a great and glorious adventure, was never the same again'. He expressed his forebodings in a private letter to Willie at the time. And while the press response was not exactly apocalyptic, there were clear symptoms of unease. *The Times* editorial noted that 'There is now no one in the Cabinet who could reasonably affect the title of elder statesman. There is no statesman of any kind without a personal interest in the future leadership of the country. An important source of advice has been stemmed. It is hard to see it reopening.' For the *Daily Telegraph* Willie's departure was 'the sharpest personal loss the Prime Minister has suffered while in office'. One minister was quoted as saying that 'until the stroke we did not realise how much we loved him, or just how indispensible he was'. Mrs Thatcher herself had coined the most appropriate phrase, when during a speech-writing session at a Party Conference she had declared that 'Every Prime Minister needs a Willie'. Disconcerted by the laughter of her team, she extracted a promise that the remark would not be repeated. Inevitably, it soon leaked out; when he heard about it, Willie wept with laughter. But the phrase has survived because of the truth it conveyed; even Tony Blair has been advised that he needs his own Willie Whitelaw.[5]

Most of Willie's fellow peers recognised their loss. At the start of business on 11 January there were twenty minutes of tributes from all sides of the Lords. The Opposition leader Lord Cledwyn described Willie as 'a man for all seasons'. Lord Boyd-Carpenter spoke for many when he said that 'in my recollection, no leader of the House has enjoyed so much affection from your Lordships as does the noble Viscount'. All the speakers hoped that Willie would be back among them very soon; Lord Paget even suggested that in a few years he might feel well enough to resume his office, since 'Doctors' advice is wrong about four times out of five'. From the cross-benches Baroness Hylton-Foster assured Willie's successor, Lord Belstead, that no one expected him to be 'a second Lord Whitelaw'. But at least Belstead was well liked in a House he had served for many years, having been Willie's Deputy since 1983. Lord Young had been touted for this job, too, but he would have had his work cut out to convince sceptical peers that he could prioritise the interests of the House in the way Willie had done. Within the government as a whole Willie's jobs were divided among several ministers. But his successor as Lord President, John Wakeham, had already blotted his copy-book in Mrs Thatcher's eyes with an indifferent radio performance during the 1987 general election. In any case, one of Willie's key assets had been the stature he had already earned before Mrs Thatcher became leader. Wakeham only joined the Cabinet in 1987.[6]

The genuine affection expressed in the Lords at this time – and again after his death more than ten years later – was in its own way almost as great a testimony to Willie's personal qualities as the reaction to his departure from Northern Ireland. Not only had he mastered the procedure of the second chamber, after so many years in the very different House of Commons; he had also responded to the changing mood. He had, in short, fulfilled the promises he made in the early days of his Leadership, striking the correct balance between defending the Lords and upholding the government's authority. He had also ensured that television cameras were a permanent fixture in the Lords, speaking on behalf of an experiment proposed by his friend Lord Soames, then reassuring the remaining sceptics once this trial period had elapsed in May 1986. Although the Commons narrowly rejected televising its proceedings in November 1985 – and Mrs Thatcher was very uneasy about it – the arguments that Willie had advanced since the 1960s were now difficult to resist. The first broadcast was transmitted on 21 November 1989, again as an experiment, which was soon extended indefinitely.

In his memoirs Willie defended the composition of the Lords as it existed at the time of his resignation, writing that 'No one starting afresh could ever devise a House of Lords with its present membership. But in its strange way it works.' He had no sympathy for the idea of an elected second chamber, arguing that this would inevitably lead to clashes with the Commons. If there was an irresistible demand for change he was prepared to consider a reduction in the number of hereditary peers, who might choose a proportion of their more active members to continue serving in the House. But he would be reluctant to tamper even to that extent; although he made little use of this argument once he sensed that opinion was against him, he felt that even the most obscure hereditary peer could make a useful contribution on specific subjects. Significantly, although he served for a while on an informal and high-powered committee created in 1995 to discuss options for change, he used a minor procedural disagreement as a pretext for stepping down. Willie was too ill to contribute to debates by the time the Blair Government introduced its proposals after the 1997 general election, but he would not have been happy with the outcome. Almost certainly he would have backed Viscount Cranborne's attempts to secure a compromise on the position of the hereditary peers, even though the party leader William Hague later sacked Cranborne for his insubordination. But to secure any kind of compromise that preserved the traditional nature of the Lords, in the face of a government which was determined to camouflage its lack of radicalism elsewhere by reducing the British constitution to rubble, would surely have over-taxed even Viscount Whitelaw's powers.

After his resignation Willie told Nigel Lawson that 'I shall never interfere but will equally come if wanted'. He made the same offer to Mrs Thatcher. Before the end of January 1988 he had helped to host a lunch at Number 10, and it seemed that he would become a regular visitor. But as the government's difficulties grew he felt that he was not being consulted. When the *Sunday Times* serialised Willie's memoirs Andrew Neil was disappointed by the lack of sensational stories to justify his newspaper's substantial investment. Brian Walden was sent to interview Willie, and prised out of him the admission that 'nothing that was basically social could go on' between himself and the Prime Minister: 'In fact,' he added, 'over the years, we have both made positive efforts to see that a purely social meeting does not take place.' The interview probably did more damage to Willie than to Mrs Thatcher. Criticised for his snobbish phrases, he claimed that he could not remember having used those words, which only amounted to a more brutal expression of what he had said many times – that he and the Prime Minister were very different people, with no mutual interests outside politics. Walden, however, insisted that he had a full transcript of the interview; whenever Willie had said something controversial he had expressly confirmed that he could be quoted. Ironically, after the Downing Street dinner that Willie helped to arrange in January 1988, Mrs Thatcher had written 'what a pity we don't meet together more often for convivial occasions. But perhaps there isn't time.' Woodrow Wyatt detected that the Walden interview had upset Mrs Thatcher, but she understood why he had made his comments. In public her response was equally dignified; she said that 'Willie is pure gold' and hinted that she would be consulting him more often in the future. Unfortunately Walden later confirmed to Wyatt that Willie really had meant what he said, adding the even more unwelcome news that he had also deprecated Mrs Thatcher's reliance on advisers like Wyatt.[7]

At least Willie had avoided any direct criticism of Mrs Thatcher's policies, and had praised her achievements warmly in his memoirs. But during the round of interviews to publicise the book he risked further displeasure from Downing Street, airily predicting that Mrs Thatcher's leadership was 'bound to end in a muddle because she's been so dominant for so long'. He suggested that some people might prefer 'a certain hesitancy' in a leader to a constant hectoring style. He seemed to be taking pains to give every remark a double edge; 'it's not quite true that she has no sense of humour at all,' he mused. In another coded criticism of his leader (which also indicated that he still saw a key role for himself, at least until the unavoidable transition was over) Willie revealed that there was no obvious successor in sight. Elsewhere he committed the ultimate sin of praising the most unpalatable of all the aspirants to Number 10, saying that although he still had reservations about Michael Heseltine's judgement, he thought that he might turn out to be an excellent Prime Minister. Up to then Heseltine's opponents had complacently assumed that Willie's hostility would prevent his succession, if all else failed. No one was more surprised than Heseltine himself when he learned of this interview; he dashed off a note to express his gratitude.[8]

Perhaps Willie thought he could afford to risk a serious breach with the Prime Minister because she was getting on so badly with her other senior colleagues. Relations between Mrs Thatcher and Geoffrey Howe continued to deteriorate, and now Lawson was also out of favour. The issue dividing Prime Minister and Chancellor was the possibility of Britain joining the Exchange Rate Mechanism (ERM) of the European Monetary System (EMS). Far from being an advocate of a European 'superstate', Lawson had a pragmatic interest in a system that could act as a far more reliable weapon against inflation, and economic stability in general, than monetarism had proved to be. As early as November 1985 Willie had attended an ad hoc meeting of ministers and officials on the subject. After hearing Lawson, Howe and Robin Leigh-Pemberton, the Governor of the Bank of England, all arguing in favour of ERM membership, Willie said that this combination should be conclusive, even if the Prime Minister herself was still very doubtful. However, on this occasion he had misjudged the strength of Mrs Thatcher's feelings. According to one report, 'with venom in her voice' she said, 'Ayes seven, Noes one – the Noes have it.'[9]

When the long-delayed recovery led some commentators to hail a fragile 'boom' as an 'economic miracle', the problem seemed less urgent. But towards the end of the decade inflation, which had supposedly been vanquished by the miracle-workers, surfaced once again. The Chancellor had been widely regarded as the architect of the 1987 election victory, but now his stock was falling dramatically. Willie had become very fond of him, advising him on one occasion not to leave the Treasury even for another senior government post unless he felt that the economy was in good shape. In June 1989 Lawson asked Willie for a private chat. He confided that he was minded to resign, feeling that Mrs Thatcher's economic adviser, Professor Alan Walters, was undermining his position. Willie said that he hoped Lawson would not resign but made no attempt to dissuade him, stressing that he himself no longer had influence over the Prime Minister. It was a significant response. Willie had always thought that a government was doomed if the authority of the Chancellor was questioned. In the past he had tried to ensure that the Treasury view prevailed over spending ministers. But it was a very different matter when the attack was being led by the Prime Minister herself. When the crisis had been resolved a few months later, robbing Mrs Thatcher of her Chancellor, her adviser and much of her remaining reputation for prudent leadership, Norman Tebbit claimed that it would have been nipped in the bud if Willie had still been in the Cabinet. But Willie must have felt a measure of relief at not having to act as umpire. In his discussion with Lawson in June 1989 he agreed that Mrs Thatcher 'had become impossible'.[10]

A fortnight after this tête-à-tête, Lawson and Howe returned from the European Council at Madrid with what they considered to be a satisfactory agreement on ERM membership. There was no timetable for British entry, but detailed conditions had been established. Unfortunately, Mrs Thatcher felt that she had been 'ambushed' by her senior colleagues, who had both hinted at resignation if they did not get their way. On 24 July the Prime Minister struck back, demoting Howe from the Foreign Office. Later Howe felt that he should have resigned at this point, but he agreed to stay in the Cabinet provided that in addition to the leadership of the Commons he was given the title of Deputy Prime Minister. Howe was right in thinking that anything less would be a humiliation; but even in the heat of the moment he should have realised that recent events made a constructive partnership with Mrs Thatcher impossible. For her own part, the Prime Minister thought that 'Something had happened to Geoffrey' since he had been at the Foreign Office, and subsequently she regretted that she had not sacked him outright. Instead, he was rubbished by the government's supporters in the media. Much was made, for example, of his supposed insistence that he should take over Dorneywood from Nigel Lawson. In fact, Willie's old residence had been freely offered to Howe by Mrs Thatcher.[11]

Bernard Ingham was pleased when Willie confirmed that the title of Deputy Prime Minister had no constitutional standing, and would be meaningless in the absence of trust between the top two. But Willie's real feelings were reflected in reported comments to friends, in which he lambasted the reshuffle as 'a ghastly mistake'. It was impossible for 'anyone in their right mind' to imagine that Howe and Thatcher could work together happily, he was quoted as saying. Significantly, he placed the responsibility for rebuilding the relationship on the Prime Minister, warning that 'she will have to work very hard to restore any trust in Geoffrey Howe'. In addition, he felt that the new Foreign Secretary, John Major, had been promoted too quickly. Subsequently he denied making the remarks, but the main themes were reported accurately. His own view was that if Howe had to be moved at all, he should have been made Lord Chancellor. In substance, his 'denial' only added up to the qualification that he was pleased with one or two of the other appointments arising from the reshuffle, including Kenneth Baker's promotion to Party Chairman.[12]

Unfortunately for Willie, he had been nominated as President of the National Union for 1989, and in that capacity he had to preside over the Party Conference in October. In an unhappy moment, Baker had decided that the theme of the gathering should be 'The Right Team', just as the wrangling between manager and players was spilling onto the pitch. By contrast, Labour had enjoyed an unusually harmonious conference, and the Conservatives were now 11 per cent behind in the polls. Mrs Thatcher's own speech was followed by chants of 'Ten More Years' from the besotted audience, in defiance of the fact that 58 per cent of the public wanted her to step down immediately. It took eleven minutes of 'bell-ringing and bellowing' for Willie to restore order; his performance amused the platform and the audience so much that it actually prolonged the ovation.[13]

But Nigel Lawson had an unhappy conference – Willie's attempt to rouse the audience after the Chancellor's speech was even less effective than his bell-ringing – and he decided to resign on 26 October after further friction with Alan Walters. In his letter of sympathy, Willie told Lawson, 'She could so easily have got rid of Walters, but increasingly I fear that she simply cannot bring herself to be on the losing side in any argument. That failing may ditch us all.' Despite these opinions, Willie issued a public call for loyalty when it became clear that Mrs Thatcher's leadership would be challenged by Sir Anthony Meyer, who emerged as a 'stalking horse' in November 1989. At least his plea for an end to the plotting was more sincere than similar pledges of loyalty from Howe and Heseltine, who were both awaiting a better opportunity. Yet Mrs Thatcher's vulnerability was exposed by the failure of sixty MPs to support her in the ballot itself, on 5 December. Willie's friend George Younger, who had helped with the campaign, advised the Prime Minister to drop her unpopular advisers, Ingham and Charles Powell. Younger had promised wavering MPs that Mrs Thatcher would pay more attention to backbench opinion in future; when his advice on Powell and Ingham was rejected he must have guessed that the Prime Minister would ignore the rest of his message. The problem that had been foreseen back in January 1988 was destroying the Thatcher premiership; in the absence of Willie, or an adequate substitute, the Prime Minister had felt free to ignore any source of counsel with the slightest claim to be independent.[14]

In an interview for this book Willie hotly denied a well-sourced story that he had advised Mrs Thatcher against retirement in May 1989 – the tenth anniversary of her first general election victory. But in any case that was before the 'ghastly' reshuffle, and Lawson's resignation. Although Conservative popularity had been sliding since the beginning of the year, the two main parties were neck-and-neck in the polls at the time of the anniversary. But by March

1990 the government was more than 20 per cent behind Labour. That month the Conservatives lost the Mid-Staffordshire by-election on a 22 per cent swing; it ended with the Trafalgar Square anti-Poll Tax riot, which led to 339 arrests and even more injuries. On 2 April a horrified Woodrow Wyatt heard Lady Aldington suggesting that the time had come for Willie to visit Downing Street and say, 'You must go now because your time is up.' Given Wyatt's reputation as a man whose loyalty to Mrs Thatcher made Greyfriars Bobbie look like a snivelling turncoat, it was particularly significant that people were now willing to speak out in his presence. The loudest alarm bell of all had already sounded; Alec Home predicted that Mrs Thatcher would be out of office before the next election. Probably Home was less conscious of Wyatt's feelings than some of his younger friends; the *News of the World*, in which the former Labour MP expounded his views, was unlikely to be consulted very often at the Hirsel. But if the master of the timely resignation felt that way, then his former Chief Whip was unlikely to be more positive. With Mrs Thatcher's encouragement, Wyatt directly asked for Willie's opinion. 'He was not exactly equivocal,' Wyatt confided to his diary, 'but he said he thought that when people went mad it was very difficult to do anything about them.' If those were Willie's precise words, his message was not 'equivocal' at all. He went on to say that it would be 'very bad for the party' if Mrs Thatcher clung on after a narrow victory in another leadership election. Even so, the infatuated Wyatt concluded that 'Willie was no longer in some plot with Alec Home'. In fact the only evidence that there had ever been such a thing was a story that they had met at the Farmers' Club after the Meyer challenge and concluded that Mrs Thatcher was in serious trouble.[15]

But if there was any concerted 'Establishment Plot' at this time it was designed to block Heseltine rather than to unseat Mrs Thatcher. Despite his earlier warm words about the former Defence Secretary, Willie thought that a Heseltine leadership would be too unsettling for the party; and he had not been impressed by Heseltine's cunning mantra that he 'could not foresee the circumstances' under which he might launch a challenge. Early in 1990 Willie told John Cole that, despite everything, Mrs Thatcher offered her party the best chance of winning the next election, and presumably this judgement arose from a dim view of the alternatives rather than from any confidence in the appeal of the current leader. He did feel that the summer of 1990 would be crucial, but some skilful news management by Kenneth Baker convinced the media that a net loss of 200 seats in that May's local elections really represented a vindication of the Poll Tax. When Willie visited Central Office a few days later he congratulated Baker on 'a real coup'; the result (or rather its presentation) had 'certainly saved Margaret', he thought. Although the Conservatives were still behind in the opinion polls, the gap had narrowed slightly and by the time of the 1990 Party Conference a small majority of voters thought that the government would retain power at the next election. Since this did not have to be called for another two years there were good reasons for trying to damp down speculation about another leadership challenge.[16]

Even this relatively unpromising situation was blown away by Geoffrey Howe's resignation on 1 November 1990, followed twelve days later by a Commons statement that made Willie wince as he listened in the public gallery. During the interval between these events Willie – who sent Howe a letter which echoed his previous message to Lawson – was invited to Downing Street. It was said that the meeting was pre-arranged, but the fact that Willie was wearing his Guards tie was taken as an ominous sign. Apparently Mrs Thatcher wanted to discuss her plans for the next ten years, but as Julia Langdon reported in the *Sunday Telegraph* it was far more likely that they focused on the next ten days. After the meeting it was announced that the date of any Conservative leadership election would be brought forward, to disrupt the calculations of Heseltine or any stalking-horse. If Willie was a party to that tactical ruse he had every reason to be dismayed by Howe's resignation speech, which could be read as a further instalment of Heseltine's post-Westland attack on Mrs Thatcher's style of government.[17]

The day after Howe's speech Heseltine threw his hat into the ring. Willie told Wyatt that the situation was 'so absolutely ghastly and they are behaving so abominably'. 'They' presumably included his own former campaign manager, Michael Mates, who was now acting in the same capacity for Heseltine (the team even tempted fate by taking Interview Room J, which Willie's supporters had used in 1975, as its Commons base). Willie went on to confide that he felt Mrs Thatcher 'ought to win. She must win. But I am very worried that she is not going to win by enough. I don't know what her friends and advisers are telling her.' Having dismissed as 'nonsense' the idea that he would go and tell her to stand down, he proceeded to hint that if she failed to win a clear majority on the first ballot he might do exactly that. This suggestion worried Wyatt, and rightly so; when Willie referred to 'friends and advisers' he was obviously hoping that Wyatt would transmit his message back to Downing Street. It was hardly necessary for him to add, 'Whatever happens we can't have her humbled. But then she is wise enough to know that.'[18]

In fact Mrs Thatcher showed no such wisdom after the ballot on 20 November. Like Heath in 1974–5, she had isolated herself too much to grasp what was really going on. She was tantalisingly close to winning outright, and immediately declared her intention of fighting on; but Heseltine had received 152 votes and there were sixteen abstentions. 'Alec's Revenge' had been exercised again; and this time the much-maligned leadership rules proved their worth. The extra hurdles that had been introduced to make life harder for Heath now hobbled his assassin. Without the Home Committee's insistence on a 15 per cent margin of victory based on all who were *entitled* to vote, rather than those who had actually voted, Mrs Thatcher would have retained her position, albeit horribly mauled.

The fact that the Thatcher camp had made no secret of their detestation of Heseltine rebounded on them. If almost half of the parliamentary party could take their dissatisfaction to the length of voting for a man who was regularly denounced as an egomaniac and (at least) a semi-socialist, it was obvious that the Conservatives could not continue under their present management. Without the 'payroll vote' of ministers – and those MPs who had only backed Mrs Thatcher because they would never have been able to face their constituency associations had they deserted her – Heseltine might even have won. Before Howe's speech Willie had told Kenneth Baker that the Prime Minister should stand aside if one-third or more of Tory MPs voted against her, and this total had been comfortably exceeded. Even so, a challenger who was already divisive enough among the Conservative grass roots would be even less likely to unite the party if he won on a fiercely fought second ballot. Somehow a candidate had to be found who aroused none of the passions surrounding both of the first-round contestants.[19]

Very early in the morning of Wednesday 21 November the government's Chief Whip, Tim Renton, called on Willie at Clabon Mews. The previous evening Conservative MPs had been meeting all over London, and this day would be filled with consultations. Asked by reporters if he was one of the 'Men in Grey Suits', Willie showed his irritation, replying, 'No, I'm not, for the very simple reason that I am wearing a blue suit.' This was not very reassuring, and when Cecil Parkinson learned that Renton had seen Willie he was dismayed, feeling certain that 'the Chief Whip was wobbling'. Sure enough, when Renton appeared at Downing Street he reported a general view at Westminster that Mrs Thatcher should resign. He went on to convey a message from Willie, which turned out to be, almost word for word, the advice that he had tried to pass on through the medium of Woodrow Wyatt. By the time she came to write her memoirs, Mrs Thatcher was so absorbed in her self-adopted role as Julius Caesar that she classed Willie with others who had used the 'humiliation' argument as a polite pretext for coaxing her out of Number 10 with the minimum of fuss. Whatever his private opinion, Willie had supported her so often in the past that his verdict ought to have been treated with more respect than this. In his eyes, at least, her refusal to go quietly when her time was obviously up merely confirmed that she was no longer fit to be leader.[20]

After all the talk of the omnipotent 'Men in Grey Suits', Willie's advice had weighed no more heavily than that of other departed ministers, such as Norman Tebbit and George Younger (who had been roped into the campaign team despite his unhappy experience in 1989). After hearing Willie's message, Mrs

Thatcher could still tell reporters that she was determined to 'fight to win'. Only a series of interviews with her ministers, backed by John Wakeham's assessment that she had lost the support of the Cabinet, persuaded her that the game was up; she resigned on the morning of Thursday, 21 November. Ironically, the Thatcherites had branded Heath a 'bad loser' when, after winning more votes than Labour in February 1974, he had delayed his resignation until he had put out the obvious feelers for support from other parties. Even if Mrs Thatcher had intimidated her ministers into backing her, she would still have faced the problem of convincing MPs that the party could recover under her leadership. Despite the heroic status accorded to her during these hours by her admirers, her behaviour could be compared unfavourably with Heath's refusal to resign straight away after the general election of February 1974. At that time she had thought that Heath's 'horse trading' had made the party 'look ridiculous', and she had left Downing Street 'with some sense of relief' when the negotiations failed, feeling that 'it was time not just for a change of government but for a change in the Conservative Party'. In her eyes, those who shared that view in November 1990 were traitors, to herself, her party and the country.[21]

If he had been thinking only of his own future influence, Willie might have been well advised to march into Downing Street at the head of a grey-suited delegation, rather than letting the Cabinet take on the responsibility. But if even Mrs Thatcher could ignore his judgement of party opinion, it was unlikely that his word on those matters would count for very much again. Nevertheless, before the second ballot he gave public support to Douglas Hurd, who had stepped forward with John Major as challengers to Heseltine. As Home Secretary from 1985 to 1989 Hurd had been, if anything, more successful than Willie in defending his patch. Since Lawson's resignation he had served as Foreign Secretary, a job for which he was perfectly fitted. These qualifications, plus the intimate knowledge of life at Number 10 that he had gained from working with Ted Heath, made Hurd the best candidate to succeed Mrs Thatcher. Unfortunately his campaign quickly stalled, amid jibes against Hurd's (relatively) privileged background, which Willie tried to rebuff himself, from the dubious sociological vantage point of Winchester, Cambridge and the Guards.

The real trouble with Hurd as a candidate, Willie told Kenneth Baker, 'was the same with me in 1975. He doesn't really want the job.' Hurd certainly gave this impression during his media appearances. But the parallel with 1975 was more exact than Willie seemed to realise. Like Willie, Hurd was a viable contender for the leadership – and would have accepted the job with pleasure – only if the party could be persuaded to return to a 'national' approach and he could 'emerge' without an unseemly squabble. Since Conservative MPs had spurned this prospectus in 1975 they were unlikely to snatch at it in 1990. Instead, as Willie went on to hint, the winning candidate would have to convince the right wing that he was 'One of Us', and Hurd's supporters knew in advance that he could never manage this. He was badly beaten on the second ballot, in which Major came only two votes short of the majority demanded by the rules. Before this second vote Willie had met Wakeham to discuss the arrangements for a further contest; they had agreed that, notwithstanding Willie's continued misgivings about Major, they would both throw their weight behind him if he won something less than a decisive victory. This last instalment of the 'Establishment Plot' proved unnecessary; Heseltine and Hurd conceded defeat after the first ballot, handing the succession to Major.[22]

Like Hurd, Major had held two of the most senior government positions. But he had only joined the Cabinet for the first time in June 1987; even then he was Nigel Lawson's second choice for the job of Chief Secretary to the Treasury (Willie and Mrs Thatcher had argued that Major would be better as Chief Whip). This meant that Willie had spent a few months in Cabinet with Major, and he had special reasons for admiring him because the spending round of 1987 was entirely settled through bilateral meetings, sparing Willie the tiring Star Chamber process for that year. But apart from the obvious handicap of Major's relative inexperience, Willie had already detected his fatal flaw as a successful leader of the party. 'Many will vote for him because they think he's on the right wing,' he told Baker before Major was even a candidate. 'They'll be disappointed and soon find out he isn't.'[23]

Willie's most successful political partnerships had been forged with people who shared his general outlook, or with those who provided constructive contrasts to his own personality. John Major fell between these stools. In some ways the pair were strikingly similar. The new Prime Minister was very good with people, and believed that good-humoured negotiations were far more likely to produce results than all-out confrontation. Instinct, rather than dogma, was his political guide; and like Willie he seemed to belong in the 'One Nation' bracket even when he was drifting along in the 'Thatcherite' tide. Neither of them could be described as 'intellectuals', but here lay an important difference. While Willie instinctively distrusted intellectuals in politics, Major seemed most happy in the company of people like William Waldegrave and Viscount Cranborne (who learned much from Willie, but remained a far more cerebral operator). Their approach complemented Major's own way of thinking; in important respects Willie merely duplicated it.

But the most important barrier to a fruitful relationship was the generation gap, accentuated by the recent history of the party. First elected in 1979, Major had never been an Opposition MP. If he wore battle-scars, they had been inflicted during internal faction-fights, as the 1979 intake scrambled for the best jobs. In the general election of 1992 the Tories completed the fight-back that began as soon as Mrs Thatcher was deposed. More than ever, after that fourth consecutive Tory victory ministers were tempted to assume an unlimited tenure of power, and to concentrate on party management rather than governing the country. It was a tendency that Willie warned about as early as June 1991, and which was later echoed in one of the telling phrases of the Major years – the parting accusation of Major's first Chancellor, Norman Lamont, that 'We give the impression of being in office, and not in power.'[24]

The disunity that bedevilled Major's premiership was brought into the open by sharply divergent attitudes towards European integration. After leaving office Mrs Thatcher had thrown off the flimsy restraints which had partly checked her Euro-scepticism. In October 1991 – two months before the crucial negotiations at Maastricht – Willie issued a stern rebuke to his former leader, saying that once someone has given up a position they should allow their successors to get on with the job. He had advised her to quit the Commons at the next election, but when she took her seat in the Lords she stepped up her battle against a government that she accused of betraying her legacy across the board. Such were the passions involved that neither Willie nor anyone else could have acted as an intermediary.

As a veteran of so many debates before Britain's accession to the Treaty of Rome, Willie was well aware of the strong feelings within his party on Europe. But he confessed to bewilderment as the Conservatives tore themselves apart over Maastricht. He felt that Major had negotiated shrewdly, and that if Lady Thatcher had still been Prime Minister she would have returned with a similar deal: after all, 'She always realised we had to be part of Europe.' He was particularly angry when she backed an attempt in the Lords to force the government to call a referendum on Maastricht. Ratification of the treaty had been a manifesto commitment. This was an argument he had used many times in the Lords to discourage rebellions against the Thatcher Government; but the Tory opponents of Maastricht, who had been quite happy when the backwoodsmen flooded in to push through bills that destroyed the autonomy of local government, now felt that the traditional reticence of the Lords should be abandoned in the face of a treaty which, in itself, barely affected the British constitution. In his own contribution to the debate of 7 June 1993 – which for knowledge and good humour easily outstripped anything the Commons could offer – Willie described the Euro-sceptics as 'narrow-minded'. Some criticisms of the European Community were justified, he said, 'but, goodness me, one can justify criticism of all kinds of institutions which one supports and believes in. Yet that will not do, and carping criticism from the sidelines can do Britain nothing but harm.'[25]

Willie's last public word on Europe came in September 1996, when he joined his old friends Geoffrey Howe, Leon Brittan, Douglas Hurd, Peter

Carrington and Edward Heath in signing a letter to the *Independent* newspaper. The Euro-sceptic press denounced the six elder statesmen (unimaginatively dubbed 'Grandees'), who were inevitably accused of having 'plotted' an initiative which threatened to bring new life to the European controversy just before the Conservative Party Conference. Yet the text of the letter hardly justified the hysterical reaction; it merely argued that it would be a catastrophe for Britain to rule out membership of a single currency, and claimed that 'To countenance withdrawal from the European Union would be to court disaster'.[26]

Willie could sign up happily to all that. But whether or not the label of unthinking 'Euro-fanatic' would fit any of his co-signatories, it would have been difficult for someone with Willie's ingrained constitutional conservatism – and his dislike of grandiose blueprints – to feel happy at the prospect of a European federal union. During his lifetime he could avoid awkward questions on this subject by saying that only if it took a full, constructive part in debate could Britain ensure that European institutions developed in a congenial direction. But Major's experience at Maastricht suggested that the damage had already been done, and that other European leaders were intent on proceeding with their own vision, whether Britain's leaders shared it or not. Major himself became increasingly sceptical over time, despite his original desire to place Britain 'at the very heart of Europe'. Willie might easily have retreated into a position best described as one of 'benevolent neutrality' had his health held up in his final few years.[27]

The 1992 general election was swiftly followed by Britain's exit from the ERM. In April 1993 Willie spoke of 'The worst first year of a government I can recall', adding Michael Heseltine's mishandling of pit closures to the charge sheet. Kenneth Baker's Dangerous Dogs Bill was 'too absurd', and Willie doubted the wisdom of other pending legislation. His final commendation of Major was a perfect, double-edged 'Willie-ism': 'I am an enormous admirer of John Major, and I desperately hope that he will be as good a prime minister as I believe he will be.' Major, of course, had already had the chance to prove himself during two and a half years in Downing Street.[28]

The views attributed to Willie were outspoken enough, but in private he was even more scathing. In June 1993 he declared that the Tories were 'the most worthless party he ever could remember'; it was clear from his comments that he thought little of Major as Prime Minister. Two years later Willie delivered even more damaging criticisms. By now the political problems of the Conservative Party had been reinforced by allegations of sexual and financial misconduct; Willie was relatively relaxed about the first, but the idea of MPs receiving 'cash for questions' was further evidence of a collapse in public standards. As Willie had told Lord Nolan, who was conducting an inquiry into these scandals, he also felt that ministers should not take up an appointment in a privatised company for at least two years. Someone as talkative – and noisy – as Willie ran an obvious risk of inadvertent leaking. But generally the press had protected him with anonymity in the past because they regarded him as an invaluable source. By 1995 the cloak had slipped. In March the *Sun* quoted him as describing the government as 'a complete shower . . . one of the worst governments I can remember'. The privatisations of electricity and the railways were singled out, but Willie was reported to have said that the government was 'incompetent on pretty well everything'. Major himself was criticised for his 'feeble leadership'.[29]

Papers like the *Sun* had been reliable supporters of Mrs Thatcher, but now their priority was to prosecute their anti-European agenda, no matter which government was in power. The sceptical strategy deployed by Major at Maastricht was nowhere near enough for Lady Thatcher's media allies. Journalists were prepared to use any weapon to strike at Major. As one of the few Thatcher ministers publicly to defend her successor – and as a pro-European – Willie was an ideal (if involuntary) recruit to the cause. And if he retaliated to the breach of confidence by refusing to deal with the *Sun* in future, clearly the editor believed that the loss would be sustainable. Willie still provided good copy on occasions, but he was not privy to the big secrets any more.

Willie's remarks had been overheard in a London club – probably the Carlton, where he was Chairman and often entertained members with stories about the government. In the past a gentleman could let off steam in his fireside chair without fear of any disclosures. But times were changing and news of his outburst – or others of a similiar tendency – had circulated even before the article. Lord Tebbit had written at the beginning of March 1995 suggesting a talk, since 'From what I hear you have formed the same opinion of this government that I have done'. But after the *Sun* article Willie was furious at what he regarded as 'very strange journalism'. In his anger he telephoned the newspaper's editor, Stuart Higgins, and followed up with a letter protesting that 'the comments made are not my views'. Higgins sent back a half-hearted apology, merely 'to emphasise the value of our continued healthy professional relationship'. Both men knew that the remarks had been a fair reflection of Willie's opinion. This was tacitly confirmed when Willie wrote to Major, expressing his deep regret for having been 'very cleverly duped'. 'I have been trying for a long time to stand up for you in different ways,' he continued. 'I have done so, and now I have let you down and feel very unhappy about it.'[30]

Before this incident Willie had been a fairly regular visitor to Number 10, taking advantage of Major's offer to see him whenever he felt it necessary. In accepting this arrangement Willie showed that he had learned from his experience after his resignation; if Mrs Thatcher had called him only when others prompted her, John Major was unlikely to be more solicitous. The Prime Minister sent a generous reply to Willie's apology, putting it all down to 'dirty tricks' on the part of the press. Obviously it would be important to remain on good terms; Willie had indeed 'stood up' for Major in various ways, for example visiting the editor of the *The Times* in an attempt to rally support. But the relationship could only be weakened, at a time when the Prime Minister was convinced that Cabinet dissidents were using the press to undermine him. By mid-June 1995 Major had decided to put a stop to the sniping, one way or another. At exactly the same time Willie had reached the conclusion that something had to be done. He telephoned Viscount Cranborne, who now had Willie's old job of Leader in the Lords. An appointment with Major and Cranborne was arranged for the evening of Wednesday 21 June.[31]

Willie arrived at Downing Street wearing the ominous Guards tie. Sitting at the Cabinet table, he said, 'It's very good of you to see me. Things are very bad. Very very bad. My message is that you're going to have to do something. I don't know what it is, but you'll have to do something.' Major replied that Willie was quite right: 'I have something in mind, and I'll do it this week.' Willie said that he was very glad, and there was no need to tell him what it was. Before he left he raised the question of a new Chief Whip (the present incumbent, Richard Ryder, had not been fully fit for some time and was now anxious to step down). 'I don't know who it should be,' Willie said, 'but I am entitled to say this. Never choose a man who is against fox hunting.'[32]

Cranborne and Major, who had been sitting opposite each other, had continually made eye contact and found it hard not to laugh. In fact, although Major had almost made up his mind to steal a march on his critics by resigning as party leader (though not as Prime Minister), he probably would not have felt able to confide in his visitor even if the *Sun* incident had never happened. The need for secrecy – with the corresponding concern that an unprecedented gamble was about to be taken after only minimal consultations – may help to account for Major's mood. But the suppressed laughter does reinforce the impression that Willie no longer counted in Downing Street – except, perhaps, as a monitor of opinion in the Lords. While Major himself praised Willie in his memoirs, there was certainly a different attitude among the Prime Minister's circle. When two close advisers wrote their account of life at Number 10, they claimed that 'Legend has turned Lord Whitelaw into a cross between Merlin and Dr Watson, but contemporary observers give a more modest account of his role in Margaret Thatcher's Government'. Richard Ryder was more directly cutting, telling the ubiquitous Woodrow Wyatt that Willie was 'extremely two-faced; he leaked enormously to the press, showing them how wise he was and how he managed to keep a check on Margaret's excesses . . . it was really all drivel about his great influence on her, although he may have had a little'.[33]

Major's gamble failed. More than a hundred MPs refused to support him in the contest against John Redwood, and although loyal ministers briefed the press that this was a decisive victory, it was nowhere near enough to restore the image of a united party. In November 1995 Lord Carr told Willie, 'I have never since the war been so worried about the Conservative Party – about the depth of its unpopularity and where the party is heading.' He feared 'not just losing the next election, but losing it so badly that we shall suffer a long painful sojourn in the wilderness'. The difficulty was finding a way to act on Carr's accurate analysis of a party that was now identified with extremism and personal excesses; despite the leadership contest, the Prime Minister was still under pressure to appease the right wing, who were largely responsible for creating the problem in the first place. Probably Willie would have advised Major against his gamble, and he must have left Downing Street on that June evening hoping that the Prime Minister was about to purge his Cabinet of dissenters. But even this might not have worked. In reality Major could only hope for a quiet life if he sacked the majority of his parliamentary party and purged the grass-roots membership. As Willie had told another disillusioned Tory back in June 1993, 'I am sure that the best way [of escaping the current difficulties] is firmly to stand up for what we have believed in the party for a long time. Alas, we have all too many difficult young men who have very different views to what we have all lived with for a long time.'[34]

If these reasons for pessimism were not enough, the government continued to tax Willie's patience by bombarding the Lords with over-hasty legislation. There were regular reports of Lord Whitelaw's unhappiness with various measures. His preferred method was to raise these objections privately with the minister concerned, in the hope that bills would be amended with government agreement; but he found this increasingly difficult after he left the Cabinet. Just before Mrs Thatcher fell from office he was particularly exercised by an attempt (partly inspired by Lord Wyatt) to enforce impartiality on commercial broadcasters. He told the Lords that when he read of Wyatt's plan he could not believe that it was serious. On this occasion the offending amendment was withdrawn. But Willie's negotiations behind the scenes were less successful over defence policy. In October 1991 he criticised plans to reorganise several regiments, which would deprive the Scots Guards of one battalion as well as merging other units. He had known in August 1991 that he would have to make his misgivings public, and he quietly resigned as Deputy Leader of the party. Most people had forgotten that he still held this position, but the resignation was a typically honourable action on Willie's part. A lesser man would have timed the announcement to ensure the widest publicity for his views; instead, two months before the defence debate, Willie simply explained away his decision by saying that the position was pretty meaningless anyway.[35]

Certainly the *Sun* had correctly reported Willie's views on rail privatisation; his grandfather, who had run one of the original independent companies, would have endorsed his opposition to the break-up of British Rail. But Willie was not interested in building up a new reputation for futile dissent, and by the beginning of 1994 he could still boast that he had never actually voted against any Conservative legislation. A more serious test of loyalty was about to emerge. Sensing that a tough line on law and order might appease some of his right-wing critics, Major encouraged successive Home Secretaries to challenge the liberal 'consensus' that Willie had protected, notwithstanding his own 'short, sharp shock'. A Police and Magistrate's Court Bill came up for its second reading on 19 January 1994. In the debate Willie attacked a provision that allowed the Home Secretary to appoint the salaried chairmen of local police authorities. The bill was also criticised by Carr and Callaghan, both former Home Secretaries, and by the Lord Chief Justice. Willie carefully drew attention to the feelings of Carr and Callaghan: 'We may, of course, as a body be wrong. We may as a body be silly, but we have kept the tradition of our country in [independent] police services over many years which I think should be recognised as being right.' It was a familiar form of words for the Willie-watchers. As William Rees-Mogg put it, 'The thunderbolt of meaning emerges out of a cloud of syntax.'[36]

The right-wing press had not been prominent defenders of local authorities of any kind since 1979. But the government's critics wanted blood, and now they would attack on any issue. Rees-Mogg argued that ministers should apply 'the Whitelaw test' to all of their policies: 'if it will not wash with Willie, it will not wash at all'. This did not stop Rees-Mogg suggesting that Major should listen more carefully to the extreme Euro-sceptic case, which had no chance at all of 'washing with Willie'. But Willie himself was not concerned to inspect the credentials of his allies, so long as the government retreated from its centralising course. His speech had concentrated minds in Whitehall; as one source put it, there was 'No one worse to have against you. It's unpleasant and nasty.' The current Home Secretary, Michael Howard, had initially rebuffed Willie, claiming that the objectionable new powers were 'essential' to the legislation. Willie had then visited Major, who had refused to intervene despite Willie's warning that he would have to make his views public. Now Howard bowed to the inevitable, sending Willie a copy of his revised proposals on 25 January. In his reply, Willie promised that he would support the amended bill, but warned that his advocacy might not win the day in the face of a 'head of steam' in the Lords against remaining proposals that would still increase the Home Secretary's powers of patronage. It was an excellent example of plain dealing, based on an intimate knowledge of the way the Lords operated; the only shame from Willie's point of view was that the Upper House had been presented with such a flawed piece of legislation in the first place.[37]

To Willie's former admirers among the 'wets' it was ironic that the man they had looked to for support against 'Thatcherism' had finally taken up the cudgels against a Prime Minister who genuinely wanted 'a nation at ease with itself'. But in John Major this worthy aspiration was not matched by a strategy to repair the social damage of the preceding decade. In this sense, at least, Willie had been right to throw his weight behind Hurd in the leadership contest, on the grounds that Major needed more time. During his rapid rise through the ranks there had been no opportunity for him to examine the impact of Thatcherism, let alone develop a distinctive philosophy of his own. Without real direction from the top, ministers like Howard tried to raise their standing in the Conservative Party with measures that either centralised administrative power, increased the scope of the 'free market', or both – possibly in the expectation that they would be promoted to better things before the impact of their changes was felt. As a result, the overall approach of the Major Governments could be described as 'Thatcherism on auto-pilot'.

Even so, the main reason for Willie's new readiness to criticise was the change in his perspective. The most telling evidence here is his 1993 comment about 'too many difficult young men' in the party. These had not appeared overnight; but he only seemed to notice them once he had left the government. During the 1992 general election he was so outraged by racist comments made by the MP Nicholas Fairbairn that he cancelled a campaigning visit to his constituency. Yet Fairbairn had been an MP since October 1974, and had actually been Solicitor-General for Scotland until quite recently. While he was Home Secretary Willie had been exposed to several very troublesome characters; but Ivor Stanbrook et al. were not exactly 'young'. As Leader of the Lords he had regularly dined with Tory MPs to keep in touch with the mood. But during that period the government rarely had much difficulty with its backbenchers; the most spectacular revolt, against Keith Joseph's plans to replace student grants with loans, was a self-inflicted 'banana skin' which Willie had been unable to prevent in difficult negotiations over the education budget.

Even in his relative detachment as a retired Leader of the Lords, Willie could never quite bring himself to accept that the advent of the 'difficult young men' was a direct consequence of Mrs Thatcher's leadership victory in 1975. The party was no longer a natural home for people who shared his own outlook – a group that was declining anyway, for other reasons. For the new generation of MPs, Willie's idol Stanley Baldwin was either an appeaser or an irrelevance; nor would they genuflect at the name of Alec Home. Their preferred model was the crusading style of Margaret Thatcher; and when the remnants of the 'old guard' collaborated with electoral opportunists in securing her removal, these MPs were unlikely to forgive. Euro-scepticism provided them with an ideal rallying cry; although Mrs Thatcher herself had signed the 1986 Single European Act which paved the way for further integration, the issue had played a significant role in her downfall and could serve as a replacement for the old Cold War categories, which had allowed right-wingers to ask, 'Are you one of us?'

The interviews Willie gave for this book were conducted in the closing months of the Major Government. Determined to shun the possibility that the Conservative Party was finished as an institution, Willie persisted in blaming specific individuals for mounting chaos. Despite his experience at the hands of the *Sun*, he confirmed that the Major Government was the worst he had ever known; the BSE crisis (which affected so many of his friends, although he had disposed of his own valuable herd) was 'the worst political disaster I've ever experienced'. He revealed that he had asked a former ministerial colleague if he intended to stand for the Commons again in 1997. 'You must be mad,' was the reply, 'I don't want anything to do with this lot, and hope I'll never see them again.' Elsewhere Willie was less eloquent, but he only needed a couple of words to convey his feelings. Tristan Garel-Jones last saw him in a Westminster lobby when things were particularly bad for the government. 'Well, Willie, how do you think it's all going?' he asked brightly. Willie shook his head sadly. 'Oh dear. Oh dear. Oh dear,' he muttered. Garel-Jones watched him walk away; Willie was still shaking his head as he disappeared down one of the corridors he had paced so often.[38]

Willie had been among the first senior Tories to offer public praise to Tony Blair and Gordon Brown, warning an audience of Young Conservatives in February 1989 that the modernising duo were 'becoming a little dangerous'. After the 1997 general election – which fully verified Robert Carr's prophecy – there was a further setback for Willie, when Kenneth Clarke, the candidate he backed, failed in his bid to succeed John Major. He hardly knew William Hague, who had joined the Commons, and then the Cabinet, after Willie had departed from both. Having been Chief Whip on the last occasion that his party was faced by a Labour government with a large, disheartening majority, Willie's age should not have deterred the new leader from consulting him on a regular basis; and Hague showed that he was happy to call in experienced hands who posed no threat to his own position when he appointed Lord Parkinson as his first Party Chairman. Just conceivably, Willie might have helped to avert the furore over Cranborne's resignation. By now, though, the impassable obstacle was his deteriorating health, and this spared him from what would have been a thankless task.[39]

There was little political news to cheer Willie in his last decade, but at least he had more time for genuine relaxation. He developed an obsession with televised snooker – only golf on another channel could drag him away from it. When neither of those athletic spectacles was available, he went for long walks in all weathers. This exercise, combined with a strict daily ration of only two glasses of champagne brought his weight under control. But there were constant interruptions, not just from his regular attendance at the Lords but also from his work for dozens of charities. Society might have changed beyond recognition since his grandfather's day; but Willie was determined to persevere in the role he had been born to. He was a vigorous fund-raiser for local organisations, and he patronised institutions such as the National Portrait Gallery (where he and Celia held a memorable party to mark their fiftieth wedding anniversary in 1993). His period as Home Secretary was reflected in his association with groups offering support to victims of crime and to injured policemen; he helped several railway preservation societies; and for ten years he was President of the British and International Golf Greenkeepers Association, a body that enjoyed his special affection. Another golfing role which gave him great pleasure was the Presidency of the Nairn club; the only pity was that he did not live to see the Walker Cup played on his favourite course. He was always in great demand for after-dinner speeches; he must have hoped that no one would ever hear him more than once because he relied rather heavily on a limited stock of jokes. But Willie had never thought of himself as an orator. The real value of his speeches came from his obvious integrity. As Charles Moore commented after reading Willie's paean to loyalty, delivered at Glenalmond School on the day after the Fagan break-in, 'It comes straight from a heart free from egotism and rancour. It is the speech of a Tory Englishman, the more eloquent because it is not always lucid.'[40]

Willie himself considered that he had been blessed with great good fortune throughout his life. Just before Mrs Thatcher's fall the 'Tory Englishman' had been offered the highest honour available to a Scot – the Order of the Thistle. When he received this award at St Giles' Cathedral, the scene of his marriage nearly half a century before, the only thought that marred his happiness was the fact that the death of an old friend, 'Chips' Maclean, had created the vacancy for him. The lonely boy on the beach at Nairn had certainly come a long way. But he had made his own luck; the real key to his success – apart from having met and married someone who suited him so perfectly – was having a temperament that allowed him to ride out the storms which he had encountered through his own choice. In any case, Willie's brief brush with the Classics at Winchester ought to have left him with the knowledge that no man can safely reflect on a happy life until he is on his deathbed.

In November 1996 Willie was driving back from Silloth Golf Club when his Range Rover was in collision with a BMW. Willie was technically at fault, having crossed a junction without noticing the oncoming vehicle. But he had been distracted by a low sun, which made driving difficult for everyone in the area that day. The occupants of the BMW survived, but had to be cut free from the wreckage. Willie himself was trapped upside down in the driver's seat. He was taken to hospital, but quickly discharged.

Willie's family believe that he was never the same again after the accident, which resulted in a fine. Not only was he very badly shaken, but as with his shooting mishap he could blame himself for causing physical injuries, which could have resulted in something even more serious. But nothing could stop him from contributing his mite to the Conservative cause, and before the general election of May 1997 he campaigned in southern Scotland. However, there were no set-piece speeches – just a final walk to meet the voters. Until October 1997 he continued to appear in the Lords, but he was clearly no longer the man he had been and his condition caused increasing sorrow to his friends. At the end of that year he fell on the stairs at Ennim, and after that there could be no more of the rounds of golf he had been enjoying with Celia. By the summer of 1999 he was under constant medical care; a series of strokes gradually eroded his faculties. He could still walk and speak, but made little sense; although there were occasional signs of frustration, for the most part his face was lit by something like his old benevolent smile when visitors arrived. The occasional glass of white wine that enlivened his spartan diet would be greeted even more warmly. But his sharpest moments came when Celia took him for drives around his much-loved Cumbrian countryside; on those occasions he was always ready with directions.

The nature of the illness was a particularly cruel fate for a man who had won so much admiration for his sound judgement. But just before illness shut his senses, his reputation was attacked in a way that was entirely unexpected. A middle-aged man living near Glasgow claimed to be Willie's secret son. At the time of Willie's death the family thought the allegation had died away without publicity; but within a few days of his funeral the press had been alerted, carrying pictures of the man, who bore a superficial similarity to Willie. His mother, apparently, had never divulged the identity of her lover; and she had lived on the Gartshore estate. These romantic details hardly counted as evidence, against the fact that the Whitelaws had moved away from Gartshore a few years before the child was conceived.[41]

Willie passed away quietly, at home in his beloved Cumbria, on 1 July 1999 – three days after his eighty-first birthday. He was buried in the beautiful churchyard of Dacre, where he had been a faithful parishioner despite his time-consuming political duties. Two memorial services were held. Both Sir Edward Heath and Lady Thatcher attended the gathering at Carlisle Cathedral; at least in death Willie had managed to bring under the same roof the leaders he had served so well. At the Guards' Chapel on Birdcage Walk in London, Carrington and Major both gave addresses, while Michael Bonnalack of the Royal and Ancient and Sir Brian Hayes, formerly of the Metropolitan Police, provided several characteristic anecdotes. The service was conducted with great dignity by Robert Runcie, who was mortally ill himself.

None of the speakers on that day referred to Enoch Powell's famous dictum that 'all political lives, unless they are cut off in midstream at a happy juncture, end in failure, because that is the nature of politics and human affairs'.[42] Perhaps it would have been inappropriate to refer to Powell, who had never been a favourite with Willie. But it was a sentiment that chimed in with Willie's own sceptical conservatism; and in a final reckoning it is tempting to apply it to the latter's own career. Far from being cut short in mid-stream, he had been just short of three-score and ten when he retired. From his own point of view, he had succeeded well beyond his original hopes. Unlike most politicians, whose ambitions grow as they ascend the ladder, he had been more than content with the deputy's role. And he had done more than anyone else to secure his primary objective – to keep his party together. Even he could not entirely overlook the symptoms of decay in January 1988. But to say that he had 'failed' when he had contributed so much to the cause would be to reduce Powell's rule to a mere truism.

But if Willie Whitelaw's political career gives the lie to Powell's pessimism, he had been an unusual politician from the outset and by the time of his death he could almost be regarded as the type of exception which proves the rule after all. Had Willie Whitelaw been struck down nearer his prime – if the surprise attack at St Margaret's had felled him, perhaps – those who attended the London service would have marked the loss of a unique individual, and a great servant to both party and country. As it was, the presence of Lord Runcie, and others of a fading generation, provoked thoughts that made it difficult to grieve for Willie alone. More than is usual on these occasions, there was a sense of something missing. It was painfully clear on that day that Willie had been the last of his kind, and that his passing had left a hole too big for anyone to fill. He had loved the Guards, and the other institutions that were represented in the distinguished audience; he would have roared with laughter at the funny stories in the speeches. But it was too late even to mourn for the values that had guided a truly 'splendid' career.

Introduction

1   *Sun*, 29 January 1989.
2   WW, *The Whitelaw Memoirs* (Aurum Press, 1989), 261–5; hereafter referred to as *Memoirs*.
3   Ibid., 262.
4   Interview with Lord Whitelaw.
5   *Spectator*, 15 January 1983.
6   Ibid.
7   Interviews with Major Charles Farrell and Sir Fraser Noble.

Chapter 1   An Orphan of the Great War

1   Contemporary newspaper report, reprinted in Mrs Frank Russell, *Fragments of Auld Lang Syne* (Hutchinson, no date), 308. The epic painting was by Thomas Henty; Rudyard Kipling was among the poets who celebrated the heroism of Ensign Russell.
2   WW, *Memoirs*, 1.
3   Speech at Glenalmond School, reprinted in the *Spectator*, 15 January 1983.
4   Paul Langford, *Public Life and the Propertied Englishman 1689–1798* (Clarendon Press, 1991), 288–97.
5   WW, interview for 'The Thatcher Factor', LSE archives, 06/8; interview with Petronella Wyatt, *Daily Telegraph*, 17 May 1996; WW, *Memoirs*, 2.
6   David Cannadine, *The Decline and Fall of the British Aristocracy* (Papermac ed., 1990), 83.
7   Information taken from H. Vincent Whitelaw, *The House of Whitelaw* (Jackson, Wylie & Co, 1928), and from correspondence with Stella

Thomas, a relative of the family. Although the precise family connection has not been established, a milk jug that belonged to the stool-hurling Jenny Geddes has been passed down to Mrs Thomas.

8   H. Vincent Whitelaw, op. cit., 130–1. WW, *Memoirs*, 33–4.

9   *The Times* obituary, 21 January 1946; Tom Stacey and R. St Oswald, *Here Come the Tories* (Tom Stacey, 1970), 68; interview with Lord Whitelaw; *The Times*, 12 June 1895; *Daily Review*, 15 January 1875; George Earl Buckle, *The Life of Benjamin Disraeli, Earl of Beaconsfield*, vol. V (John Murray, 1920), 362.

10   Robert Blake, *Disraeli* (Eyre & Spottiswoode, 1966), 126. The police prevented the duel from taking place.

11   Mrs Russell, op. cit., 35, 114. The Baillies (and Willie Whitelaw) were thus related to the family who founded Balliol College, Oxford.

12   Richard Faber, *Young England* (Faber & Faber, 1987), 11. For Smythe's social ideas, see John Morrow (ed.), *Young England: The New Generation* (Leicester University Press, 1999).

13   Quoted in Blake, op. cit., 170.

14   WW, *Memoirs*, 42–3.

15   *Don Juan*, 1st Canto, XXXVII.

16   Information from scrap books in possession of the Whitelaw family, interview with Lady Caroline Gilmour; *Sunday Telegraph*, 19 June 1983.

17   See Lucy Iremonger, *The Fiery Chariot: A Study of Prime Ministers and the Search for Love* (Secker & Warburg, 1970). Among those who lost their fathers before they reached maturity were Canning, Wellington, Peel, Rosebery and Lloyd George.

18   Interview with Lord Campbell of Croy.

19   Various untraced newspaper cuttings in the Whitelaw scrapbooks; Cecil King, *Diary 1965–1970* (Jonathan Cape, 1972), 257; Jack Page, *A Page at a Time* (Wilton 65, 2000), 158.

20   Private information.

21   Interview with Sir Fraser and Lady Noble.

22   Margach in Stacey and St Oswald, op. cit., 68; *Daily Telegraph*, 17 May 1996.

23   WW, *Memoirs*, 2.

24   Speech at Glenalmond School, *Spectator*, 15 January 1983.

25   WW in *The House Magazine*, 25 July 1988, 10.

26   Noel Annan, *Our Age: The Generation that Made Post-War Britain* (Fontana ed., 1991), 50; Anthony Sampson, *Anatomy of Britain Today* (Hodder & Stoughton, 1965), 202. Among the Wykehamists who were prominent Conservatives during Whitelaw's career were Sir David Eccles (Minister

of Education from 1959 to 1962 and Willie's Cabinet colleague as Minister of Arts in the Heath Government), Mrs Thatcher's best-known PPS, Ian Gow, and her long-serving Secretary of State for Scotland (and later for Defence), George Younger. Tellingly, Eccles was nicknamed 'Smarty Boots' by his fellow Conservatives.

27 Information kindly supplied by David Wilson, *Evening Standard*, 17 October 1967.

28 WW, *Memoirs*, 5–6.

29 Undated cutting [1936?] in Whitelaw Scrapbook I.

30 WW, *Memoirs*, 4; letter to the authors from Sir Carol Mather.

31 WW, *Memoirs*, 6; interviews with Lord Aldington and David Wilson (both of whom protested when the memoirs were published).

32 Interview with Sir Fraser Noble; *Evening News and Star*, 24 January 1994; WW, *Memoirs*, 21–2.

33 Various unsourced newspaper cuttings in Whitelaw scrapbooks; *Daily Telegraph*, 6 May 1991.

34 Various undated cuttings in the Whitelaw scrapbooks; *Glasgow Herald*, 1 December 1964; *Daily Telegraph*, 6 May 1991; Ian Nalder, *Pride in the Pedigree: The Story of Nairn Golf Club and Tales of the Famous Who Came to Play* (Gopher Publishers, 2001).

35 Information supplied by David Wilson.

36 *Sunday Telegraph*, 21 June 1970; Henry Pelling, *Social Geography of British Elections 1885–1910* (Macmillan, 1967), 390–1.

37 WW, *Memoirs*, 8.

Chapter 2   'Never Look Back . . .'

1 Hansard, vol. 570, cols 326–7, 14 May 1957.

2 WW, *Memoirs*, 11.

3 Ibid., 12; interviews with Majors Peter Balfour and Charles Farrell; Rev. George Reid, MC, to WW, 20 June 1983, Whitelaw Papers.

4 Christopher Martin-Jenkins and Pat Gibson (eds), *Summers will never be the same: A Tribute to Brian Johnston* (Partridge Press, 1994), 20–1; Tim Heald, *Brian Johnston: The Authorised Biography* (Methuen, 1995), 73–4; cf. William Douglas-Home, *Old Men Remember* (Collins & Brown, 1991), 160–1. Willie's military service records cast another faint shadow on the story. His performance on the Bovington course earned the remark 'satisfactory' from his commanding officer, Sidney Cuthbert. Admittedly this was a come-down from his previous course, in which he had 'qualified with distinction'; but it seems that he did better at Bovington than on his next course, at Stafford, after which Cuthbert

could only bring himself to write 'attended' (service book in possession of the Whitelaw family).

5   Charles Farrell, *Reflections 1939–1945: A Scots Guards Officer in Training and War* (Pentland Press, 2000), 41–2, 55; Jeremy Paxman, *Friends in High Places: Who Runs Britain?* (Penguin ed., 1991), 82.

6   Patrick Forbes, *6th Guards Tank Brigade: The Story of Guardsmen in Churchill Tanks* (Sampson Low, Marston & Co., no date), 17.

7   WW, *Memoirs*, 14.

8   Ibid., 15.

9   Ibid.

10 Interview with Major Charles Farrell.

11 WW, *Memoirs*, 16.

12 Ibid.

13 Interview with Lord Runcie.

14 Private information.

15 Farrell, op. cit., 55–7, 129; Farrell, obituary of WW in *Scots Guards Magazine*.

16 Woodrow Wyatt, *The Journals of Woodrow Wyatt*, Vol. One (Pan ed., 1999), 98.

17 WW, *Memoirs*, 17.

18 Ibid., 17–18.

19 Ibid., 18–19; Kenneth O. Morgan, *Labour in Power 1945–1951* (Clarendon Press, 1984), 208; interview with Lord Merlyn-Rees.

20 WW, *Memoirs*, 31.

21 Private information.

Chapter 3   A Gentleman in Politics

1   Interview with Lord Whitelaw.

2   Unsourced newspaper cuttings in Whitelaw scrapbooks; *Nairnshire Telegraph*, 16 August 1949.

3   *Sunday Telegraph*, 21 June 1970; WW, *Memoirs*, 43.

4   WW, *Memoirs*, 34.

5   See his speech as President of the Institute of Transport, reported in *The Times*, 10 October 1933. Willie Whitelaw senior hoped, however, that there would be no political interference with the management of a nationalised railway.

6   WW, *Memoirs*, 36.

7   Unsourced newspaper cuttings in Whitelaw scrapbook.

8   James Stuart, *Within the Fringe* (Bodley Head, 1967), 153.

9   Unsourced newspaper cuttings in Whitelaw scrapbook.

10 In an interview for this book Willie suggested that James Stuart wanted him as his successor at Moray and Nairn, but Stuart did not step down until 1959. Ironically, Gordon Campbell, who succeeded Stuart in the seat, did become Secretary of State for Scotland in 1970.

11 See *Dictionary of National Biography* entry for Sir James Graham, who is described as a typical patrician: 'he was convinced that he was one of the class who had the right to govern England'.

12 Letter of 25 May 1954 in CCO 1/10/45, Conservative Party Archive (CPA), Bodleian Library.

13 Stuart Ball (ed.), *Parliament and Politics in the Age of Churchill and Attlee: The Headlam Diaries 1935–1951* (Royal Historical Society, 1999), 311.

14 Private information; Fetherstonehaugh to Hare, 27 June 1954, CCO 1/10/45, CPA, Bodleian Library.

15 Unsourced newspaper cuttings in Whitelaw scrapbook.

16 Letter of 24 September 1953, in CCO 1/10/45, CPA, Bodleian Library.

17 WW, *Memoirs*, 40.

18 Ibid., 39–40.

19 Unsourced newspaper cuttings in Whitelaw scrapbook.

20 Unsourced newspaper cuttings in Whitelaw scrapbook.

21 Unsourced newspaper cuttings in Whitelaw scrapbook.

22 Ibid., 41.

Chapter 4   In and Out of Office

1 Interview with Lord Whitelaw. Unsourced newspaper cuttings in Whitelaw scrapbooks.

2 *Newcastle Journal*, 20 June 1955.

3 Interview with Lord Whitelaw; Hansard, vol. 545, cols. 423–6, 27 October 1955.

4 Stuart, *Within the Fringe*, 179.

5 WW, *Memoirs*, 42–3.

6 Ibid., 43.

7 Unsourced newspaper cuttings in Whitelaw scrapbook.

8 CAB CC (58) 3, 5 January 1958, PRO.

9 WW to Powell, 7 January 1958, quoted in Simon Heffer, *Like the Roman: The Life of Enoch Powell* (Weidenfeld & Nicolson, 1998), 237; interview with Lord Whitelaw.

10 *Daily Telegraph*, 1 August 1958.

11 Peter Rawlinson, *A Price Too High: An Autobiography* (Weidenfeld & Nicolson, 1989), 131; *The Times*, 21 October 1968.

12 Interview with Sir Robin Chichester-Clark.

13   Hansard, vol. 582, cols 652–8, 13 February 1958.
14   Letter from C.A.J. Norton, 14 April 1958, CCO 1/12/44, CPA, Bodleian Library.
15   Correspondence in Whitelaw scrapbooks.
16   Unsourced newspaper cuttings in Whitelaw scrapbooks.
17   Unsourced newspaper cuttings in Whitelaw scrapbooks; campaign notes in Whitelaw papers.
18   WW in *The House Magazine*, 25 July 1988, 10.
19   Hansard, vol. 663, col. 28, 30 July 1962; Official Report of Standing Committee on Offices, Shops and Railway Premises Bill, 12th sitting, 7 February 1963, col.538.
20   Private information.
21   Lord Rodgers, tribute to the late Lord Whitelaw, *House of Lords Debates*, vol. 603, col. 423, 1 July 1999.
22   John Hare to WW, 21 October 1963; Jo Godber to WW, 20 October 1964 (correspondence in possession of the Whitelaw family); Hansard, vol. 667, cols 672–84, 15 November 1962; *Manchester Guardian*, 12 March 1963.
23   WW, *Memoirs*, 46.
24   Report of Parliamentary delegation to Soviet Union, 1964, in Whitelaw papers.
25   Correspondence and unsourced newspaper cuttings in Whitelaw scrapbooks.
26   D.R. Thorpe, *Alec Douglas-Home* (Sinclair-Stevenson, 1997), 68; WW interviewed by Michael Wolff in *Crossbow*, July–September 1965, 45–6.

Chapter 5   'A Tower of Strength'

1   Private information.
2   WW, *Memoirs*, 35; information from Lord Pym's privately printed *Sentimental Journey: Tracing an Outline of Family History* (1998); interview with Lord Pym.
3   Ian Aitken in the *Guardian*, 5 May 1965; interview with Sir Jack Page; Philip Goodhart, *The 1922: The Story of the Conservative Backbenchers' Parliamentary Committee* (Macmillan, 1973), 200.
4   WW interviewed by Michael Wolff in *Crossbow*, July–September 1965, 45–6; Lord Weatherill, tribute to the late Lord Whitelaw, *House of Lords Debates*, vol. 603, col. 424, 1 July 1999.
5   Edward Short, *Whip to Wilson: The Crucial Years of Labour Government* (Macdonald, 1989), 109, 139, 268.
6   *Sunday Times*, 11 July 1965.
7   Private information; Lord Weatherill, *House of Lords Debates,* vol. 603, col. 424, I July 1999; WW, *Memoirs*, 119; *Sunday Times*, 11 July 1965;

Andrew Roth, *Heath and the Heathmen* (Routledge & Kegan Paul, 1972), 183.

8   Hansard, vol. 715, cols 1809–10, 8 July 1965; Short, op. cit., 135–6.

9   *Crossbow*, July–September 1965, 45.

10   Home to WW, 20 February 1965 (in possession of the Whitelaw family); Kenneth Young, *Sir Alec Douglas-Home* (J.M. Dent, 1970), 225.

11   Private information.

12   Young, op. cit., 230; interview with Lord Gilmour.

13   WW to Swinton, 1 July 1965, Swinton Papers, SWIN I, 7/12, Churchill College archive; Nigel Fisher, *The Tory Leaders: Their Struggle for Power* (Weidenfeld & Nicolson, 1977), 121; Home quoted in James Margach, *The Abuse of Power* (W.H. Allen, 1978), 135; WW, Nuffield College interview, 24 May 1966; cf. for example, John Ramsden (*The Winds of Change: Macmillan to Heath, 1957–1975*, Longman, 1996, 236), who records that Whitelaw and du Cann urged Home to 'stand firm'.

14   Private information.

15   Letters in possession of the Whitelaw family; WW, *Memoirs*, 53–5; Nuffield College interview, 24 May 1966. The only suggestion that, after all, the Homes might have continued to resent Willie is the surprising fact that he is not mentioned at all in the ex-Prime Minister's memoirs.

16   WW, Nuffield College interview, 24 May 1966.

17   Robert Shepherd, *Iain Macleod* (Hutchinson, 1994), 403; interview with Sir Robin Chichester-Clark; Sarah Curtis (ed.), *The Journals of Woodrow Wyatt*, vol. 1 (Pan ed., 1999), 652.

18   Patrick Cosgrave, *Margaret Thatcher: Prime Minister* (Arrow ed., 1979), 38–9.

19   WW, Nuffield college interview, 1 May 1967.

20   Lord Carrington, *Reflect on Things Past* (Fontana ed., 1989), 192; interview with Lord Carrington.

21   Margaret Laing, *Edward Heath: Prime Minister* (Sidgwick & Jackson, 1972), 119.

22   WW, speech at Glenalmond School, quoted in the *Spectator*, 15 January 1983.

23   Willie immediately regretted this remark; see WW to Swinton, 17 October 1967, Swinton Papers, SWIN I, 9/16, Churchill College archives; *Evening Standard*, 17 October 1967.

24   Donald McLachlan in the *Sunday Telegraph*, 21 June 1970.

25   Jim Prior, *A Balance of Power* (Hamish Hamilton, 1986), 42; Earl Swinton to WW, 4 April 1966, Swinton Papers, SWIN I, 7/12, Churchill College archive.

26   Short, op. cit., 191.

27   WW, *Memoirs*, 60.

28   Nigel Fisher, *Iain Macleod* (André Deutsch, 1973), 276; Andrew Alexander and Alan Watkins, *The Making of the Prime Minister 1970* (Macdonald, 1970), 94; interview with Lord Jenkin. Humphry Berkeley depicted a Chief Whip on the verge of a breakdown: 'At one point he had a physical spasm of shivering and trembling which brought him close to physical collapse.' Only Berkeley seems to have interpreted Whitelaw's behaviour at this time in this way, and since his disagreement with the party leadership was irreconcilable, it may be that his account was a reflection of his own feelings rather than an accurate diagnosis of the Chief Whip's mental and physical health. See Humphry Berkeley, *Crossing the Floor* (Allen & Unwin, 1972), 112.

29   Lord Denham, tribute to the late Lord Whitelaw, *House of Lords Debates*, vol. 603, col. 424, 1 July 1999; private information; letter to authors from Liz Huckle.

30   Short, op. cit., 207.

31   WW, *Memoirs*, 60; *Daily Telegraph*, 13 February 1966; Berkeley, op. cit., 116; interview with Lord Biffen.

32   Ramsden, op. cit., 261.

33   WW, Nuffield college interview, 24 March 1966.

34   Prior, op. cit., 39; interview with Lord Biffen.

35   Interview with Lord Jopling.

36   Richard Crossman, *The Diaries of a Cabinet Minister: Volume Two, Lord President of the Council and Leader of the House of Commons 1966–68* (Hamish Hamilton and Jonathan Cape, 1978), 625, 283–4, 292.

37   Richard Crossman, *The Diaries of a Cabinet Minister: Volume Three, Secretary of State for Social Services 1968–70* (Hamish Hamilton and Jonathan Cape, 1977), 104, 109. In fact the source of the leak was a member of Wilson's 'kitchen cabinet', who briefed Ian Aitken.

38   Ibid., 396.

39   Carrington, op. cit., 214.

40   George Hutchinson, *Edward Heath: A Personal and Political Biography* (Longman, 1970), 171.

41   Heath to WW, 30 December 1967; letter in the possession of the Whitelaw family.

42   WW to Swinton, 15 April 1968, Swinton Papers, SWIN I, 7/17, Churchill College archives.

43   Powell's speech reprinted in full in Humphry Berkeley, *The Odyssey of Enoch: A Political Memoir* (Hamish Hamilton, 1977), 129–37.

44   WW, *Memoirs*, 64; interview with Lord Whitelaw.

45   Shepherd, op. cit., 500, 325; WW, *Memoirs*, 64–5; Edward Heath, *The Course of My Life* (Hodder & Stoughton, 1998), 293.

46   Ironically, when writing his memoir the former Chief Whip stated that Boyle had voted with the government – a common error in accounts of Boyle's conduct at this time; see WW, *Memoirs*, 65.

47   *Observer*, 25 July 1982.

48   LCC (68) 244, 19 June 1968, CPA, Bodleian Library.

49   Alexander and Watkins, op. cit., 94–6; Heffer, *Like the Roman*, 473–4; *Daily Telegraph,* 11 July 1968; T.F. Lindsay and Michael Harrington, *The Conservative Party 1918–1970* (Macmillan, 1974), 257.

50   Interview with Lord Whitelaw; Crossman, op. cit., Vol. Three, 75.

51   King, *Diary 1965–1970*, 292.

52   Prior, op. cit., 56–7; Alexander and Watkins, op.cit., 166; *The Times*, 19 December 1969.

53   King, op. cit., 213, 72, 264.

Chapter 6   'Mud – Filthy Mud'

1   Unsourced newspaper cuttings in Whitelaw scrapbook.

2   WW, *Memoirs*, 69–70; WW, Nuffield College interview, 29 July 1970; Geoffrey Tucker to WW, 23 June 1970, Whitelaw papers.

3   WW, Nuffield College interview, 29 July 1970.

4   Alexander and Watkins, *The Making of the Prime Minister 1970*, 166; David Butler and Michael Pinto-Duschinsky, *The British General Election of 1970* (Macmillan, 1971), 220.

5   WW, Nuffield College interview, 29 July 1970; Prior, *Balance of Power*, 60; Cecil King, *Diary 1970–1974* (Jonathan Cape, 1975), 21; Alexander and Watkins, op. cit., 165; Roth, *Heathmen*, 15.

6   Alexander and Watkins, op. cit., 191–2; cf. Robert Rhodes James, *Ambitions and Realities: British Politics 1964–70* (Weidenfeld & Nicolson, 1972), 246–7; WW, Nuffield College interviews, 29 July, 8 October 1970; *Daily Record*, 21 June 1972.

7   Heffer, *Like the Roman*, 806–7, 913 (Lady Thatcher herself is cited as the source for the dubious peerage story).

8   John Ranelagh, *Thatcher's People* (HarperCollins, 1991), 95; Thorpe, *Alec Douglas-Home*, 402–3; Heath, *The Course of My Life*, 307; interview with Lord Carrington. In his memoirs Carrington does admit that he discussed with Willie 'the ineffably depressing prospect of another Wilson government'; see *Reflect on Things Past*, 214.

9   WW, Nuffield College interview, 23 April 1970.

10   Jean Campbell in the *Evening Standard*, 12 October 1970.

11 Among those who congratulated Willie were Rab Butler, John Hare (now Lord Blakenham) and military friends, including the war hero Douglas Bader. Fred Peart and John Silkin also wrote; Silkin remarked of Willie's Cabinet posting that 'Next to being Leader of the House myself, I cannot imagine anyone I would have liked to have had it more' (letter of 23 June 1970 in the Whitelaw papers).

12 Rawlinson, *A Price too High*, 142; Heath, op. cit., 308–9; WW, *Memoirs*, 90. Douglas Hurd thought that Isserlis produced 'beer and pork pies' rather than sandwiches; if so, there might have been a little more justification for his outburst. Jim Prior remembers 'warm beer and sandwiches'. See Douglas Hurd, *An End to Promises* (Collins, 1979), 31; Prior, op. cit., 61.

13 WW, *Memoirs*, 72, 229; interview with Kenneth Clarke.

14 Hansard, vol. 803, col. 191, 3 July 1970.

15 Prior, op. cit., 78; remark of a Shadow Cabinet colleague before the 1970 election, quoted in *Here Come the Tories*, 71; 'Crossbencher' in the *Sunday Express*, 19 March 1972. Heath set up the Central Policy Review Staff (CPRS) to provide ministers with an 'early warning system' for likely pitfalls. The similarity with Whitelaw's role led members of the CPRS to use 'Mr Whitelaw's bath' as a shorthand description for forward strategic thinking. The assumption was that the bath was the most likely place for Willie to muse on possible difficulties; had they known him better, the CPRS might have referred instead to 'Mr Whitelaw's golf course'. See Tessa Blackstone and William Plowden, *Inside the Think Tank: Advising the Cabinet 1971–1983* (Mandarin ed., 1990), 39.

16 Private information.

17 *Golf Illustrated*, 29 May 1969.

18 WW, *Memoirs*, 26–7; interview with Lord Whitelaw.

19 WW, *Memoirs*, 28.

20 Michael Bonallack, address at WW's memorial service, 27 October 1999.

21 *The Times*, 1 October 1973; interview with Lady Whitelaw. But cf. John Junor's account (in *Memoirs: Listening for a Midnight Tram*, Pan ed., 1991, 187–8) in which the Japanese Foreign Secretary suddenly hits form and defeats his premier. Perhaps the reported result was a product of some diplomatic 'spinning' by the British. Tanaka was later implicated in a corruption scandal.

22 Derek Marks in the *Evening Standard*, 29 June 1971. In his memoirs Michael Heseltine records that there was talk of Whitelaw replacing Heath as leader even while the campaign was still in progress. This speculation might have arisen from the secret contingency planning

over what the party should do in the event of a defeat; if nothing else, given the availability of other Conservatives who had already held high office, the rumour is evidence of Willie's high standing within the party; see Michael Heseltine, *Life in the Jungle* (Hodder & Stoughton, 2000), 103.

23 Hansard, vol. 797, col. 765, 5 March 1970.

24 Hansard, vol. 803, cols 973–82, 9 July 1970.

25 *Sunday Express*, 19 March 1972.

26 Hansard, vol. 827, col. 1297, 8 December 1971; vol. 825, cols 949–58, 9 November 1971; Alan Watkins in the *New Statesman*, 18 December 1970; interview with Andrew Alexander.

27 Philip Norton, *Conservative Dissidents: Dissent within the Parliamentary Conservative Party 1970–74* (Temple Smith, 1978); John Boyd-Carpenter, *Way of Life* (Sidgwick & Jackson, 1980), 223–5; Hansard, vol. 801, col. 201, 12 January 1971; vol. 808, cols 1566–7, 17 December 1970.

28 King, *Diary 1965–1970*, 263, 292, *Diary 1970–1974*, 98; Alan Watkins in the *New Statesman*, 2 July 1971; Hurd, op. cit., 98. For a concise argument of the case in favour of Conservative support over *In Place of Strife*, see Prior, op. cit., 42.

29 Robert Taylor, 'The Heath Government and Industrial Relations: Myth and Reality', in Stuart Ball and Anthony Seldon (eds), *The Heath Government 1970–74* (Longman, 1996), 170.

30 *The Times*, 22 January 1971; Hansard, vol. 810, col. 46, 25 January 1971; Selwyn Lloyd, *Mr Speaker, Sir* (Jonathan Cape, 1976), 66, 69, 64.

31 *Sunday Express*, 31 January 1971.

32 John Young, 'The Heath Government and British entry into the European Community', in Ball and Seldon, op. cit., 275; WW, speech at Manchester reported in *The Times*, 30 January 1972; WW, Nuffield College interview, 27 March 1969.

33 David Owen, *Time to Declare* (Penguin ed., 1992), 181.

34 Patrick Gordon-Walker, *Political Diaries 1932–1971* (Historians' Press, 1991), 327; King, *Diary 1970–1974*, 81, 144–5; Owen, op. cit., 181.

35 One of Pym's successors considers this to have been perhaps the greatest feat of whipping in the post-war period; interview with Lord Jopling.

36 Geoffrey Howe, *Conflict of Loyalty* (Macmillan, 1994), 67–9.

37 Hansard, vol. 833, cols 1498–9, 22 March 1972.

38 Ian Gilmour, *The Body Politic* (Hutchinson, 1971 ed.), 287 note.

39 WW, Nuffield College interview, 8 October 1970; Edward du Cann, *Two Lives* (Images Publishing, 1995), 175–84.

40 Frank Stacey, *British Government 1966–1975: Years of Reform* (Oxford University Press, 1975), 28–36; interview with Lord Whitelaw.

41 King, *Diary 1965–1970*, 241; *The Times*, 22 July 1971; Donald Searing, *Westminster's World: Understanding Political Roles* (Harvard University Press, 1994), 432.

42 Lloyd, op. cit., 69–70; interview with Sir Robin Chichester-Clark; Hansard, vol. 830, cols 32–3, 31 January 1972.

Chapter 7 'Willie Whitewash'

1 WW, interview with David Butler, 19 February 1972; Hurd, *An End to Promises*, 103.

2 For these and other details see the *Sunday Times*' 'Insight' team's investigation, reprinted as *Ulster* (Penguin, 1972), esp. ch. 2.

3 King, *Diary 1965–1970*, 323; Martin Dillon and Denis Lehane, *Political Murder in Northern Ireland* (Penguin ed., 1973), 34; interview with Sir Robin Chichester-Clark.

4 CM (70), 1–3, PRO.

5 Trend memos of 21 June and 9 July 1970, PREM 15/100, PRO.

6 Hansard, vol. 822, cols 1950, 1954, 5 August 1971; Brian Faulkner, *Memoirs of a Statesman* (Weidenfeld & Nicolson, 1978), 118; John Cole, *As it Seemed to Me: Political Memoirs* (Phoenix ed., 1996), 137.

7 *Guardian*, 16 June 2001.

8 Faulkner, op. cit., 129. For Heath's acknowledgement that Maudling had to be moved, see for example King, *Diary 1970–1974*, 165 (entry for 5 January 1972).

9 WW, *Memoirs*, 82; Maudling, *Memoirs*, 188; Heath, *Course of My Life*, 436; King, *Diary 1970–1974*, 138, 144, 80; interview with Lady Whitelaw; interview with Sir Robin Chichester-Clark.

10 Faulkner, op. cit., 158, 145.

11 Ibid., 149; F.S.L. Lyons, *Ireland since the Famine* (Fontana ed., 1973), 15; Peter Taylor, *Provos: The IRA and Sinn Fein* (Bloomsbury, 1997), 135; Gerry Adams, *Before the Dawn: An Autobiography* (William Morrow, 1996), 186.

12 Taylor, op. cit., 134.

13 Paul Arthur, 'The Heath Government and Northern Ireland', in Ball and Seldon, *The Heath Government 1970–74*, 242; Ramsden, *Winds of Change*, 342.

14 Heath, op. cit., 436.

15 Maudling, op. cit., 183.

16 King, *Diary 1970–1974*, 211, 207; Patrick Mayhew to WW, 1 August 1994, Whitelaw papers.

17   Interview with Sir Robin Chichester-Clark.

18   King, *Diary 1970–1974*, 185.

19   Sean MacStiofáin, *Memoirs of a Revolutionary* (Gordon Cremonesi, 1975), 184.

20   Faulkner, op. cit., 122.

21   WW, *Memoirs*, 81–3.

22   Interviews with Lord Merlyn-Rees and Sir Robin Chichester-Clark; Crossman to WW, 24 March 1972, Whitelaw papers; King, *Diary 1970–1974*, 177.

23   Undated leter to WW from Lord Mountbatten, Whitelaw papers; interview with Keith McDowall.

24   *The Times*, 25 March 1972.

25   Interview with Lord Windlesham; King, *Diary 1970–1974*, 188, 207.

26   Robert Fisk in *The Times*, 3 December 1973; interviews with Lord Brittan and Lord Windlesham.

27   Interview with Keith McDowall; Ken Bloomfield, *Stormont in Crisis: A Memoir* (Blackstaff Press, 1994), 173.

28   Faulkner, op. cit., 79.

29   WW, *Memoirs*, 85–6, 92, 101.

30   Private information.

31   Interviews with Lord Merlyn-Rees and Lord Windlesham.

32   *The Times*, 30 March 1972; Norton, *Conservative Dissidents*, 84–6, 193–4.

33   WW, interview with Julian Norridge, *Evening Standard*, 24 April 1972.

34   Interview with Lord Howell; James Downey, *Them and Us: Britain-Ireland and the Northern Question, 1969–1982* (Ward River Press, 1983), 9.

35   King, *Diary 1970–1974*, 194–5, 214–15.

36   WW, *Memoirs*, 85.

37   Downey, op. cit., 54.

38   *The Times*, 25 March 1972.

39   Faulkner, op. cit., 123; WW, *Memoirs*, 93; Robert Fisk in *The Times*, 3 December 1973.

40   Martin Wallace, *British Government in Northern Ireland: From Devolution to Direct Rule* (David & Charles, 1982), 70–1; Adams, op. cit., 191.

41   Robert Fisk in *The Times*, 3 December 1973; *Guardian*, 10 November 1972; MacStiofáin, op. cit., 242, 246–7.

42   MacStiofáin was right about the women. When one veteran of the civil-rights campaign was asked many years later to evaluate the various Secretaries of State, she singled out Willie for praise; see Fionnuala O'Connor, *In Search of a State: Catholics in Northern Ireland* (Blackstaff Press, 1993), 200.

Chapter 8   Bad Day at Cheyne Walk

1   Ian Waller in the *Sunday Telegraph*, 28 May 1972.

2   King, *Diary 1970–1974*, 188.

3   *The Times*, 22 May 1972.

4   WW, interview with Alastair Hetherington and John Cole, 12 June 1972, LSE archives, Hetherington 11/18.

5   Heath, interview with Alastair Hetherington, 14 June 1972, LSE archives.

6   WW, *Memoirs*, 94.

7   *The Times*, 19 May 1972.

8   Steve Bruce, *The Red Hand: Protestant Paramilitaries in Northern Ireland* (Oxford University Press, 1992), 1–6, 209–10; *Private Eye*, 5 May 1972.

9   Cole, *As it Seemed to Me*, 136.

10   Simon Winchester in the *Guardian*, 22 May 2002.

11   *Observer*, 28 May 1972; General Sir Walter Walker, quoted in *The Times*, 20 May 1972.

12   King, *Diary 1970–1974*, 207–8; Paul Routledge, *John Hume* (HarperCollins, 1997), 115; *The Times*, 9 June 1972; Adams, *Before the Dawn*, 198–9; notes of interview with WW, 19 June 1973, in Andrew Roth's archive.

13   WW, speech reprinted in the *Guardian*, 17 June 1972.

14   MacStiofáin, op. cit., 268.

15   WW, *Memoirs*, 96.

16   Ibid., 98; Bruce, op. cit., 62; Adams, op. cit., 200–1.

17   This account of the Cheyne Walk meeting is based on MacStiofáin, op. cit., 280–6, Adams, op. cit., 202–5, and Tim Pat Coogan, *The IRA* (Fontana ed., 1987), 490–5; WW, interview with John Graham, *Sunday Mirror*, 1 April 1973; WW, interview with Ian Aitken.

18   Taylor, *The IRA*, 143.

19   WW, *Memoirs*, 100. In blaming the UDA for the ceasefire breakdown, Steve Bruce refers to the Cheyne Walk meeting as a decisive factor in enraging the UDA. This might be a slip, because news of the talks had yet to leak out. On the other hand, sources friendly to the UDA might have revealed the secret, and this was another consideration that Willie might have pondered over before going ahead with the meeting. See Bruce, op. cit., 63.

20   MacStiofáin, op. cit., 288–9; Taylor, op. cit., 144–5; *Sunday Times*, 16 July 1972.

21   Quoted in M.L.R. Smith, *Fighting for Ireland: The Military Strategy of the Irish Republican Movement* (Routledge, 1995), 119.

22   WW, *Memoirs*, 100.

23   John Simpson, *Strange Places, Questionable People* (Pan ed., 1999), 113; WW, *Memoirs*, 101.

24   Garret Fitzgerald, *All in a Life: An Autobiography* (Gill & Macmillan, 1991), 104; King, *Diary 1970–1974*, 215–16, 415.

25   WW, *Memoirs*, 100.

26   *The Times*, 11, 12 July 1972: Hansard, vol. 840, cols 1188–9, 10 July 1972; Wilson, record of an interview with Alastair Hetherington, 19 July 1972, LSE archives.

27   Minutes of Northern Ireland Committee, 12 July 1972, CCO CRD 3/18/1, CPA, Bodleian Library; *The Times*, 12, 14, 21 July 1972.

28   *The Times*, 22 July 1972; interview with Lord Howell; MacStiofáin, op. cit., 295–6.

29   Ibid., 297; Adams, op. cit., 208; Bloomfield, *Stormont in Crisis*, 176

30   Interview with Sir Robin Chichester-Clark; Faulkner, op. cit., 172.

31   WW, *Memoirs*, 104–5.

32   Ibid., 105; *Sunday Mirror*, 1 April 1973.

33   M.L.R. Smith, op. cit., 110; WW, *Memoirs*, 105; Adams, op. cit., 209.

34   Since the chairman of the committee was Willie's friend Bill Deedes, he must have been given a detailed account of proceedings.

35   Minutes of Northern Ireland Committee, 3 August 1972, CCO CRD 3/18/1, CPA, Bodleian Library.

36   Correspondence with Sir Ludovic Kennedy.

37   Interview with Lord Howell; King, *Diary 1970–1974*, 280, 221.

38   Robert Mark, interview with Alastair Hetherington, 2–3 March 1973, Hetherington MS 20/23, LSE archives; Simpson, op. cit., 108; WW, *Memoirs*, 79. Cf. Heath, *Course of My Life*, 437. Heath follows Willie's formula, but his book was written after a new inquiry into Bloody Sunday had been called, so he had reason to be more careful. However, unlike Willie he seemed confident that Widgery had reached the right conclusions. Typically, Reginald Maudling omits Bloody Sunday altogether. A later Secretary of State, Merlyn Rees, found that his own inquiries only led to a series of attempts to pass the buck (interview with Lord Merlyn-Rees).

Chapter 9   Hero for a Day

1   Interview with Lord Whitelaw.

2   WW, *Memoirs*, 111; King, *Diary 1970–1974*, 360. Carrington must have been even more robust in previous conversations, because King took this remark as a sign that relations were improving.

3   *Guardian*, 27 October 1972.

4   Downey, *Them and Us*, 125.

5 Speech of 14 October 1972, *Conservative Party Conference Report* (1972), 128.

6 David Wood in *The Times*, 12 October 1972; David McKie in the *Guardian*, 12 October 1972; *Daily Telegraph*, 12 October 1972.

7 Faulkner, *Memoirs of a Statesman*, 185.

8 Hansard, vol. 853, cols 1589–95, 29 March 1973; Heffer, *Like the Roman*, 666; unnamed official quoted in Arthur, 'The Heath Government and Northern Ireland', 252; *The Economist*, 24 March 1973.

9 Faulkner, op. cit., 188; King, *Diary 1970–1974*, 272; Campbell, *Heath* (Jonathan Cape, 1993), 546–7.

10 Faulkner, op. cit., 193.

11 King, *Diary 1970–1974*, 296.

12 Ibid., 296, 272; *The Times*, 23 April, 9 June 1973; Andrew Roth's note of an interview with WW, 19 June 1973.

13 WW, *Memoirs*, 176; *The Times*, 5 April, 9 August 1973.

14 Private information.

15 King, *Diary 1970–1974*, 309–10; Fitzgerald, *All in a Life*, 207–8; private information.

16 WW, *Memoirs*, 115.

17 Faulkner, op. cit., 209–10.

18 *Financial Times*, 13 October 1973.

19 Charles Moore and Simon Heffer (eds), *A Tory Seer: The Selected Journalism of T. E. Utley* (Hamish Hamilton, 1989), 256.

20 Faulkner, op. cit., 219–20.

21 Heath, *Course of My Life*, 442; WW, *Memoirs*, 118.

22 Faulkner, op. cit., 223–4; Paddy Devlin, *Straight Left: An Autobiography* (Blackstaff, 1993); WW, *Memoirs*, 116.

23 Interview with Sir Frank Cooper.

24 Devlin, op. cit., 199–200.

25 *The Times*, 3 December 1973; Bloomfield, *Stormont*, 185; Hansard, vol. 864, col. 1610, 22 November 1973.

26 WW, *Memoirs*, 119; *The Times*, 11 December 1973.

Chapter 10 . . . So Lost a Business

1 *Evening Standard*, 24 September 1973.

2 Interview with Lord Whitelaw.

3 *Evening Standard*, 24 September 1973.

4 Interview with Lord Carr.

5 Anthony Barber, *Taking the Tide: A Memoir* (Michael Russell, 1996), 91; interview with Lord Pym.

6   Robert Fisk in *The Times,* 3 December 1973.

7   C.V. Wedgwood, *Strafford* (Jonathan Cape ed., 1938), 218, 254. Contrary to a common assumption, John and Francis Pym were not blood relatives.

8   *The Times,* 8 November 1973; Howe, *Conflict of Loyalty,* 76.

9   Hurd, *Promises,* 114.

10 Campbell, *Heath,* 582.

11 King, *Diary 1970–1974, 327.*

12 WW, *Memoirs,* 123–4.

13 Ibid., interview with Lord Whitelaw.

14 Interview with Lord Whitelaw.

15 Robert Harris, *Good and Faithful Servant: The Unauthorized Biography of Bernard Ingham* (Faber & Faber, 1991 ed.), 58.

16 Interview with Lord Whitelaw.

17 '. . . And he wrote in the letter, saying, Set ye Uriah in the forefront of the hottest battle, and retire ye from him, that he may be smitten and die', II Samuel, 11:15.

18 Campbell, op. cit., 592; King, *Diary 1970–1974,* 342; Tony Benn, *Against the Tide: Diaries 1973–76* (Arrow ed., 1990), 75.

19 Interview with Lord Prior.

20 Joe Gormley, *Battered Cherub* (Hamish Hamilton, 1982), 132; Richard Clutterbuck, *Britain in Agony: The Growth of Political Violence* (Faber & Faber, 1978), 109.

21 WW, *Memoirs,* 127–8; cf. *Socialist Worker,* 22 June 1974.

22 Gormley, op. cit., 132–3.

23 Ibid., 133.

24 Campbell, op. cit., 580–2, Barber, op. cit., 91; WW, *Memoirs,* 131–2; Gormley, op. cit., 137.

25 Interview with James Douglas.

26 WW, Nuffield College interview, 21 March 1973.

27 Campbell, op. cit., 585.

28 See WW's letter to Earl Swinton, 30 July 1968: '[Heath] needs time and hates feeling he is being pushed by his advisers': Swinton Papers, SWIN I, 7/17, Churchill College archives.

29 Interview with Lord Whitelaw; Prior, *Balance of Power,* 90–2; Phillip Whitehead, *The Writing on the Wall: Britain in the Seventies* (Michael Joseph, 1985) 109.

30 Hansard, vol. 867, col. 190, 10 January 1974.

31 Interview with Lord Whitelaw.

32 Hansard, vol. 867, cols 188–90, 10 January 1974; Barbara Castle, *The Castle Diaries 1974–76* (Weidenfeld & Nicolson, 1980), 25, 27; Campbell, op. cit., 590.

33 WW, Nuffield College interview, 21 March 1974; Prior, op. cit., 93; Benn, *Against the Tide*, 104; interview with Lord Pym.

34 WW, *Memoirs*, 131.

35 WW, text of a party political broadcast, 14 February 1974; David Butler and Dennis Kavanagh, *The British General Election of February 1974* (Macmillan, 1974), 159–60.

36 Lord Home, *The Way the Wind Blows: An Autobiography* (Collins, 1976), 274; Heath, *Course of My Life*, 513–14; interview with Lord Carr.

37 WW, *Memoirs*, 133.

38 Home, op. cit., 275; Martin Holmes, *The Failure of the Heath Government* (Macmillan, 1997 ed.), 116–17; WW, interview with David Butler, 26 February 1974; *The Times*, 27 February 1974.

39 WW, Nuffield College interview, 21 March 1974.

40 Both the reporter for this story and his informant (Alan Clark and Julian Amery) disliked Willie at the time. Alan Clark, *Diaries: Into Politics* (Weidenfeld & Nicolson, 2000), 151.

41 See Alan Clark, *The Tories: Conservatives and the Nation State 1922–1997* (Phoenix ed., 1998), 439; King, *Diary 1970–1974*, 348.

42 WW, *Memoirs*, 133–4; Nuffield College interview, 23 March 1973. In retirement Willie also revealed that he had never favoured formal cooperation with the Liberals, a view that is quite consistent with his behaviour at the time; interview with Lord Whitelaw.

43 *The Times*, 22, 28 February 1974.

44 WW, *Memoirs*, 134.

Chapter 11   The Poisoned Chalice

1 WW, *Memoirs*, 121. In September 1974 the loss of Heath's yacht *Morning Cloud* also cost the life of a godson, and in December the IRA launched a bomb attack on his London home.

2 Campbell, *Heath*, 624–5.

3 Clark, *The Tories*, 436; Campbell, op. cit., 626.

4 Interview with Robert Jackson.

5 Ian Gilmour, unpublished diary, 12, 14 March 1974; *The Times*, 2, 26 March 1974; WW, interview with John Cole and Alastair Hetherington, 17 July 1974, LSE archives.

6 In fact, as John Ramsden has pointed out, there was a fairly recent precedent: in 1930 Stanley Baldwin had given the chairmanship to his most likely successor, Neville Chamberlain; see Ramsden, *Winds of Change*, 411.

7 *The Times*, 15 June 1974.

8   WW, *Memoirs*, 136–9; interview with Alastair Hetherington and John Cole, 17 July 1974.

9   Interview with Sara Morrison.

10 WW, Nuffield College interview, 25 October 1974; WW, Nuffield College interview, 22 October 1974; interview with Lord Waldegrave.

11 Sir Richard Webster, Nuffield College interview, 18 October 1974. Webster's testimony is the more important given that he had been unsettled by recent developments at Central Office and was vehemently opposed to the idea of a coalition, which was so closely associated with Willie; see Ramsden, op. cit., 412.

12 Ibid., 412–13; Minutes of Breakfast Meetings of 24 September and 5 October 1974, in the papers of Geoffrey Tucker; Chairman's Department file, CCO 20/17/51, CPA, Bodleian Library. The *Daily Mirror* was slightly more demanding, at around 1,700 words.

13 WW, Nuffield College interview, 17 September 1974; WW, *Memoirs*, 138; Julian Critchley, *A Bag of Boiled Sweets: An Autobiography* (Faber & Faber, 1994), 139; private information.

14 *Putting Britain First*, 2–4; Minutes of Leader's Consultative Committee Meeting, 26 July 1974, CPA, Bodleian Library.

15 Butler and Kavanagh, *The British General Election of October 1974*, 44. See also, for example, Campbell, op. cit., 647: 'For the second time in six months the party committed itself to a risky but potentially popular strategy, then threw away the dividend by presenting its case weakly.'

16 WW, interview with John Cole and Alastair Hetherington, 17 July 1974.

17 WW, text of speech at Alnwick Castle, 31 July 1974.

18 Butler and Kavanagh, op. cit., 117.

19 Ibid., 125.

20 William Waldegrave, Nuffield College interview, 25 October 1974; Butler and Kavanagh, op. cit., 126, 264 note.

21 Ibid., 264, 129; Nigel Fisher, *The Tory Leaders: Their Struggle for Power* (Weidenfeld & Nicolson, 1977), 146; Minutes of a tactical meeting chaired by WW, 17 September 1974, CCO 20/17/49, CPA, Bodleian Library.

22 WW, text of a speech at Dryburgh Hall, Putney, 8 October 1974; Miles Hudson's diary, 23 October 1974.

23 Butler and Kavanagh, op. cit., 264–5; WW, Nuffield College interview, 22 October 1974; Ramsden, *Winds of Change*, 429–31. Back in July Willie had urged that 'we should be a national party looking after the national interest'; text of a speech at Dover, 26 July 1974.

24 Interview with Sara Morrison; WW, *Memoirs*, 138.

25 WW, text of a speech at Upminster, Monday 7 October 1974.

26 Minutes of a breakfast meeting, 27 September 1974, Tucker papers.

27 Butler and Kavanagh, op. cit., 131; Clark, *Diaries: Into Politics*, 55–6; Clark, *The Tories*, 448 note.

28 Miles Hudson's diary, 4 October 1974.

29 Ibid.; Fraser in CCO 20/17/64, CPA, Bodleian Library.

30 WW, *Memoirs*, 139; Miles Hudson's diary, 24 September 1974; WW, Nuffield College interview, 22 October 1974; Simon Hoggart, *On the House* (Robson Books, 1981), 37–8.

31 Miles Hudson's diary, 10 October 1974.

32 WW, *Memoirs*, 139; Nuffield College interview, 22 October 1974; Butler and Kavanagh, op. cit., 136.

33 WW, *Memoirs*, 140; Butler and Kavanagh, op. cit., 136; Patrick Cosgrave, *Carrington: A Life and a Policy* (Dent, 1985), 112; Kenneth Baker, *The Turbulent Years: My Life in Politics* (Faber & Faber, 1993).

34 Miles Hudson's diary, 23 October 1974.

Chapter 12   'Alec's Revenge'

1 For example, Heath's biographer names Francis Pym as one who urged him to submit himself for re-election as quickly as possible; but Heath himself claims that Pym urged him to 'tough it out'; see Campbell, *Heath*, 656, and Heath, *Course of My Life*, 528.

2 Prior, *Balance of Power*, 98; Heath, op. cit., 528.

3 Clutterbuck, *Britain in Agony*, 123.

4 Critchley, *A Bag of Boiled Sweets*, 141–2.

5 Critchley, op. cit., 140; *Daily Telegraph*, 11 October 1974; WW, statement of 17 October 1974, CCO handout; *Sunday Express*, 27 October 1974.

6 *Sunday Express*, 20 October 1974.

7 WW, *Memoirs*, 141; Fisher, *Tory Leaders*, 154.

8 Interview with Sir Paul Bryan.

9 Heath, op. cit., 532.

10 *Sunday Express*, 15 December 1974; Fisher, op. cit., 145–9; Clark, *The Tories*, 458.

11 *The Times*, 15 October 1974; Fisher, op. cit., 155; Critchley, op. cit., 141.

12 Campbell, op. cit., 663.

13 Interview with James Douglas.

14 Fisher, op. cit., 157; Campbell, op. cit., 664.

15 Michael Heseltine, *Life in the Jungle: My Autobiography* (Hodder &

Stoughton, 2000), 164; John Campbell, *Margaret Thatcher, Volume One: The Grocer's Daughter* (Jonathan Cape, 2000), 301.

16   Prior, op. cit., 100.

17   Fisher, op. cit., 173. The present account differs slightly from Philip Cowley and Matthew Bailey's 'Peasant Uprising or Religious War? Re-examining the 1975 Conservative Leadership Contest', *British Journal of Political Science*, vol. 30, 599–629. Although the authors have produced very interesting evidence, this is open to question insofar as it relies on the distant memories of participants who proved themselves to be unreliable even at the time.

18   Interview with Michael Mates; Fisher, op. cit., 176. The 'bandwagon' explanation has been criticised by Mark Wickham-Jones in 'Right Turn: A Revisionist Account of the 1975 Conservative Party Leadership Election', *Twentieth Century British History*, vol. 8, no.1 (1997), 74–89.

19   Howe, *Conflict of Loyalty*, 91.

20   Interview with Michael Mates.

21   Patrick Cosgrave, *Margaret Thatcher: Prime Minister* (Arrow ed., 1979), 39; Fisher, op. cit., 175; Robert Shepherd, *The Power Brokers: The Tory Party and its Leaders* (Hutchinson, 1991), 19. Showing a refreshing lack of superstition, Michael Heseltine's campaign team chose the same room when he ran against Thatcher in 1990.

22   Fisher, op. cit., 173, 176; *The Times*, 5 February 1975; Nicholas Wapshott and George Brock, *Thatcher* (Futura ed., 1983), 136–8; interviews with Michael Mates and Sir Dennis Walters; Ramsden, op. cit., 452.

23   George Hurchinson in *The Times*, 1 February 1974; *The Times*, 5, 7 February 1974; *Daily Telegraph*, 1 February 1975.

24   *The Times*, 8 February 1974.

25   Campbell, *Grocer's Daughter*, 304.

26   Interview with Lord Biffen.

27   Alastair Hetherington, note of a lunch with Willie Whitelaw, 9 April 1975, LSE archives.

28   In November 1974 Willie made a speech to the Bow Group, which in those days was regarded as a leading intellectual forum for the Conservatives. Afterwards 'all agreed that his speech had been impressive, but nobody could remember precisely what he had said'; *The Times*, 6 November 1974.

29   WW, *Memoirs*, 142.

30   Hansard, vol. 883, cols 631–2, 11 December 1974; Roy Jenkins, *A Life at the Centre* (Macmillan, 1991), 401; *The Times*, 12 December 1974.

31   Minutes of the Shadow Cabinet of 6 November 1974, LCC (74) 37, CPA, Bodleian Library.

32 Ramsden, op. cit., 438.

33 Margaret Thatcher, *The Path to Power* (HarperCollins, 1995), 279.

34 Ibid.; *The Times*, 10 December 1974; Castle, *Diaries 1974–76*, 303.

35 Clutterbuck, op. cit., 142.

36 Interview with Lord Merlyn-Rees; Bruce, *Red Hand*, 98; David Howell, 'The policies which prepared the ground for trust in Ulster', *The Times*, 10 February 1975. One of the present authors bought a second-hand copy of Nigel Fisher's *The Tory Leaders*. On page 154, beside a reference to Willie's 'success in Northern Ireland', the previous owner had written 'What success?'

37 WW, interview in the *Daily Mail*, 25 January 1988.

38 WW, *Memiors*, 142; *The Times*, 6 February 1975; Fisher, op. cit., 180.

39 WW, *Memoirs*, 143.

40 Interviews with Michael Mates and Sir Dennis Walters; private information.

41 Tricia Murray, *Margaret Thatcher* (Star, 1978), 140; Ramsden, op. cit., 450; Thatcher, op. cit., 291.

42 Thatcher, op. cit., 249.

Chapter 13 'That Awful Woman'

1 Ranelagh, *Thatcher's People*, 157; Campbell, *Grocer's Daughter*, 309.

2 WW, letter to Robert Carr, 19 February 1975: letter in the possession of Lord Carr.

3 WW, *Memoirs*, 144, 262; Murray, *Margaret Thatcher*, 139; interview with John Cole. When they finally met Winnie Whitelaw forgave Mrs Thatcher for beating her son and soon became 'an immense fan' – probably recognising a kindred spirit.

4 WW, speech of 20 February 1975, CCO handout.

5 WW, speech at Shap, 3 March 1975, CCO handout.

6 Benn, *Against the Tide*, 366–7.

7 Philip Goodhart, *Full-Hearted Consent* (Davis-Poynter, 1976), 125; interview with Geoffrey Tucker.

8 Jenkins, *A Life at the Centre* (Macmillan, 1991), 416.

9 Ibid., 416, 409; David Butler and Uwe Kitzinger, *The 1975 Referendum* (Macmillan, 1976), 246–9.

10 WW, speech at Mansion House, 26 February 1975; Butler and Kitzinger, op. cit., 132; Goodhart, op. cit., 187–8.

11 WW, Nuffield College interview, 12 May 1975.

12 Almost two-thirds said that they disliked Paisley, making him almost twice as unpopular as Tony Benn, his nearest rival for the title of Britain's best-hated politician; Butler and Kitzinger, op. cit., 256.

13   Geoffrey Lewis, *Lord Hailsham* (Jonathan Cape, 1997), 326.

14   Hailsham Papers, 1/1a, Churchill College.

15   Campbell, *Grocer's Daughter*, 344; text of WW broadcast, *Birmingham Post*, 22 August 1975; Thatcher, *Path to Power*, 304; Castle, *Diaries 1974–76*, 473.

16   Lewis, op. cit., 327.

17   Hailsham to Heath, 29 July 1975, Hailsham Papers, 1/1a, Churchill College.

18   Note of a lunch with WW, 9 April 1975, Hetherington Papers, LSE archive.

19   *The Times*, 21, 28 June 1975; Thatcher, op. cit., 282–3; Heath, *Course of My Life*, 537.

20   Thatcher, op. cit., 307; Alistair McAlpine, *Once a Jolly Bagman* (Phoenix ed., 1998), 210–11.

21   Campbell, *Grocer's Daughter*, 315; WW, Nuffield College interview, 29 June 1978; WW, interview with Lynda Lee-Potter in the *Daily Mail*, 25 January 1988; private information.

22   *The Times, Daily Mail, Financial Times*, 9 October 1975.

23   *The Times, Daily Mail*, 9 October 1975.

24   Campbell, *Grocer's Daughter*, 352; Jenkins, op. cit., 426.

25   Joseph Papers, CPA, Bodleian Library, 15/1.

26   Interview with Lord Pym; Trevor Russel, *The Tory Party: Its Policies, Divisions, and Future* (Penguin ed., 1978), 124; Hailsham to Maude, 12 December 1976, Hailsham Papers, 1/2, Churchill College.

27   Campbell, *Grocer's Daughter*, 397.

28   *A Better Tomorrow* (Conservative Central Office, 1970s), 24.

29   Minutes of the Shadow Cabinet meeting of 11 April 1975, LCC (75), 57, CPA, Bodleian Library. In rejecting Joseph's suggestions that he should chair committees on parliamentary reform and public spending, Willie made the predictable suggestion that Francis Pym could do these jobs.

30   Norman Tebbit, *Upwardly Mobile* (Futura ed., 1989), 203; Neave to WW, undated letter, in possession of Whitelaw family.

31   Peter Hennessy, *Whitehall* (Fontana ed., 1990), 28.

32   *Guardian*, 4 February 1978.

33   *Guardian*, 20 January 1978; *Sunday Times*, 5 February 1978.

34   *Express & News*, 4 March 1977; Roy Jenkins, *European Diary 1977–1981* (Collins, 1989), 215; Campbell, *Grocer's Daughter*, 399–400; *Sunday Times*, 5 February 1978.

35   *The Right Approach* (CCO, 1976), 47–8; Advisory Committee on Policy, minutes of a meeting held on 12 January 1977, ACP (77) 148, CPA, Bodleian Library.

36 *Sunday Times*, 5 February 1978; WW, speech at Loughborough University, 3 February 1978, CCO handout; *Guardian*, 4 February 1978.

37 *Express & News*, 4 March 1977; *The Times*, 8 April 1978.

38 *The Times*, 24, 28 July 1978; *Birmingham Post*, 8 July 1978; interview with Kenneth Clarke.

39 *Guardian*, 7 March 1979; *Observer*, 25 February 1979. For Clark, Budgen and Stanbrook, see Philip Norton, *Dissension in the House of Commons 1974–1979* (Clarendon Press, 1980); interview with Sir Roger Sims; *Observer*, 17 July 1977; interview with Andrew Alexander.

40 WW, speech at Conservative Party Conference, 13 October 1977, CCO handout.

41 WW, speech at Conservative Party Conference, 11 October 1978, CCO handout; *Daily Mail*, 12 October 1978; *Guardian*, 20 June 1978.

42 Thatcher, op. cit., 403; Campbell, *Grocer's Daughter*, 390.

43 Interview with Lord Gilmour; WW, Nuffield College interview, 29 June 1978; note of 6 October 1977, Hailsham Papers, 1/3, Churchill College.

44 Patrick Hutber (ed.), *What's Wrong With Britain?* (Sphere ed., 1978), 7–9, 41–6.

45 Alan Watkins in the *Observer*, 7 July 1985; John Hoskyns, *Just in Time: Inside the Thatcher Revolution* (Aurum Press, 2000), 47.

46 Murray, op. cit., 139–44; interview with John Cole.

47 Interview with Lord Whitelaw; *Daily Telegraph*, 27, 29 March 1979.

48 Ibid.

Chapter 14   *'Of Course It Won't Work!'*

1   Interview with Lord Waldegrave.

2   *Guardian*, 24 April 1979; Craig Brown in the *Sunday Times*, 6 June 1987.

3   Interview with Lord Garel-Jones; McAlpine, *Once a Jolly Bagman*, 214.

4   Thatcher, *Path to Power*, 456, 444; WW, *Memoirs*, 157.

5   WW, *Memoirs*, 160.

6   Peter Walker, *Staying Power* (Bloomsbury, 1991), 144, 146; interview with Lord Peyton.

7   Nicholas Ridley, *My Style of Government: The Thatcher Years* (Hutchinson, 1991), 26; Ian Gilmour, *Dancing with Dogma: Britain under Thatcherism* (Simon & Schuster, 1992), 3.

8   Heath, *Course of My Life*, 574; Campbell, *Heath*, 716.

9   Private information; WW, *Memoirs*, 164.

10 *The Art of the Possible: The Memoirs of Lord Butler* (Hamish Hamilton, 1971), 198.

11   Hennessy, *Whitehall*, 634.

12   Interview with Sir Roger Sims; Alan Clark, *Diaries: Into Politics*, 277.

13   Interview with Sir Roger Sims; Anthony Seldon, *Major: A Political Life* (Weidenfeld & Nicolson, 1997), 56; John Major, *The Autobiography* (HarperCollins, 1999), 73–4; Clark, *Into Politics*, 292.

14   Major, op. cit., 74; Clark, *Into Politics*, 196; Clark, *Diaries* (Weidenfeld & Nicolson, 1993), 200.

15   WW, *Memoirs*, 167; Tony Benn, *The End of an Era: Diaries 1980–90* (Arrow ed., 1994), 299. This figure probably included letters signed by junior ministers (interview with Sir Timothy Raison).

16   WW, speech to the 1980 Conservative Party Conference, 9 October 1980.

17   *Guardian*, 22 May 1980; interview with Sir John Chilcot.

18   *The Times*, 22 March 1980; *Yorkshire Post*, 2 April 1980.

19   *The Conservative Manifesto 1979*, 19–20.

20   WW, *Memoirs*, 171.

21   *Yorkshire Post*, 2 April 1980; *Sunday Telegraph*, 2 November 1980.

22   *Yorkshire Post*, 29 October 1980.

23   *Yorkshire Post*, 23 October 1980.

24   Hoskyns, *Just in Time*, 275.

25   *Conservative Manifesto 1979*, 20–1; *Guardian*, 24 April 1979.

26   Heffer, *Like the Roman*, 838; *Daily Mail*, 12 July 1980.

27   *Birmingham Post*, 31 July 1980; Zig Layton-Henry, *The Politics of Immigration* (Blackwell, 1992), 192–3.

28   Ibid., 194; *The Times*, 9 February 1980.

29   Martin Kettle and Lucy Hodges, *Uprising! The police, the people and the riots in Britain's cities* (Pan ed., 1982), 23–5; WW, *Memoirs*, 185; *The Times*, 3, 5 April 1980.

30   Kettle and Hodges, op. cit., 25, 33; *The Times*, 3 April 1980; *Scotsman*, 8 April 1980.

31   Private information.

32   Note of a conversation of 31 January 1981 in the Hailsham Papers, 1/5, Churchill College.

33   Mark Stuart, *Douglas Hurd: The Public Servant* (Mainstream, 1998), 108–9; WW, *Memoirs*, 181; *Observer*, 11 May 1980.

34   After both had retired, Willie was instrumental in the award of an MBE to this remarkable public servant.

35   WW, *Memoirs*, 181; interview with Jack Liddiard.

36   General Sir Peter de la Billière, *Looking for Trouble: An Autobiography – from the SAS to the Gulf* (HarperCollins, 1994), 322; interview with Lord Whitelaw; *Observer*, 11 May 1980.

37 De la Billière, op. cit., 329.

38 Ibid., 331–5; interview with Lord Whitelaw; Hennessy, op. cit., 634.

39 WW, *Memoirs*, 183.

40 Ibid., 221.

41 *Guardian*, 16 September 1980; Nicholas Crickhowell, *Westminster, Wales and Water* (University of Wales Press, 1999), 18–21.

42 WW, *Memoirs*, 226–9.

43 *Sunday Times*, 13 September 1982; note of a conversation of 11 December 1980, Hailsham Papers, 1/5, Churchill College; Hansard, vol. 42, col. 388, 4 May 1983.

44 Kettle and Hodges, op. cit., 104–6.

45 WW, *Memoirs*, 186–8; Kettle and Hodges, op. cit., 118.

46 *The Times*, 7 October 1982.

47 Kettle and Hodges, op. cit., 70, 62.

48 Ibid., 156–62; Hansard, vol. 8, col. 1397, 16 July 1981.

49 Kettle and Hodges, op. cit., 162–8.

50 *The Times*, 8 July 1981; WW, *Memoirs*, 190–1.

51 Thatcher, *Downing Street Years* (HarperCollins, 1993), 142–7.

52 Clark, *Diaries*, 140; letters to authors from Liz Huckle.

53 WW, *Memoirs*, 191–2.

54 WW, text of the inaugural Stanley Baldwin lecture, 14 October 1980, CCO handout.

55 Hansard, vol. 8, cols 1397–1405, 1421, 1411–17, 16 July 1981; Robert Shepherd, *Enoch Powell: A Biography* (Hutchinson, 1996), 484–5; cf. Heffer, *Like the Roman*, 846–7.

56 WW, *Memoirs*, 192; Hoskyns, *Just in Time*, 322; Michael Crick, *Michael Heseltine: A Biography* (Penguin ed., 1997), 228; note of 3 July 1980, Hailsham Papers, 1/5, Churchill College.

57 Benn, *End of an Era*, 299.

58 Hugo Young, *One of Us* (Pan ed., 1990), 234; Kettle and Hodges, op. cit., 223.

59 Benn, op. cit., 299; Young, op. cit., 234.

Chapter 15   Holding the Line

1 Gilmour, *Dancing with Dogma*, 36–7.

2 Interviews with Lord Howe and Sir John Chilcot; *Guardian*, 5 September 1982.

3 Gilmour, op. cit., 38; Thatcher, *Downing Street Years*, 148; Hoskyns, *Just in Time*, 320–3.

4   Prior, *Balance of Power*, 142; Thatcher, op. cit., 149, 139 note.
5   Private information.
6   Young, *One of Us*, 221; private information.
7   Gilmour, op. cit., 42; Prior, op. cit., 142; interview with Lord Whitelaw.
8   Hoskyns, op. cit., 334, 323; interview with Lord Gilmour; Thatcher, *Downing Street Years*, 151–2.
9   Hoskyns, op. cit., 332.
10   Prior, op. cit., 171–2.
11   *The Times*, 15 September 1981; Thatcher, op. cit., 152–3.
12   Interviews with Sir Dennis Walters and Lord Garel-Jones.
13   WW, *Memoirs*, 196; *Sunday Times*, 8 October 1989.
14   WW, *Memoirs*, 197; *Searchlight*, 1 March 1984.
15   WW, *Memoirs*, 197–8.
16   Campbell, *Heath*, 731.
17   WW, *Memoirs*, 198.
18   Peter Stothard in *The Times*, 16 December 1981; Clark, *Into Politics*, 256; Young, op. cit., 236.
19   Private information.
20   Clark, *Into Politics*, 300–2.
21   *Daily Mail*, 19 March 1982; 19 March 1983. Willie confided that his daughter had kept him well informed about the previous deficiencies of policing in Brixton; interview with John Cole.
22   Clark, *Into Politics*, 302–3; WW, *Memoirs*, 236; interview with Lord Whitelaw.
23   Ivor Crewe and Anthony King, *SDP: The Birth, Life and Death of the Social Democratic Party* (Oxford University Press, 1995), 144.
24   *Daily Telegraph*, 22 March 1982; *Western Mail*, 19, 23 March 1982; WW, *Memoirs*, 200.
25   Clark, *Into Politics*, 305.
26   WW, *Memoirs*, 203.
27   Clark, *Into Politics*, 313; WW, *Memoirs*, 203–4; interview with Lord Cranborne; Lord Carrington, *Reflect on Things Past* (Fontana ed., 1989), 371.
28   WW, *Memoirs*, 206–8.
29   Ibid., interview with Lord Parkinson; Thatcher, op. cit., 206–7.
30   Interview with Lord Pym; *Mail on Sunday*, 23 May 1982.
31   Max Hastings and Simon Jenkins, *The Battle for the Falklands* (Michael Joseph, 1983), 254, 169; Michael Leapman, *The Last Days of the Beeb* (Coronet ed., 1987), 235–7.
32   Interview with Lord Garel-Jones.
33   Hastings and Jenkins, op. cit., 300–3; WW, *Memoirs*, 19–20.

34   Nicholas Wapshott and George Brock, *Thatcher* (Futura ed., 1983), 250; Clark, *Into Politics*, 333.

35   WW, *Memoirs*, 211–12; private information. Sir David McNee acknowledges in his memoirs that he and Willie 'had our disagreements', and these did not end when the Commissioner left office. Personal differences may help to explain some of the contrasts between the accounts of key events provided by Lord Whitelaw in interviews and Sir David in his own memoir, *McNee's Law* (Collins, 1983).

36   *Observer*, 16 August 1992; interview with Lord Cranborne.

37   Clark, *Into Politics*, 344–6; letter to the authors from Sir Jack Page; Richard Shepherd in the *Birmingham Post*, 19 July 1982.

38   *Daily Telegraph*, 7 October 1994; interview with Lord Whitelaw.

39   See the excellent discussion in Diana Woodhouse, *Ministers and Parliament: Accountability in Theory and Practice* (Clarendon Press, 1994), 136–43; Andrew Alexander in the *Daily Mail*, 3 February 1981.

40   *The Times*, 16 July 1982; *Financial Times*, 22 July 1982; WW, *Memoirs*, 215–16; *Daily Telegraph*, 6 April 1988.

41   *In Conference*, October 1982, 4.

42   *Daily Telegraph*, *Daily Mail*, 7 October 1982.

43   *Daily Mail*, 22, 14 October 1982.

44   *Daily Mail*, 22 October 1982.

45   Geoffrey Smith in *The Times*, 3 April 1982.

46   *Sunday Times*, 21 March 1982; *Daily Mail*, 12 November 1982.

47   *Financial Times*, 7 December 1982; Ian Aitken in the *Guardian*, 13 December 1982.

48   *Sunday Express*, 28 November 1982.

49   Hugo Young in the *Sunday Times*, 19 December 1982.

50   Ibid.; interview with Sir Timothy Raison; *Daily Telegraph*, 17 December 1982.

51   *Guardian*, 16 February 1983.

52   See K.D. Ewing amd C.A. Gearty, *Freedom under Thatcher: Civil Liberties in Modern Britain* (Oxford University Press, 1990), ch. 2; WW in the *Daily Express*, 29 April 1983.

53   Ewing and Gearty, op. cit., 47; *Daily Telegraph*, 3 May 1983.

54   Parkinson, *Right at the Centre* (Weidenfeld & Nicolson, 1992), 223–4.

55   *Observer*, 5 June 1983.

56   James Barr, *The Bow Group: A History* (Politicos, 2001), 184; *Guardian*, 4 May 1983.

57   John Cole, *The Thatcher Years: A Decade of Revolution in British Politics* (BBC Books, 1987), 57.

58   WW, *Memoirs*, 236–8.

Chapter 16   'The Empire Strikes Back'

1   Private information; correspondence with Lord Tebbit.

2   Sir Brian Hayes, address at WW's memorial service, 27 October 1999.

3   WW, *Memoirs*, 167; interviews with Sir John Chilcot and Sir Roger Sims.

4   WW, *Memoirs*, 167; Hansard, vol. 986, col. 793, 12 June 1980; *Guardian*, 11 June 1982, 13 June 1980.

5   *The Times*, 30 July 1983; interview with Lord Parkinson.

6   *Guardian*, 19 July 1983.

7   *Daily Telegraph*, 13 June 1983.

8   WW, *Memoirs*, 241.

9   WW, *Memoirs*, 239–42; *Financial Times*, 21 December 1984.

10   Thorneycroft to WW, 13 June 1983, Whitelaw Papers.

11   WW, text of a speech to the Press Gallery, 28 March 1984.

12   Adam Raphael in the *Observer*, 6 November 1983; Prior, *Balance of Power*, 150.

13   Howe, *Conflict of Loyalty*, 342; *Sunday Telegraph*, 22 July 1984.

14   Adam Raphael in the *Observer*, 6 November 1983.

15   Ian Aitken in the *Guardian*, 20 January 1984; Colin Brown in the *Guardian*, 20 August 1984.

16   *Guardian*, 29 June 1984.

17   Ian Aitken in the *Guardian*, 5 July 1984; *The Times*, 17 July 1984.

18   *Guardian*, 26 April, 9 May, 21 June 1985; Kenneth Baker, *The Turbulent Years: My Life in Politics* (Faber & Faber, 1993), 104.

19   Alan Travis in the *Guardian*, 20 October 1987; *The Times*, 9 October 1987.

20   Interview with Peter Hennessy, *Financial Times*, 5 November 1987; Baker, op. cit., 230.

21   Clark, *Diaries*, 195.

22   David Butler, Andrew Adonis and Tony Travers, *Failure in British Government: The Politics of the Poll Tax* (Oxford University Press, 1994), 32–3.

23   Nigel Lawson, *The View From No.11: Memoirs of a Tory Radical* (Bantam Press, 1992), 561–2, 578–9.

24   Baker, op. cit., 124, 127; Lawson, op. cit., 291.

25   Interview with Lord Garel-Jones.

26   *Mail on Sunday*, 28 July 1985.

27   *Sunday Times*, 21 October 1984; *The Times*, 26 April 1985; *Daily Mirror*, 26 April 1986.

28   Interview with Lord Tebbit.

29   WW, *Memoirs*, 254–5.

30   Heseltine, *Life in the Jungle*, 312; Crick, *Michael Heseltine*, 182.

31   Private information; Magnus Linklater and David Leigh, *Not with Honour: The inside story of the Westland Scandal* (Sphere ed., 1986), 99–101.

32   Ibid., 165; *Observer*, 26 January 1986.

33   Linklater and Leigh, op. cit., 131; *Yorkshire Post*, 24 January 1986; Woodrow Wyatt, *Journals*, Vol. One, 71.

34   Wyatt, op. cit., 71; Linklater and Leigh, op. cit., 111–12.

35   *The Times*, 8 February 1986.

36   *Daily Mail*, 2 February 1986.

37   Interview with Trevor Kavanagh.

38   Thatcher, *Downing Street Years*, 440–1.

39   Ibid.; interview with Lord Tebbit; *The Times*, 23 February 1986; Lewis, *Hailsham*, 328; Baker, op. cit., 269.

40   *Observer*, 15 June, 13 July 1986.

41   Adam Raphael in the *Observer*, 20 July 1986.

42   Andrew Neil, *Full Disclosure* (Macmillan, 1996), 205.

43   Interviews with Sir Roger Sims and Robert Jackson; WW, *Memoirs*, 260; Denis Healey, *The Time of My Life* (Penguin ed., 1990), 529.

44   Sara Keays, *A Question of Judgement* (Quintessential Press, 1986), 22; Cecil Parkinson, *Right at the Centre* (Weidenfeld & Nicolson, 1992), 236; Clark, *Diaries*, 56.

45   Malcolm Rutherford in the *Financial Times*, 6 September 1985; Alan Watkins in the *Observer*, 28 July 1985; *Sunday Telegraph*, 10 August 1986; John Junor, *Listening for a Midnight Tram: Memoirs* (Pan ed., 1991), 235.

46   *Daily Telegraph*, 8 October 1987; Ian Aitken in the *Guardian*, 10 October 1985; Junor, op. cit., 230–1.

47   Michael Crick, *Jeffrey Archer: Stranger than Fiction* (Fourth Estate ed., 1999), 260; interview with Lord Parkinson.

48   Interview with Lord Whitelaw; *Financial Times*, 27 January 1986.

49   Remarks on WW's involvement in the 1987 election taken from Lord Young's invaluable (but unpublished) diary; *Sunday Times*, 17 May 1987; Michael Dobbs in Iain Dale (ed.), *Memories of Maggie* (Politicos, 2000), 171–2; interview with Michael Dobbs.

50   Craig Brown in *The Times*, 6 June 1987.

51   WW, *Memoirs*, 267; Lord Young, *The Enterprise Years* (Headline, 1990), 255–7; *Guardian*, 29 October, 7 November 1987.

52   *Sunday Times*, 20 September 1987.

53   Ian Aitken in the *Guardian*, 6 November 1987.

54   *Financial Times*, 18 December 1987; *Daily Mail*, 25, 11 January 1988.

55   *Evening News and Star*, 27 August 1986; private information.

56   Baker, op. cit., 251; WW, *Memoirs*, 268; interviews with Lord Jenkin

and Dr John Gayner; Norman Fowler, *Ministers Decide: A Memoir of the Thatcher Years* (Chapmans, 1991), 225; Norman Fowler to WW, 16 January 1988, Whitelaw Papers.

57   WW, *Memoirs*, 268–9.

Chapter 17   *Too Late to Mourn*

1   Interview with Lady Whitelaw.

2   WW, *Memoirs*, 30; correspondence in possession of the Whitelaw family.

3   Interview with Dr John Gayner.

4   WW, *Memoirs*, 269–70; Woodrow Wyatt, *Journals*, Vol. One, 467; interviews with John Cole and Dr John Gayner.

5   Lawson, *View from No.11*, 708; Lawson to WW, 11 January 1988, Whitelaw Papers; *The Times*, *Daily Telegraph*, 11 January 1988; *Sunday Telegraph*, 10 January 1988; *The Times* editorial, 22 December 1997; Ronald Millar, *A View From the Wings: West End, West Coast, Westminster* (Weidenfeld & Nicolson, 1993), 319.

6   *House of Lords Debates*, vol. 491, cols 915–18, 11 January 1988.

7   WW, *Memoirs*, 246; Lawson, op. cit., 709; *Sunday Times*, 23 April 1989; Bruce Anderson in the *Sunday Telegraph*, 30 April 1989; Margaret Thatcher to WW, 28 January 1988 (letter in possession of the Whitelaw family); Sara Curtis (ed.), *The Journals of Woodrow Wyatt*, vol. II (Macmillan, 1999), 72–3, 93; *Mail on Sunday*, 30 April 1989.

8   *Observer*, 1 May 1988; *Sunday Telegraph*, 24 April 1988; Michael Heseltine to WW, 25 April 1988, letter in possession of the Whitelaw family.

9   Lawson, op. cit., 708–9, 928; William Keegan and Nicholas Wapshott in the *Observer*, 7 October 1990.

10   Interview with John Cole; Lawson, op. cit., 928; Tebbit in the *Evening Standard*, 30 October 1989.

11   Howe, *Conflict of Loyalty*, 590, 587; Thatcher, *Downing Street Years*, 756–7.

12   Interviews with Lord Whitelaw and Sir Bernard Ingham; *Observer*, 30 July 1989; *Sunday Times*, 30 July 1990.

13   *Guardian*, 14 October 1989; *Observer*, 8 October 1989; Parkinson, *Right at the Centre*, 6.

14   Lawson, op. cit., 969; *The Times*, 23 November 1989; Howe, op. cit., 609–11.

15   Interview with Lord Whitelaw; Wyatt, *Journals*, Vol. Two, 267, 245, 290–1.

16   Cole, *As it Seemed to Me*, 355; Baker, *Turbulent Years*, 341.

17   Howe, op. cit., 656; *The Times*, 14 November 1990; *Sunday Telegraph*, 11 November 1990.

18   Wyatt, *Journals*, Vol. Two, 388–9; Robert Shepherd, *The Power Brokers: The Tory Party and its Leaders* (Hutchinson, 1991), 19.

19   Baker, op. cit., 383.

20   *Guardian*, 7 August 1991; Parkinson, op. cit., 34; Thatcher, *Downing Street Years*, 848.

21   Thatcher, *Path to Power*, 239.

22   Shepherd, op. cit., 77.

23   Lawson, op. cit., 710–12; Baker, op. cit., 396.

24   *Mail on Sunday*, 23 June 1991.

25   *Sunday Telegraph*, 4 April 1993; *House of Lords Debates*, vol. 546, col. 729, 8 June 1993.

26   *Independent*, 19 September 1996.

27   Interview with Lord Brittan.

28   *Sunday Telegraph*, 4 April 1993.

29   WW to Lord Nolan, 8 February 1995; *Sun*, 22 March 1995.

30   Lord Tebbit to WW, 8 March 1995; WW to Stuart Higgins and John Major, 22, 23 March 1995; Higgins to WW, 22 March 1995, Whitelaw papers.

31   Interview with Peter Stothard.

32   Interview with Viscount Cranborne.

33   Sarah Hogg and Jonathan Hill, *Too Close to Call: Power and Politics – John Major in No.10* (Little, Brown, 1995), 10; *The Journals of Woodrow Wyatt: Volume Three, From Major to Blair* (Macmillan, 2000), 659.

34   Lord Carr to WW, 22 November 1995; WW to Sir Robert Rhodes-James, 10 June 1993, Whitelaw papers.

35   *Daily Telegraph*, 6 August 1991.

36   *The Times*, 20 January 1994.

37   Ibid., 20 January 1994; *Evening Standard*, 21 March 1994; correspondence between WW and Michael Howard in Whitelaw papers.

38   Interviews with Lord Whitelaw and Lord Garel-Jones.

39   *Mail on Sunday*, 12 February 1989.

40   *Spectator*, 15 January 1983.

41   See, for example, the *Daily Mail*, 26 July 1999.

42   Enoch Powell, *Joseph Chamberlain* (Thames and Hudson, 1977), 151.

INDEX